T0236409

Lecture Notes in Artificial Intelligence 9662

Subseries of Lecture Notes in Computer Science

More information about this series at http://www.springer.com/series/1244

Yves Demazeau · Takayuki Ito
Javier Bajo · Maria José Escalona (Eds.)

Advances in Practical Applications of Scalable Multi-agent Systems

The PAAMS Collection

14th International Conference, PAAMS 2016
Sevilla, Spain, June 1–3, 2016
Proceedings

 Springer

Editors

Yves Demazeau
Laboratoire d'Informatique de Grenoble
Centre National de la Recherche Scientifique
Grenoble
France

Takayuki Ito
Department of Computer Science
and Engineering
Nagoya Institute of Technology
Nagoya
Japan

Javier Bajo
Departamento de Inteligencia Artificial
Universidad Politécnica de Madrid
Boadilla del Monte, Madrid
Spain

Maria José Escalona
ETS Ingenieria Informatica
Universidad de Sevilla
Sevilla
Spain

ISSN 0302-9743   ISSN 1611-3349 (electronic)
Lecture Notes in Artificial Intelligence
ISBN 978-3-319-39323-0   ISBN 978-3-319-39324-7 (eBook)
DOI 10.1007/978-3-319-39324-7

Library of Congress Control Number: 2016939381

LNCS Sublibrary: SL7 – Artificial Intelligence

Printed on acid-free paper

This Springer imprint is published by Springer Nature
The registered company is Springer International Publishing AG Switzerland

Preface

Research on agents and multi-agent systems has matured during the last decade and many effective applications of this technology are now deployed. An international forum to present and discuss the latest scientific developments and their effective applications, to assess the impact of the approach, and to facilitate technology transfer became a necessity and was created a few years ago.

PAAMS, the International Conference on Practical Applications of Agents and Multi-Agent Systems, is the international yearly tribune to present, to discuss, and to disseminate the latest developments and the most important outcomes related to real-world applications. It provides a unique opportunity to bring multi-disciplinary experts, academics, and practitioners together to exchange their experience in the development and deployment of agents and multi-agent systems.

This volume presents the papers that were accepted for the 2016 edition of PAAMS. These articles report on the application and validation of agent-based models, methods, and technologies in a number of key application areas, including: daily life and real world, energy and networks, humans and trust, markets and bids, models and tools, negotiation and conversation, scalability and resources. Each paper submitted to PAAMS went through a stringent peer review by three members of the Program Committee composed of 97 internationally renowned researchers from 24 countries. From the 45 submissions received, nine were selected for full presentation at the conference; another 10 papers were accepted as short presentations. In addition, a demonstration track featuring innovative and emergent applications of agent and multi-agent systems and technologies in real-world domains was organized. In all, 16 demonstrations were shown, and this volume contains a description of each of them.

We would like to thank all the contributing authors, the members of the Program Committee, the sponsors (IEEE SMC Spain, IBM, AEPIA, AFIA, APPIA, Polytechnic University of Madrid, University of Seville, and CNRS) and the Organizing Committee for their hard and highly valuable work. Their work contributed to the success of the PAAMS 2016 event. Thanks for your help – PAAMS 2016 would not exist without your contribution.

April 2016

Yves Demazeau
Takayuki Ito
Javier Bajo
Maria José Escalona

Organization

General Co-chairs

Yves Demazeau	Centre National de la Recherche Scientifique, France
Takayuki Ito	Nagoya Institute of Technology, Japan
Javier Bajo	Polytechnic University of Madrid, Spain
Maria José Escalona	University of Seville, Spain

Advisory Board

Keith Decker	University of Delaware, USA
Frank Dignum	Utrecht University, The Netherlands
Toru Ishida	University of Kyoto, Japan
Jörg P. Müller	Technische Universität Clausthal, Germany
Juan Pavón	Universidad Complutense de Madrid, Spain
Michal Pěchouček	Czech Technical University in Prague, Czech Republic
Franco Zambonelli	University of Modena and Reggio Emilia, Italy

Program Committee

Carole Adam	University of Grenoble, France
Emmanuel Adam	University of Valenciennes, France
Frederic Amblard	University of Toulouse, France
Francesco Amigoni	Politecnico di Milano, Italy
Bo An	Nanyang Technological University, Singapore
Javier Bajo	Polytechnic University of Madrid, Spain
Matteo Baldoni	University of Turin, Italy
Jeremy Baxter	QinetQ, UK
Michael Berger	DocuWare AG, Germany
Olivier Boissier	Ecole Nationale Superieure des Mines de Saint Etienne, France
Rafael Bordini	Pontifical University of Rio Grande do Sul, Brazil
Vicente Botti	Polytechnic University of Valencia, Spain
Oliver Bown	University of Sydney, Australia
Lars Braubach	Universität Hamburg, Germany
Sven Brueckner	Axon AI, USA
Longbing Cao	University of Technology Sydney, Australia
Javier Carbó	University Carlos III of Madrid, Spain
Luis Castillo	University of Caldas, Colombia
Wei Chen	Intelligent Automation Incorporated, USA
Caroline Chopinaud	MASA, France

Helder Coelho	University of Lisbon, Portugal
Juan Manuel Corchado	University of Salamanca, Spain
Rafael Corchuelo	University of Seville, Spain
Julie Dugdale	University of Grenoble, France
Amal Elfallah	University of Paris 6, France
Johannes Fähndrich	Technical University of Berlin, Germany
Jose Luis Fernandez-Marquez	University of Geneva, Switzerland
Rubén Fuentes	Complutense University of Madrid, Spain
Katsuhide Fujita	Tokyo University of Agriculture and Technology, Japan
Naoki Fukuta	Shizuoka University, Japan
Aditya Ghose	University of Wollongong, Australia
Daniela Godoy	University of Tandil, Argentina
Jorge J. Gómez-Sanz	Complutense University of Madrid, Spain
Charles Gouin-Vallerand	Télé-Université du Québec, Canada
Kasper Hallenborg	University of Southern Denmark, Denmark
Vincent Hilaire	University of Belfort-Montbeliard, France
Koen Hindriks	University of Delft, The Netherlands
Benjamin Hirsch	EBTIC / Khalifa University, UAE
Martin Hofmann	Lockheed Martin, USA
Tom Holvoet	Catholic University of Leuven, Belgium
Shinichi Honiden	National Institute of Informatics Tokyo, Japan
Jomi Hübner	Universidad Federale de Santa Catarina, Brazil
Vicente Julian	Polytechnic University of Valencia, Spain
Achilles Kameas	University of Patras, Greece
Ryo Kanamori	Nagoya University, Japan
Takahiro Kawamura	Toshiba, Japan
Franziska Kluegl	University of Örebro, Sweden
Matthias Klusch	DFKI, Germany
Martin Kollingbaum	University of Aberdeen, UK
Ryszard Kowalczyk	Swinburne University of Technology, Australia
Jaroslaw Kozlak	University of Science and Technology in Krakow, Poland
Miguel Angel Lopez-Carmona	University of Alcala, Spain
Rene Mandiau	University of Valenciennes, France
Ivan Marsa-Maestre	University of Alcala, Spain
Philippe Mathieu	University of Lille, France
Eric Matson	Purdue University, USA
Cetin Mericli	Carnegie Mellon University, USA
José M. Molina	Carlos III University of Madrid, Spain
Mirko Morandini	University of Trento, Italy
Bernard Moulin	University of Laval, Canada
Jean-Pierre Muller	CIRAD, France
Joerg Mueller	Clausthal University of Technology, Germany

Itsuki Noda	Advanced Institute of Science and Technology, Japan
Michael North	University of Chicago, USA
Ingrid Nunes	Universidad Federal de Rio Grande do Sul, Brazil
Akihiko Ohsuga	University of Electro-Communications, Japan
Eugenio Oliveira	University of Porto, Portugal
Andrea Omicini	University of Bologna, Italy
Mehmet Orgun	Macquarie University, Australia
Sascha Ossowski	University of Rey Juan Carlos, Spain
Juan Pavon	Complutense University of Madrid, Spain
Terry Payne	University of Liverpool, UK
Pascal Perez	University of Wollongong, Australia
Sébastien Picault	University of Lille, France
David Pynadath	University of Southern California, USA
Alessandro Ricci	University of Bologna, Italy
David Robertson	University of Edinburgh, UK
Juan Rodriguez Aguilar	Artificial Intelligence Research Institute, Spain
Nicolas Sabouret	University of Paris 11, France
Silvia Schiaffino	University of Tandil, Argentina
Leonid Sheremetov	Instituto Mexicano del Petróleo, Mexico
Elizabeth Sklar	City University of New York, USA
Graeme Stevenson	University of Saint Andrews, UK
Sonia Suárez	University of La Coruna, Spain
Toshiharu Sugawara	Waseda University, Japan
Katia Sycara	CMU, USA
Patrick Taillandier	UMR IDEES, MTG, France
Viviane Torres da Silva	Universidad Federal Fluminense, Brazil
Paolo Torroni	University of Bologna, Italy
Rainer Unland	University of Duisburg, Germany
Domenico Ursino	University of Reggio Calabria, Italy
Laszlo Varga	Computer and Automation Research Institute, Hungary
Wamberto Vasconselos	University of Aberdeen, UK
Laurent Vercouter	University of Rouen, France
José R. Villar	University of Oviedo, Spain
Wayne Wobcke	University of New South Wales, Australia
Franco Zambonelli	University of Modena, Italy

Organizing Committee

María José Escalona Cuaresma Chair	University of Seville, Spain
Javier Bajo Chair	Technical University of Madrid, Spain
Carlos Arevalo Maldonado	University of Seville, Spain
Gustavo Aragon Serrano	University of Seville, Spain
Irene Barba	University of Seville, Spain
Miguel Ángel Barcelona Liédana	Technological Institute of Aragon, Spain

Juan Manuel Cordero Valle	University of Seville, Spain
Francisco José Domínguez Mayo	University of Seville, Spain
Juan Pablo Domínguez Mayo	University of Seville, Spain
Manuel Domínguez Muñoz	University of Seville, Spain
José Fernández Engo	University of Seville, Spain
Laura García Borgoñón	Technological Institute of Aragon, Spain
Julian Alberto García García	University of Seville, Spain
Javier García-Consuegra Angulo	University of Seville, Spain
José González Enríquez	University of Seville, Spain
Tatiana Guardia Bueno	University of Seville, Spain
Andrés Jiménez Ramírez	University of Seville, Spain
Javier Jesús Gutierrez Rodriguez	University of Seville, Spain
Manuel Mejías Risoto	University of Seville, Spain
Laura Polinario	University of Seville, Spain
José Ponce Gonzalez	University of Seville, Spain
Francisco José Ramírez López	University of Seville, Spain
Isabel Ramos Román	University of Seville, Spain
Jorge Sedeño López	University of Seville, Spain
Nicolás Sánchez Gómez	University of Seville, Spain
Juan Miguel Sánchez Begines	University of Seville, Spain
Eva-Maria Schön	University of Seville, Spain
Jesús Torres Valderrama	University of Seville, Spain
Carmelo Del Valle Sevillano	University of Seville, Spain
Antonio Vázquez Carreño	University of Seville, Spain
Carlos Torrecilla Salinas	University of Seville, Spain
Ainara Aguirre Narros	University of Seville, Spain
Diana Borrego	University of Seville, Spain
Fernando Enríquez de Salamanca Ros	University of Seville, Spain
Juan Antonio Alvarez García	University of Seville, Spain
Antonio Tallón	University of Seville, Spain

PAAMS 2016 Sponsors

Contents

Demo Papers

Regular Papers

An Agent-Based Application for Automatic Classification of Food Allergies and Intolerances in Recipes

José Alemany[(⊠)], Stella Heras, Javier Palanca, and Vicente Julián

Departamento de Sistemas Informaticos y Computacion,
Universitat Politècnica de València, Valencia, Spain
{jalemany1,sheras,jpalanca,vinglada}@dsic.upv.es

Abstract. The automatic recommendation of recipes for users with some kind of food allergies or intolerances is still a complex and open problem. One of the limitations is the lack of databases that labels ingredients of recipes with their associated allergens. This limitation may cause the recommendation of inappropriate recipes to people with specific food restrictions. In order to try to solve this, this paper proposes a collaborative *multi-agent system* that automatically detects food allergies in nutrients and labels ingredients with their potential allergens. The proposed system is being employed in `receteame.com`, a recipe recommendation system which includes persuasive technologies, which are interactive technologies aimed at changing users' attitudes or behaviors through persuasion and social influence, and social information to improve the recommendations.

Keywords: Recommendation system · Food allergy · Multi-agent system

1 Motivation

Nowadays, food allergies and intolerances are a common problem that affect to people of our society (up to 8 % in children and 2 % in adults)[1]. Even if an individual is not directly affected by them, many have relatives or friends who are. Although the World Allergy Organization (WAO) regulated the terminology used to characterize allergies, the information is difficult to understand because its complexity. In particular, food allergies are one of the most complex allergies.

The impact caused by food allergies in the population is high, since food is part of the daily routine of all people, and their prevalence is growing exponentially. People with allergies are forced to constantly revise the composition of what they will eat. This is an awkward situation, especially when one (or a relative) has been recently diagnosed with a food allergy or intolerance. Furthermore, the lack of experience in nutrition and allergens complicates daily life

---

[1] WAO World Allergy Organization, Food allergy statistics: http://www.worldallergy.org/public/allergic_diseases_center/foodallergy/.

© Springer International Publishing Switzerland 2016
Y. Demazeau et al. (Eds.): PAAMS 2016, LNAI 9662, pp. 3–12, 2016.
DOI: 10.1007/978-3-319-39324-7_1

of allergy sufferers. Therefore, many turn to the Web to find information about allergen-free recipes that allows them to eat in a safe and varied form.

In recent years, social networks have changed the way users perform many everyday Internet activities. Specifically, the direct interaction between users has gained ground to the traditional activities of search and navigation. Users have gone from being mere consumers of information to be their real producers. In Spain, for example, 93 % of Internet users access social networking sites every day; 2 out of 3 takes into account the recommendations of other users to make decisions (about products, treatments, entertainment, etc.); and of these, 69 % gives a lot or some credibility to what their friends or acquaintances say on social networks.

However, the growing number of users and information generated, the heterogeneity of users, their unpredictable behavior, and the dynamism of the structure of social networks cause users a high degree of uncertainty when choosing with whom to interact and what information they should consume [1]. To reduce this uncertainty, tools that help users in their decision-making processes are required. A promising solution is the use of recommendation systems [2,3], which are able of performing effective recommendations to help users to make appropriate decisions.

In [4], we presented `receteame.com`, a persuasive social recommendation system whose goal is to recommend the most appropriated recipe to each specific user, taking into account their preferences, food restrictions and social context. In this work, we propose an improvement of the system to automatically detect allergens in recipes, based on their ingredients composition, and to prevent the system from recommending inappropriate recipes to people with specific food restrictions. `receteame.com` uses the USDA[2] nutrient database to provide more detailed nutritional information about the ingredients of the recipes. However, this database does not include full information about the potential allergies associated with each ingredient and, to the best of our knowledge, there is no reference database that labels ingredients with their associated allergens.

This is a major problem for our system, since an accurate and reliable detection of recipe allergens must be performed each time a new recipe is uploaded or updated in the system, and always before the system can provide a specific recommendation. Thus, the system must avoid errors in the classification of allergens in a recipe, as this may drastically decrease its reputation among users affected by food allergies (a population that is particularly reluctant to rely on information from the Web or computer systems) and even, in the worst case, could cause serious health problems to their users. The solution that we propose in this paper consists on a collaborative *multi-agent expert system* that is able to automatically detect food allergies in nutrients and label ingredients with their potential allergens.

---

[2] USDA National Nutrient Database for Standard Reference: http://ndb.nal.usda. gov/.

2   Related Work

As the prevalence of diet-related diseases (either those directly caused by poor nutrition or those that condition the diet of their affected patients) is growing, the interest of the artificial intelligence community to develop intelligent systems to help humans with their food needs is also on the rise.

Early research on planning meals was started in the area of case-based reasoning, where the system JULIA [5] created plan meals and the system CHEF [6] created new recipes based on those it already knew about. More recently, the recommender systems community has also paid attention to this topic, and we can find in the literature some recipe recommendation systems that focus on specific diseases. The food recommendation system presented in [7], which uses food clustering analysis for diabetic patients to recommend the proper substituted foods in the context of nutrition and food characteristic, is an example of this type. Others try to predict recipe ratings, as the system proposed in [8], which illustrates how these ratings can be predicted with features derived from combinations of ingredient networks and nutrition information.

Even when people do not have specific food restrictions, the improvement of their diet and health is a hot topic. With this aim, the recipe recommendation system proposed in [9] makes tailored recommendations of healthy recipes; in [10] authors created a personalized recipe recommendation method that is based on the user's food preferences from his/her recipe browsing and cooking history; in [11] authors presented a system that learns user tastes for improving the rating prediction and make better recommendations of recipes; and in [12] the system recommends recipes that users will like and that fit into a balanced diet.

In the area of persuasion technologies, the *Portia* system [13] used relevant arguments, both rational and emotional, to persuade people to change their eating habits.

However these proposals do not follow a social network-based recommendation approach [14] and are not able to automatically detect and classify allergens in the recipes ingredients. The approach proposed in this work deals with the latter challenge and, to the best of our knowledge, is the first attempt in a recommendation system to include this interesting functionality.

3   Application Design

receteame.com is a persuasive social recommendation system that has been designed following the MVC (Model-View-Controller) model. The design of the application is shown in Fig. 1. The database contains information about the model. This is the information about our users (personal information, their tastes, preferences, allergies, etc.), and the recipes and ingredients (calories and nutritional information, allergens and others) that we recommend. Moreover, the application includes a front-end (web interface) that allows users to interact with the recommender, and ultimately, with the application. The front-end represents the view and the controller.

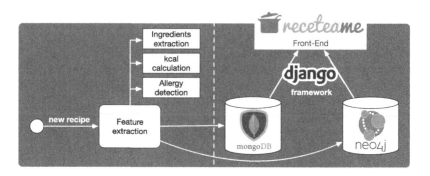

Fig. 1. Receteame.com platform: components and services.

Our system can register new recipes in two ways: via other web sites or through new registered entries by users. Each time a new recipe is uploaded in the system, a process for the extraction of characteristics thereof is performed. This process extracts the ingredients of the recipe, detects potential allergens and calculates the kilocalories of the recipe. We use a heuristic to match the ingredients of our recipes with those corresponding ingredients of the USDA nutrient database, which contains detailed data of 8789 food items.

In order to allow the system to detect and classify ingredients according to their potential food allergies, we have designed a collaborative multi-expert-system. Figure 2 shows its design. In the figure, each expert represents a machine learning technique that we have trained to label the ingredients of our recipes with their associated allergens. When a new ingredient is extracted from a new recipe, each expert analyses the ingredient separately. After that, the experts inform to the decision-maker agent whether or not the ingredient has potential food allergens. The decision-maker, according to the opinion of each expert, is then in charge of labeling the ingredient with the set of detected allergens. We have implemented three experts for our collaborative multi-expert-system, each representing one of the best machine learning techniques (decision trees, logistic regression and K nearest neighbors) that we have tested for our system.

Since an ingredient may contain more than one allergen, our experts are binary classifiers that the system calls for each specific allergen that we want to detect. As will be explained in the next section, the use of separated classifiers allows us to improve the detection of allergens and also to increase the accuracy and reliability of our system, relying in the vote of the majority to discard individual classification errors in such a sensible domain.

4   Evaluation

As has already been mentioned, the persuasive social recommendation system receteame.com uses the USDA nutrient database to provide more detailed nutritional information about recipes. The USDA national nutrient database is an

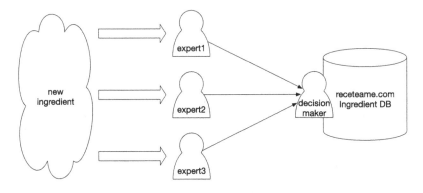

Fig. 2. Collaborative multi-expert-system.

Statistics Report: 01035, Cheese, provolone
Return to Search Results ▦ Basic Report ▦ Full Report (All Nutrients) 📊 Download (CSV) 🖶 Print (PDF)

Nutrient values and weights are for edible portion.

Nutrient	Unit	Value (100g)	Data Points	Std. Error	Min	Max	df	LB	UB	# Studies	Source	NDB Ref	Last Modified
Proximates													
Water	g	40.95	21	0.661	--	--	--	--	--	--	Analytical or derived from analytical	--	11/1976
Energy	kcal	351	--	--	--	--	--	--	--	--	Calculated or imputed	--	02/2009
Energy	kJ	1471	--	--	--	--	--	--	--	--	Calculated or imputed	--	02/2009
Protein	g	25.58	18	0.349	--	--	--	--	--	--	Analytical or derived from analytical	--	11/1976
Total lipid (fat)	g	26.62	24	0.341	--	--	--	--	--	--	Analytical or derived from analytical	--	11/1976
Ash	g	4.71	14	0.155	--	--	--	--	--	--	Analytical or	--	11/1976

Fig. 3. USDA National Nutrient Database: Example of nutritional information.

open database produced by the US Department of Agriculture that provides nutritional data of generic and proprietary-branded foods. It is the major source of information with data about 8789 food items and up to 150 food components per item. Most of these values have been calculated analytically or derived from analytical processes by scientists. However, there are still many entries with unknown values in food components. The USDA nutrient database is updated regularly and may be searched or downloaded through a REST API. In Fig. 3 you can see an example of one entry of the database.

With the nutritional food information acquired by the USDA nutrient database and the tools and algorithms explained in the Sect. 3, we are going to classify the ingredients (and in consequence the recipes) by their potential allergens.

According to the WAO and AEPNAA[3] (the most important agency in Spain that provides information about food allergies and helps to improve the safety and quality of life of individuals affected by food allergies) among the most common food allergies in the Spanish population are milk, egg, fish, and wheat.

---

[3] Asociación Española de Personas con Alergia a Alimentos y Látex: http://www.aepnaa.org.

Therefore, in this work we have focused on the automatic detection of these food allergies in the ingredients of the recipes of our system.

4.1 System Implementation

As shown in Fig. 1, we used the `django` framework to implement `receteame.com`. Furthermore, the `mongodb` and `neo4j` technologies have been used to implement the database. The `mongodb` database technology provides quick access and supports high loads of requests. It has been used to store the information used by `receteame.com` to display the information about the recipes. The `neo4j` database provides flexibility and easy queries. Therefore, it has been used to implement the logic of our recommender system.

The implementation of the collaborative multi-agent expert system has been performed by programming a different machine learning technique in each expert. We tested a wide range of techniques, including decision trees, linear regression, logistic regression, support vector machines and k nearest neighbors (see Sect. 4.2). The better classification results were obtained by the following techniques: the decision trees, which allows us to build a rule-based model to predict allergies in the ingredients; logistic regression, which is a linear model where the probabilities describing the possible outcomes of a single trial are modeled using a logistic function; and K nearest neighbors, a classifier based on instances which is computed from a simple majority vote of the nearest neighbors of each point, so finally our system includes an expert for each of these three techniques.

To implement the experts, we have used `scikit-learn`[4] and `bigml`[5], which provide simple and efficient tools for data mining and analysis. By using these tools, we have trained a binary classifier, one for each of the food allergies that we want to detect in our ingredients. In addition, to increase the quality of the classification, we have elicited in each agent a dictionary of keywords with basic ingredients that contain the allergies (according to information provided by WAO, AEPNAA, FARE[6] among others). We have included all the models created with each machine learning technique in an individual agent. Therefore, each expert agent has a different model for each allergy, but all allergy models have been trained by using the same machine learning technique in the agent.

The operation of our system is performed as follows: when a new recipe is uploaded or updated in `receteame.com`, the system detects its ingredient composition and sends the list of ingredients to the three expert agents. Then, for allergy to detect, they use the learned models to classify the ingredient (as having or not such allergy) and send a message to the decision-maker agent with the results of the classification. Finally, the decision-maker agent implements a voting system by which the classification agreed by the majority is selected as the final classification for each allergy in each ingredient (see Fig. 4 for an example). As will be shown in the next section, with this simple voting technique, our

---

[4] http://scikit-learn.org/.
[5] https://bigml.com/.
[6] Food Allergy Research & Education: http://www.foodallergy.org.

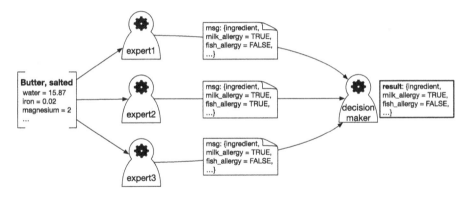

Fig. 4. Food allergy detection: Example of collaboration.

systems reaches good allergy-detection results and is robust against individual misclassification errors.

4.2   Results

To test our system, for each allergy to detect we have created a set of ingredients with and without the allergen. Also, each set has been divided into two subsets: 65 % for training and 35 % for testing under different machine learning techniques. The results are shown in Table 1[7].

Table 1. Accuracy of the different models applied to sets of each food allergy test.

	Milk allergy	Egg allergy	Fish allergy	Gluten allergy
Logistic regression (1)	**95.15 %**	**96.50 %**	**98.18 %**	**96.97 %**
Decision tree (2)	**89.91 %**	**90.33 %**	**96.04 %**	**89.01 %**
K nearest neighbors (3)	**87.67 %**	**86.08 %**	**93.12 %**	**86.97 %**
Support vector machines	79.66 %	80.85 %	81.46 %	76.08 %
Linear regression	74.58 %	84.01 %	79.93 %	83.61 %

From the results, we can observe how the logistic regression, decision-tree and k nearest neighbors techniques achieve the best classification results, so we included these techniques in our expert agents. In addition, Table 2 shows more detail regarding the percentages of ingredients that have been correctly classified as having the allergen (true positives, labeled as true in the table) or not having the allergen (true negatives, labeled as false in the table).

---

[7] We only show in the table a subset of all machine learning techniques that we tested.

Table 2. Accuracy of collaborative multi-expert system compared to each expert individually (for food allergies treated).

		Milk allergy	Egg allergy	Fish allergy	Gluten allergy
Collaborative multi-expert system	True	**97.72 %**	94.20 %	**99.12 %**	**96.27 %**
	False	**96.91 %**	95.58 %	98.45 %	95.03 %
Expert1 (1)	True	92.91 %	**95.24 %**	94.51 %	95.05 %
	False	95.82 %	**96.92 %**	**98.58 %**	**97.76 %**
Expert2 (2)	True	87.50 %	82.27 %	93.85 %	86.47 %
	False	90.38 %	93.30 %	98.24 %	91.56 %
Expert3 (3)	True	73.88 %	75.68 %	73.33 %	76.38 %
	False	91.74 %	89.56 %	95.28 %	91.29 %

In our domain, to correctly detect those ingredients that can provoke an allergic reaction in our users is crucial. Therefore, although we achieved quite good classification results with the logistic regression technique alone, we needed to increase the accuracy in detecting true positives and we developed the collaborative multi-expert system presented in Sect. 3. The results obtained by each expert agent alone and by the collaborative system can be seen in Table 2.

Results demonstrate that the collaborative system, where the classification of the majority is selected as the final classification, improves the percentage of true positives (the detection of the ingredients that have the allergen) for almost all allergy tested. Only in the case of the egg allergy, the logistic regression technique (implemented in expert 1) gets better results alone, but the collaborative technique still achieves similar good results. Therefore, this technique improves the reliability of our system and provides better allergy-detection results.

5   Conclusions and Future Work

This paper has presented a *multi-agent system* that is able to automatically detect food allergies in nutrients and label ingredients with their potential allergens. The system has been designed as a set of experts, where each expert represents a machine learning technique that tries to label new ingredients. Moreover, the system includes a decision-maker agent which, according to the opinion of each expert, makes a decision about the allergens associated to the new recipes uploaded or updated in the system. At this moment, the number of expert agents implemented is three, but it could be easily extended if other new labeling techniques get better classification results in the future. The proposed system has been integrated into `receteame.com`, a website that uses a persuasive social recommendation system to recommend recipes taking into account the preferences and food restrictions of its users.

Some experiments have been performed in order to validate the proposal. Results show that the combination of separated classifiers into a collaborative technique allows the system to improve the detection of allergens and also to increase the accuracy and reliability, relying in the vote of the majority to discard individual classification errors. In our system, the reliability of the allergens information provided is crucial, since misclassifications could seriously compromise the reputation of the system and in the worst case, could cause serious health problems to our users. Therefore, future work will be performed to investigate new machine learning techniques and voting mechanisms that could decrease classification errors.

Acknowledgments. This work was supported by the projects TIN2015-65515-C4-1-R and TIN2014-55206-R of the Spanish government and by the grant program for the recruitment of doctors for the Spanish system of science and technology (PAID-10-14) of the Universitat Politècnica de València.

References

1. van der Aalst, W.M.P., Song, M.S.: Mining social networks: uncovering interaction patterns in business processes. In: Desel, J., Pernici, B., Weske, M. (eds.) BPM 2004. LNCS, vol. 3080, pp. 244–260. Springer, Heidelberg (2004)
2. Adomavicius, G., Tuzhilin, A.: Toward the next generation of recommender systems: a survey of the state-of-the-art and possible extensions. IEEE Trans. Knowl. Data Eng. **17**(6), 734–749 (2005)
3. Zhou, X., Yue, X., Li, Y., Josang, A., Cox, C.: The state-of-the-art in personalized recommender systems for social networking. Artif. Intell. Rev. **37**(2), 119–132 (2012)
4. Palanca, J., Heras, S., Botti, V., Julián, V.: receteame.com: a persuasive social recommendation system. In: Demazeau, Y., Zambonelli, F., Corchado, J.M., Bajo, J. (eds.) PAAMS 2014. LNCS, vol. 8473, pp. 367–370. Springer, Heidelberg (2014)
5. Kolodner, J.L.: Capitalizing on failure through case-based inference. Technical report, DTIC Document (1987)
6. Hammond, K.J.: Case-based Planning: Viewing Planning As a Memory Task. Academic Press Professional Inc., San Diego (1989)
7. Phanich, M., Pholkul, P., Phimoltares, S.: Food recommendation system using clustering analysis for diabetic patients. In: 2010 International Conference on Information Science and Applications (ICISA), pp. 1–8. IEEE (2010)
8. Teng, C.-Y., Lin, Y.-R., Adamic, L.A.: Recipe recommendation using ingredient networks. In: Proceedings of the 4th Annual ACM Web Science Conference, pp. 298–307. ACM (2012)
9. Freyne, J., Berkovsky, S.: Intelligent food planning: personalized recipe recommendation. In: Proceedings of the 15th International Conference on Intelligent User Interfaces, pp. 321–324. ACM (2010)
10. Ueda, M., Takahata, M., Nakajima, S.: User's food preference extraction for personalized cooking recipe recommendation. In: Semantic Personalized Information Management: Retrieval and Recommendation SPIM 2011, p. 98 (2011)
11. Harvey, M., Ludwig, B., Elsweiler, D.: You are what you eat: learning user tastes for rating prediction. In: Kurland, O., Lewenstein, M., Porat, E. (eds.) SPIRE 2013. LNCS, vol. 8214, pp. 153–164. Springer, Heidelberg (2013)

12. Elsweiler, D., Harvey, M.: Towards automatic meal plan recommendations for balanced nutrition. In: Proceedings of the 9th ACM Conference on Recommender Systems, pp. 313–316. ACM (2015)
13. Mazzotta, I., De Rosis, F., Carofiglio, V.: Portia: a user-adapted persuasion system in the healthy-eating domain. IEEE Intell. Syst. **22**(6), 42–51 (2007)
14. Schall, D.: Social network-based recommender systems (2015)

Multi-agent Retail Energy Markets: Contract Negotiation, Customer Coalitions and a Real-World Case Study

Hugo Algarvio[1,2($\boxtimes$)], Fernando Lopes[2], and João Santana[1]

[1] Instituto Superior Técnico, Universidade de Lisboa, INESC-ID, Lisboa, Portugal
hugo.algarvio@tecnico.ulisboa.pt, jsantana@ist.utl.pt
[2] LNEG–National Research Institute, Est. Paço do Lumiar 22, Lisboa, Portugal
fernando.lopes@lneg.pt

Abstract. The participants in energy markets (EMs) can purchase and sell electricity through a few basic instruments, notably spot markets and bilateral contracts. This work aims at using software agents to help manage the complexity of EMs. Specifically, this paper centers on contract negotiation between a single retailer and a coalition of end-use customers—that is, two or more customers ally into a coalition to strengthen their bargaining positions and obtain better tariffs. It extends our previous work on bilateral contracting and customer coalition by considering a different interaction process between a trusted coordinator agent and the coalition members (end-use customers). Also, it presents a case study involving three schools for children located in England. The schools decide to ally into a coalition and rely on a coordinator agent, who takes decisions according to either a "majority" decision rule (two of the customers must are in agreement) or an "unanimity" rule (all customers must are in agreement). Although preliminary, the results do suggest that the formation and management of coalitions during bilateral contracting of electricity is indeed beneficial to end-use customers.

Keywords: Agent-based system · Electricity markets · Bilateral contracting · Customer coalitions · Trading strategies · Decision rules

1 Introduction

Electricity markets (EMs) are systems for effecting the purchase and sale of electricity using supply and demand to set energy prices. The participants in EMs can purchase and sell electrical energy through a few basic instruments, notably spot markets and bilateral contracts [1]. Spot markets involve no direct negotiations between the parties—all market participants who wish to either sell or buy electricity on a specific delivery day submit their price and quantity offers, and the entire market settles simultaneously, usually following a marginal pricing algorithm. Bilateral contracts are essentially agreements between buyers and sellers to trade electricity at negotiated terms and conditions.

© Springer International Publishing Switzerland 2016
Y. Demazeau et al. (Eds.): PAAMS 2016, LNAI 9662, pp. 13–23, 2016.
DOI: 10.1007/978-3-319-39324-7_2

This work focuses on retail markets, which differ from their more traditional counterparts because energy cannot be efficiently held in stock or stored (as tangible goods can). Consequently, retailers are forced to work with consumption prognoses (demand estimations). They typically sign mid-term contracts with producers and most tariffs do not reflect the pressure of competition. Furthermore, whereas classical pricing policies encourage discounts on quantity (the more you buy, the cheaper the unit price becomes), the terms and conditions of most actual electricity contracts are negotiated directly between retailers and single customers, thus oversimplifying or even ignoring such pricing policies. Simply put, most end-use customers only partially enjoy the benefits of deregulation.

Against this background, an ongoing study is looking at using software agents to help manage the complexity of energy markets. The following two types of agents are of particular importance to this paper: retailer or supplier agents (representing business units that sell electricity to end-use customers) and consumer or customer agents (including commercial, industrial and other electricity consumers). The agents are computer systems capable of flexible action in order to meet their design objectives. Also, they are equipped with a bilateral negotiation model [2]. They are able to negotiate and sign forward contracts—that is, agreements between two parties to exchange electric power under a set of specified terms and conditions, typically including energy price, energy quantity, time of delivery, potential penalties and duration. Negotiation involves an iterative exchange of offers and counter-offers.

This paper centers on contract negotiation between a single retailer and a coalition of end-use customers—that is, two or more customers ally into a coalition to strengthen their bargaining positions, and also the customers rely on a trusted coordinator to pursue a superior negotiation outcome. It is an extension of the work presented in [3] in that it considers a different interaction process between the coordinator and the coalition members. Typically, whenever the coordinator receives an offer from the retailer, it communicates the offer to all customers (coalition members) and opens a voting process, where each customer states whether or not the offer is acceptable. Also, whenever a new offer has to be proposed to the retailer, the coordinator often opens a call for proposals among all customers (but see, e.g., [4]). In this paper, we consider a slightly different interaction process—whenever the coordinator receives an offer from the retailer, this agent prepares a new offer (counter-offer) and opens a voting process among all customers, where both offers are made public among them.

Furthermore, this paper presents a case study involving three schools for children located in England. The schools have signed up for different time-of-use tariffs characterized by two energy prices for two blocks of time (peak and off-peak) of a 24-h day. They decide to ally into a coalition and to negotiate a better energy tariff. To this end, they rely on a coordinator agent who interacts and negotiates directly with a retailer agent. The coordinator takes decisions about the submission of new offers and the acceptance of incoming offers according to either a "majority" decision rule (two of the customers must are in agreement) or an "unanimity" rule (all customers must are in agreement).

2   Bilateral Contracting in Electricity Markets

Derivatives are contracts whose values depend on (or derive from) the values of other, more basic, underlying variables, typically the prices of traded assets. The term "derivative" is used to refer to a set of financial instruments, notably forwards. Specifically, forward bilateral contracts are agreements to sell or buy a specific amount of electricity at a certain future time for a specific price. One of the parties assumes a long position and agrees to buy the energy on a future date for a predetermined price, and the other assumes a short position and agrees to sell the energy on the same date for the same price. The payoff from a long position in a forward contract on one unit of electricity is the difference between the spot price (SP) at maturity date and the delivery price (DP). Similarly, the payoff from a short position is the difference: $DP - SP$. These payoffs can be positive or negative.

This work uses the potential of agent-based technology to develop a computational tool to support coalitions of end-use customers in bilateral contracting of electricity. In particular, this section presents several key features of a bilateral negotiation model (see also our previous work in the areas of automated negotiation [2] and EMs [5]). Let $\mathcal{A} = \{a_1, \ldots, a_m\}$ be the set of agents. For each issue X in the agenda $\mathcal{I} = \{X_1, \ldots, X_n\}$, the range of acceptable values is represented by the interval $D = [x_{min}, x_{max}]$. The priority $prt \in \mathbb{N}$ of X is a number that represents its importance. The limit lim of X is the point beyond which an agent $a \in \mathcal{A}$ is unwilling to concede on X.

2.1   A Bilateral Negotiation Model

Two agents, say $a_i \in \mathcal{A}$ and $a_j \in \mathcal{A}$, negotiate by alternately submitting offers (or proposals) at times in $T = \{1, 2, \ldots\}$. The rules of trading are settled by an alternating offers protocol [6]. This means that only one proposal is submitted in each period, with an agent a_i, offering in odd periods $\{1, 3, \ldots\}$, and the other agent $a_j \in A$ offering in even periods $\{2, 4, \ldots\}$. In period $t \in T$, a proposal submitted by a_i to a_j is a vector of issue values:

$$p_{i \to j}^t = (x_1, \ldots, x_n) \tag{1}$$

where x_1 and x_n are values of issues $X_1 \in I$ and $X_n \in I$, respectively. The agents have the ability to unilaterally opt out of the negotiation when responding to a proposal made by the opponent.

The negotiation process starts with a_i submitting a proposal $p_{i \to j}^1$ to a_j in period $t = 1$. The agent a_j receives $p_{i \to j}^1$ and can either accept the offer, reject it and opt out of the negotiation, or reject it and continue bargaining. trading. In the first two cases, negotiation comes to an end. Specifically, if $p_{i \to j}^1$ is accepted, negotiation ends successfully and the agreement is implemented. Conversely, if $p_{i \to j}^1$ is rejected and a_j decides to opt out, negotiation terminates with no agreement. In the last case, negotiation proceeds to the next time period $t = 2$, in which a_j makes a counter-proposal $p_{j \to i}^2$. This process repeats until one of the outcomes mentioned above occurs.

The preferences of the agents are represented by a utility function $U(\mathbf{x})$ with the following properties:

(1) $U(x_1, \ldots, x_n) > U(x_1', \ldots, x_n')$ if agents prefer $(x_1, \ldots, x_n)$ to $(x_1', \ldots, x_n')$;
(2) $U(x_1, \ldots, x_n) = U(x_1', \ldots, x_n')$ if agents are indifferent between $(x_1, \ldots, x_n)$ and $(x_1', \ldots, x_n')$.

Thus, when the utility from one offer is greater than from another offer, we assume that an agent a_i prefers the first outcome over the second. The most common form of the utility function is as follows [7]:

$$U(x_1, \ldots, x_n) = \sum_{i=1}^{n} w_i \times V_i(x_i) \tag{2}$$

where w is the weight for an issue X (a number representing the preference of an agent $a \in \mathcal{A}$ for X) and $V(x)$ is the marginal utility function that gives the score a assigns to a value of X.

Negotiation strategies are computationally tractable functions that define the tactics to be used during the course of negotiation. The agents can pursue several strategies that model typical patterns of concessions. For instance, they can start with ambitious demands, well in excess of limits and aspirations, and concede slowly. High demands and slow concessions, also referred to as "starting high and conceding slowly", are often motivated by concern about position loss and image loss. A formal definition of a negotiation strategy that models this and other existing forms of concession making is presented elsewhere [8]. Also, the agents can have different strengths of preference for the issues at stake—they can place greater emphasis on some key issues and make significant efforts to resolve them favorably. Hence, they may be more willing to make larger concessions on less important issues. The strategy of "low-priority concession making" involves changes of proposals in which larger concessions are made on low-priority than on high-priority issues (see [8] for a formal definition).

Concession tactics are functions that model the specific concessions to be made throughout negotiation—that is, they generate new values for each issue at stake. Let $X \in I$ designate an issue and denote its value at time t by x. Consider that an agent $a \in \mathcal{A}$ wants to maximize the value of X. Formally, a concession tactic Y is a function with the following general form:

$$Y(x) = x - C_f(x - lim) \tag{3}$$

where $C_f \in [0,1]$ is the concession factor of the agent a and lim is the limit of a for X.

The concession factor C_f can be simply a positive constant independent of any objective criteria. Alternatively, C_f can be modelled as a function of a single criterion. Typical criteria include the total concession made on each issue throughout negotiation [9] and also [10]: the time elapsed since the beginning of negotiation, the quantity of resources available, and the previous behavior of the opponent.

For bilateral contracting in EMs, a useful criterion is the amount or quantity of energy for a specific trading period (e.g., peak or mid-peak period). The associated "energy dependent concession making" strategy involves individual decisions to make concessions based on the (expected) quantity of energy to be consumed in a given block of time (but see [11]). A different criterion was introduced in [3], namely the total amount of energy that two or more end-use customers are willing to purchase in a given daily pricing period. In particular, if the total amount of energy to sell increases, then the likelihood of a seller agent making substantial concessions and thereby adopting a large concession factor also increases.

The concession factor can be represented by considering either a polynomial or an exponential function. A generic exponential function follows [3]:

$$C_f = 1 - e^{-K(\epsilon-1)\left(\frac{q}{q_{ref}}\right)^{\frac{\epsilon}{2}}} \tag{4}$$

where q is the (expected) total amount of energy to sell in a specific trading period, q_{ref} is the seller's reference quantity for the trading period, $K \in [0,1]$ is a constant, and $\epsilon > 1$ is a parameter that determines the convexity degree of the curve. As shown in [3], for small values of ϵ (e.g., $\epsilon = 1.1$), C_f is very small and slightly changes as energy quantity increases. If ϵ increases to values close to 2.0, C_f increases linearly with the energy quantity. For higher values of ϵ (e.g., $\epsilon = 3.0$), C_f increases very rapidly in response to a small increase in energy quantity.

3   Customer Coalitions and Bilateral Trading

In Sect. 2, we focused on two parties—a seller (e.g., a retailer) and a buyer (e.g., a customer)—to set the terms and conditions of forward bilateral contracts. In this and the next sections, we extend the analysis to situations that involve multiple buyers, notably multiple end-use customers. Two or more customers ally into coalitions to strengthen their bargaining positions and negotiate better agreements.

In general, coalition formation is likely to occur when the parties need to add the resources or support of others to enhance the likelihood of achieving their own individual objectives. Two critical aspects of coalition formation are [12]: what each member brings to the coalition and what each member should receive if the coalition forms. Coalition decision rules focus on the standards for which members of the coalition advocate and how the output or results should be allocated. They tend to parallel three standards of fairness: equity, equality, and need. Parties arguing for an equity standard consider that anyone who contributed more should receive more, in proportion to the magnitude of the contribution. Those arguing for an equality standard consider that all should receive the same, and those arguing for a need standard consider that members should receive more in proportion to some demonstrated need for the resource.

Now, the members of a coalition may simply select one of them to act as a representative. However, in this work we consider that the members rely on a trusted coordinator or mediator. The coordinator interacts with a seller agent according to the rules of an alternating offers protocol, i.e., bilateral trading proceeds by an iterative exchange of offers and counter-offers. In particular, the coordinator sends offers and team decisions to the seller and broadcasts offers from this agent to the members of the coalition. The seller can pursue the strategies described in Sect. 2 or any other similar strategies (see, e.g., [10]).

The coordinator also interacts with all coalition members—that is, all end-use customers. Specifically, it helps them in two key decisions: whether an offer (counter-offer) received from the seller agent should be accepted and which a new offer should be sent to the seller. Typically, whenever the mediator receives an offer from the seller, say at time period $t-1$, it communicates the offer to all customers and opens a voting process, where each customer states whether or not the offer is acceptable. The votes can be either positive (1), if the offer is acceptable, or negative (0), if the offer is not acceptable. The votes are submitted to the coordinator, who counts the number of acceptances (positive votes) and makes a decision based on a specific decision rule. A common rule is the "simple majority" rule (or just "majority" for short): offers supported by more than half of the customers are accepted, otherwise they are rejected. If the number of customers is even and a tie has been produced, a random decision is taken by the coordinator. Another common rule is the "unanimity rule": offers supported by all customers are accepted, otherwise they are rejected (but see, e.g., [4]).

The other key decision is related to new offers to submit to the seller agent. Typically, whenever a new offer has to be proposed to this agent, the coordinator opens a call for proposals among all customers. Next, each customer prepares and submits a specific proposal to the coordinator. Following this, the coordinator reveals the proposals to all customers (i.e., the proposals are made public), and opens a voting process—again, the votes for each proposal can be either positive (offer acceptance) or negative (offer rejection). The mediator gathers all votes and then makes a decision based on a specific decision rule. In this case, a common rule is the "plurality" rule (or "relative majority"): the most supported proposal is selected, made public among all customers, and sent to the seller agent. When the decision results in a tie, one of the most supported proposals is selected randomly (but see, e.g., [4]).

In this work, we consider a slightly different interaction process between the coordinator and the coalition members. Whenever the coordinator a_c receives an offer $p_{s \to c}^{t-1}$ from the seller agent a_s, say at time period $t-1$, a_c prepares a new offer $p_{c \to s}^{t}$, and opens a voting process among all members, where the offers $p_{s \to c}^{t-1}$ and $p_{c \to s}^{t}$ are made public. The votes can be either positive (acceptance of $p_{s \to c}^{t-1}$, and consequent rejection of $p_{c \to s}^{t}$) or negative (acceptance of $p_{c \to s}^{t}$, and rejection of $p_{s \to c}^{t-1}$). The decision depends on both the utility $U(p_{s \to c}^{t-1})$ of $p_{s \to c}^{t-1}$ and the utility $U(p_{c \to s}^{t})$ of $p_{c \to s}^{t}$, i.e., a vote is positive if $U(p_{s \to c}^{t-1}) \geq U(p_{c \to s}^{t})$. Thus, each member receives both offers, rates them using its own utility function, and votes accordingly.

The votes are submitted to the coordinator, who sums up the number of positive votes and makes a decision based on a specific decision rule. In this work, we consider three different decision rules: a "'simple majority" or just "majority" rule (a specific proposal receives more than half of the votes), a "qualified majority" or "supermajority" rule (a proposal receives a number of votes above a specified percentage, set to 75 %), and an "unanimity" rule (a proposal receives all votes). Thus, if the number of positive votes is greater than half of the votes plus one, then the offer $U(p_{s \to c}^{t-1})$ is accepted at period $t-1$, and negotiation ends successfully in an agreement. Otherwise, if the coordinator and the coalition members decide to continue bargaining, negotiation passes to period t, and the coordinator submits the offer $p_{c \to s}^t$ to the seller agent.

4 Case Study

This section presents a case study to analyze the impact of customer coalitions on energy tariffs during bilateral contracting of electricity. The agents are three end-use customers (a_1, a_2 and a_3), a coordinator (a_c), and a retailer (a_s). More specifically, the customers are three schools for children (ages three to sixteen) located in England:

- a_1: St George's College, Weybridge Road, Addlestone, Surrey;[1]
- a_2: St George's Junior School, Thames Street, Weybridge, Surrey;[2]
- a_3: Ludgrove School, Ludgrove, Wokingham, Berkshire.[3]

We consider that the schools decide to negotiate a new contract and ally into a coalition to strengthen their bargaining positions. To this end, they rely on the coordinator agent who interacts and negotiates directly with the retailer agent a mutually acceptable agreement and, hopefully, a better tariff for all end-use customers—that is, all members of the coalition. The contract duration is set to 365 days.

Table 1 presents the daily average energy quantities, the electricity tariffs and the annual average costs for all customers. The data in the Table is based on real consumption data and tariffs.[4] We consider that each customer has signed up for a time-of-use (TOU) tariff characterized by two different energy prices for two different blocks of time (peak and off-peak) of a 24-h day. The corresponding blocks of time are as follows:

- Peak hours: 8 a.m.–5 p.m.
- Off-peak hours: 12 midnight–8 a.m. and 5 p.m.–12 midnight

Thus, the electricity tariffs of the customers present two different rates: a day rate and a night rate—that is, when demand is high (i.e. during the day) the price is higher and when demand is low (i.e. at night) the price is also low.

The negotiating agenda includes the energy prices for the two periods of a 24 h day (peak and off-peak). Negotiation proceeds by an iterative exchange of

---

[1] http://www.stgeorgesweybridge.com/college/why-st-georges-college.
[2] http://www.stgeorgesweybridge.com/junior-school.
[3] http://www.ludgrove.net/.
[4] http://www.ecodriver.co.uk (accessed on January 2016).

Table 1. Customers: daily average energy quantities, tariffs and annual costs

	Period	End-use Customer		
		St George's College (a_1)	St George's Junior School (a_2)	Ludgrove School (a_3)
Daily average energy (MWh)	Peak	0.980	0.365	0.138
	Off-peak	0.629	0.220	0.072
Energy tariff (£/MWh)	Peak	96.00	96.00	94.00
	Off-peak	60.00	60.00	69.00
Annual cost (thousand £)		48.11	17.60	6.548

offers and counter-offers. At a specific period of the negotiation process, each agent prepares a new offer by considering its previous offer and also a specific negotiation strategy. The coordinator pursues a "low-priority concession making" strategy (see Sect. 2 and also [8]). This means that this agent (and naturally all customers) places greater emphasis on the key negotiation issue—that is, the peak price. In other words, whenever a new offer has to be prepared, the coordinator often yields on the less important or low-priority issue (i.e., the off-peak price). Also, the coordinator takes decisions about the submission of new offers and the acceptance of incoming offers according to either a "majority" decision rule (two of the customers must are in agreement) or an "unanimity" decision rule (all customers must are in agreement).

The retailer agent pursues a concession strategy based on Eqs. (3) and (4). Thus, this agent makes concession throughout negotiation according to the total amount of energy that the customers are expecting to consume in a given daily pricing period—that is, 1.483 MWh in the peak period and 0.921 MWh in the off-peak period. Naturally, the amount of energy to sell increases when the customers ally into a coalition (when compared with each isolated customer), increasing the likelihood of the retailer to make substantial concessions.

The simulation results are presented in Table 2, namely the new energy tariffs, the corresponding average annual costs, and the annual financial benefits. The case study involved two different simulations: a simulation where the coordinator adopts a majority decision rule, and a simulation where this agent adopts an unanimity decision rule. Clearly, each of the two new tariffs is better for customer a_3, since the new peak and off-peak prices are lower than the current peak and off-peak prices, respectively. The annual gains are 165.83£ (majority rule) and 184.55£ (unanimity rule).

Also, the new tariffs are significantly better for customer a_2—in both simulations, the new peak prices are considerably lower than the current peak price (although the new off-peak prices are higher than the current off-peak price). The annual gains are 20.66£ (majority rule) and 76.01£ (unanimity rule). For customer a_1, the tariff resulting from the second simulation (unanimity rule) is

Table 2. Simulation results: energy tariffs, annual costs and financial benefits

Decision rule		Period	End-use customer		
			St George's College	St George's Junior School	Ludgrove School
Majority	Energy tariff (£/MWh)	Peak	92.56	92.56	92.56
		Off-peak	65.45	65.45	65.45
	Annual cost (thousand £)		48.13	17.58	6.382
	Annual financial benefit (£)		−20.75	20.66	165.83
Unanimity	Energy tariff (£/MWh)	Peak	92.47	92.47	92.47
		Off-peak	64.91	64.91	64.91
	Annual cost (thousand £)		47.97	17.53	6.363
	Annual financial benefit (£)		135.42	76.01	184.55

significantly better than the current tariff—the annual gain is 135.42£. However, the tariff resulting from the first simulation (majority rule) is slightly worse than the current tariff (the annual loss is 20.75£).

Overall, the technical decision of the three end-use customers to ally into a coalition may be considered a high-quality group decision—the new tariffs resulting from coalition formation and contract negotiation are more favorable to all customers when an "unanimity" decision rule is adopted (although they are more favorable to only two customers when a "majority" rule is adopted). Furthermore, the customers may voluntarily adjust their demand based on the new prices, to avoid consuming at the higher-priced hours and/or take advantage of the lower-priced hours. Specifically, they may adopt one (or both) of the following two basic load response strategies [13]:

1. Foregoing: involves reducing the electricity usage at times of the high price without changing the consumption pattern during the other periods;
2. Shifting: involves rescheduling usage away from times of the high price to the other periods.

For each strategy, inconveniences to building occupants are likely to be important considerations and may be an important part of the cost-benefit decision.

At this stage, we hasten to add two explanatory and cautionary notes. First, the simulation results presented in Table 2 are initial results. There is a need to perform more detailed simulations and even to conduct experiments to evaluate the effect of coalition formation on contract negotiation. Nevertheless, although the results are preliminary, they do suggest the formation and management of customer coalitions during bilateral contracting of electricity. Second, the above statement: "the schools decide to... ally into a coalition to strengthen their bargaining positions" requires some qualification. Since the retailer makes concessions according to Eq. (4), that is, by taking into account the total amount of energy in a given daily pricing period, the best we can hope for is to model bargaining power by considering only a single criterion, namely the total amount of energy that the customers are willing to purchase. Certainly, bargaining power is a more complex negotiation factor. Broadly speaking, bargaining power is the potential to alter the attitudes and behaviors of others that an individual brings to a given negotiation situation (but see, e.g., [12]).

5   Conclusion

This paper has described research work that uses the potential of agent-based technology to develop a computational tool to support both bilateral contracting of electricity and coalition formation and management, particularly coalitions of end-use customers. Specifically, the paper has described a bilateral negotiation model, and mainly presented some key features of a model for coalition formation and decision making.

From the perspective of end-use customers, it has investigated how coalitions could strengthen their bargaining positions and lead to superior negotiation outcomes. To this end, it has presented a case study involving three schools for children (ages three to sixteen) located in England. The schools decided to negotiate a new contract and to ally into a coalition to strengthen their bargaining positions. They have relied on a trusted coordinator agent who has negotiated directly with a retailer agent a mutually acceptable agreement. Although preliminary, the simulation results do suggest that coalition formation during bilateral contracting of electricity is indeed beneficial to end-use customers. In other words, the technical decision of the three schools to ally into a coalition may be considered a high-quality group decision—the new tariffs resulting from coalition formation and contract negotiation are indeed more favorable to all customers when an "unanimity" decision rule was adopted (although they are more favorable to only two customers when a "majority" rule was adopted).

In the future, we intend to study other types of coalitions, especially coalitions involving entities from the primary and domestic sectors, and also to analyze the impact of new decision rules on contract negotiation outcomes. Furthermore, we intend to perform a number of inter-related experiments to empirically evaluate the benefits of coalitions in bilateral contracting of electricity. The experimental method will be controlled experimentation.

Acknowledgement. This work was supported by "Fundação para a Ciência e a Tecnologia" with references UID/CEC/50021/2013 and PD/BD/105863/2014 (H. Algarvio).

References

1. Kirschen, D., Strbac, G.: Fundamentals of Power System Economics. Wiley, Chichester (2004)
2. Lopes, F., Mamede, N., Novais, A.Q., Coelho, H.: Negotiation in a multi-agent supply chain system. In: Third International Workshop of the IFIP WG 5.7 Special Interest Group on Advanced Techniques in Production Planning & Control, pp. 153–168. Firenze University Press (2002)
3. Algarvio, H., Lopes, F., Santana, J.: Multi-agent retail energy markets: bilateral contracting and coalitions of end-use customers. In: 12th International Conference on the European Energy Market (EEM 2015), pp. 1–5. IEEE (2015)
4. Sánchez-Anguix, V., Julián, V., Botti, V., García-Fornes, A.: Studying the impact of negotiation environments on negotiation teams performance. Inf. Sci. **219**, 17–40 (2013)
5. Lopes, F., Rodrigues, T., Sousa, J.: Negotiating bilateral contracts in a multi-agent electricity market: a case study. In: Hameurlain, A., Tjoa, A., Wagner, R. (eds.) 23rd Database and Expert Systems Applications (DEXA 2012), pp. 326–330. IEEE (2012)
6. Osborne, M., Rubinstein, A.: Bargaining and Markets. Academic Press, London (1990)
7. Raiffa, H.: The Art and Science of Negotiation. Harvard University Press, Cambridge (1982)
8. Lopes, F., Coelho, H.: Concession behaviour in automated negotiation. In: Buccafurri, F., Semeraro, G. (eds.) EC-Web 2010. LNBIP, vol. 61, pp. 184–194. Springer, Heidelberg (2010)
9. Lopes, F., Mamede, N., Novais, A.Q., Coelho, H.: Negotiation among autonomous agents: experimental evaluation of integrative strategies. In: Bento, C., Cardoso, A., Dias, G. (eds.) 12th Portuguese Conference on Artificial Intelligence (EPIA 2005), pp. 280–288. IEEE Computer Society Press (2005)
10. Faratin, P., Sierra, C., Jennings, N.: Negotiation decision functions for autonomous agents. J. Robot. Auton. Syst. **24**(3–4), 159–182 (1998)
11. Lopes, F., Algarvio, H., Coelho, H.: Bilateral contracting in multi-agent electricity markets: negotiation strategies and a case study. In: 10th International Conference on the European Energy Market (EEM 2013), pp. 1–8. IEEE (2013)
12. Lewicki, R., Barry, B., Saunders, D.: Negotiation. McGraw Hill, New York (2010)
13. Benefits of Demand Response in Electricity Markets and Recommendations for Achieving them. Report to the United States Congress, US Department of Energy, February 2006

Fair Multi-agent Task Allocation for Large Data Sets Analysis

Quentin Baert, Anne Cécile Caron, Maxime Morge$^{(\boxtimes)}$,
and Jean-Christophe Routier

Univ. Lille, CNRS, Centrale Lille, UMR 9189 - CRIStAL - Centre de Recherche en
Informatique Signal et Automatique de Lille, 59000 Lille, France
quentin.baert@etudiant.univ-lille1.fr,
{anne-cecile.caron,maxime.morge,jean-christophe.routier}@univ-lille1.fr

Abstract. Many companies are using MapReduce applications to
process very large amounts of data. Static optimization of such applications is complex because they are based on user-defined operations,
called map and reduce, which prevents some algebraic optimization. In
order to optimize the task allocation, several systems collect data from
previous runs and predict the performance doing job profiling. However
they are not effective during the learning phase, or when a new type of
job or data set appears. In this paper, we present an adaptive multi-
agent system for large data sets analysis with MapReduce. We do not
preprocess data and we adopt a dynamic approach, where the reducer
agents interact during the job. In order to decrease the workload of the
most loaded reducer - and so the execution time - we propose a task
re-allocation based on negotiation.

Keywords: Multi-agent system · Negotiation · Big data · MapReduce

1 Introduction

Data Science aims at processing large volumes of data to extract knowledge or
insights. Since the technological potential and the societal demand increase, new
methods, models, systems and algorithms are developed. The volume and velocity of available data requires new forms of processing to enable their analysis.
For this reason the MapReduce design pattern [1] is very successful. The most
popular MapReduce framework is Hadoop, but numerous implementations exist,
as the cluster computing framework Spark [2], or the distributed NoSQL database Riak built from Amazon Dynamo [3]. In these approaches, the extraction
and processing techniques are distributed and operated without sampling.

Data flows can have periodic (daily, weekly or seasonal) and event-triggered
peak data loads. These peaks can be challenging to manage. In the existing
frameworks, an efficient task distribution (i.e. the key partitioning) requires prior

---

This work is part of the PartENS research project supported by the Nord-Pas de
Calais region (researcher/citizen research projects).

Y. Demazeau et al. (Eds.): PAAMS 2016, LNAI 9662, pp. 24–35, 2016.
DOI: 10.1007/978-3-319-39324-7_3

knowledge of the data distribution. The partitioning is *a priori* fixed and so the workload is not necessarily uniformly distributed. By contrast, multi-agent systems are inherently adaptive and thus particularly suitable when workloads constantly evolve.

In this paper, we propose an adaptive multi-agent system for large data sets analysis based on the MapReduce paradigm. The data processing is distributed among two kinds of agents: (i) the mapper agents filter data; (ii) the reducer agents aggregate the data. In order to balance the workload between reducers, the tasks are dynamically re-allocated among reducers during the process without sampling. For this purpose, reducers are involved in multiple concurrent auctions. Our agents negotiate tasks based on their individual workload in order to decrease the workload of the worst-off agent, i.e. the one which delays the data processing. We prove that the negotiation process terminates and improves the fairness which measures if the processing is performed at the expense of the worst-off agent. We have experimented our multiagent system over real-world data and our observations confirm the added-value of negotiation.

This paper is structured as follows. Section 2 overviews relevant related works and introduces the MapReduce design pattern in the background of our work. Section 3 describes the core of our proposal. Then, we present in Sect. 4 our empirical results. Finally, Sect. 5 concludes.

2   Related Works

In [1], the authors present the MapReduce programming model and its implementation for processing large data sets. In this model, while the map function plays the role of filtering data, the reduce function aggregates data. It allows programmers without any experience with parallel and distributed systems to easily use the resources of a large distributed system. MapReduce jobs are divided into a set of *map* tasks and *reduce* tasks that are distributed on a cluster of computers. The MapReduce programming model calls for two user-provided functions with the following types:

map: $(K1, V1) \rightarrow list[(K2, V2)]$

$reduce$: $(K2, list[V2]) \rightarrow list[(K3, V3)]$

The partitioner takes the intermediate key-value pairs from the mapper and splits them into subsets, one subset per reducer such that all values associated with the same key $K2$ are grouped into a sequence and passed to a reducer. By default the partitioner performs a modulo operation of the number of reducers (`key.hashCode() % numberOfReducers`) whatever the used partitioner (e.g. `YARN` or `MESOS`). Additionally, the partitioner can be customized in order to specify which keys need to be processed together in a single reducer. In this way, the reducer takes pairs of the form $(K2, list[V2])$ and run the reduce function once per key grouping. Once it is done, the final key-value pairs $(K3, V3)$ are written to a file.

Whether a default function or a special one is used, the partitioning is *a priori* fixed. It means that this function does not depend on the data, and so the workload is not necessarily uniformly distributed among the reducers. It results that the computation time is determined by the most loaded reducer.

In this paper, we focus on reducing the workload of the most loaded reducer. Several systems have studied the reduce phase optimization, for instance by predicting the performance with job profiling, collecting data from previous runs (see [4] or [5]). We do not want to preprocess data (e.g. with a machine learning phase using a sample dataset) and we prefer a dynamic approach where adaptive reducers interact during the job. In [6], the authors study unbalanced situations between mappers or between reducers. They design a system named SkewTune, which mitigates two types of skew: skew due to an uneven distribution of data and skew due to some subsets of the data taking longer to process than others. When a resource is available because its task is completed, SkewTune identifies the slowest reducer and re-partitions its unprocessed input data. Our approach is similar but, by contrast, we want the partitioning to be a collective choice of workers. Moreover, we intend to deal with partitioning a set of values associated with the same key, and not only partitioning a set of keys. In [7], the authors propose adaptive mappers to decrease the startup overhead. Such optimization is complementary to our approach and could be implemented by a MAS.

In our work, the dynamic allocation of tasks is based on a negotiation between reducers. Social choice theory provides methods for designing and analyzing collective decision by combining individual preferences or welfares. Computational social choice is often considered as an optimization problem solved by a centralized approach (e.g. an auction) where agents report their preferences to the central and omniscient auctioneer that determines the allocation consequently [8]. Indeed, such an approach makes important assumptions that correspond to severe drawbacks: (i) it may be too expensive to gather all information in a single place; (ii) if data evolve during the solving process, it must restart in order to take the new data into account; (iii) it assumes that agents are fully connected without restriction and that they can communicate with all others. Typically in a distributed system, the communication cost depends on the topology of the network, i.e. physical constraints. We consider here multiple distributed concurrent auctions. By contrast, [9] considers MRF in the domain application of UAV where the underlying assumptions are quite different. For instance, the acquaintance network is highly dynamic and the cost of tasks are different from one agent to another.

3   Proposal

We aim at reducing the workload of the most loaded reducer. For this purpose, we consider dynamic task re-allocation with a multi-agent system which does not require a centralized supervision.

In this section, we present our core proposal. First, we overview the proposal. Second, we present our reducer agent architecture. Third, we introduce the different interaction protocols in which reducer agents are involved. Fourth, we detail their behaviour. Finally, we present some formal properties.

3.1   Overview

Our contribution aims at providing a balanced reducer tasks partitioning. In this purpose we propose a task re-allocation based on local decisions where each reducer is embodied by an agent. This agent is characterized by the bundle of tasks it must achieve. We assume that each task has a cost, i.e. an intrinsic characteristic. Therefore, all the agents, with the same capabilities, estimate their own contributions to the global resolution as the costs of their bundles.

Definition 1 (Allocation/Contribution). *Given a set $\mathcal{T}$ of m tasks $\tau_1, \ldots, \tau_m$ with the associated costs $c_{\tau_1}, \ldots, c_{\tau_m}$ and a population $\Omega = \{1, \ldots, n\}$ of n reducer agents, a task allocation A is represented by an ordered list of pairwise disjoint task bundles $\mathcal{T}_i \subset \mathcal{T}$, such that $\biguplus \mathcal{T}_i = \mathcal{T}$, describing the subset of tasks owned by each agent i:*

$$A = [\mathcal{T}_1, \ldots, \mathcal{T}_n] \text{ with } 1, \ldots, n \in \Omega$$

The contribution of the agent i at time t within the allocation A is defined such that:

$$c_i^A(t) = \sum_{\tau \in \mathcal{T}_i} c_\tau + w_i(t)$$

where w_i is the estimated cost of the work-in-progress of agent i. Before starting the reduce phase, $w_i(0) = 0$.

Mapper phase does not differ from the classical MapReduce model. Mappers deliver intermediate key-values pairs to the reducers. However for each key-values, the mappers add information on the cost of a task for these (partial) values. The default partitioning is then used to achieve the initial distribution to the reducers.

Reducers receive their pairs $(K2, list[V2])$ and start their reduce work. Simultaneously, the negotiation phase begins in order to decrease the contribution of the most loaded reducer, such that the reducing phase finishes earlier. The reducer agents communicate with each other to negotiate task delegation. Actually, they request their peers through cfp (call-for-proposal) in order to alleviate their contributions. A cfp includes the cost of the submitted task and the proposer's contribution.

A reducer bids to take the responsibility of the task in order to decrease the worst contribution. A bidder makes a proposal iff, after the task transfer, the worst resulting contribution is smaller than the worst initial one. Formally, its decision is based on the following local criteria:

Definition 2 (Acceptability Criteria). *Let A be an allocation of tasks at time t between n agents Ω. The agent j will accept the transfer of the task $\tau \in \mathcal{T}_i$ from i iff:*

$$c_j^A(t) + c_\tau < c_i^A(t).$$

In other words, a participant agrees to be involved as bidder in a negotiation iff, in case of successful negotiation, its resulting contribution would be strictly smaller than the initial initiator contribution. Then, for the two involved agents, the greatest contribution after the transfer is smaller than the greatest one before. It results that through repeated negotiations, the highest contributions decrease then the most loaded agents will finish its tasks earlier.

Reciprocally, the initiator of a negotiation can potentially receive several bids replying to its cfp. A bid includes the contribution of the potential supplier. The initiator selects the winner with the smallest contribution. Formally,

Definition 3 (Selection Criteria). *Let A be an allocation of m tasks $\mathcal{T}$ between n agents in Ω at time t. If the agent i has proposed to delegate the task τ and it has received some bids from the agents $\Omega' \subset \Omega$, it selects:*

$$\operatorname{argmin}(\{c_j^A(t) \mid j \in \Omega'\}).$$

In this way, the task transfer allows to load the least loaded reducer in order to balance the workload. It is worth noticing that evaluating the decision criteria for the task transfer only requires local information.

The reducers send cfp as long as their previous cfp has not been denied by all their acquaintances. The protocol ensures that when negotiations stop, there is no task transfer that could lead to a decrease of the highest contribution. A reducer resumes sending cfp when it acquires knowledge that some of its acquaintances are liable to accept it.

3.2   Reducer Agent Architecture

Inspired by [10], we consider that an agent: (i) has a unique *id*; (ii) is triggered by messages delivered in its mailbox; and (iii) can create other agents. The reducer agent creates three agents:

1. a worker agent which locally computes several tasks;
2. a broker agent which negotiates tasks in order to delegate them and potentially adopt additional ones;
3. a manager agent which is responsible of the task bundle to be distributed between the worker and the broker. The task bundle is sorted based on the task costs. In order to increase the likelihood to find a supplier, the manager tries to delegate the task with the lowest cost. By contrast, the task with the highest cost is locally performed by the worker.

Contrary to the worker agent, the two other ones can both communicate with other agents via their reducer. While the manager agent receives the mapper output, the broker negotiates with other brokers. Actually, the reducer agent plays the role of proxy to forward messages from/toward other agents.

3.3 Protocols

The manager interacts with the worker in order to locally perform some tasks (cf Fig. 1a). The manager assigns a task to the worker through a `Request` message and the worker replies with `Done` when the task is performed. Then, the manager is able to send a new task. In order to know the estimated cost of the work in progress, the manager can also send an `Evaluation` message to the worker, and the worker replies with `Remaining`.

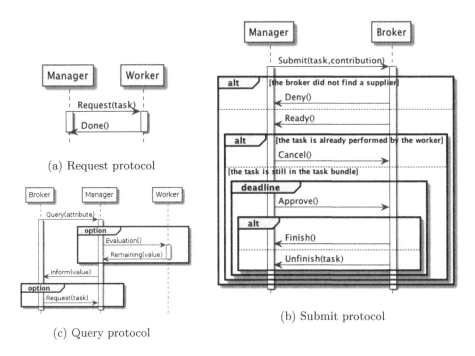

(a) Request protocol

(b) Submit protocol

(c) Query protocol

Fig. 1. Protocols regulating interactions between the manager, the worker and the broker of the same reducer agent

The manager interacts with the broker in different ways depending on its role in the negotiations: a broker can be either the initiator of a negotiation or it can be one of the bidders.

If the broker acts as a bidder (cf Fig. 1c), then it needs to know the local contribution in order to reply to a `Cfp`. For this purpose, the broker sends a `Query` to the manager which replies with an `Inform`. Eventually, the broker can request to the manager a task to perform if it has won the auction. In this case, this task is added to the bundle.

To delegate a task the manager sends a `Submit`, then the broker initiates a negotiation (cf Fig. 1b). If the broker does not find any potential supplier, it replies to the manager with a `Deny`. Otherwise, the broker replies with a `Ready` message. In the latter case, it is still possible that meanwhile the manager has given the task, which had been submitted, to the worker. For this reason the manager can Cancel it. Otherwise, the manager sends an Approve which confirms the successful delegation with a Finish message. If it is not the case, the manager receives an Unfinish message and the task returns to the bundle.

Finally, brokers can negotiate a task delegation through an auction (cf Fig. 2). Such a negotiation is initiated by a broker with a call-for-proposal (Cfp) which contains the cost of delegated task and its own contribution. Depending on its own acceptability criteria (cf Definition 2) each of the m participants can either decline (Decline) or accept the cfp. In the latter case, the participant sends a Propose containing its contribution. Only the proposal with the smallest contribution is selected as the auction winner (cf Definition 3). The others are notified by a Reject while the winner receives an Accept and must then definitely acknowledge the delegation with a Confirm.

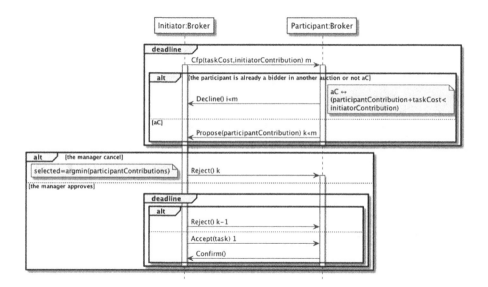

Fig. 2. Negotiation protocol

3.4   Behaviours

Manager. The manager coordinates the activities of the worker and the broker: it provides some tasks to the worker and it triggers the broker to emit Cfp. This coordination is based on some principles: (i) the manager gives priority to the worker: a task is delegated only if the worker is busy. As soon as the worker is free, the manager gives a new task to it; (ii) the manager ensures that a broker is involved in at most one Cfp; (iii) the task bundle operates as a priority queue: the manager gives to the worker the task with the highest cost, and tries to delegate the task with the lowest cost via the broker. This task bundle is filled initially by the mappers, and by the broker when it accepts a `Cfp`.

Additionally, the manager interacts with the supervisor to detect the termination of the data processing. The manager is idle when both the worker and the broker are free and the task bundle is empty. The manager is reactivated when it receives a `Request` for the broker.

Worker. The worker, which is initially free, becomes busy as soon as it receives a `Request`. When the task has been performed, the worker informs the manager and it becomes free. During its work, a worker can tell to its manager the estimated remaining cost of the work in progress

Broker. The broker can act as a bidder or as an initiator in a negotiation.

Broker as a Bidder. When the broker receives a `Cfp`, it queries the local contribution to the manager in order to participate in the auction. If the acceptability criteria, denoted aC (cf Definition 2), is fullfilled, then a proposal is sent. If it is not the case, then the broker declines to enter the auction and informs the manager that it is free. Since a broker can be a bidder only in one negotiation at a time, it does not reply to all the other `Cfp` but stores them in order to respond as soon as possible. This mechanism prevents livelocks. When the bidder is informed (or not) by the initiator of the negotiation outcome: (i) either the bidder wins the auction and it requests the task to its manager and confirms the task delegation to the initiator; (ii) either the bidder does not win the auction (the deadline is reached or `Reject` is received) and it informs its manager it becomes free.

Broker as an Initiator. When the broker receives a `Submit` from the manager, it sends a `Cfp` to the other brokers. Each reply, whether it is a proposal or declination, is notified in a map. When all of them are received (or the deadline is reached), the best proposal (with the lowest contribution) is selected. Obviously, if no proposal is received the negotiation is cancelled and the broker sends a `Deny` message to the manager. Otherwise, the broker selects the auction winner and rejects the losers. It notifies (`Ready`) the manager that is has found a supplier. In return the manager tells if the task is still available or not, resp. `Approve` or `Cancel`. If it is not the case the negotiation is canceled and the winning bid is rejected. Otherwise, an acceptance is sent and a confirmation is expected.

Halting cfp. When a reducer receives `decline` messages from all its acquaintances in response to its `Cfp`, it is useless to emit again the `Cfp` if the context does not change. The reducer can then enter in a *paused state* to prevent sending useless `Cfp`. In this state the reducer can still respond to other's `Cfp`. It leaves this state only if the context changes. The handling of this state is not detailed here due to lack of space. But the principle is the following: the context change means that an unfulfilled acceptability criteria can become fulfilled. The only possibilities are: (i) one new task is added to the bundle and then the reducer's contribution increases; (ii) the reducer is informed that some acquaintance's contribution has decreased (one of its acquaintances has delegated a task or its worker has done a task). Even if one of these events occurs, there is no guarantee that the satisfiability criteria becomes satisfied. However the reducer can estimate whether there is a chance this happens since it keeps track of its acquaintances contributions. This is done by storing (and updating) information on contributions received through acquaintances `Cfp`. Thus, the reducer can estimate the chance for the satisfiability criteria to become fulfilled by one of its acquaintance and therefore for its `Cfp` to be successful. When it is the case, the reducer leaves the *paused state*. In the next section, Theorem 3 tells that after a finite number of negotiations, every agent will be in paused state. Theorem 4 tells that this happens only when no task transfer could produce a better task partitioning.

With workers accomplishing their tasks, the context changes and some new task transfer could be possible. For instance, this can be the case if one of the worker works more slowly that expected. In this case, agents will un-pause and begin a new negotiation phase that will produce a better new task distribution, i.e. a distribution for finishing the job earlier.

3.5   Results

First of all, we can remark that a negotiation improves the fairness which measures if the processing is performed at the expense of the worst-off agent. The tasks are distributed in a more egalitarian way after a negotiation.

Property 1. *The variance of the reducers contributions decreases after one successful negotiation.*

Proof 1. *Let $\Omega = \{1, \ldots, n\}$ be a set of n reducer agents. Let us consider a successful negotiation led by the agent 1. We denote:*

- *$(c_i)_{i \in \Omega}$, the contributions of the agents before the negotiation;*
- *$(c'_i)_{i \in \Omega}$, the contributions of the agents after the negotiation;*
- *$\bar{c} = \frac{1}{n}\Sigma_{i=1}^{n}c_i = \frac{1}{n}\Sigma_{i=1}^{n}c'_i$ the mean contribution[1];*
- *$Var = \Sigma_{i=1}^{n}(c_i - \bar{c})^2$ the variance of the contributions before negotiation;*
- *$Var' = \Sigma_{i=1}^{n}(c'_i - \bar{c})^2$ the variance of the contributions after negotiation.*

Let $c > 0$ be the cost of the negotiated task and k the reducer agent which has won the negotiation. Due to the acceptability criteria of the participant k, $c_k + c < c_1$, so $c_k + c - c_1 < 0$. Then $Var' - Var < 0$.

It is worth noticing that the whole process also improves the fairness.

Property 2. *The successful iterated negotiations make the variance of the contributions decrease.*

---

[1] It is worth noticing that the negotiation is conservative.

Proof 2. *The protocols ensure that no agent is simultaneously involved in several negotiations: bidder and initiator roles are mutually exclusive for the broker agent; when committed as bidder in negotiation the broker agent does not reply to the requests for other negotiations.*

It results that every negotiation is independent. Then the outcome of a negotiation does not impact another one. According to Theorem 1 every successful negotiation makes the variance of contributions decrease, independently of other negotiations, then during the iteration of such negotiations the variance decreases.

Finally, the negotiation process terminates.

Property 3. *The iteration of successful negotiations terminates.*

Proof 3. *According to Theorem 2, the variance strictly decreases (and is positive) during iterated successful negotiations, and the number of tasks is finite, then after a finite number of negotiations the variance can no more decrease then successful negotiation are no more possible.*

Negotiation process is correct: when it halts, no other task transfer could alleviate the most loaded agent.

Property 4. *When iteration of successful negotiations terminates, there exists no task transfer that could decrease the most loaded agent contribution.*

Proof 4. *Let agent j be the most loaded and τ be the smallest task of agent j. Let us assume that there exists some agent i, with contribution c_i, such that i accepting the transfer of task τ results in a decrease of the highest contribution. This implies that $c_i + c_\tau < c_j$.*

Then i would have make a proposal to a cfp from j for task τ. This cfp would have been successful which is a contradiction.

4   Experiments

In order to evaluate our proposition, we have reimplemented the classical MapReduce using the default partitioning function and our multiagent system with the Scala programming language and Akka's actor implementation.

We have performed several experiments. In all of them, our adaptive process leads to a better task allocation. Due to the lack of space, we have chosen to present a particular illustrative one. It considers the historical weather data in France available since 1996. It contains more than 3 millions of observations over 62 stations (800 Mo). We aims at counting the number of observations per half degree of temperature (cf Fig. 3).

We consider 10 mappers and 20 fully connected reducers. Figure 4 shows the contributions of reducers in both cases. On the left, the default partitioning function leads to an unfair distribution of tasks where only a few reducers are committed to perform tasks. We can observe that the MAS balances the workload between reducers since the tasks are dynamically re-allocated among

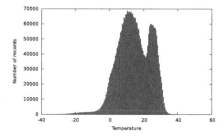

Fig. 3. The number of records per half degree of temperature.

reducers during the process. The overloaded reducers delegate some of their tasks to unoccupied agents. Actually, the contributions of the worst-off agent is reduced by 72 %, and then the fairness which measures if the processing is performed at expense of the worst-off agent is improved in proportion. Moreover the ratio between the least loaded reducer and the most loaded one shift from 0 to 0.7.

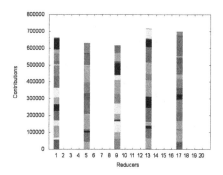 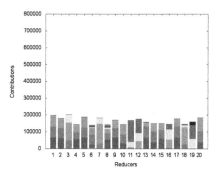

Fig. 4. The contributions of reducers for the classical MapReduce (at left) and for our multi-agent system (at right).

5   Conclusion

MapReduce applications are complex to optimize, because they are based on user-defined operations and the programmer need to understand the implementation of the framework (for instance, Hadoop). In particular, it is difficult to manage the allocation of work among reducers, since the distribution of tasks is statically fixed. This can lead to an unfair distribution. Our MAS consists of a distributed model of computation, inherently adaptive. Therefore, we have defined in this paper an implementation of MapReduce where task allocation is the result of negotiations between agents during the reduce phase, with only local decisions taken by reducer agents (i.e. no global supervisor), and without preprocessing the data. More precisely, our model is based on reducers composed of three coordinated agents, manager, worker and broker. In order to balance the workload, these complex reducer agents negotiate tasks based on their individual contributions in order to decrease the contribution of the worst-off agent, i.e. the one which delays the data processing. Our experiments over real-world data confirm that MAS are suitable to design such adaptive allocation.

We consider several perspectives for this work. We are currently distributing the implementation of the framework. Then, we will be able to compare with other skew reduction techniques and measure the communication cost. Another improvement we consider is to split the large key tasks such that the subtasks can be negotiated. Our long-term project consists of tackling complex workflows of jobs and adapting the network of acquaintances to the physical constraints.

References

1. Dean, J., Ghemawat, S.: MapReduce: simplified data processing on large clusters. In: Sixth Symposium on Operating System Design and Implementation, pp. 137–150 (2004)
2. Zaharia, M., Chowdhury, M., Das, T., Dave, A., Ma, J., McCauley, M., Franklin, M.J., Shenker, S., Stoica, I.: Resilient distributed datasets: a fault-tolerant abstraction for in-memory cluster computing. In: Proceedings of the 9th USENIX Conference on Networked Systems Design and Implementation, pp. 15–28. USENIX Association (2012)
3. DeCandia, G., Hastorun, D., Jampani, M., Kakulapati, G., Lakshman, A., Pilchin, A., Sivasubramanian, S., Vosshall, P., Vogels, W.: Dynamo: Amazon's highly available key-value store. In: Proceedings of the 21st ACM SIGOPS Symposium on Operating Systems Principles (SOSP 2007), pp. 205–220 (2007)
4. Lama, P., Zhou, X.: Aroma: automated resource allocation and configuration of mapreduce environment in the cloud. In: Proceedings of the 9th Internatinal Conference on Autonomic Computing (ICAC 2012), pp. 63–72 (2012)
5. Verma, A., Cherkasova, L., Campbell, R.H.: Aria: automatic resource inference and allocation for mapreduce environments. In: Proceedings of the 8th Internatinal Conference on Autonomic Computing (ICAC 2011), pp. 235–244 (2011)
6. Kwon, Y., Balazinska, M., Howe, B., Rolia, J.: Skewtune: mitigating skew in mapreduce applications. In: Proceedings of the 2012 ACM SIGMOD International Conference on Management of Data, SIGMOD 2012, pp. 25–36 (2012)
7. Vernica, R., Balmin, A., Beyer, K.S., Ercegovac, V.: Adaptive mapreduce using situation-aware mappers. In: Proceedings of the 15th International Conference on Extending Database Technology, EDBT 2012, pp. 420–431 (2012)
8. Brandt, F., Conitzer, V., Endriss, U.: Computational social choice. In: Weiss, G. (ed.) Multiagent Systems, pp. 213–380. MIT Press, Cambridge (2013)
9. Pujol-Gonzalez, M., Cerquides, J., Meseguer, P., Rodríguez-Aguilar, J.A., Tambe, M.: Engineering the decentralized coordination of UAVs with limited communication range. In: Bielza, C., Salmerón, A., Alonso-Betanzos, A., Hidalgo, J.I., Martínez, L., Troncoso, A., Corchado, E., Corchado, J.M. (eds.) CAEPIA 2013. LNCS, vol. 8109, pp. 199–208. Springer, Heidelberg (2013)
10. Hewitt, C., Bishop, P., Steiger, R.: A universal modular actor formalism for artificial intelligence. In: Proceedings of the 3rd International Joint Conference on Artificial Intelligence, pp. 235–245 (1973)

Location-Aware Social Gaming with AMUSE

Federico Bergenti and Stefania Monica[✉]

Dipartimento di Matematica e Informatica, Università degli Studi di Parma,
Parco Area delle Scienze 53/A, 43124 Parma, Italy
{federico.bergenti,stefania.monica}@unipr.it

Abstract. This paper focuses on a novel software module that allows
agents running on smart appliances to estimate their location in the
physical environment thanks to an underlying ranging technology and a
specific localization algorithm. The proposed module is an add-on of the
AMUSE platform which allows agents to estimate their position in the
physical environment and to have it readily available as a specific game
element in the scope of location-aware games. The module first acquires
range estimates between the appliance where the agent is running and
the access points of the WiFi network, and then it properly processes
such range estimates using a localization algorithm. In order to prove
the validity of the proposed approach, we show experimental results
obtained in an illustrative indoor scenario where four access points have
been accurately positioned. The position estimates of the appliance are
obtained by applying the Two-Stage Maximum-Likelihood localization
algorithm to the range estimates from the four access points. According
to the results presented in this paper, the proposed agent-based localization approach guarantees sufficiently accurate position estimates for
many indoor applications.

1 Introduction

The adoption of agent technology on mobile devices dates back to the very first
prototypes of cellular telephones capable of hosting Java applications, and *JADE*
(*Java Agent and DEvelopment framework*) [1] was one of the first tools that
enabled agents on the appliances that we used to call *Java-enabled phones* [2,3].
The recent porting of JADE to Android devices [4] allows us to deploy IEEE
FIPA (www.fipa.org) agents on a wide variety of smart appliances and it finally
provides concrete opportunities to use agents and multi-agent systems to support
users in their daily activities. Notably, the appliances of today—and even more
the appliances of tomorrow—offer much more resources than in the past and the
development of agents for mobile devices is no longer about managing the lack
of resources; rather it is about interfacing agents with the physical world they
live in, to ensure the user is provided with context-aware services.

One of the two major evolutions of JADE is *WADE* (*Workflows and Agents
Development Environment*) [5,6], an open-source platform for agent-based *BPM*
(*Business Process Management*). WADE extends JADE to support the execu-
tion of tasks defined according to the workflow metaphor, and it also provides

© Springer International Publishing Switzerland 2016
Y. Demazeau et al. (Eds.): PAAMS 2016, LNAI 9662, pp. 36–47, 2016.
DOI: 10.1007/978-3-319-39324-7_4

a set of mechanisms that help managing the inherent complexity of large-scale multi-agent systems both in terms of administration and of non-functional characteristics like scalability, fault tolerance and load balancing. WADE is now a mature technology and its non-functional characteristics are the reason why WADE was chosen to support the construction of a significant part of a large-scale network management service that has been in daily use for more than 5 years [7] to support the core business of Telecom Italia.

Recently, a second major evolution of JADE has been provided to address a specific, yet very important, application area, where agents have shown their benefits [8]. *AMUSE (Agent-based Multi-User Social Environment)* [9] is an open-source platform that extends WADE to tackle specific issues of online social games and it offers a set of functionality that free developers from the burden of implementing—and possibly reimplementing over and over again—horizontal features that are common to most, if not all, online social games. The approach that AMUSE fosters lets developers concentrate on game-specific features, ensures solidity, and, ultimately, reduces time-to-market with increased product quality. AMUSE is implemented on top of WADE to benefit from the interesting non-functional characteristics of WADE in terms of scalability, fault-tolerance and load-balancing. In detail, just like any other possible verticalization of WADE, AMUSE can be smoothly deployed in a local setting to support initial development, and it can then be scaled up to meet the requirements of large-scale service providers.

One of the most interesting characteristics of online social games specifically intended for mobile users is that the physical world of the user can be embedded in the game as an effective game element. In particular, geo-localized games use the physical location of the user (acquired via the GPS) and the pointing direction of his or her smart appliance (acquired via compass and accelerometer) as essential game elements. An obvious generalization of geo-localized games, which we call *location-aware games*, is based on the availability of a ranging technology capable of supporting the localization of a device with respect to a fixed reference frame in an indoor environment where the GPS and its envisioned improvements are not available.

This paper tackles the problem of interfacing agents on a mobile appliance with the physical world where they live in by introducing a novel AMUSE add-on that can be used to provide AMUSE agents with the ranging and localization capabilities needed to support location-aware games. We have already extended JADE agents with the possibility of sensing their physical location [10] using a dedicated technology called *UWB (Ultra-Wide Band)* which has been recently made available on some smart appliance. The work presented in this paper differs from that experience because we make no particular assumption on the targeted appliance and we provide a tool tightly integrated with AMUSE and with the game-related abstractions that it provides to ease the construction of social games. In detail, we prototyped a software module that can be used to develop AMUSE agents capable of sensing their location with respect of a fixed reference frame by measuring the distances between the appliance where the agent is running and the *APs* (*Access Points*) of the WiFi network using standard network scanning techniques available to all smart appliances. The measured distances are then fed to a localization algorithm that provides the agent with an estimate of its location and that allows using such an estimate as a major game element for location-aware games.

The considered module enables all location-based augmented reality applications in indoor scenarios with no need of dedicated infrastructure. Possible realistic applications of the localization module described in this paper involve large indoor areas with high concentrations of potential users, like the halls of shopping malls, the waiting areas of airports, and the covered markets often found in historic cities. Nowadays, the majority of such areas offers dedicated WiFi coverage and the knowledge of the positions of APs together with the possibility of estimating the distance between each AP and the user's appliance allow reproducing a sort of GPS for the area with no need for a new infrastructure. It is worth noting that the implemented prototype does not assume that the appliance is connected to one of the WiFi networks of the area; rather it only assumes that the WiFi receiver is enabled on the appliance.

In details, we target scenarios where users in one of the indoor areas mentioned above receive discounts by playing location-aware games, e.g., one of the many possible variations of a treasure hunt. For such scenarios the GPS is out of question because we assume an indoor environment and because the typical accuracy of the GPS (typically 5 m for civilian applications) is not sufficient to ensure that the user is, for example, in front of a specific shop window. A localization accuracy of less than 2 m is needed to discriminate the shop window in front of which the user is and in this paper we show, through illustrative examples, that such an accuracy can be achieved by using the presented AMUSE add-on. It is worth noting that the use of a ranging technology with higher accuracy, like the UWB [11], is an overkill that cannot trade off with the general availability of WiFi support on all smart appliances.

For the sake of brevity, this paper mainly concentrates on the implemented localization algorithm and validates its characteristics in terms of localization accuracy. In Sect. 2, the localization framework is introduced and the algorithm implemented in AMUSE is summarized. In Sect. 3, a few illustrative experimental results are shown. Section 4 concludes the paper.

2   Position-Aware AMUSE Agents

In order to provide information on the position of the appliance that hosts an agent in the scope of a location-aware game, ranging and localization capabilities have been integrated in AMUSE by means of a dedicated add-on module. The implemented localization algorithm is based on the range estimates between some APs with known positions and the user appliance, denoted as *TN* (*Target Node*) in the following. Such range estimates are derived from the received power of the WiFi signal using the Friis formula, according to which the average received power $\bar{P}(r)$ at distance r can be expressed as

$$\bar{P}(r) = P_0 - 10\beta \log_{10} \frac{r}{r_0} \tag{1}$$

where P_0 is the known power at the reference distance r_0. An estimate of the average received power $\bar{P}(r)$ yields the value of the distance r by inverting (1).

The considered localization approach involves two steps. First, the agent in charge of performing localization needs to acquire the range estimates between itself and a sufficiently large number of APs. In particular, at least four range estimates from four different APs need to be acquired in order to perform localization in a three-dimensional environment. Each communication between the TN and any of the AP in range allows obtaining an estimate of the distance between them, and other valuable information, such as the *BSSID (Basic Service Set IDentification)* of the responding AP. By associating each mapped BSSID with the coordinates of the corresponding AP, each range estimate can be related to the coordinates of the corresponding AP. This possibility is crucial to apply the second step, where the agent responsible for localization uses a proper localization algorithm which relies on the range estimates and on the APs coordinates acquired in the first step to estimate the TN position.

Various range-based localization algorithms have been proposed in the literature [12]. Such algorithms can be roughly classified into active and passive methods. Passive localization methods are based on the analysis of the scattering caused by targets during signal propagation and/or of the variance of a measured signal. Relying on the strong dependence of wireless communications on the environment, changes in the received physical signals can be analyzed and used to locate a target [13]. Active localization methods, instead, require that all nodes are equipped with sensors and with an electronic device able to send information [14]. The experimental setup considered in this paper involves active nodes, namely the device where the AMUSE agent runs and the WiFi APs.

Among the wide variety of active localization algorithms known in the literature [15], we decided to implement the *TSML (Two-Stage Maximum-Likelihood)* algorithm [16] in the presented AMUSE add-on module. Such method is considered optimal because it can attain the Cramer-Rao lower bound, which is a lower bound for the variance of an estimator [16]. However, any other range-based active localization algorithm could be easily implemented because the module is intentionally extensible and customizable.

In this paper we do not discuss the details of the implementation of the agent behaviours which have been provided to add localization capabilities. Instead, we are more interested in briefly describing the localization approach and, most of all, in showing experimental results, which have been obtained in a real indoor scenario, and which validate the proposed approach. In order to do so, let us first introduce some notation. In the remaining of the paper, we indicate the coordinates (in a three-dimensional environment) of the APs as

$$\underline{s}_i = [x_i, y_i, z_i]^T \qquad i \in \{1, \ldots, M\} \tag{2}$$

where M is the number of available APs. We remark that we assume that the coordinates of the APs are known to the agent in charge of the localization.

In the following, the Euclidean norm of the coordinate vector of the i-th AP is denoted as $\{a_i\}_{i=1}^M$, namely

$$a_i \triangleq ||\underline{s}_i|| = \sqrt{x_i^2 + y_i^2 + y_z^2} \qquad i \in \{1, \dots, M\}. \qquad (3)$$

The (unknown) position of the TN is denoted as $\underline{u} = [x, y, z]^T$ so that the exact distance between the TN and the i-th AP can be written as

$$r_i \triangleq ||\underline{u} - \underline{s}_i|| = \sqrt{(\underline{u} - \underline{s}_i)^T (\underline{u} - \underline{s}_i)} \qquad i \in \{1, \dots, M\}.$$

Observe that if the coordinates of the APs and the true values of the distances $\{r_i\}_{i=1}^M$ are known, the true position of the TN can be found by intersecting the spheres $\{S_i\}_{i=1}^M$, centered in $\{\underline{s}_i\}_{i=1}^M$ with radii $\{r_i\}_{i=1}^M$. In other words, the TN coordinates satisfy the following quadratic system of equations

$$\begin{cases} (x - x_1)^2 + (y - y_1)^2 + (z - z_1)^2 = r_1^2 \\ \dots \\ (x - x_M)^2 + (y - y_M)^2 + (z - z_M)^2 = r_M^2. \end{cases} \qquad (4)$$

Unfortunately, the true values of the distances $\{r_i\}_{i=1}^M$ are unknown and, therefore, localization must be performed only relying on range estimates, which will be denoted as $\{\hat{r}_i\}_{i=1}^M$. The equations of the M spheres $\{\hat{S}_i\}_{i=1}^M$ centered in $\{\underline{s}_i\}_{i=1}^M$ with radii $\{\hat{r}_i\}_{i=1}^M$ are shown in the following system

$$\begin{cases} (\hat{x} - x_1)^2 + (\hat{y} - y_1)^2 + (\hat{z} - z_1)^2 = \hat{r}_1^2 \\ \dots \\ (\hat{x} - x_M)^2 + (\hat{y} - y_M)^2 + (\hat{z} - z_M)^2 = \hat{r}_M^2. \end{cases} \qquad (5)$$

While the system of Eq. (4) has a unique solution, corresponding to the TN position, the spheres $\{\hat{S}_i\}_{i=1}^M$ would hardly intersect in a unique point since the radii (namely, $\{\hat{r}_i\}_{i=1}^M$) are affected by errors. For this reason, proper localization algorithms, such as the TSML algorithm, are needed. Here we consider a simplified version of the TSML algorithm described in [16].

According to the TSML algorithm, the quadratic system (5) is solved using a two-step approach. Denoting as $\underline{\hat{u}} = [\hat{x}, \hat{y}, \hat{z}]^T$ the vector representing the coordinates of the TN position estimate and as

$$\hat{n} \triangleq ||\underline{\hat{u}}||^2 = \hat{x}^2 + \hat{y}^2 + \hat{z}^2 \qquad (6)$$

its Euclidean norm, the system (5) can be reformulated in matrix notation as

$$\underline{G}_1 \hat{\underline{\omega}} = \hat{\underline{h}}_1 \qquad (7)$$

where $\hat{\underline{\omega}} = [\hat{x}, \hat{y}, \hat{z}, \hat{n}]$ and

$$\underline{G}_1 = -2 \begin{pmatrix} x_1 & y_1 & z_1 & -0.5 \\ \vdots & \vdots & \vdots & \\ x_M & y_M & z_M & -0.5 \end{pmatrix} \qquad \hat{\underline{h}}_1 = \begin{pmatrix} \hat{r}_1^2 - a_1^2 \\ \vdots \\ \hat{r}_3^2 - a_3^2 \end{pmatrix}. \qquad (8)$$

Observe that (7) is not a linear system. As a matter of fact, the fourth element of the solution vector $\hat{\underline{\omega}}$ depends on the first three according to (6). However, according to the TSML algorithm, the solution $\hat{\underline{\omega}}$ of the system (7) is determined, neglecting this dependence, through a Maximum-Likelihood (ML) approach and it can be expressed as

$$\hat{\underline{\omega}} = (\underline{\underline{G}}_1^T \, \underline{\underline{W}}_1 \, \underline{\underline{G}}_1)^{-1} \underline{\underline{G}}_1^T \, \underline{\underline{W}}_1 \, \hat{\underline{h}}_1 \tag{9}$$

where $\underline{\underline{W}}_1$ is a positive definite matrix [16]. In the current implementation of the TSML localization algorithm, the weighting matrix $\underline{\underline{W}}_1$ is set equal to the identity matrix, which is the simplest choice one can make. Possible different choices are shown in [16].

The second stage of the TSML algorithm is meant to take into account the dependence of $\hat{n}$ on the other elements of the solution vector $\hat{\underline{\omega}}$ of (7). This is done by solving the following system of equations

$$\underline{\underline{G}}_2 \, \hat{\underline{\phi}} = \hat{\underline{h}}_2 \tag{10}$$

where $\hat{\underline{\phi}} = [\hat{x}^2, \hat{y}^2, \hat{z}^2]^T$ and

$$\underline{\underline{G}}_2 = \begin{pmatrix} 1 & 0 & 0 \\ 0 & 1 & 0 \\ 0 & 0 & 1 \\ 1 & 1 & 1 \end{pmatrix} \qquad \hat{\underline{h}}_2 = \begin{pmatrix} \hat{\omega}_1^2 \\ \hat{\omega}_2^2 \\ \hat{\omega}_3^2 \\ \hat{\omega}_4 \end{pmatrix} \tag{11}$$

where $\hat{\omega}_j$ denotes the j-th component of $\hat{\underline{\omega}}$. The rectangular linear system (10) can be solved, once again, through the ML technique, obtaining

$$\hat{\underline{\phi}} = (\underline{\underline{G}}_2^T \, \underline{\underline{W}}_2 \, \underline{\underline{G}}_2)^{-1} \underline{\underline{G}}_2^T \, \underline{\underline{W}}_2 \, \hat{\underline{h}}_2. \tag{12}$$

As done when solving (7), in the implemented version of the TSML algorithm the weighting matrix $\underline{\underline{W}}_2$ is the identity matrix. Finally, the position estimate can be expressed as

$$\hat{\underline{u}} = \underline{\underline{U}} \left[\sqrt{\hat{\phi}_1}, \sqrt{\hat{\phi}_2}, \sqrt{\hat{\phi}_3} \right]^T \tag{13}$$

where $\underline{\underline{U}} = \mathrm{diag}(\mathrm{sign}(\hat{\underline{\omega}}))$ and $\hat{\phi}_j$ denotes the j-th component of $\hat{\underline{\phi}}$.

In Sect. 3, experimental results obtained using the proposed localization framework are shown. The number of APs in the considered setup is four, which, as already remarked at the beginning of this section, is the minimum number of APs that guarantees localization in a three dimensional environment. Three different TN positions are considered. For each of them, 50 localization estimates have been performed. In the following, the position estimates of the considered TN in the j-th iteration are denoted as

$$\hat{\underline{u}}^{(j)} = [\hat{x}^{(j)}, \hat{y}^{(j)}, \hat{z}^{(j)}] \qquad j \in \{1, \ldots, 50\}. \tag{14}$$

The accuracy of the considered localization approach is analyzed in terms of the average distance between the true TN position $\underline{u}$ and its estimates $\hat{\underline{u}}^{(j)}$.

More precisely, as discussed in previous sections, for the considered application we are interested in the x and y coordinates of the position estimates, since we are interested in locating the TN on the xy-plane. For this reason, let us define the vector

$$\underline{u}_{[1,2]} = [x, y] \tag{15}$$

which contains the true abscissa and ordinate of the TN. Similarly, we denote as

$$\hat{\underline{u}}^{(j)}_{[1,2]} = [\hat{x}^{(j)}, \hat{y}^{(j)}] \tag{16}$$

the vector containing the abscissa and the ordinate of the TN position estimate in the j-th iteration. Using this notation, one can define

$$d^{(j)} = ||\hat{\underline{u}}^{(j)}_{[1,2]} - \underline{u}_{[1,2]}|| \qquad j \in \{1, \ldots, 50\} \tag{17}$$

which represents the distance between the projections of the true TN position and the projection of the TN position estimate in the j-th iteration on any plane $\{z = k\}$, with constant k. In Sect. 3, the performance of the proposed localization framework is investigated in terms of $\{d^{(j)}\}_{j=1}^{50}$.

3   Experimental Results

In order to test the validity of the agent-based localization framework previously described, we performed a tests in an illustrative indoor scenario, namely a room whose sides are 5 m long. Four APs, denoted as $\{AP_i\}_{i=1}^{4}$, were positioned in the room and their coordinates, expressed in meters in a proper coordinate system, are

$$\begin{aligned} \underline{s}_1 &= [2.5, 0, 2.5]^T & \underline{s}_2 &= [0, 2.5, 2.5]^T \\ \underline{s}_3 &= [2.5, 5, 1.5]^T & \underline{s}_4 &= [5, 2.5, 2.5]^T. \end{aligned} \tag{18}$$

With this configuration of APs, we positioned the target smartphone in three different positions inside the room. The coordinates of such positions, expressed in meters, are

$$\underline{u}_1 = [1, 1.5, 1]^T \qquad \underline{u}_2 = [2.5, 2.5, 1]^T \qquad \underline{u}_3 = [2.5, 0.1, 1]^T. \tag{19}$$

Figure 1 shows the positions of the four fixed APs (black squares) and the three different positions of the TN (red stars), denoted as $\{TN_i\}_{i=1}^{3}$.

First, the TN is positioned in the point with coordinates $\underline{u}_1$ defined in (19). Such a point is denoted as TN_1 in Fig. 1. In this case, the true distances $\{r_i\}_{i=1}^{4}$ between the i-th AP and the TN, expressed in meters, are

$$r_1 \simeq 2.59 \text{ m} \qquad r_2 \simeq 2.06 \text{ m} \qquad r_3 \simeq 3.84 \text{ m} \qquad r_4 \simeq 4.38 \text{ m}.$$

Range estimates from each of the four APs are acquired and used to estimate the position TN_1. This procedure is iterated 50 times, thus obtaining 50 position estimates $\{\hat{\underline{u}}^{(j)}\}_{j=1}^{50}$ for TN_1.

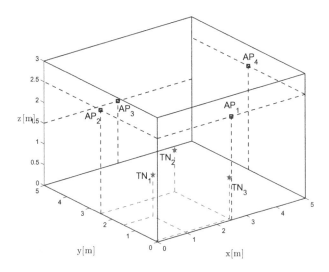

Fig. 1. The positions of the four considered APs (black squares) and three different TN positions (red stars) are shown. (Color figure online)

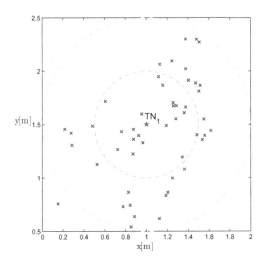

Fig. 2. The projection on the plane $z = 1$ of the 50 position estimates of TN_1 (blue crosses), together with the true TN position (red stars). (Color figure online)

Figure 2 shows the projections of such position estimates on the plane $\{z = 1\}$ (blue crosses), namely the plane, parallel to the floor, where the TN lies. The TN position is also shown (red star). In order to emphasize the values of the distance errors $\{d^{(j)}\}_{j=1}^{50}$ between $\underline{u}_{[1,2]}$ and $\{\hat{\underline{u}}_{[1,2]}^{(j)}\}_{j=1}^{50}$, Fig. 2 also shows two circumferences centered in $[x_1, y_1]$ with radii 0.5 m (dashed green line) and 1 m (dash-dotted cyan line), respectively. The presence of such circumferences

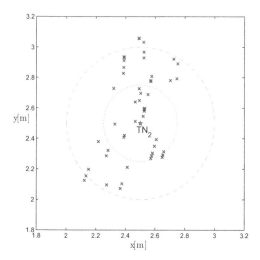

Fig. 3. The projection on the plane $z = 1$ of the 50 position estimates of TN_2 (blue crosses), together with the true TN position (red stars). (Color figure online)

allows emphasizing that the values of the distance errors $\{d^{(j)}\}_{j=1}^{50}$ are smaller than 0.5 m for 20 times, namely in 40 % of the cases. Moreover, the values of $\{d^{(j)}\}_{j=1}^{50}$ are smaller than 1 m for 49 times, corresponding to 98 % of the cases. The value of the distance between the true TN position and the projection of the TN position estimate on the plane $\{z = 1\}$ in the remaining case is 1.12 m and it also corresponds to the maximum value of $\{d^{(j)}\}_{j=1}^{50}$. The average of $\{d^{(j)}\}_{j=1}^{50}$, expressed in meters, is

$$\frac{1}{50} \sum_{j=1}^{50} d^{(j)} \simeq 0.54 \text{ m}$$

meaning that, on average, the distance error between the exact TN position and their estimates on the xy-plane is nearly half a meter. Such a precision is satisfying for the considered application.

Let us now consider the results relative to the TN positioned in the point denoted as TN_2 in Fig. 1, whose coordinates are denoted as $\underline{u}_2$ in (19). In this case, the TN is positioned in the middle of the room and the values of the true distances $\{r_i\}_{i=1}^{4}$ between the i-th AP and TN_2, expressed in meters, are

$$r_1 = r_2 = r_4 \simeq 2.91 \text{ m} \qquad r_3 \simeq 2.54 \text{ m}.$$

In Fig. 3 the projections $\{\underline{\hat{u}}_{[1,2]}^{(j)}\}_{j=1}^{50}$ of the 50 position estimates on the plane $\{z = 1\}$ (blue crosses) and the true TN position (red star) are shown. Figure 3 also shows two circumferences centered in $[x_2, y_2]$ with radii 0.25 m (dotted magenta line) and 0.5 m (dashed green line), so that we can visually conclude that the values of $\{d^{(j)}\}_{j=1}^{50}$ are smaller than 0.5 m in the 90 % of the cases, namely 45 times. Moreover, 20 position estimates (40 % of the cases) correspond

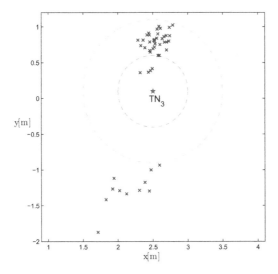

Fig. 4. The projection on the plane $z = 1$ of the 50 position estimates of TN_3 (blue crosses), together with the true TN position (red stars). (Color figure online)

to values of $\{d^{(j)}\}_{j=1}^{50}$ which are also smaller than 0.25 m. With this node config-uration, the maximum value of $\{d^{(j)}\}_{j=1}^{50}$ is 0.55 m and it is nearly a half of the corresponding value relative to TN_1. As expected, also the average of the values $\{d^{(j)}\}_{j=1}^{50}$ is reduced with respect to the previous case. As a matter of fact, the following holds

$$\frac{1}{50} \sum_{j=1}^{50} d^{(j)} \simeq 0.30 \text{ m}$$

so that the distance error on the xy-plane is, on average, 30 cm. It can then be concluded that the position estimates relative to TN_2 are more accurate than those relative to TN_1. However, in both cases the localization accuracy is sufficient for the considered application.

Finally, we consider the TN denoted as TN_3 in Fig. 1, which is near a wall, under the AP denoted as AP_1. With this configuration, the values of the true distances $\{r_i\}_{i=1}^{4}$ between the i-th AP and TN_3, expressed in meters, are

$$r_1 \simeq 1.50 \text{ m} \qquad r_2 \simeq 3.77 \text{ m} \qquad r_3 \simeq 4.92 \text{ m} \qquad r_4 \simeq 3.77 \text{ m}.$$

Figure 4 shows the true TN position (red star) and the projections $\{\hat{\underline{u}}_{[1,2]}^{(j)}\}_{j=1}^{50}$ of its 50 estimates on the plane $\{z = 1\}$ (blue crosses). The two circumferences centered in $[x_3, y_3]$ with radii 0.5 m (dashed green line) and 1 m (dash-dotted cyan line) are also shown in Fig. 4. It can then be easily concluded that, in this case, the values of $\{d^{(j)}\}_{j=1}^{50}$ are smaller than 0.5 m only 4 times and they are smaller than 1 m for 39 times. In the remaining cases, which represent 22 % of the cases, Fig. 4 shows that the TN position estimates have a negative ordinate, which corresponds to saying that the TN position estimates fall outside the considered indoor environment. In such cases, the agent can easily determine that the position estimate is wrong (as it knows to be inside the considered environment) and it can drop the estimate and wait for the next one. According to previously shown results, the accuracy obtained with the proposed framework is sufficient for the considered application which requires, for instance, to know if a person holding an appliance is close to a specific shop in a shopping mall in order to receive discounts from the shop by playing proper location-aware games.

4   Conclusion

In this paper we presented a novel AMUSE add-on which allows implementing agents that can interact with the physical world where they live in by using information on their location. Such information is provided to agents as a specific game element and game developers can use it to support the construction of location-aware games with AMUSE.

In detail, the proposed software module allows an AMUSE agents to acquire range estimates from a number of network nodes with known locations (namely, the known APs of the WiFi network) and to use them to estimate its location. Even if WiFi-based localization does not guarantee the same accuracy obtained with other kinds of wireless communications, such as UWB signaling, it has the advantage of being easily implemented since WiFi APs are now available in the majority of indoor environments and, therefore, it does not require any new infrastructure.

Such new ranging and localization abilities of AMUSE agents are necessary to support location-aware games as envisioned in large indoor environments like the halls of shopping malls, the waiting areas of airports, and the covered markets of historic cities. For each of these scenarios, proper variants of known location-based games, such as treasure hunt, could be implemented using the proposed AMUSE add-on. Experimental results obtained in an illustrative, yet meaningful, indoor environment are shown in the last part of the paper to prove that the proposed agent-based localization approach guarantees sufficiently accurate position estimates to support the envisioned applications.

References

1. Bellifemine, F., Caire, G., Greenwood, D.: Developing multi-agent systems with JADE. Wiley Series in Agent Technology. Wiley, Chichester (2007)
2. Adorni, G., Bergenti, F., Poggi, A., Rimassa, G.: Enabling FIPA agents on small devices. In: Klusch, M., Zambonelli, F. (eds.) CIA 2001. LNCS (LNAI), vol. 2182, pp. 248–257. Springer, Heidelberg (2001)
3. Bergenti, F., Poggi, A.: LEAP: a FIPA platform for handheld and mobile devices. In: Meyer, J.-J.C., Tambe, M. (eds.) ATAL 2001. LNCS (LNAI), vol. 2333, pp. 436–446. Springer, Heidelberg (2002)
4. Bergenti, F., Caire, G., Gotta, D.: Agents on the move: JADE for Android devices. In: Proceedings of Workshop From Objects to Agents (2014)

5. Banzi, M., Caire, G., Gotta, D.: WADE: a software platform to develop mission critical, applications exploiting agents and workflows. In: Proceedings of International Joint Conference on Autonomous Agents and Multi-Agent Systems, pp. 29–36 (2008)
6. Bergenti, F., Caire, G., Gotta, D.: Interactive workflows with WADE. In: Proceedings of IEEE International Conference on Enabling Technologies: Infrastructures for Collaborative Enterprises, pp. 10–15 (2012)
7. Bergenti, F., Caire, G., Gotta, D.: Large-scale network and service management with WANTS. In: Industrial Agents: Emerging Applications of Software Agents in Industry, pp. 231–246. Elsevier (2015)
8. Bergenti, F., Franchi, E., Poggi, A.: Agent-based interpretations of classic network models. Comput. Math. Organ. Theory **19**, 105–127 (2013)
9. Bergenti, F., Caire, G., Gotta, D.: Agent-based social gaming with AMUSE. In: Proceedings of the 5th International Conference on Ambient Systems, Networks and Technologies (ANT 2014) and 4th International Conference on Sustainable Energy Information Technology (SEIT 2014). Procedia Computer Science, vol. 32, pp. 914–919 (2014)
10. Monica, S., Bergenti, F.: Location-aware JADE agents in indoor scenarios. In: Proceedings of 16th Workshop "Dagli Oggetti agli Agenti" (WOA 2015), Napoli, Italy, June 2015
11. Monica, S., Ferrari, G.: An experimental model for UWB distance measurements and its application to localization problems. In: Proceedings of the IEEE International Conference on Ultra Wide Band (ICUWB 2014), pp. 297–302 (2014)
12. Monica, S., Ferrari, G.: Accurate indoor localization with UWB wireless sensor networks. In: Proceedings of the 23rd IEEE International Conference on Enabling Technologies: Infrastructure for Collaborative Enterprises (WETICE 2014), Parma, Italy, pp. 287–289, June 2014
13. Dardari, D., D'Errico, R.: Passive ultrawide bandwidth RFID. In: Proceedings of the IEEE Global Telecommunications Conference (GLOBECOM 2008), New Orleans, LA, pp. 1–6, December 2008
14. Liu, H., Darabi, H., Banerjee, P., Liu, J.: Survey of wireless indoor positioning techniques and systems. IEEE Trans. Syst. Man Cybern. Part C Appl. Rev. **37**(6), 1067–1080 (2007)
15. Monica, S., Ferrari, G.: Swarm intelligent approaches to auto-localization of nodes in static UWB networks. Appl. Soft Comput. **25**, 426–434 (2014)
16. Shen, G., Zetik, R., Thomä, R.S.: Performance comparison of TOA and TDOA based location estimation algorithms in LOS environment. In: Proceedings of the 5th Workshop on Positioning, Navigation and Communication (WPNC 2008), Hannover, Germany, pp. 71–78, March 2008

Dealing with Large MDPs, Case Study of Waterway Networks Supervision

Guillaume Desquesnes[1,2(✉)], Guillaume Lozenguez[1,2], Arnaud Doniec[1,2], and Eric Duviella[1,2]

[1] Mines Douai, IA, 59508 Douai, France
[2] Univ. Lille, 59500 Lille, France
{guillaume.desquesnes,guillaume.lozenguez,arnaud.doniec,
eric.duviella}@mines-douai.fr

Abstract. Inland waterway networks are likely to go through heavy changes due to a will in increasing the boat traffic and to the effects of climate change. Those changes would lead to a greater need of an automatic and intelligent planning for an adaptive and resilient water management. A representative model is proposed and tested using MDPs with promising results on the water management optimization. The proposed model permits to coordinate multiple entities over multiple time steps in order to avoid a flood in the waterway network. However, the proposed model suffers a lack of scalability and is unable to represent a real case application. The advantages and limitations of several approaches of the literature are discussed according to our case study.

Keywords: Markov Decision Process · Inland waterway network · Large model

1 Introduction

Climate change is a main concern in our modern society. In the last years, the effects of global change on the inland waterway network has been studied. The general agreement is that the intensity and the occurrence of flood and drought periods will increase [17].

In parallel, the use of inland navigation to decongest road and railway traffic is in vogue. An increase of ships traffic is thus expected in the coming years. All these evolutions tend to complicate the water management in inland waterway networks and make human planning less and less relevant.

An inland waterway network is an artificial water system interacting with the natural environment. Most of these interactions are only partially known: illegal discharges, exchanges with groundwater tables, local weather influence, . . . The control of a such a network is thus subjected to uncertainties and a stochastic modeling seems therefore more adapted.

Markov Decision Processes (MDPs) are widely used for planning on stochastic models and provide plan for all configurations of the model. To the best of

© Springer International Publishing Switzerland 2016
Y. Demazeau et al. (Eds.): PAAMS 2016, LNAI 9662, pp. 48–59, 2016.
DOI: 10.1007/978-3-319-39324-7_5

our knowledge, MDPs have not yet been used to model the inland waterway network in order to make them resilient and more stable. However previous work has been made on this topic, using flow network with the strong hypothesis of a deterministic model [16].

MDP framework permits to model the evolution of an uncertain system but induces intractable model in most of the applications. Those large MDPs make the policies of an optimal control hard to compute and require specific algorithms [3,15]. A stochastic modeling of the network is proposed, allowing to plan a coordination of all entities in the network. The main complexity comes from the distribution of water transfer possibilities over a territory. An optimal control represents all possible join water transfers considering all complete network situations. This paper aims to draw back the limitations of such an optimal centralized model applied to waterway network and to discuss about approaches that take advantage of distributed control.

In this paper, the problem of inland waterway network management in a context of climate change is presented in Sect. 2. A naive modeling of the network using MDP is proposed in Sect. 3 and some results and the limitations are shown in Sect. 4. Finally a description and comparison of MDP approaches for large scale and distributed model is proposed in Sect. 5 with regard to inland waterway network supervision.

2 Waterway Network Supervision

An inland waterway network, see Fig. 1a is a large scale system, mostly used for navigation. It provides both economic and environment benefits [13,14] while providing quiet, efficient and safe transports of goods [5]. It is mostly composed of canalized rivers and artificial channels, and is divided by locks. Any part between two locks is called a navigational reach. For the sake of simplicity, navigational reach will be called reach on the rest of this paper.

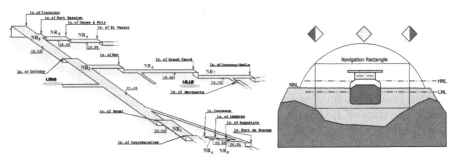

(a) Small part north of France inland waterway network

(b) Navigation rectangle

Fig. 1. (a) Part of north of France waterway network, (b) Navigation rectangle

The water level of a reach must respect the conditions of the navigation rectangle, see Fig. 1b, and be as close as possible from the Normal Navigation Level (NNL). The lower and upper boundaries of the rectangle are respectively the Lower and Higher Navigation Level (LNL & HNL). The main concern of the operator consists in maintaining acceptable water level in all the reaches of the inland waterway network.

In normal situation, having a boat crossing a lock is the main disturbance of the water level, since using a lock drains water from the upstream reach and release water to the downstream reach. Furthermore the water level is affected by ground exchanges, natural rivers, weather and other unknown factors, like illegal discharges. Locks are not dedicated to control the water level, so gates are used to send water downstream and pumps can be used to send some upstream.

At the moment, the navigation is only allowed during daytime, with few exceptions, notably on Sunday. Reaches management is based on human expertise gathered over the time. But in a context of climate change, that will increase the effect of floods and droughts, and with a will to increase the traffic, notably by allowing 24 h a day traffic, those methods start to show their limits.

The objective is to determine a global planning, to maintain the navigation conditions in the entire network, by taking into account uncertainties of the problem, such as weather and traffic in a context of climate change and increasing navigation traffic. Planning over multiple time steps allows a better anticipation of possible events and a better reaction over unexpected events, using real-time information of the network using level sensors spread through the reaches.

3   Using Markov Decision Process

Markov Decision Process (MDP) is a generic framework modeling control possibility of stochastic dynamic system as probabilistic automaton. The framework is well adapted to Waterway Network Supervision while the state of the network is fully observable (in term of water volumes) and the control is uncertain due to uncontrolled water transit.

3.1   MDP Model

A MDP is defined as a tuple $\langle S, A, T, R \rangle$ with S and A respectively, the state and the action sets that define the system and its control possibilities. T is the transition function defined as $T : S \times A \times S \rightarrow [0, 1]$. $T(s, a, s')$ is the probability to reach the state s' from s by doing action $a \in A$. The reward function R is defined as $R : S \times A \times S \rightarrow \mathbb{R}$, $R(s, a, s')$ gives the reward obtained by attaining s' after executing a from s.

A policy function $\pi : S \rightarrow A$ assigns an action to each system state. Optimally solving a MDP consists in searching an optimal policy π^* that maximizes the expected reward. π^* maximizes the value function of Bellman Eq. [1] defined on each state:

$$V^{\pi}(s) = \sum_{s' \in S} T(s, a, s') \times (R(s, a, s') + \gamma V^{\pi}(s')) \quad \text{with} \quad a = \pi(s) \quad (1)$$

$$\pi^*(s) = \underset{a \in A}{\operatorname{argmax}}(\sum_{s' \in S} T(s, a, s') \times (R(s, a, s') + \gamma V^{\pi^*}(s'))) \quad (2)$$

The parameter $\gamma \in [0, 1]$ balances the importance between future and immediate rewards. With γ set close to 0 the immediate action with the maximal reward will be taken while a γ close to 1 will permit the control to accept penalties if future gains could be important. Multiple algorithms exist to solve optimally a MDP, a notable version is *Value Iteration* [19]. It constructs iteratively the value function V, using Eq. 3, until convergence or until a specified number of iterations has been done. The last V_i obtained is then used to generate the optimal policy with Eq. 2. The first value function, V_0 is initialized at 0.

$$V_{i+1}(s) = \max_{a \in A}(\sum_{s' \in S} T(s, a, s') \times (R(s, a, s') + \gamma V_i(s'))) \quad (3)$$

3.2   Naive Waterway Network Control

The objective is to plan the best course of actions for the whole network over t time steps, knowing that some conditions may differ on each time step and can affect the inland navigation. For instance the weather might become rainy which will increase the water volume of affected reaches or more boats than expected could traverse the reach resulting in an higher lock usage.

N represents the number of reaches in the network. Since large time steps are used, we make the assumption that the water level is the same or nearly same at all point in a reach.

A state of the model is defined as an assignation of volume for all the reaches in the network at a given time. Similarly an action is defined as an assignation of volume for each controlled point of transfer (locks, pumps and gates). The MDP formalism requires discrete set of states and actions, but since the volumes are continuous, we discretized them using intervals.

Each reach is divided in intervals, all of the same size, except the first and the last intervals which gather values that are outside of the navigation rectangle. Those two are considered to be of infinite size and represents everything that must be avoided at all cost. The water transfer points use a similar partition as the reaches, except that there is no infinite size intervals, since it is supposed to be fully controlled. More formally, the set of states S of the model is defined as the combination of all possible reaches volumes intervals for all time steps.

For a reach i, the intervals result from a regular discretization of volumes from less water than minimal authorized 0 to more than the maximal authorized ri_{out}.

$$S = \{1, \ldots, t\} \times \prod_{i=1}^{N} [0, ri_{out}] \quad (4)$$

In a similar way, we define the set of actions A as the discretized volumes planed for transfer between between two adjacent reaches. Action is time independent, so we simply have

$$A = \prod_{i,j\in[0,N]^2} L_{i,j} \tag{5}$$

where $L_{i,j}$ represent the set of all possible volume transfer of the transfer point linking reach i to reach j and reach 0 represents external rivers linked to the reaches. In fact, there is only a limited number of transfer points and most of the $L_{i,j}$ do not permit any controlled transfer ($L_{i,j} = \emptyset$).

We denote $a_{i,j} \in L_{i,j}$ the transfer volume planed from reach i to reach j in the action $a \in A$. To simplify the notation, a_i defines the part of the action affecting the reach i as

$$a_i = \sum_{j=0}^{N}(a_{i,j} \ominus a_{j,i}) \tag{6}$$

We define two operators $\oplus$ and $\ominus$ on $(\mathbb{R} \cup \mathcal{I})^2 \rightarrow \mathbb{R}$, that can respectively add and substract intervals of numbers and/or numbers, the result being alway a real.

$\mathcal{I}$ being the set of all possible intervals of our network. Our operators are respectively a simple addition and subtraction using the value of the member if it is a real, or its average value if it is an interval.

Our transition function $T(s, a, s')$ represent the probability to reach the state s' by doing action a from the state s and taking into account the possible temporal variation. It results from discussions with experts of the north of France waterway network. Trivially, for s at time step t and s' at time step t', s' is only reachable if $t' = t + 1$.

Since the transition of each reach is independent from other reach, it only depends on the previous state and its incoming and outgoing water. A first source of uncertainty comes from the uncontrolled water modeled as a list of the temporal variations, noted Var.

Temporal variations are local changes to one or more reaches or transfer points during one or more time steps with some probabilities, for example rain on a reach is a temporal variation. Since those temporal variations are not represented in the action space nor in the state space, they only affect the transition function. The uncontrolled volume of water affecting the reach i is noted $v_i \in Var$ and $P(v_i|t)$ represents the probability that the random variable v_i occurs in time step t. $P(v_i|t)$ is built based on data of uncontrolled water displacement combined with weather forectasts.

The second source of uncertainty results from the discretization in interval of volume, causing an approximation in the state representation.

Let define $P(ri_{s'}|ri_s, a_i + v_i)$ the probability that the volume of water in reach i at time step $t_s + 1$ will be included in interval $ri_{s'}$ if the action a_i is performed and with v_i uncontrolled transfer on i:

$$P(ri_{s'}|ri_s, \, a_i + v_i) = \begin{cases} p_= & \text{if} \quad ri_s \oplus a_i + v_i \in ri_{s'} \\ p_+ & \text{if} \quad ri_s \oplus a_i + v_i \in ri_{s'} + 1 \\ p_- & \text{if} \quad ri_s \oplus a_i + v_i \in ri_{s'} - 1 \\ 0 & \text{else} \end{cases} \tag{7}$$

where $p_=$ is the probability to get the expected volumes by taking into account intervals approximations and, p_+ (resp. p_-) is the probability to get the interval corresponding to a superior (resp. inferior) water level, with respect to

$$p_+ + p_- + p_= = 1 \quad \text{and} \quad p_+ = p_-$$

The transition function states the product of the two sources of uncertainty:

$$T(s, a, s') = \prod_{i=1}^{N} \left(\sum_{\forall v_i \in Var} P(v_i|t) \times P(ri_{s'}|ri_s, \, a_i + v_i) \right) \tag{8}$$

Finally, we define a reward function, representing the current goal of the operators, to greatly penalize the distance to the normal navigation level for each reach with a small cost for all water movement. More formally we define:

$$R(s, a, s') = -1 \times \left(\sum_{i=1}^{N} (NNL_i \ominus ri_{s'})^2 + a_i \right) \tag{9}$$

where NNL_i is the volume corresponding to reach i being at normal navigation level. If $ri_{s'}$ is outside the navigation rectangle we replace it by a large value c and half this value if $ri_{s'}$ is only partially outside the navigation rectangle.

4   Test on a Network

To test this approach, we made a realistic waterway network (see Fig. 2), with two reaches and six transfer points. Then the MDP is solved and the policy is tested on several scenarios.

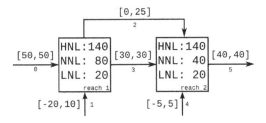

Fig. 2. Waterway network

4.1   Network Characteristics

On Fig. 2, the reaches represented by squares, with a specified volume range, in units of volume, and the arcs correspond to the transfer point with a minimum and maximum capacity. A negative value meaning this transfer point can be used to import and export water. We simulate this network for 8 day and night periods, with locks closed during the night, giving us 16 time steps.

The two reaches volumes are divided in 9 intervals, 7 of size 20 and 2 of infinite size. The points of transfer 1, 2 and 4 are divided in intervals of size 5 (respectively 6, 5 and 2 intervals). The points of transfer 0, 3 and 5 transfer a constant amount of water. Since we were planning on 16 time steps, we had $9 \times 9 \times (16+1) = 1377$ states. An extra time step is added to mark the end of the last planning step, all states within this time step are absorbing, which means $T(s, a, s) = 1$ and have $R(s, a, s) = 0$ to have no influence on the planning. In a similar way, the number of actions is $6 \times 5 \times 2 = 60$.

We used $c = 10000$ as an arbitrary large value for being outside of the navigation rectangle. To valide the performances of our model, the probabilities of the intervals has been set arbitrarily to $p_= = 0.9$ and $p_+ = p_- = 0.05$.

4.2   Some Results

To analyze empirically the quality of the policy generated, we made a few simulations. We made 4 scenarios, the first one being an ideal scenario: both reaches start from their NNL and there is no perturbation. The second scenario consists of the first reach starting from its lowest bound and the second from its highest bound, still with no temporal perturbation. The third one is the opposite of the second one first reach from its highest, second from its lowest. And finally the last scenario is similar to the first one, except that during one time step an heavy rain may happen, with high probability, and would overflow the first reach if nothing is done to prevent it.

Since the policy actions are intervals, we decided to test our scenarios using random values from the chosen intervals to apply to the transfer points, rather than the best at the moment or the average value of the interval to test the quality of the chosen interval. Running each simulation 5 times allowed us to reduce the randomness impact while preserving clarity. It is important to note that the simulations use a continuous modeling of the systems, in both reaches volumes and transfered volumes.

We created our network so that the optimal policy of the first scenario would allow to maintain both NNL at all time steps. We can see in Fig. 3a, that we are only close from it. This is caused by our discretization. Since we represent an interval by its average value, it is possible for a reach to reduce or increase its level while not changing its state causing the reach to continue to decrease or increase its level.

The reaction of the network to some event that put the two reaches on the extremity of their navigation levels, is visible in Fig. 3b and c. We notice that the recovery is way faster in the second case because the upstream reach has to

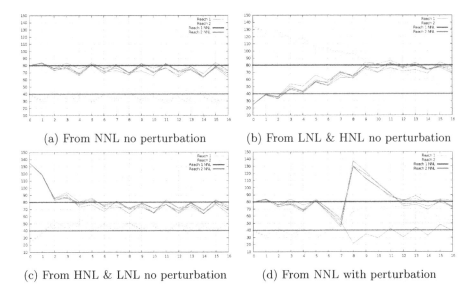

(a) From NNL no perturbation   (b) From LNL & HNL no perturbation

(c) From HNL & LNL no perturbation   (d) From NNL with perturbation

Fig. 3. Different scenarios

empty itself and the downstream needs to be filled unlike the second case where the opposite scenario is happening and each reach has to maintain a minimum impact on the other one to avoid making the other outside of its navigation level.

In the last scenario, heavy rain is supposed to happen between step 7 and 8 causing the first reach to overflow if it is close to its NNL. And to prevent that we see that, few time steps before the event, the first reach will empty itself in the second reach, making it go further from its NNL but by doing that preserving the integrity of the system, if the perturbation happens.

4.3   Limitations in Scaling up

A naive implementation of the transition function consists in creating a $|S|^2 \times |A|$ matrix, which would contain $1377^2 \times 60 = 1.137\,677\,40 \times 10^8$ values, assuming 8 bytes to store each value would mean approximatively $0.91\ GB$ of memory space only for the transition function.

Since, doing an action means that the time step will change, except on the dummy time step, only a small subset of the states, containing at most $\frac{|S|}{t+1}$ states can be reached. A sparse matrix would allow us to reduce drastically the size of the matrix, since only non zero values and their indices has to be stored, so as long as more than half of the matrix is empty, using the sparse matrix is beneficial. By calculating the optimal policy of our example, we have been able to observe a few results. Firstly it converges very fast and works as intended but the construction of the transition function takes most of the time. Since time isn't cyclic, it is possible to find the optimal action for all states corresponding to a certain time step, if it is the last one or if the next one already has optimal action for the states. This allow us to add a max bound to the number of iterations required to find the optimal policy to the number of time steps, here 17.

5 Approaches to Workaround Naive Model Limitation

By increasing the size of our example or its precision, we quickly encounter memory limitations. Furthermore, the state domain, by construction, grows exponentially in the number of reaches and, real application such as the inland waterway network in north of France contains around 50 reaches. Our naive approach wouldn't be able to calculate an optimal policy for this application.

To workaround spatial limitations, some extensions of the MDP have been defined in the literature such as a factored representation of the model. An other technique consist in decomposition where the MDP is split into local sub-MDPs.

Investigation focus on approaches permitting to plan a policy covering the entire state space. For now, we are not interested in approximation as based on Monte-Carlo tree-search [11] where the computed policy fit only probable states. This approach requires to know the initial states and a continuous mechanism if the system derives toward uncover states.

5.1 Factored MDP

The factored MDP approach aims to represent in a compact way the transition and reward functions, as introduced by *Boutilier, Dearden, Goldszmidt et al.* [4]. For that purpose states are represented by an assignation of variables. Every variables may have no influence on the value of a specific variable at the next time step. The idea behind factored MDPs is to explode the state space to group similar part of states in the transition and reward functions.

Hoey et al., [10] use algebraic decision diagram (ADD) to represent in a more compact way transition, reward and value functions by capturing regularity in the respective function.

Guestrin et al., used factored MDP to solve multi agent planning in [8]. They approximate the value function as a linear combination of localized value functions. Their method exploits both state and action space structure. This allows to solve problems with over 10^{28} states and a 10^9 actions. Furthermore agents need a coordination graph, to decide their action on runtime. However this approach assumes that agents interact only with a few of other agents.

This limitation is bypassed by a rule-based approach introduced by *Guestrin et al.*, in [9], this approach worst case being faster than the previous approach worst case, nevertheless in some case the previous approach is faster. Furthermore the rule-based approach doesn't require the rules to be mutually exclusive unlike tree or ADD representation.

In our case, the state space (resp. action space) results in the cartesian product of the state space (resp. action space) of each reach. But the state of a reach usually doesn't depends directly on the state of nearby reaches, only their action matters, when a reach receive water, the volume of the source isn't used to determine its new level. Since we assume moving water is always possible, reach never full nor empty, because such action are forbidden in the model, the state of reaches are independant and we could exploit it to factorize our MDP.

5.2   Decomposed MDP

The decomposition of an MDP permits to decrease the complexity of the policy computation by building a hierarchy between local problems and a global solution [3,7]. It is particularly efficient in spatial problems as it is based on the topological aspect of transitions.

Decomposed MDP splits the state spaces into sub-MDPs in a way the union of sub-MDPs cover the total MDP. *Dean et al.* [7] proposed two approaches to solve Decomposed MDP. The first iterative approach consists in solving each sub-MDP iteratively until a stable point is reached. A stable point match that all the sub-policies are coherent among each other. This solution do not guaranty to speed-up the policy computation but guaranty the optimality of the total policy (the union of sub-policies).

The second hierarchical approach consists in defining a set of parameters for each sub-MDPs in order to compute a finite collection of sub-policies. Then, a high level global MDPs is defined on "macro-states" to select the appropriates sub-policies to apply in order to have a coherent global behavior. This solution permits to control the policy computation but does not guaranty the optimality of the solution. The quality of the total policy take benefit from rich parameter definition but, with a cost on the computation resources.

In most real problems, Decomposed MDP could reduce policy computation (with or without optimal guaranty) but require to compute a partition in the state space [18,20]. If there are no evident decomposition, partitioning is a very hard [2], and could penalize a decomposition approach.

Waterway MDP is not easily decomposable while each state represents a snapshot of the entire networks. However, an option exists in considering severals levels of deterioration of navigation conditions. Each sub-MDP matching deteriorate condition will produce a policy of supervision oriented to the normal navigation conditions. For example with a Waterway MDP decomposed in tree sub-MDP: normal, flood and drought, we can expect that the supervision policy will keep the system in normal states (close to *NNL*) with spare dependencies between the tree sub-MDPs. This way, solving first the normal sub-MDP and them the two deteriorate sub-MDP will speed-up the policy computation. However, decomposition will not impact transition function construction and storage.

5.3   Distributed MDP

Distributed MDPs appear as ad-hoc solution to solve cooperative problems on agent based modeling. Such an approach is developed to solve Decentralized MDP [6,15] (a framework where the policy have to be distributed over agents and performed in a decentralized way). Each agent is responsible in computing its own policy considering its part of a mission. Protocols based mechanisms allow the agents to adapt their policies to reach a common interest. Distributed MDP is used for example in robotic mission to deal with traveling salesmen coordination [12].

This approach combines factorization and decomposition ideas. The total MDP is split in several sub-MDP by partitioning the set of variables defining the states and actions. Each sub-MDP is responsible for a subset of problem variables and ignores the others. In agent based modeling, each sub-MDP will match agent capability in the group (individual perceptions and actions).

An iterative approach is used to solve Distributed MDP while each iteration will modify each sub-MDP structure (transition and/or reward values). The computation is stopped when policies are stable for all the sub-MDPs (agents). The state space explored to compute the policy could be significantly reduced. That permit to speed-up computation, however, they are no guaranty on the optimality of the solution.

Waterway network would be easily distributable as the transit points are already distributed over a territory. An agent in the agent based model will be responsible for the control of one or few connected transit points and the coordination mechanism will be based on the reaches which are common to two or more agents. Distributed MDP seems very promising, for our problematic, because it can significantly decrease computation complexity and it allows flexible network definition. However, the result by using such an approach remain uncertain considering that distributed MDP solving is a young approach with mostly ad-hoc contribution to specific application and no generic framework established yet.

6 Conclusion

In this paper, we present a MDP based approach to optimize the water management in inland waterway network with a global view and planning on a given horizon. This approach aims to reduce the impact of drought and flood that may be increased by climate change in the next years.

Using MDPs, it is possible to model the dynamic and the uncertainty in such a system to optimize navigation conditions. However, this model is quickly limited by the size of the state space and thus we presented possible trails to circumvent this limitation. We investigated Factored MDP, Decomposed MDP and Distributed MDP. Factored and Distributed MDP take advantage to variable correlations in state and action definitions. Variable correlation is relevant in distributed problems as water management in inland navigation.

In future works, we plan to explore Distributed MDP based on an agent modeling of the waterway network even though this solution does not guarantee the optimality. We expect a better control of the required computation resources which is required to handle any size of networks. Determining the probability to reach the expected interval will also be explored, alongside the discretization.

References

1. Bellman, R.: A Markovian decision process. J. Math. Mech. **6**, 679–684 (1957)
2. Bichot, C.E., Siarry, P.: Graph Partitioning. Wiley-ISTE (2011)

3. Boutilier, C., Dean, T., Hanks, S.: Decision-theoretic planning: structural assumptions and computational leverage. J. Artif. Intell. Res. **11**, 1–94 (1999)
4. Boutilier, C., Dearden, R., Goldszmidt, M., et al.: Exploiting structure in policy construction. In: IJCAI, vol. 14, pp. 1104–1113 (1995)
5. Brand, C., Tran, M., Anable, J.: The uk transport carbon model: an integrated life cycle approach to explore low carbon futures. Energy Policy **41**, 107–124 (2012)
6. Chades, I., Scherrer, B., Charpillet, F.: A heuristic approach for solving decentralized-POMDP: assessment on the pursuit problem. In: SAC 2002: Proceedings of the 2002 ACM Symposium on Applied Computing, pp. 57–62. ACM, New York (2002)
7. Dean, T., Lin, S., Lin, S.: Decomposition techniques for planning instochastic domains. In: 14th International Joint Conference on Artificial Intelligence (1995)
8. Guestrin, C., Koller, D., Parr, R.: Multiagent planning with factored mdps. In: NIPS, vol. 1, pp. 1523–1530 (2001)
9. Guestrin, C., Venkataraman, S., Koller, D.: Context-specific multiagent coordination and planning with factored mdps. In: AAAI/IAAI, pp. 253–259 (2002)
10. Hoey, J., St-Aubin, R., Hu, A., Boutilier, C.: Spudd: stochastic planning using decision diagrams. In: Proceedings of the Fifteenth Conference on Uncertainty in Artificial Intelligence, pp. 279–288. Morgan Kaufmann Publishers Inc. (1999)
11. Kocsis, L., Szepesvári, C.: Bandit based Monte-Carlo planning. In: Fürnkranz, J., Scheffer, T., Spiliopoulou, M. (eds.) ECML 2006. LNCS (LNAI), vol. 4212, pp. 282–293. Springer, Heidelberg (2006)
12. Lozenguez, G., Adouane, L., Beynier, A., Mouaddib, A.I., Martinet, P.: Punctual versus continuous auction coordination for multi-robot and multi-task topological navigation. Auton. Robots **40**, 599–613 (2016)
13. Mallidis, I., Dekker, R., Vlachos, D.: The impact of greening on supply chain design and cost: a case for a developing region. J. Transp. Geogr. **22**, 118–128 (2012)
14. Mihic, S., Golusin, M., Mihajlovic, M.: Policy and promotion of sustainable inland waterway transport in europe-danube river. Renew. Sustain. Energy Rev. **15**(4), 1801–1809 (2011)
15. Nair, R., Varakantham, P., Tambe, M., Yokoo, M.: Networked distributed POMDPs: a synthesis of distributed constraint optimization and POMDPs. In: National Conference on Artificial Intelligence, p. 7 (2005)
16. Nouasse, H., Rajaoarisoa, L., Doniec, A., Duviella, E., Chuquet, K., Chiron, P., Archimede, B.: Study of drought impact on inland navigation systems based on a flow network model. In: 2015 XXV International Conference on Information, Communication and Automation Technologies (ICAT), pp. 1–6. IEEE (2015)
17. Pachauri, R.K., Allen, M., Barros, V., Broome, J., Cramer, W., Christ, R., Church, J., Clarke, L., Dahe, Q., Dasgupta, P., et al.: Climate change 2014: synthesis report. contribution of working groups i, ii and iii to the fifth assessment report of the intergovernmental panel on climate change (2014)
18. Parr, R.: Flexible decomposition algorithms for weakly coupled Markov decision problems. In: 14th Conference on Uncertainty in Artificial Intelligence, pp. 422–430 (1998)
19. Puterman, M.L.: Markov Decision Processes: Discrete Stochastic Dynamic Programming. Wiley, New York (1994)
20. Sabbadin, R.: Graph partitioning techniques for Markov Decision Processes decomposition. In: 15th Eureopean Conference on Artificial Intelligence, pp. 670–674 (2002)

An Agent-Based DSS Supporting the Logistics of Cruise Passengers Arrivals

Claudia Di Napoli[1], Pol Mateu Santamaria[2], and Silvia Rossi[3(✉)]

[1] Istituto di Calcolo e Reti ad Alte Prestazioni, C.N.R., Napoli, Italy
claudia.dinapoli@cnr.it
[2] Facultat d'Informatica de Barcelona, Polytechnic University of Catalonia,
Barcelona, Spain
[3] Dipartimento di Ingegneria Elettrica e Tecnologie dell'Informazione,
Università degli Studi di Napoli "Federico II", Napoli, Italy
silvia.rossi@unina.it

Abstract. The arrival of cruises in a city represents an unmissable opportunity for the city economy to increment its tourist market penetration. Nevertheless, the management of an unforeseen number of passengers that need to visit the city in short time may have a negative impact on the city, so reducing the expected benefits. This is mainly due to the difficult in taking the right decisions when organizing the dispatching of passengers in different city areas, since these decisions depend on several conditions, that can also dynamically occur, and may impact different city sectors. In order to address the problem of organizing transportation and city tours for cruise passengers in a city, a Decision Support System is proposed to help both planning passengers transportation in the city, and also to evaluate the consequences for the city if the plans are really implemented. The system is designed according to the multi-agent paradigm, so allowing to easily manage the necessary coordination among different entities and data sources that are usually involved in the considered application domain.

Keywords: Decision Support Systems · Multi-agent systems · Cruises logistics

1 Introduction

Usually, the arrival of cruises in a port city is a chance for the city to increase its tourist market not be missed. Nevertheless, the simultaneous arrival of cruises with the disembarkation of several passengers and their consequent visit of the city impact the city in many aspects: traffic, transportation needs, tour planning.

A static plan to manage the arrival and the distribution in the city of a considerable amount of people could fail due to dynamic events that may happen in the city interfering with the plan, e.g. a public transportation strike, a protest and/or unplanned building works preventing the transit in specific areas of the city, or particular events that may be a touristic attraction at a specific time.

© Springer International Publishing Switzerland 2016
Y. Demazeau et al. (Eds.): PAAMS 2016, LNAI 9662, pp. 60–71, 2016.
DOI: 10.1007/978-3-319-39324-7_6

In this work a system to support the decision making process necessary to organize the transportation of cruise passengers to reach areas of touristic interest in the city is proposed. The system is designed as a Decision Support System (DSS) [7,9] that gives suggestions on how to organize the transportation of cruise passengers in the city taking into account the number of passengers, their touristic needs, and specific city events. The proposed suggestions contain also information on their impact on the city logistics that can be used by the system users to make decisions that limit, as much as possible, negative outcomes for the city. The core modules of the system responsible for "reasoning" on the available information in order to infer possible plans for passengers transportation, are designed as software agents able to communicate with each other to exchange information, to process and analyze the gathered information and, more importantly, to compute suggestions by applying codified logical rules. These rules model the behavior of the considered application domain by describing in declarative terms the evolution of identified situations in determined conditions.

Our work was inspired by the use of DSS in the domain of traffic and transportation optimization problems. Systems for traffic management [1,4,6] aim at avoiding as much as possible traffic congestion, while the ones for transportation management aim at providing suggestions to improve the efficiency of the service even when unexpected situations occur. Nevertheless, in these works a specific goal is considered, and it addressed as an optimization problem over a set of computed alternatives. Instead, the system proposed in the present work aims at addressing a variety of goals, i.e. limit traffic congestion, maximize tourism penetration, limit the impact on city transportation capacity, and so on, depending on both the different potential end users of the system, and on the priorities that end users assign to the different goals, i.e. limit traffic congestion, maximize tourism penetration, limit the impact on city transportation capacity, and so on. So, traffic and transportation management represent only sub-modules of the proposed system.

2   CAMS: An Agent-Based DSS

The system proposed in the present work, named the Cruise Arrival Management System (CAMS), is a DSS responsible for computing suggestions concerning the organization of transportation of cruise passengers arriving in a port city.

The types of suggestions are categorized according to the potential users of the system, that are:

1. public and/or private transportation companies that manage buses services;
2. travel agencies that organize cruises and provide passengers with city tour proposals;
3. city council and port authorities that are responsible for managing city logistics affected by the arrival and the transit of several passengers.

Suggestions for transportation companies concern the possibility to plan a schedule for specified bus services according to the needs of cruises, and the port and city logistics. Suggestions for travel agencies concern the possibility to offer city tours proposals to cruise passengers that are compatible with the city needs upon cruises arrival. Suggestions for city council and port authorities concern the signaling of the most affected city areas upon cruise arrivals, so that suitable corrective actions may be taken, such as to plan more security measures in specific city areas, or to avoid access to areas where specific events will take place. At its current stage, CAMS provide suggestions concerning mainly the allocation of buses to cruises, and the city areas worth to visit, taking into account the current city state upon cruise arrivals.

In order to plan the assignment of buses to passengers of the different cruises that arrive at the port in a considered time interval, it is necessary to take into account the number of passengers requiring the service, the port transportation restrictions provided by the port authority, the possible destinations of the planned buses, and information about specific events taking place in the city. On one hand, port restrictions impose constraints on the number of buses that can access the port area at the same time. These restrictions may require to plan a different scheduling of passenger transportation in the case more cruises arrive simultaneously at the port, in order to make decisions on the buses distribution among cruises. On the other hand, bus destinations may be planned by taking into account predicted disruptions in specific city areas, so to avoid, or at least limit, traffic congestion.

In order to plan possible city tours for passengers, it is necessary to take into account the touristic attractiveness of city areas (in terms of points of interests, facilities such as bus parking, special events occurring in the area, and so on), but also the time of the tour, and the city events that may influence the planning of the tour.

As described, there are different potential users of the system, but at the moment a single user approach was adopted, assuming that a user representing a local authority is allowed to access and manage all the information, to propose city tours to travel agencies, to interact with transportation companies, to plan buses provisions, to take decisions to resolve conflicting situations that may impact the city livability, evaluating the priorities to be considered. However, the system is designed in such a way that it can be easily extended to allow different types of users to access it, by granting them different access rights according to their roles.

2.1   The CAMS Architecture

The system proposed in this work is designed according to the DSS methodology allowing to decompose the decision problem into simpler components taking into account the different aspects that, as described earlier, need to be taken into account when making decisions on how to organize the transportation of a considerable number of cruises passengers arriving in a city. It is designed as a web-based application, developed within a Tomcat server container[1], so to allow different users to access it, and also from different devices. This choice makes it possible to include external services/information sources to gather more information to refine the provided suggestions when necessary. For example, in some cases it could be of relevance to inquire whether forecast services or city planned events services to increase the knowledge base of the system used to derive suggestions.

The architecture, illustrated in Fig. 1, is designed according to the layered architecture introduced in [5], and it is composed of the typical layers of a DSS:

- the **Presentation Layer**, it is responsible for presenting the systems results to end users, and for the user interaction with the system through easily to use graphical interfaces;
- the **Process Layer**, it is the core of the system responsible for processing the data by applying the knowledge models in order to compute suggestions consisting in value added information that is used by users to make decisions;
- the **Data Layer**, it is composed of a DataBase Management System (DBMS) responsible for storing and managing uniform access to the different data sources used to compute suggestions, and of a Model Base Management System (MBMS) that manages the knowledge models used to represent real world aspects that are relevant for the application domain. Models are used to transform the raw data of the DBMS in structured and added value information useful for the decision making process.

Of course, the more complete the models for representing the knowledge relevant for the considered application domain are, the more accurate the suggestions computed by the system are. A model consists of variables and statistical indicators providing measures of user preferences over the identified variables and decision objectives. Model design is a complex task requiring the cooperation of several disciplines, ranging from economics, operations research, decision theory, decision analysis, statistics to be efficiently used by DSSs.

In CAMS, two basic models are introduced. The *Zone Model*, processes information data regarding an area of the city, such as special events, traffic and public transportation state, congestion level at specific time of the day, number of points of touristic interest, dimensions, capacity in terms of the number of people that can circulate in the area without overcrowding. The obtained structured information is used to derive the consequences of events and tourist arrivals in a specific zone. The *Port Model* is used to structure information about cruise arrivals and departures, and to manage the circulation of buses in the city port (in terms of number of buses entering and leaving the port) and the restrictions regarding circulation in the port zone.

2.2 The Multi-agent Process Layer

The core of the system is the Process Layer and it is designed as a multi-agent system, following an agent-oriented system engineering approach, as in [6]. The

---

[1] http://tomcat.apache.org.

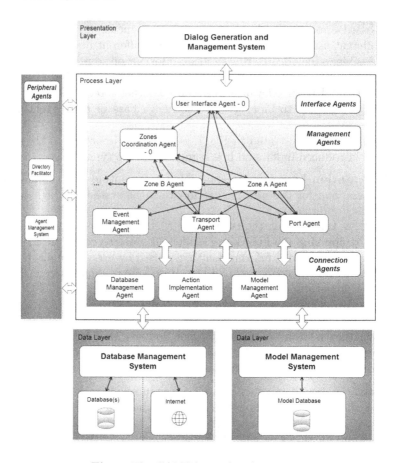

Fig. 1. The CAMS layered architecture.

rationale of this choice is to guarantee the autonomy of the different components of the system, the possibility to communicate and exchange data among them, and to clearly distinguish the different functionalities provided by the layer. In fact, the characterizing features of a multi-agency approach allow for several advantages in DDS [3].

For the CAMS system the following agents features were exploited:

– modularity: making it possible to structure the systems according to the different functions, and the different types of information to be processed;
– distribution: making it possible to distribute the management of information sources according to their type, complexity, and location;
– openness: making it possible to add new agents to the system in order to include both new functionality and new sources of information, when they become available;
– proactivity: making it possible the autonomous processing of information on demand to increase the reasoning capabilities;

– communication: making it possible to exchange processed information and to reason cooperatively

The application domain considered in the present work is characterized by the dynamic heterogeneous nature of the information necessary to derive decisions, by different levels of complexity in the reasoning necessary to provide suggestions, by the different world models that can be used to refine the decision making process, so the multi-agent approach allows to have a modular and distributed system architecture, and more importantly to add additional components and even to access external data sources where necessary.

As reported in Fig. 1, four groups of agents are introduced according to their functionality: the *Peripheral Agents*, *Interface Agents*, the *Connection Agents*, the *Management Agents*, and the *Action Implementation Agents*. They are BDI agents [8] with a reasoning module based on production rules that communicate according to he FIPA specification communication protocol. They are implemented using the JADE development framework [2].

The Peripheral Agents provide administrative support to the multi-agent system, and they are in charge of exerting supervisory control to access and use the JADE platform, for maintaining a directory of available agents, and for handling their life cycle.

The Interface Agent is responsible for the interaction between the user and the system, by processing user requests, and displaying system suggestions.

The Connection Agents are responsible for information management. They include two different types of agents: Database Management Agents that are responsible for retrieving and storing information in the different data sources when requested by other agents; Model Management Agents that process requests concerning the models stored in the system.

The Management Agents are the most complex ones since they are responsible for computing suggestions for the users. They include three different types of agents according to the models and the information they are responsible for, that are: *Port Agent*, *Zone Agent*, and *Zones Coordination Agent* (ZCoordAgent).

The Port Agent is responsible for managing information about the organization of the port area, the cruise arrivals, and the number of buses allowed to enter and leave the port. It suggests the buses that could be assigned to cruise tourists by making it sure that congestion is not created and that all passengers from the same cruise have the same transportation method (on foot or bus). The agent is also responsible for processing user requests regarding the assignment of buses to cruises, and to determine the consequences of such assignments. Finally, it also provides information regarding the number of tourists that will arrive at or leave the city from/to the port at each hour.

The Zone Agent processes the raw data of the area it is responsible for, including events, points of interest and the maximum capacity in terms of people circulating in the area. It uses this information together with the information coming from other Zone Agents and from the Port Agent to compute the impact of cruise passenger arrivals in its area. It is also responsible to inform Zone Agents

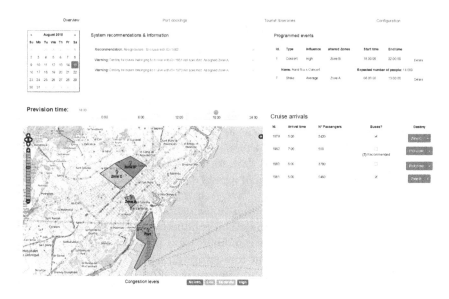

Fig. 2. The *Overview* layer of the CAMS GUI. (Color figure online)

of its neighbor areas (i.e., areas that are connected) when congestion problems are predicted.

The Zones Coordinator Agent is the one that computes the final suggestions by applying logical rules on the forecasts it collects from the Port Agent and the different Zone Agents involved in a specific query. The computed suggestions include the assignment of buses to cruises, destinations for the buses leaving the port, and information about critical congestion conditions in each city area. These suggestions are transmitted to Interface Agent.

Finally, the Action Implementation Agents are in charge of simulating the implementation of the decisions computed by the system and selected by the user, so to derive the consequences of such decisions on city congestion if they were concretely taken.

2.3   The CAMS User Interface

The Presentation layer of CAMS is a web-based graphical user interface (GUI) responsible for displaying the computed suggestions and the corresponding possible consequences, through the Dialog Generation and Management System. It uses the Open-StreetMap (OSM) application for the visualization of the city streets and zones data. The GUI is organized in different presentation layers offering different functionalities: the *Overview*, the *Port dockings*, the *Touristic Itineraries*, and the *Configuration*. At the current stage, the Touristic Itineraries layer is not implemented since the system provides only the destination areas selected for the buses without detailed tourist itineraries within the area.

The Overview interface of the system (see Fig. 2) provides a general sketch of the CAMS functionalities. Once a specific day is selected on the calendar (on the top left of the interface), a map reporting the average congestion levels in the areas (reported in different colors) is shown together with the planned cruise arrivals (at the bottom right) and the programmed event data for the selected day (at the top right). By clicking on a specific zone, the detailed data on the evolution of the congestion in time is shown. Finally, it shows suggestions and alerts provided by the system.

The Port docking is the layer used to plan the bus assignment to the cruises (see Fig. 4), while the Configuration layer is used to interact with the database management system, and to store and retrieve information.

3   A Running Example

In order to show the behavior of CAMS, a simulation example based on real data is carried out. The example consists in providing suggestions to organize the dispatching of cruise passengers arriving at a port in the same day, and that need to visit the city. The considered city for the experimentation is Barcelona[2] and the information regarding the cruises arrivals is extracted from the official prevision of the "Port de Barcelona"[3]. The city is split in zones, each one managed by a Zone Agent and described according to the Zone Model.

Three touristic areas A, B and C and the port area, shown in Fig. 2 are considered. The information for each area is characterized by the following parameters: **Capacity**, the maximum number of people allowed in an area without collapsing; **Stops**, the number of public transport stops in the area, including metro, bus and tram; **POI**, the number of points of interest in the area; **Attractiveness (0–100)**, a score describing how likely a tourist is going to visit the area; **Events**, the description of the events programmed inside the area; **Neighbor areas**, areas which have at least one delimiting edge in common.

Parameters values for the three zones used in the experiments are reported in Table 1, and they can be set through a window obtained by clicking on a chosen zone. Points of Interest and the public transport stops are real data provided by local authorities, while the attractiveness and capacity values are estimated.

The zones B and C, as shown in Fig. 2, share a delimiting edge, hence events or congestion problems in one area will impact the other one. That mean that the Zone Agents responsible for zones B and C will communicate with each other to share this kind of information, so modifying the parameters values when computing congestion levels according to the Zone Model. The day chosen to carry out the simulation is the 15 August 2015, when the arrival of four cruises with the schedule reported in Table 2 was planned, with two of them arriving at exactly the same time, that is a quite common situation.

---

[2] Open Data BCN http://opendata.bcn.cat/.

[3] Port de Barcelona - Cruises consultation http://www.portdebarcelona.cat/en/web/ port-del-ciudada/consulta-cruceros.

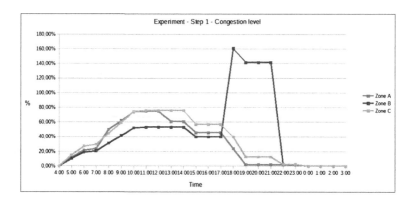

Fig. 3. Day congestion levels evolution for zones A, B and C.

Table 1. Parameter values used in the simulation.

Parameter	Zone A	Zone B	Zone C
Capacity	7000	10000	14000
Stops	27	32	60
POI	1	3	10
Attractiveness (0–100)	28	35	70
Events	Strike (8:00 to 13:00)	Concert (18:00 to 22:00)	-
Neighbor areas	-	Zone C	Zone B
Relative distance to port	89	122	114

Table 2. Cruises arrival and departure information.

Cruise	Identifier	Arrival	Departure	# Passengers
Disney Magic	1979	5:00 on 15/08/2015	17:00 on 15/08/2015	5420
Costa Fascinosa	1980	8:00 on 15/08/2015	14:30 on 15/08/2015	3780
Sovereign	1981	8:00 on 15/08/2015	18:00 on 15/08/2015	5460
Europa 2	1982	7:00 on 15/08/2015	12:00 on 15/08/2015	500

In our tests, we consider as a programmed events, a *Strike* taking place early in the morning in the A area, and a *Concert* taking place in the evening in the B area. The strike has an impact both on street traffic and public transportation, while the concert has effect only on the traffic (see Table 1), as specified in the considered models.

The information for the Port Zone is characterized by the following parameters: **Capacity**, defined as the maximum number of people that can enter or leave the port on foot per hour; **Bus restriction**, the number of buses that can access the port in an hour with respect to their own capacity.

Fig. 4. The *Port dockings* layer of the CAMS GUI.

In the case studied, a port capacity of 3000 persons, and a maximum number of 100 buses per hour with a capacity of 65 seats are set. In addition, note that the model specifies that commonly a part of tourists may not want to join the guided tour since they want to visit the city on their own. In particular, the portion of tourists joining the guided tour, and therefore that will need a seat in a bus, is set to 85 %.

CAMS is an event-based system that compute suggestions and alerts each time an event occurs. The first event is the selection of a specific day on the calendar by the user. In the experiment carried out, once the day is selected (the 15th of August), the system elaborates the congestion levels for that day with the information retrieved from the database. In particular, the congestion states due to the planned events are computed, and the user is informed about the planned events, the cruise arrivals and the evolution of congestion for the considered zones. Information on cruises and events is visually shown in Fig. 2, while the evolution of congestion levels is shown in Fig. 3. The congestion level for a zone in a time interval and the number of expected people in the zone with respect to its capacity are evaluated by the corresponding Zone Agent.

With the available information provided by the system, the user decides to assign buses to the most crowded cruises (see Fig. 4), i.e., cruises with id 1979 and 1981. The system reports that 71 buses for the cruise number 1979 and 72 buses for the cruise 1981 are needed, where each bus has a capacity for 65 persons. Moreover, the system notifies that cruise with number 1980, after this assignment, is not a candidate to receive buses anymore, because it arrives at the same hour of 1981 cruise, and if buses were assigned to both cruises the port bus restriction would be violated. Since the cruise number 1982 arrives at a different time, the system suggests to assign buses to it. However, the user decides to reject the suggestion since this number of tourists is not expected to congest the port or the public transport.

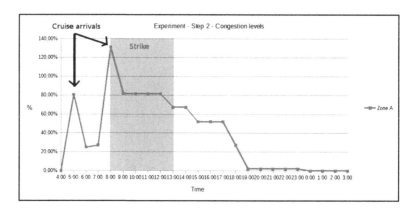

Fig. 5. Day congestion levels evolution for zone A after cruise arrivals.

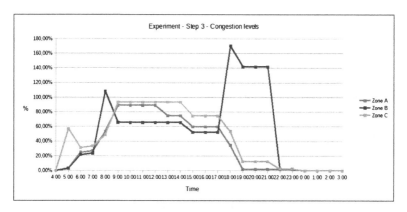

Fig. 6. Day congestion levels evolution for zone A, B and C after destinations changes.

Then, the system automatically assigns as destination zone for the buses the closest one, i.e., the A zone. The remaining passengers (the ones not allocated to buses) are expected to go on their own to visit city areas, and so the system distributes them to zones according to their "attractiveness" score. New city congestion levels previsions are computed and the results obtained for the A zone are shown in Fig. 5. Furthermore, since a strike is programmed at 8 am in the A zone, the system notifies a high congestion level (130 % of the zone capacity) in such zone, and so the user decides to change the buses destinations to different areas. In such a way, the user takes the decisions that have a less negative impact on the congestion levels in the city. Indeed, following the suggestions, the user chooses as destinations for the buses assigned to cruises arriving at 5 am and 8 am the zones C and B respectively. The new assignment produces the congestion levels shown in Fig. 6 resulting in a more acceptable congestion level for the A zone compared to the one reported in Fig. 5.

4 Conclusions

To our knowledge, the use of DSS systems for supporting a decision making process related to the transport organization of cruise passengers arriving in a city is a novel approach. The novelty of the approach proposed in the present work is to adopt a system design methodology that allows to clearly separate the different knowledge sources and domain models that contribute to come up with helpful suggestions in the chosen application domain. In addition, the multi-agent approach adopted for designing and implementing the core of the system (i.e., the Process Layer) allows to guarantee the autonomy of the different system components, together with necessary communication among them to exchange information, and to incrementally and cooperatively "reason" on the available models to compute both suggestions and their consequences. The system is intended to be used by different types of users since the suggestions it provides can be useful for improving different aspects of a city logistics. The experiment carried out was based on simple models, and it uses both simulated and real data. The rationale of the experimentation was to show the behavior of the system, and its potential uses. Finally, its modular design allows to easily extend it with more functionalities, more models, and more information sources by adding new Management Agents.

References

1. Almejalli, K., Dahal, K.P., Hossain, M.A.: Intelligent traffic control decision support system. In: Giacobini, M. (ed.) EvoWorkshops 2007. LNCS, vol. 4448, pp. 688–701. Springer, Heidelberg (2007)
2. Bellifemine, F., Poggi, A., Rimassa, G.: JADE - a FIPA-compliant agent framework. In: Proceedings of the Practical Applications of Intelligent Agents (1999)
3. Gao, Y., Shang, Z., Kokossis, A.: Agent-based intelligent system development for decision support in chemical process industry. Expert Syst. Appl. **36**(8), 11099–11107 (2009)
4. Hasan, M.: A framework for intelligent decision support system for traffic congestion management system. Engineering **2**(4), 270–289 (2010)
5. Minch, R.P., Burns, J.R.: Conceptual design of decision support systems utilizing management science models. IEEE Trans. Syst. Man Cybern. **SMC–13**(4), 549–557 (1983)
6. Ossowski, S., Hernandez, J.Z., Belmonte, M.V., Maseda, J., Fernandez, A., Garcia-Serrano, A., Triguero, F., Serrano, J.M., de-la Cruz, J.L.P.: Multi agent systems for decision support: a case study in the transportation management domain. Appl. Artif. Intell. **18**(9–10), 779–795 (2004)
7. Power, D.J.: Decision support systems: a historical overview. In: Handbook on Decision Support Systems 1. International Handbooks Information System, pp. 121–140. Springer, Heidelberg (2008)
8. Rao, A.S., Georgeff, M.P.: Readings in agents. In: Modeling Rational Agents with a BDI-Architecture, pp. 317–328. Morgan Kaufmann Publishers Inc. (1998)
9. Turban, E., Aronson, J., Liang, T.P.: Decision Support Systems and Intelligent Systems, 7th edn. Pearson Prentice Hall, Upper Saddle River (2005)

An Open Platform for Customized Corpus Browsing Using Agents and Artifacts Approach

Zina EL Guedria$^{(\boxtimes)}$ and Laurent Vercouter

INSA Rouen, LITIS, Normandie Univ, 76000 Rouen, France
{zina.el_guedria,laurent.vercouter}@insa-rouen.fr

Abstract. Document research in a digital corpus can be considered as a browsing process driven by some information needs. Such browses require the use of traditional information retrieval tools to select relevant documents based on a query. But they can be improved by the use of customization and adaptation mechanisms in order to refine the representation of information needs. Several factors are useful to influence this customization: user profiles, browsing profiles, semantic proximity of documents, recommendations from other similar users, ... Existing multiagent approaches for document research have proposed an agent model of resources and processes of a given system. We propose in this article a general model for agent-based document research decoupling browsing management and customization or recommendantion decisions. We follow a stigmergic approach in which agents implement different customization factors and modify their shared environment to influence the browsing results. The openness of this architecture is shown by presenting several variants that can be obtained by the dynamic addition of agents or resource artifacts.

Keywords: Customized document research · Agent and Artifact · Stigmergic approach · Information need

1 Introduction

Accessing documents from a digital corpus raises problems related to information retrieval, visualisation of query results and navigation between documents. Some of these problems are similar to those encountered in the field of information retrieval on the web (e.g. the calculation of the relevance of documents in response to a query) but others are specific to the fact that we consider a closed, finite corpus in which documents, queries and users are specific to a given domain. In this context, the recognition of distinctive users or uses may be interesting to improve the documents retrieval process.

We are interested in this article in the customization of browsing inside a digital document corpus. There are many factors that can be taken into account for customizing: a user-specific profile, a recognized browsing use case, a semantic proximity between documents or a recommendation built on the navigation history.

© Springer International Publishing Switzerland 2016
Y. Demazeau et al. (Eds.): PAAMS 2016, LNAI 9662, pp. 72–83, 2016.
DOI: 10.1007/978-3-319-39324-7_7

One can find many works in the literature a adopting multiagent approach within information retrieval problem. These systems implement each task of IR in a distinct agent. Thus, they are designed for a specific use and resources. Also, the agents and their interactions are defined according to the information systems component. However, we propose in this article to treat this diversity of influence by a multiagent system interacting with a shared environment representing the users browsing. It is a global architecture decoupling the management of browsing of decisions related to the customization and the recommendation, allowing a dynamic composition of the content of these two layers.

We follow a stigmergic approach in which the agents implement different customization factors and modify their shared environment to influence the representation of users needs and the browsing. This environment, implemented in a layer of artifacts, is thus an object built and adapted by the collective activity of agents and the user, implementing the decision layer. Compared to existing works, the use of stigmergy increases the autonomy of decision processes. Thus, our architecture is open and expandable as it is not attached to a specific information system. It allows the addition/removal of information retrieval processes such as various customization factors.

The contributions described in this article are:

- An agent-artifact model of a multiagent system to achieve customized browsing (work presented in details in [11]);
- A recommendation process based on similar profiles;
- An extension of the proposed Agent-Artifact architecture.

This article is organised as follows: Sect. 2 provides an overview of related research work being carried out concerning customized information retrieval. In particular, we present researches using a multiagent approach for information retrieval and customization and recommender systems. Section 3 presents our multiagent model of a customized browsing platform composed of two layers: a browsing layer and a decision layer. Section 4 presents an application case that has been realized for a High-Normandy regional project, PlaIR 2.0, using a digital corpus from the field of international transportation law. Section 5 presents a possible extension of our agent and artifact model by taking into account the annotations of users and a more sophisticated recommendation process is presented. Finally, the conclusion summarizes the work described in this article and our prospects for future work.

2   Related Work

2.1   Multiagent System for Information Retrieval

The first multiagent approaches for information retrieval have focused on the distribution of information retrieval tasks. Generally, these tasks are assigned to different agents that can perform them in sequence or in competition. These multiagent models propose distinct agents in charge of different entities: users, resources, ontology etc. Among the first multiagent systems for information retrieval we can cite for example: InfoSleuth [1], the AgentSeek system [6], RETSINA model [5], and the digital library UMDL [2]. Customization has been addressed in more recent approaches such as SARIPOD (An Intelligent Possibilistic Web Information Retrieval using multiagent system) [3] and the SWAPP platform (Search based Web AdaPtive Platform) [7]. Each of the systems shown above, propose a multiagent model for a specific information retrieval system. Thus, they are designed for a specific use and resources and the agents and their interactions are defined according to the information system components. In this article, we propose a more general approach, based on a general information retrieval process that allows open customization by adding customization factors according to the current needs.

2.2 Stigmergy, Agent, and Artifcat

Stigmergy was formally defined by Grassé [10] as "the phenomenon of indirect communication mediated by modifications of the environment." In a MAS, stigmergy could be defined as indirect coordination between agents. The main idea is that a trace left, by an agent action, in the environment stimulates the performance of a subsequent action, whether by the same agent or a different agent. In that way, each action tends to build and reinforce on each other. It leads to the spontaneous appearance of seemingly coherent systematic activity. Direct coordination wastes a lot of time and resources to discuss and coordinate the discussions. In a stigmergic system, all agents have full autonomy to act as they wish. In this system based on action, what counts is action on the environment, i.e. the trace left by an agent on the environment leads to further actions of this agent or other agents.

As defined by Ricci et al. [18], "The artifacts are entities modelling systems (or parts of a system) that are better characterised as resources or tools used by agents for their own aims."

The notion of artifact has been introduced as a first-class abstraction in MAS. It represent tools or objects that agents can use to sustain their activities in an individual or collective way, and can be designed to provide and encapsulate different types of functionalities or services to agents [8]. The cognitive stigmergy introduced in [18] is an extended definition of stigmergy where we could preserve the ant-based mechanism generally adopted in the field of multi-agent systems and exploit the cognitive abilities of agent in an environment defined by artifacts in the stigmergic process.

2.3 Recommender Systems

Among the ways to expand this approach, recommendation processes may be used for assisting the user's browsing. A recommender system (RS) helps users who have not enough experience or the necessary competence to evaluate potentially important alternatives offered by a web site. A Recommender system [12] generates recommendations to users about various types of items.

Existing recommendation systems are generally classified into two categories: Content-based filtering and collaborative filtering. Content-based filtering tries to recommend items that correspond to the user profile. This profile is based on the items that the user has liked in the past or on the interests that he has explicitly defined. A content-based filtering RS matches the item profile with the user profile to decide its relevance for the user [13].

Collaborative filtering is one of the most popular techniques applied in recommender systems [14]. In contrast to content-based recommender systems, collaborative filtering produces recommendations by calculating the similarity between a user's preferences and those of other users. The method aims an automatic predicting (filtering) the user's interests by collecting ratings given by many users (collaborators). In practice, recommender systems often do not use one single recommendation technique but instead combine different approaches. Such recommender systems are called hybrid recommender systems [13]. They merge, for example, the results obtained by different recommendation techniques or apply a second recommendation technique to filter and refine the results provided by the first one.

3   An Open A & A Platform for Customized Corpus Browsing

This section describes the proposed multiagent system to achieve customized browsing in a digital corpus of documents. A multiagent approach has been adopted to represent the heterogeneity of customization factors. Thus, each agent applies a different influence on the selection of documents to be presented to the user. The first part of this section presents the overall architecture of the system. Then, we describe the shared environment, representing the browsing processes. Finally, we present the agent's specifications at the decision layer.

The aim of our platform is to allow users to browse sequentially through a closed, finite corpus by visualising various documents and refining or adapting their query progressively. First, it is necessary to use traditional information retrieval mechanisms to select relevant documents based on a query. We propose to complete these tools with customization and adaptation mechanisms to refine the representation of the information need. This evolution is dynamic since it is performed during a browsing session based on the user's profile, their actions, and their previous browsings. For that reason we use the term *information need* to describe the overall objective that the platform must meet rather than *query*, which is specific to a punctual search for information.

To achieve a customized browsing, the stigmergic approach allows for carrying out an open browsing system that supports independent addition of new customization factors.

We represent the informational needs within a virtual environment shared by agents. This need, initially expressed by a query composed of a set of terms, is modified through the actions of agents. The evolution of the informational need is thus the result of a co-construction process involving agents and the user and enable to integrate various sources of customization and user control. In addition, the shared environment includes useful tools for navigation (index, information search engine, user interface), as well as all documents judged relevant for the current navigation.

In order to distinguish the decision layer and the operational layers of the platform, we chose the Agent-Artifact approach [8]. Decisions about the modification of the information need are made by the multiagent system, sometimes in interaction with the user. Storage of information related to navigation and the execution of queries are the responsibility of the artifacts of the environment. This architecture is shown in Fig. 1.

In the *Browsing* layer, five types of artifacts are used. An *Interface* artifact encapsulates the capabilities of direct interaction with the user. Each instance of *Browsing* artifacts represents the informational need of a browsing session. For each session, an instance of *Search* artifact is created to run a search for information on the corresponding need. The result of a search is stored in a *Document* artifact. Finally, *Profile* artifacts collect information on user behaviours.

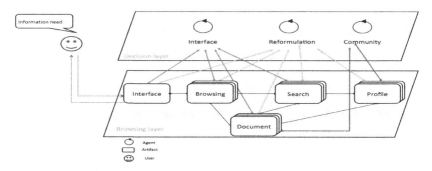

Fig. 1. Agent-Artifact proposed architecture

The *Decision* layer contains agents that will decide to act on the Browsing layer in order to modify the information need or the documents provided to the user. The *Interface* agent serves as an entry point to the user to create an initial query and change it during navigation. The *Reformulation* agent proposes to add terms to the information need on the basis of documents selected by previous searches. Finally, the *Community* agent proposes to add documents considered as relevant during past similar sessions.

More details about each agent and each artifact are presented in our previous work see [11].

4   Application to a Digital Corpus on Transportation Law

The customized browsing multiagent platform, modeled in the previous section, is intended to be implemented to access a digital prototype corpus of international transport laws. We describe in this section, the corpus used to implement the prototype using progress with the platform Cartago [9] then a usage scenario.

4.1   The IDIT Corpus

A prototype of a platform to navigate in a digital corpus in the field of international transport law is in development under the PlaIR 2.0 project (Regional Indexing Platform) in collaboration with the Institute of International Transport Law (IDIT).

The corpus created by IDIT [4], contains over 40 000 numbered references in all fields of Transport (Rail, Road, Maritime, Air, Multimodal and Logistic) of different types of documents (Court Cases, Doctrine, Legislation, ...) These documents are indexed using a terminology and a full text analysis of the documents. Customization based on the observation of users' browsing is very interesting in this type of corpus. On the one hand users do not have the same needs when expressing a given query due to different levels of expertise. On the other hand, the "typical" browsings are held without being precisely formalised by frequent practices as comparative case studies, court-case, specific research, ...

4.2   Execution Scenario

In this section, we describe a browsing scenario within the IDIT corpus.

Initial Query. Suppose a user, Paul, initiates a navigation seeking all legal decisions involving trucks. His initial query is $K_{N_1}^{INIT} = \{trucks\}$. The Interface agent creates a Browsing artifact defined by $N_1 = (\{trucks\}, Paul)$.

The Interface agent launches a first query: $Search(trucks)$ via the Search artifact, which returns two documents $D_{N_1,RI} = \{Decision_1, Decision_{10}\}$. It follows the creation of a Document artifact $D_1 = \{\{Decision_1, Decision_{10}\}, \emptyset\}$.

Reformulation. The user chooses to visualise two documents. He considers the $decision_{10}$ as a relevant result. This relevance feedback, and the first results, lead to the creation of a Profile artifact by the Reformulation agent initialized to $P_1 = (\{trucks\}, \emptyset, \emptyset, \{Decision_{10}\})$. The Reformulation agent retrieves the index terms of the $decision_{10}$, $Index(Decision_{10})$, that returns: $\{motorised\ vehicles, trucks, fruits, foods, accidents, car, motorcycles\}$.

Let's assume that the terms having the most important weight and that are not in the initial query are: *motorised vehicles, accidents,* and *fruits.*

Then, Reformulation agent suggests these terms to the user who has the choice to accept or reject them. Suppose that Paul accepts the last two ones, his profile artifact then becomes:

$P_1 = (\{trucks\}, \{accidents, fruits\}, \{motorised\ vehicles\}, \{Decision_{10}\})$.

The Reformulation agent launches a new Search:

$Search(trucks, accidents, fruits)$ which returns as results the decisions (1, 10, 15, 20, and 19). The user consults the decisions (20, 19, and 15) and judges the decisions 15 and 19 as relevant. His profile artifact then becomes:

$$P_1 = (\{trucks\}, \{accidents, fruits\}, \{motorised\ vehicles\},$$
$$\{Decision_{10}, Decision_{15}, Decision_{19}\}).$$

The terms of the index of decision$_{15}$ and the decision$_{19}$ are: *fruits, trucks, damages, goods, percentage of damage*, and *delivery time*.

The terms accepted by the user will bring new documents, that may be marked as relevant, bringing new terms proposed and so on until the set of terms remains stable.

Community Recommendation. Suppose a new user, Jean uses the platform after Paul. The associated Browsing artifact is $N_2 = (\{fruits, delivery\ time\}, Jean)$. Alongside the documents proposed by Interface and Reformulation agents, the Community agent compares this initial information need with other known profiles. As a result he finds $\{fruits, delivery\ time\} \subset \{K^{INIT} \cup T^{ACC}, Paul\}$. It can as recommendes, relevant documents according to *Paul* for this information need, namely decisions (27, 15, 19, and 10). The result to be displayed to the user includes the results of the Interface agent and the recommendations of the Community agent: Decision$_1$, Decision$_{51}$, Decision$_{11}$, Decision$_{19}$, and Decision$_{27}$, Decision$_{15}$, Decision$_{10}$, and Decision$_{19}$.

5   Extension of the Proposed Agent-Artifact Architecture

In the previous sections, we presented our model for agent-based document research and an application example. The objective of the stigmergic approach that we adopted is to allow a dynamic adaptation of the system according to the specific resources and processes of a given digital corpus. Thus, we show in this section that the system introduced in Sect. 3 can be extended with specific corpus resources or with a recommendation process. For that purpose, the first subsection introduces an artifact to deal with annotations provided by users, showing an extension of the browsing layer, while the second subsection shows an extension of the decision layer by adding a recommendation agent.

5.1   Annotation

As shown in Fig. 2, we add an Annotation artifact to our model in the Browsing layer. The role of the annotation artifact is to collect the user's annotations. Indeed, a user u_i can annotate one or several part(s) $\S \subset D$ he considers relevant in a document considered relevant D_i^{REL}. He selects a part of the relevant document and associates a comment called annotation An. The Annotation $A_{u_i}^D$ of a user involved in a browsing session N_i is composed by his relevance feedback $RF_{u_i} \in \{0, 1\}$, one or several part(s) $\S \subset D$ he considers relevant in a document considered relevant D_i^{REL} as well as the annotations An_i.

$$A_{u_i}^D = (RF_{u_i}, \S, An_i) \tag{1}$$

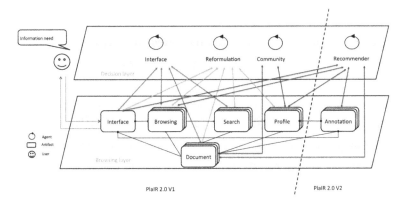

Fig. 2. Extension of the proposed Agent-Artifact architecture

where

$$RF_{u_i} \in \{0,1\} \tag{2}$$

$$\S \subset D \tag{3}$$

and

$$An_i = Message \tag{4}$$

The annotations of a document that are added by different users are stored in the annotation artifact. To integrate annotations in the Artifact layer we need first to update the Interface artifact to enable the user to perform its annotations by selecting a passage in the document and introduce his message. These modifications of the annotated documents are recorded and updated in the Document artifact. Thus, during the display of the search results, the annotated documents will have a bigger weight compared to other relevant documents.

These annotations can be used by Recommender agent since the Annotation artifact contains user's relevance feedback. As detailed thereafter, we make the assumption that an annotated document is implicitly relevant.

Example. Resuming our execution scenario. *Paul*'s profile is as follows. $P_1 = (\{trucks\}, \{accidents, fruits\}, \{motorised vehicles\}, \{Decision_{10}, Decision_{15}, Decision_{19}\})$.

Paul annotates the decision 19 in stating that the passage of the decision from line 3 to line 9 is the most relevant part. The Recommender agent then updates the Annotation artifact of the user *Paul*.

$A_{Paul}^{D_{19}} = (1, L3 - L9, $ "this part details the reasons of non delivery of merchandise") The annotations are highlighted by displaying them among the first results if the document containing the annotation meets the information need.

5.2 Recommendation

The second extension of the model is adding a Recommender agent. The Recommender agent uses collaborative filtering to recommend documents that might be relevant to users.

We formulate the recommendation of Recommender agent as a function:

$$Recommendation(\mathcal{N}, N_i, P_j, A_{u_i}^D) :\mapsto \{(D_i, Rate)\} \qquad (5)$$

This function takes as parameters as we defined in [11]: $\mathcal{N} = \{N_1, ..., N_m\}$ which is the set of all browsings, for each browsing session N_i, a user u_{N_i} has a profile P_j and can annotate documents $A_{u_i}^D$. The recommendation function returns a set of pairs of documents and their rates to be recommended to the user in the current browsing session if the rate is between 0.5 and 1 $(0, 5 < Rate < 1)$.

A Document artifact is defined as: $D_i = (D_{i,RI}, D_{i,REC})$ where $D_{i,RI}$ are documents resulting from information search and $D_{i,REC}$ are those recommended by the Community agent. Documents resulting from the Recommendation function are added to the Document artifact to update recommended document $D_{i,REC}$ as follows:

$$D_{i,REC} = (D_{i,RECC}, D_{i,RECR}) \qquad (6)$$

where the documents $D_{i,RECC}$ are those recommended by Community agent and $D_{i,RECR}$ recommended by Recommender agent. The functioning of the agent can be summarized in two steps: The first is the search for users who have similar behavior as the user to whom it wishes to make recommendations, using user profiles and browsing sessions. The second step is to use the rates and annotations of these similar users to calculate a list of recommendations for that user.

Clustering Similar Users. Given the very high number of users we have chosen to group them in groups of similar users to facilitate the comparisons. Since we don't have a predefined number of user groups, the X-Means [16] seems to be the most appropriate one to cluster users. After clustering users in X clusters defined by centroids C. We compare the current user profile with different centroids to determine to which cluster he is similar.

Collaborative Filtering. The recommendation starts when we have a current user and his group of similar users.

In general, the input of collaborative filtering problem is a simple matrix V of size $n \times m$ of rating, where n is the total number of users U and m is the total number of items (document) D.

The matrix element v_{ij} is the rate given by the user u_i to the document d_j.

If it turns out that u_i has not assigned a rating to d_j, the v_{ij} value is considered a missing value $(v_{ij} = null)$. The objective of the FC is therefore reduced to simply estimate the missing values of the matrix V.

Table 1. Filling of The Matrix

u_i	d_1	d_2	d_3	d_4	Average	u_i	d_1	d_2	d_3	d_4	Average
Rate	0	-	-	1	0.5	Rate	0	1	-	1	0.66
Annotation	-	An_2	-	An_4		Annotation	-	An_2	-	An_4	

The first step before applying collaborative filtering is to try to fill in the matrix for each case when the user makes an annotation and doesn't rate the document. We make the assumption that the document is implicitly relevant (Table 1).

The Recommender agent uses the existing values in the matrix to calculate the missing values. To calculate a value v_{ij}, it uses the neighbors of u_i who have already rated d_j. To extract them it measures the similarity between u_i and each user having rated the document d_j. The similarity measure the most frequently used is the correlation coefficient of Pearson [15]. Here is Pearson's formula to calculate the correlation between two users u_i and u_j [17]:

$$\text{Pearson}(u_i, u_j) = \frac{\sum_{d \in D_{i,j}} (v_{(u_i,d)} - \overline{v_{u_i}})(v_{(u_j,d)} - \overline{v_{u_j}})}{\sqrt{\sum_{d \in D_{i,j}} (v_{(u_i,d)} - \overline{v_{u_i}})^2 \sum_{d \in D_{i,j}} (v_{(u_j,d)} - \overline{v_{u_j}})^2}} \quad (7)$$

where $D_{i,j}$ is the sub-set of documents rated by both u_i and u_j, $v_{(u_i,d)}$ is the rate given by u_i to the document d and $\overline{v_{u_i}}$ is the average of rate given by u_i. In order to predict the rating of the current user for this document, the FC exploit the rates of other users of the same group who have rated this document.

$$v(u_i, d_j) = \overline{v_{u_i}} + \frac{\sum_{u_k \in U_{d_j}} pearson(u_i, u_k) \times (v_{(u_k,d_j)} - \overline{v_{u_k}})}{card(U_{d_j})} \quad (8)$$

where: U_{d_j} is the sub-set of users having rated d_j.

The Recommender agent will then run the FC and get the filled matrix with predicted rates of documents to be recommended to the current user.

Example. The Recommender agent starts first by filling the missing values where there is an annotation. Let the matrix in Table 2 of user ratings: Sup-

Table 2. Example of matrix

	d_1	d_2	d_3	d_4	Average		d_1	d_2	d_3	d_4	Average
Paul	0	1	-	1	0.66	Paul	0	1	0.79	1	0.66
Julien	0	1	1	0	0.5	Julien	0	1	1	0	0.5
Jean	1	1	0	-	0.66	Jean	1	1	0	0.72	0.66
u_4	0	-	-	1	0.5	u_4	0	-	-	1	0.5

pose that we want to predict the value of $v_{1,3}$. It begins by selecting the neighbors of *Paul* who have rated d_3, $D_{d_3} = \{Jean, Julien\}$ subsequently, it calculates the similarity between *Paul* and each member of D_{d_3} by using the Pearson measure. $pearson(Paul, Julien) = 0,46$ and $pearson(Paul, Jean) = 0,3$ and $v_{1,3} = 0.79$. $pearson(Jean, Paul) = -0.3$, $pearson(Jean, u_4) = (-0.46)$, $pearson(Jean, Julien) = -0.28$ and $v_{3,4} = 0.72$. Since $v_{1,3}$ and $v_{3,4}$ are both higher than 0.5, the Recommender agent adds $\{(d_3, 0.79)\}$ to recommendation list of document to be recommended to *Paul* and $\{(d_4, 0.72)\}$ to *Jean*. In addition, the list of documents to be proposed by Community agent to both *Paul* and *Jean* if there is another user having the same information need.

We have already the results to be displayed to *Jean* that includes the results of the Interface agent $D_{i,RI} = \{Decision_1, Decision_{51}, Decision_{11}, Decision_{19}\}$ and the recommendations of the Community agent: $D_{i,RECC} = \{Decision_{27}, Decision_{15}, Decision_{10}$ and $Decision_{19}\}$ to which is added $D_{i,RECR} = \{Decision_4\}$ the recommendation of Recommender agent.

6   Conclusion and Perspectives

We presented through this article an agent-based model for document research. Unlike existing works using multiagent systems for document research, we proposed a general model following a stigmergic approach in order to remain independent from any specific digital corpus. Two layers have been defined for that issue: a browsing layer composed by artifacts that represent the corpus resources and browsing processes, and a decision layer composed by agents that act on the browsing layer to influence the browsing with various factors such as query reformulation, or recommendations from the history of past browsings.

A use scenario of our architecture has been shown on a digital corpus on transportation law documents. The openness of our approach is illustrated by adding dynamically in this use case new corpus resources or new recommendation processes. As a perspective, we plan an experimental validation on a panel of users.

Acknowledgments. The work carried out in this article receives funding from the *Grand Réseau de Recherche: Logistique, Mobilité, Numérique* High-Normandy Region (PlaIR 2.0 project 2013-2016).

References

1. Nodine, M., Fowler, J., Ksiezyk, T., Perry, B., Taylor, M., Unruh, A.: Active information gathering in infosleuthTM. Int. J. Coop. Inf. Syst. **9**(01n02), 3–27 (2000)
2. Durfee, E.H., Kiskis, D.L., Birmingham, W.P.: The agent architecture of the University of Michigan digital library. IEE Proc. Softw. **144**(1), 61–71 (1997)
3. Elayeb, B., Evrard, F., Zaghdoud, M., Ahmed, M.B.: A multiagent possibilistic system for web information retrieval. In: IKE, pp. 72–78 (2007)
4. The Institute of International Transport Law (IDIT). http://www.idit.asso.fr/

5. Sycara, K., Decker, K., Pannu, A., Williamson, M., Zeng, D.: Distributed intelligent agents. IEEE Expert **11**, 36–46 (1996)
6. Grey D.J., Dunne G., Ferguson, R.I.: A mobile agent architecture for searching the WWW. In: Proceedings of Workshop on Agents in Industry, 4th International Conference of Autonomous Agents, Barcelona (2000)
7. Lemouzy, S.: Systèmes interactifs auto-adaptatifs par systèmes multiagents auto-organisateurs,: application à la personnalisation de l'accès à l'information. Ph.D thesis in computer science, Paul Sabatier University - Toulouse III, Toulouse (France) (2011)
8. Omicini, A., Ricci, A., Viroli, M.: Artifacts in the A & A meta-model for multiagent systems. Auton. Agents Multiagent Syst. **17**(3), 432–456 (2008)
9. Ricci, A., Viroli, M., Omicini, A.: CArtAgO: an infrastructure for engineering computational environments in MAS. In: Weyns, D., Parunak, H.V.D., Michel, F. (eds.) Proceedings of E4MAS, Hakodate, Japan, pp. 102–119 (2006)
10. Grassé, P.-P.: La reconstruction du nid et les coordinations interindividuelles chez Bellicositermes natalensis et Cubitermes sp. la théorie de la stigmergie: Essai d'interprétation du comportement des termites constructeurs. Insectes sociaux **6**(1), 41–80 (1959)
11. El Guedria, Z., Vercouter, L.: Customized document research by a stigmergic approach using agents and artifacts. In: Rovatsos, M., Vouros, G., Julian, V. (eds.) EUMAS 2015. LNCS, vol. 9571, pp. 50–64. Springer, Heidelberg (2016). doi:10. 1007/978-3-319-33509-4_4
12. Resnick, P., Varian, H.R.: Recommender systems. Commun. ACM **40**(3), 56–58 (1997)
13. Burke, R.: Survey and experiments. User Model. User-Adap. Inter. **12**(4), 331–370 (2002)
14. Herlocker, J.L., Konstan, J.A., Terveen, L.G., Riedl, J.T.: Evaluating collaborative filtering recommender systems. ACM Trans. Inf. Syst. **22**(1), 5–53 (2004)
15. Resnick, P., Iacovou, N., Suchak, M., Bergstrom, P., Riedl, J.: An open architecture for collaborative filtering of netnews. In: Proceedings of the 1994 ACM Conference on Computer Supported Cooperative Work, CSCW 1994, pp. 175–186 (1994)
16. Pelleg, D., Moore, A.W., et al.: X-means: extending K-means with efficient estimation of the number of clusters. In: ICML 2000, pp. 727–734 (2000)
17. Shardanand, U., Maes, P.: Social information filtering: algorithms for automating "word of mouth". In: Proceedings of the SIGCHI Conference on Human Factors in Computing Systems, pp. 210–217. ACM Press/Addison-Wesley Publishing Co, May 1995
18. Ricci, A., Omicini, A., Viroli, M., Gardelli, L., Oliva, E.: Cognitive stigmergy: towards a framework based on agents and artifacts. In: Weyns, D., Dyke Parunak, H., Michel, F. (eds.) E4MAS 2006. LNCS (LNAI), vol. 4389, pp. 124–140. Springer, Heidelberg (2007)

Which Information Sources are More Trustworthy in a Scenario of Hydrogeological Risks: A Computational Platform

Rino Falcone[✉], Alessandro Sapienza, and Cristiano Castelfranchi

ISTC-CNR of Rome, Rome, Italy
rino.falcone@istc.cnr.it

Abstract. In this work we realized a series of social simulations in order to investigate how a set of cognitive agents behave in presence of critical hydrogeological phenomena, showing some interesting results about their choices.

The paper starts with the presentation of an ad-hoc Bayesian trust model that we created and used in the simulations. Then we describe the realized platform that can be manipulated in order to shape many possible scenarios.

The simulations start with a world populated by a number of agents that have to deal with different and more or less dangerous meteorological events requiring adequate behaviors. So they need to take a decision and in order to select the right behavior they have to use the information sources they can access. Agents are also profiled into different categories, which shape how they use/trust their different sources.

They will someway interact with each other and with their information sources to finally decide how to behave.

Keywords: Trust · Social simulation · Cognitive analysis

1 Introduction

Trying to put together information coming from different information sources can be an uneasy task. It is necessary to have strategies to do it, especially in presence of critical situation, when there are temporal limits to get decision and a wrong choice can lead to an economical loss or even to risk life. So the necessity of integrating sources on different scopes can be very useful in order to make a well-informed decision. In case of the weather forecast we can consider different sources: official bulletin of authorities, the observation of other agents' behavior and of their decisions during the meteorological event, the direct evaluation and competence of the same agents as the basis for their own decisions, and so on. Some of these sources are not correlated among them (a forecast is referred to mathematical model of the weather linked to its previous data, while a direct evaluation can be based on a current human perception of the phenomenon (with its potential psychological and perceptive bias)). Then, integrating these sources becomes essential and at the same time it is necessary to identify and take into account their trustworthiness.

© Springer International Publishing Switzerland 2016
Y. Demazeau et al. (Eds.): PAAMS 2016, LNAI 9662, pp. 84–96, 2016.
DOI: 10.1007/978-3-319-39324-7_8

For trusting an information source (S) we used a cognitive model [3] based on the dimensions of competence and reliability/motivation of the source. These competence and reliability evaluations can derive from different reasons, basically:

1. Our previous *direct experience* with S on that specific kind of information content.
2. *Recommendations* (other individuals Z reporting their direct experience and evaluation about S) or *Reputation* (the shared general opinion of others about S) on that specific information content [4, 7, 11, 12, 15].
3. *Categorization* of S (it is assumed that a source can be categorized and that it is known this category), exploiting inference and reasoning (analogy, inheritance, etc.): on this basis it is possible to establish the competence/reliability of S on that specific information content [1, 2, 5, 6].

However in this paper, for the sake of simplicity, we do not analyze the agents' process for evaluating trust of the different sources, but we give directly the value of these sources as considered from the different categories of the introduced agents. This simplification is compatible with the fact that our agents do not manipulate their values of trust (we do not consider the feedback effects and the trust dynamics). Our focus is on the integration of the information sources also based on their trustworthiness. In particular, we are interested to analyze how different populations of cognitive agents (composed by different percentage of agents who rely on various sources) react to the various weather situations and how many of them take the right decision (given the real weather). Our main questions we intend investigate are: when is it better to follow the authority indications? Or the other agents' behaviors? Or our own evaluations of the situation? And again: What is the relevance of the different composition of the population (different numbers of the different agents' categories) for answering to the previous questions? In practice: Are we able to extract useful information from these simulations for situations of real cases? In the paper we show how, with a certain limit of approximation, we can give some useful and interesting indications.

2 The Trust Model

Given the complexity of simulations, we chose to use a simplified trust model, unifying many parameters in just one. Trust decision in presence of uncertainty can be handle using uncertainty theory [8] or probability theory. We decided to use the second approach, as in this platform agents know a priori all the possible events that can happen and they are able to estimate how much it is plausible that they occur. In particular we exploit Bayesian theory, one of the most used approach in trust evaluation [9, 10, 13]. In this model each information source S is represented by a trust degree called TrustOnSource, with $0 \leq$ TrustOnSource ≤ 1, plus a bayesian probability distribution PDF (Probability Distribution Function) that represents the information reported by S. The trust model takes into account the possibility of many events: it just splits the domain in the corresponding number of interval. In this work we use three different events (described below), then the PDF will be divided into three parts. The *TrustOnSource* parameter is used to smooth the information referred by S. This is the formula used for transforming the reported PDF:

$$NewValue = 1 + (Value - 1) * TrustOnSource$$

The output of this step is called Smoothed PDF (SPDF).

We will have that the greater *TrustOnSource* is, the more similar the SPDF will be to the PDF; in particular if *TrustOnSource* = 1 => SPDF = PDF and if *TrustOnSource* = 0 => SPDF is an uniform distribution with value 1.

The idea is that we trust on what S says proportionally to how much we trust it. In other words, the more we trust S, the more we tend to take into consideration what it says; the less we trust S, the more we tend to ignore its informative contribution.

We define GPDF (Global PDF) the evidence that an agent owns concerning a belief P. Once estimated the SPDFs for each information source, there will be a process of aggregation between the GPDF and the SPDFs. Each source actually represents a new evidence E about a belief P. Then to the purpose of the aggregation process it is possible to use the classical Bayesian logic, recursively on each source:

$$f(P|E) = \frac{f(E|P) * f(P)}{f(E)}$$

where:

f(P|E) = GPDF (the new one)
f(E|P) = SPDF;
f(P) = GPDF (the old one)

In this case f(E) is a normalization factor, given by the formula:

$$f(E) = \int f(E|P) * f(P)dP$$

In other words the new GPDF, which is the global evidence that an agent has about P, is computed as the product of the old GPDF and the SPDF, that is the new contribute reported by S. As we need to ensure that GPDF is still a probability distribution function, it is necessary to scale down it to[1]. This is ensured by the normalization factor f(E).

3   The Platform

Exploiting NetLogo [14], we created a very flexible platform, where a lot of parameters are taken into account to model a variety of situations.

The basic idea is that, given a population distributed over a wide area, some weather phenomena happen in the world with a variable level of criticality. These weather phenomena happen in the world in a temporal window of 16 ticks.

The world is populated by a number of cognitive agents (citizens) that react to these situations, deciding how to behave, on the basis of the information sources they have

---

[1] To be a PDF, it is necessary that the area subtended by it is equal to 1.

and of the trustworthiness they attribute to these different sources: they can escape, take measures or evaluate absence of danger.

In addition to citizens, there is another agent called authority. Its aim is to inform promptly citizens about the weather phenomena. Moreover the authority will be characterized by an uncertainty, expressed in terms of standard deviation.

3.1 Information Sources

To make a decision, each agent can consult a set of information sources, reporting to it some evidence about the incoming meteorological phenomena. We considered the presence of three kinds of information sources (whether active or passive) available to agents:

1. Their *personal judgment*, based on the direct observation of the phenomena. Although this is a direct and always true (at least in that moment) source, it has the drawback that waiting to see what happens could lead into a situation in which it is no more possible to react in the best way (for example there is no more time to escape if one realizes too late the worsening weather).
2. *Notification from authority*: the authority distributes into the world weather forecast with associated different alarm signals, trying to prepare citizens to what is going to happen. This is the first informative source that agents have.
3. *Others' behavior*: agents are in some way influenced by community logics, tending to partially or totally emulate their neighbors behavior.

The notification from the authority is provided as a clear signal: all the probability is focused on a single event. Conversely, the personal judgment can be distributed on two or three events with different probabilities. This can also be true for others' behavior estimation as the probability of each event is directly proportional to the number of neighbors making each kind of decision. If no decision is available, the PDF is a uniform distribution with value 1.

3.2 Agents' Description

At the beginning of the simulation, the world is populated by a number of agents belonging to three categories. The main difference between them lays in how much trust they have in their information sources:

1. *Self-trusting agents* prefer to rely on their own capabilities and direct experience, having a high level of self trust; they need to see the phenomena to make a decision, but as a consequence they need more time to take a decision. Their self trust (st) is high, but depending on the context, they could not be able to rely on it. In fact, if they have to take a decision before seeing a sufficient part of the event, they will be less confident on their evaluation. This is reasonable, as there is more time for the event to change type. Decreasing the part of the event they are able to see, this trust value will assume the values: 15 ticks => st = 1; 14 ticks => st = 0.9; 13 ticks => st = 0.75; 12 ticks => st = 0.55; 11 ticks => st = 0.3. The trust on the other two components will be: authority trust 0.3; community trust 0.3.

2. *Authority-trusting agents* put trust mainly on what the authority says, so they are the first to make a decision (weather forecast are distributed in advance with respect to phenomena): self trust 0.3; authority trust 0.9; community trust 0.3;
3. *Social-trusting agents* model agents that are mainly influenced by social dynamics; they need to see what other agents choose and then they follow the majority. When at least the 75 % of their neighbors decided or they reach their deadline, they take a choice: self trust 0.3; authority trust 0.3; community trust 0.9;

A special kind of social-trusting agent is *Pure Social-trusting agent*. It is just influenced by others' behavior, totally ignoring the other information sources. Plus, it will try to decide after all the other agents: self trust 0; authority trust 0; community trust 0.9.

These trust degrees are then used to apply the trust model above described.

3.3 World Description

The world is made by 32 × 32 patches, which wraps both horizontally and vertically. It is geographically divided in 4 quadrants of equal dimension, where agents are distributed in a random way. The quadrants differ in the possible weather phenomena that happen, modeled through the presence of clouds. The events are modeled so that agents cannot be completely sure of what is going to happen.

Critical events are tremendous events due to too high level of rain, with possible risks for the agents sake, presented through a 16 ticks sequence of 3 clouds. *Medium events* are defined as those events that can cause damages to houses or streets, but not to citizens' health; they are composed by a 16 ticks sequence of 2 or 3 clouds (or by a sequence of 13 ticks at the beginning followed by at least a couple of (2,3) in any sequence). To let these events be similar to the critical ones, the 50 % of the times we force the firsts 13 ticks to be equal to 3 clouds. If there is not enough rain to make any damage, it is a *light event*, composed by a 13 ticks sequence of 2/3 ticks followed by 2 ticks that can assume one of the value {0,1,2,3} and then ends with 0. This event can be confused with a medium one (if not seen in its completeness).

Figure 1 provides a graphically description of the events, to help readers understand them.

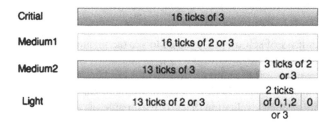

Fig. 1. Events graphical description

These phenomena are not instantaneous, but they happen progressively in time, adding a given number of clouds on each tick until the phenomenon is completed. The four quadrants are independent from each other but there can be an indirect influence as agents can have neighbors in other quadrants. These events are also correlated to the alarms that the authority raises. In fact, as previously said, the authority is characterized by a standard deviation. We use it to produce the alarm generated by the authority and from it depends the correctness of the prediction. In particular, we have considered two kinds of authorities: a reliable authority and an incompetent one.

3.3.1 Own Evaluation

How should agents evaluate the phenomena they see? We propose an empirical way to evaluate them, taking into account how phenomena are generated and how they can evolve.

Considering what we just said, agents can see a sequence of 3 clouds or a sequence of 2 and 3 clouds. The first one can lead to a critical or a medium event, the second one to a medium or light event. The following Table 1 shows a complete description of how agents evaluate what they see:

Table 1. This table provides a comprehensive description of agents' evaluation in each possible situation

Event seen	Probability of critical event	Probability of medium event	Probability of light event
15 ticks of 3	90 %	10 %	0 %
14 ticks of 3	80 %	20 %	0 %
13 ticks of 3	50 %	50 %	0 %
12 ticks of 3	10 %	80 %	10 %
11 ticks of 3	5 %	70 %	25 %
13 ticks of 3 and 1 tick of 2	0 %	80 %	20 %
13 ticks of 3 followed by (2,2), (2,3) or (3,2)	0 %	100 % (full-blowen) medium event	0 %
15 ticks of 2 or 3	0 %	90 %	10 %
14 ticks of 2 or 3	0 %	80 %	20 %
13 ticks of 2 or 3	0 %	50 %	50 %
12 ticks of 2 or 3	0 %	20 %	80 %
11 ticks of 2 or 3	0 %	10 %	90 %
Any other case	0 %	0 %	100 %

Programmatically, agents make a pattern matching of what they see, respecting the order of the table. As readers can notice, there are just a few cases in which agents are completely sure of what is going to happen.

3.4   Workflow

We start generating a world containing an authority and a given number of agents belonging to different categories. At the time t_0 the authority gives forecast for a future temporal window (composed by 16 ticks) including an alarm signal, reporting the level of criticality of the event that is going to happen in each quadrant (critic = 3, medium = 2, light = 1). Being just a forecast, it is not sure that it is really going to happen. It will have a probability linked to the precision of the authority (depending from standard deviation). However, as a forecast, it allows agents to evaluate the situation in advance, before the possible event. Event in fact starts from t_{111} to t_{115}[2] and, as previously said, lasts for 16 ticks.

During the decision making phase, agents check their own information sources, aggregating the single contributes according to the corresponding trust values. They estimate the possibility that each event happens and take the choice that minimizes the risk. Then, accordingly to their own decision-making deadlines, agents will choose how to behave. While agents collect information they are considered as "thinking", meaning that they have not decided yet. When this phase reaches the deadline, agents have to make a decision, that cannot be changed anymore. This information is then available for the other agents (neighborhood), which can in turn exploit it for their decisions.

4   Simulations

Once realized the platform, we decided to use it in order to understand which dynamics exist between the different kinds of population, analyzing individual's and crowds' behaviors and examining how they react to the presence of possible risks. To do that, we investigated a series of scenarios, populated by different percentages of agents belonging to those categories. We started studying how *SoT* agents behave in presence of *SeT* and *AT* agents. To do so, we are going to use a fixed number of SoT agents (100) and a variable percentage of SeT and AT agents.

Then in a second case we observed a similar scenario, realized using *pure social* agents. We will not provide a detailed description of each case, as we preferred focusing on just the main aspects. In order to understand agent's behavior, we will show their performance, i.e. the percentage of right decision taken by each agent's category. Results are mediated through 500 runs.

4.1   First Scenario

Simulation settings:

1. Events starting: we explored the cases in which the starting ticks are:{111, 112, 113, 114, 115}.

---

[2] This has been made in order to ensure that self-trusting agents cannot always see the whole critical event.

2. Authority reliability: we used the value 0.3 to shape a very reliable authority and 0.9 to shape an incompetent one.
3. Agents population: we tried 5 different configurations of self-trusting (SeT) and authority-trusting agents (AT), letting social-trusting agents (SoT) fixed to 100 units; (10 SeT, 90 AT, 100 SoT), (30, 70, 100), (50, 50, 100), (70, 30, 100), (90, 10, 100).
4. Event map: [1 3 3 2].
5. Decision making deadline (since the simulation starts): we decided to use this as a category parameter. As AT agents believe mainly in the authority and this kind of source is immediately available, they will quickly decide. Their deadline is fixed to 30 ticks. Conversely SeT agents need more time to decide, as they need to see a good part of the event. The same stands for SoT agents, that want to observe others behavior. Then the deadline is fixed to 125 ticks for both SeT and SoT.

First of all, notice that AT agents' performance strictly depends on what the authority says; they do not analyze the event nor look at others' behavior. Then we will focus on how SeT and SoT agents perform. Moreover in this case the Authority source has a direct influence, as source, plus an indirect influence due to the social effect. In fact AT agents decide earlier then SoT agents will mainly follow AT agents, doing most of the time what the authority says.

4.1.1 Event Starting at 111

Let us analyze the experiment considering the "event starting" parameter first. When it assumes the value 111, agents are able to see 15 ticks of event. Concerning SeT agents, they will be a lot confident on their evaluation, obtaining always-good performance. The other two information sources will be less relevant. SoT agents follow the crowd. They will be mainly influenced by AT agents as when they decide all the AT agents have decided, but SeT agents are still deciding.

4.1.2 Event Starting at 112

This case is much more relevant than the second, concerning SeT agents. Here is in fact possible to notice an interesting effect.

Let us analyze the critical event case with a reliable authority (Fig. 2). Given that the self-trust of SeT agents is 0.9 (very high) and they estimate a 80 % probability of critical event, we expect them to get a 100 % performance, but it doesn't happen. These would have happened if they had been alone. In these case the other two information sources affect them, even if they are quite irrelevant if compared to the first one (0.3 of trust).

Let us explain what happened. A single source, authority or social behavior, is not able to negatively affect the first one. But if they combine their effects, they can modify the decision. Suppose that the authority wrongly raises a medium alarm. It does with a 100 % certainty. All AT agents and the majority of SoT agents will follow what the authority states. So it can happen that both the authority source and the social source state with a 100 % probability that there will be a medium event. In this case given that own evaluation of SeT agents, even if with a high level of trust, let a possibility of 20 % of medium event, the other two sources change the outcome, letting SeT agents wrongly decide not to escape.

This is an interesting case that shows the non-linearity of information sources sum. At a cognitive level, it is possible that two sources with low trust but expressing much certainty overcome one source more trustworthy but that is less sure. The same effect happens in case of a non reliable authority (Fig. 3): we can see in fact that both the SeT curves (in red) increase when the proportion on AT agents decreases.

4.1.3   Event Starting at 113

In this case, both SeT and SoT follow the performance of AT agents. Actually, SeT agents perform a little bit better, SoT a little bit worse. Let's examine the medium event case in quadrant 4, with a reliable authority (Fig. 4).

Suppose that agents see a 13-ticks sequence of 3 (this reasoning is still valid in can of a 13-ticks sequence of 2 or 3). SeT agents estimate a 50 % probability of critical event and a 50 % probability of medium event. Being alone, they would have a 50 % performance, then the authority and social sources become essential. Their combined effect determines agents' decision between critical event of medium event **but not a light event, there wouldn't be enough evidence!** In fact in these cases, SeT agents choose randomly, with a 50 % chance of success. That is why they perform better.

The worse performance of SoT agents is due to the fact that they are influenced by agents in other quadrants, which take different decisions because of different events.

4.1.4   Event Starting at 114

Here we can see the same effect of the case 112. Again, let's look at the critical event in the second quadrant in case of reliable authority (Fig. 5).

In this case SeT agents wrongly estimate a 80 % probability of medium event, seeing just 12 ticks, but fortunately their self trust is lowered to 0.55, so that the influence of authority and social sources is greater. Conversely, this time their presence helps SeT agents in their decision. In fact decreasing the proportion of AT agents, SeT agents curve lowers. Being alone, their performance would be about 0 %.

4.1.5   Event Starting at 115

In this last case, all the curves are quite the same, choosing exactly what the authority says, meaning that its direct and indirect influence of agents is really strong.

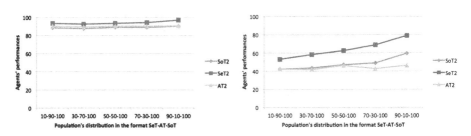

Fig. 2. Event starting at tick 112, reliable authority and critical event.

Fig. 3. Event starting at tick 112, non reliable authority and critical event

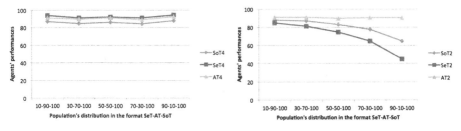

Fig. 4. Event starting at tick 113, reliable authority and medium event.

Fig. 5. Event starting at tick 114, reliable authority and critical event

4.2 Second Scenario

Here we used the same setting of the first simulation, substituting social-trusting agents with pure social-trusting agents (PST), which just rely on others behavior, completely ignoring the other information sources. Further, PST agents wait for SeT agents decision, so that they are equally influenced by SeT and AT agents.

Simulation settings:

1. Events starting: we explored the cases {111, 112, 113, 114, 115}.
2. Authority reliability: we used the value 0.3 to shape a very reliable authority and 0.9 to shape an incompetent one.
3. Agents population: we tried 5 different configurations of self-trusting (SeT) and authority-trusting agents (AT) agents, letting pure social-trusting agents (PST) fixed to 100 units; (10, 90, 100), (30, 70, 100), (50, 50, 100), (70, 30, 100), (90, 10, 100).
4. Event map: [1 3 3 2].
5. Decision making deadline (since the simulation starts): 30 ticks for AT agents, 125 ticks for SeT and PST agents.

This experiment is quite similar to the previous one. AT agents perform exactly the same, as they are not influenced by the changes. Even SeT agents perform the same: we can notice again the same effect in cases of event starting at 112 and 114; their curves tend to uniform to the AT ones.

PST agents introduce the true difference. Being equally influenced by SeT and AT, their performance depends on the proportion between them. Figure 6 shows this behavior. Further, it seems that PST agents performance has a limit (Fig. 7). This limit can be explained analyzing the differences between PST and SoT. In fact, in many cases their behavior is the same, but in two cases it completely differs. The first case occurs when their neighbors take two or three decisions with the same proportion (for example, 3 agents choose to escape and 3 agents chose to take measures). SoT agents react using the other two information sources. PST cannot, then they choose randomly, with a 50 % or 33 % of average performance, depending on if they have two choose between 2 or 3 cases. The second case is what we call the **"isolated social"**, that is a social than is not near to anyone, so that is not able to exploit its social source. Again, a SoT agent is still capable of exploiting the other two sources. A PST agent has to choose randomly, with a 33 % probability of success.

Notice that while my own evaluation of the phenomenon and the authority alarm are some way correlated with what is going to happen (even if they can be wrong), the observation of others could be completely unrelated! In fact, I could take into account the behavior of agents that belongs to other context/quadrant without considering this difference. This consideration explains why social agents performance never reaches a maximal value (although they can perform well). This aspect is less evident for SoT agents than PST agents, as SoT are able to use the other two information sources.

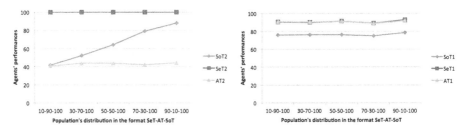

Fig. 6. Event starting at tick 111, non reliable authority and critical event.

Fig. 7. Events starting at 113, reliable authority, light event. This last picture clearly show PST agents limit.

5 Conclusion

In this work we presented an articulated platform for social simulation, particularly suited for studying agents' choice in presence of critical weather phenomena. To this aim, we realized an ad-hoc Bayesian trust model, used by agents to evaluate and aggregate information coming from different information sources. Using this framework, we were able to show some interesting result.

AT agents performance just depends on the Authority: if this one is reliable then they will perform well and vice versa.

SeT agents, mainly relying on their own evaluation, can obtain even a 100 % performance, but just observing the whole phenomenon. This could lead to situation in which they will no more be able to fulfill their decision: escaping or taking measure needs time. A very interesting case happens when they are not completely sure or their evaluation. In that case, the other two sources, even if less trusted, are able to completely change the final decision. This is due to the fact that the sum among information sources is not linear and the realized Bayesian model perfectly implements this idea.

The social source let SoT and PST agents get good performance, but they will never be able to be the best, due to some factors intrinsic in their nature. In fact, while the own-evaluation and the alarm raised by the authority are someway correlated to the event, even if they can be wrong, the social behaviour is not as they also observe what agents in other quadrant do, where there can be a completely different event. SoT agents can partially overcome this problem, exploiting the other two information sources. PST cannot, so that their maximal performance is about 80 %.

In the premise of this work we asked a set of very interesting questions on how agents should make their decisions, when they must follow a source rather than another.

It is enough easy to answer these questions considering just individuals. In fact, it is better to follow the authority when it is reliable, our own evaluation when we are good evaluator and we have the possibility to observe a good part of the phenomenon, others' behavior when we are not able to make right choice but we think that the others can. However it results really much interesting to answer these questions considering the whole population. In fact, agents following a reliable source have a positive towing effect on others. When the authority is reliable, AT agents have a very positive impact on the population. But if they are not enough they are not able to produce a significant effect, as showed by Fig. 5.

In situation in which it is possible to observe the whole event, it is better to rely on SeT agents. They, being good evaluators and observing a good part of the phenomenon, are able to produce a positive effect on the population even in case of an unreliable authority (Figs. 3 and 6). This effect is much stronger on PST agents (that however has a performance limit of about 80 %) but much more light on SoT agents, as they are mainly influenced by AT agents. In this case the benefits of having SeT agents struggle to emerge, even if there is a high percentage of them.

The conclusion is then that, being so difficult in the real world that it is possible for agents to see a good part of the phenomena and being even in that case so difficult for them to spread their effect, the best situation is when there is a reliable authority and a good part of the population relies on it.

Acknowledgments. This work is partially supported by the project CLARA—CLoud plAtform and smart underground imaging for natural Risk Assessment, funded by the Italian Ministry of Education, University and Research (MIUR-PON).

References

1. Burnett, C., Norman, T., Sycara, K.: Bootstrapping trust evaluations through stereotypes. In: Proceedings of the 9th International Conference on Autonomous Agents and Multiagent Systems (AAMAS 2010), pp. 241–248 (2010)
2. Burnett, C., Norman, T., Sycara, K.: Stereotypical trust and bias in dynamic multiagent systems. ACM Trans. Intell. Syst. Technol. (TIST) 4(2), 26 (2013)
3. Castelfranchi, C., Falcone, R.: Trust Theory: A Socio-Cognitive and Computational Model. Wiley, Chichester (2010)
4. Conte, R., Paolucci, M.: Reputation in artificial societies. Social beliefs for social order. Kluwer Academic Publishers, Boston (2002)
5. Falcone, R., Castelfranchi, C.: Generalizing trust: inferencing trustworthiness from categories. In: Falcone, R., Barber, S.K., Sabater-Mir, J., Singh, M.P. (eds.) Trust 2008. LNCS (LNAI), vol. 5396, pp. 65–80. Springer, Heidelberg (2008)
6. Falcone, R., Piunti, M., Venanzi, M., Castelfranchi C.: From Manifesta to Krypta: the relevance of categories for trusting others. In: Falcone, R., Singh, M. (eds.) Trust in Multiagent Systems, ACM Transaction on Intelligent Systems and Technology, vol.4(2), March 2013

7. Jiang, S., Zhang, J., Ong, Y.S.: An evolutionary model for constructing robust trust networks. In: Proceedings of the 12th International Conference on Autonomous Agents and Multiagent Systems (AAMAS) (2013)
8. Liu, B.: Uncertainty Theory, 5th edn. Springer, Berlin (2014)
9. Melaye, D., Demazeau, Y.: Bayesian dynamic trust model. In: Pěchouček, M., Petta, P., Varga, L.Z. (eds.) CEEMAS 2005. LNCS, vol. 3690, pp. 480–489. Springer, Heidelberg (2005)
10. Quercia, D., Hailes, S., Capra, L.: B-Trust: Bayesian trust framework for pervasive computing. In: Stølen, K., Winsborough, W.H., Martinelli, F., Massacci, F. (eds.) iTrust 2006. LNCS, vol. 3986, pp. 298–312. Springer, Heidelberg (2006)
11. Sabater-Mir, J.: Trust and reputation for agent societies. Ph.D. thesis, Universitat Autonoma de Barcelona (2003)
12. Sabater-Mir, J., Sierra, C.: Regret: a reputation model for gregarious societies. In: 4th Workshop on Deception and Fraud in Agent Societies, Montreal, Canada, pp. 61–70 (2001)
13. Wang, Y., Vassileva, J.: Bayesian network-based trust model. In: Proceedings of IEEE/WIC International Conference on Web Intelligence, WI 2003, pp. 372–378. IEEE, October 2003
14. Wilensky, U.: NetLogo (1999). http://ccl.northwestern.edu/netlogo/. Center for Connected Learning and Computer-Based Modeling, Northwestern University, Evanston, IL
15. Yolum, P., Singh, M.P.: Emergent properties of referral systems. In: Proceedings of the 2nd International Joint Conference on Autonomous Agents and MultiAgent Systems (AAMAS 2003) (2003)

Protecting the NECTAR of the Ganga River Through Game-Theoretic Factory Inspections

Benjamin Ford[1]([✉]), Matthew Brown[1], Amulya Yadav[1], Amandeep Singh[2], Arunesh Sinha[1], Biplav Srivastava[3], Christopher Kiekintveld[4], and Milind Tambe[1]

[1] University of Southern California, Los Angeles, CA, USA
{benjamif,mattheab,amulyaya,aruneshs,tambe}@usc.edu
[2] Columbia University, New York, NY, USA
as4330@columbia.edu
[3] IBM Research, New Delhi, Delhi, India
sbiplav@in.ibm.com
[4] University of Texas at El Paso, El Paso, TX, USA
cdkiekintveld@utep.edu

Abstract. Leather is an integral part of the world economy and a substantial income source for developing countries. Despite government regulations on leather tannery waste emissions, inspection agencies lack adequate enforcement resources, and tanneries' toxic wastewaters wreak havoc on surrounding ecosystems and communities. Previous works in this domain stop short of generating executable solutions for inspection agencies. We introduce NECTAR - the first security game application to generate environmental compliance inspection schedules. NECTAR's game model addresses many important real-world constraints: a lack of defender resources is alleviated via a secondary inspection type; imperfect inspections are modeled via a heterogeneous failure rate; and uncertainty, in traveling through a road network and in conducting inspections, is addressed via a Markov Decision Process. To evaluate our model, we conduct a series of simulations and analyze their policy implications.

Keywords: Game theory · Inspection · Security games · Human-robot/agent interaction · Multiagent systems

1 Introduction

The leather industry is a multi-billion dollar industry [14], and in many developing countries such as India and Bangladesh, the tanning industry is a large source of revenue. Unfortunately, the chemical byproducts of the tanning process are highly toxic, and the wastewater produced by tanneries is sent to nearby rivers and waterways. As a result, the Ganga River (along with many others) has become extremely contaminated, leading to substantial health problems for the large populations that rely on its water for basic needs (e.g., drinking, bathing, crops, livestock) [11]. Tanneries are required by law to run wastewater through

© Springer International Publishing Switzerland 2016
Y. Demazeau et al. (Eds.): PAAMS 2016, LNAI 9662, pp. 97–108, 2016.
DOI: 10.1007/978-3-319-39324-7_9

sewage treatment plants (STPs) prior to discharge into the Ganga. In many cases, however, the tanneries either do not own or run this equipment, and it is up to regulatory bodies to enforce compliance. However, inspection agencies have a severe lack of resources; the combination of tanneries' unchecked pollution and inspection agencies' failure to conduct inspections forced India's national environment monitoring agency to ban the operation of 98 tanneries near Kanpur, India while threatening the closure of approximately 600 tanneries [13]. It is our goal to provide agencies with randomized inspection plans so tanneries reduce harmful effluents and an important facet of India's economy can operate.

In this paper, we introduce a new game-theoretic application, NECTAR (**N**irikshana for **E**nforcing **C**ompliance for **T**oxic wastewater **A**batement and **R**eduction)[1], that incorporates new models and algorithms to support India's inspection agencies by intelligently randomizing inspection schedules. We build on previous deployed solutions based on Stackelberg Security Games (SSG) for counter-terrorism [17] and traffic enforcement [6]. Our SSG models are also the first to focus on the problem of pollution prevention by modeling the interaction between an inspection agency (the leader) and leather tanneries (many followers) - an interaction which poses a unique set of challenges. (i) Because there is a large disparity between the number of inspection teams and the number of tanneries, inspection plans must be efficient. (ii) We cannot assume that inspectors can catch 100 % of violations. (iii) Inspectors must travel to the tanneries via a road network so solutions must be robust to delays (e.g., traffic). Finally, current fine policies may not be sufficient to induce compliance, and (iv) it is important to investigate alternative fine structures.

NECTAR addresses these new challenges of tannery inspections. (i) Our SSG model captures the inspection process and accounts for two types of inspections: thorough inspections and simple (i.e., quick) inspections. While thorough inspections take longer to conduct (and thus less of them can be conducted), they are more likely to detect violations than simple, surface-level inspections which may only be able to check for obvious violations. To model the imperfect nature of these inspections, we (ii) introduce two failure rates: one for thorough inspections and one for simple inspections, with simple inspections failing at a higher rate. (iii) We also address the uncertainty involved with road networks by using a Markov Decision Process (MDP) that will represent and ultimately generate the game solution. Finally, (iv) we also investigate how tannery compliance is affected by two fine structures: fixed fines and variable fines, where the latter will result in larger tanneries receiving larger fines. For the evaluation of our model, we apply NECTAR to a real-world network of tanneries in Kanpur, India, we evaluate the quality of NECTAR's generated solutions, and we demonstrate how NECTAR's solutions can be visualized via a Google Earth overlay.

---

[1] Nirikshana, the Hindi word for inspect. As many mythological stories and even popular Bollywood songs attest, Ganga water is supposed to be NECTAR (or Amrit, the Hindi antonym of poison) which has inspired our project. The project name is intentionally chosen to fit this international and inter-cultural theme.

2   Related Work

Several theoretical papers have used game theory to model the impact of environmental policies. Environmental games [18] use Stackelberg Games to model interactions between a regulator and a polluting firm, while [7] used game theory to study the effect of environmental policies in the Chinese electroplating industry. *Inspection games* consider the general problem of scheduling inspections, and have been extensively studied in the literature. For example, [8] models cases where an inspector must travel to multiple sites and determine violations as a stochastic game. A general theory of inspection games for problems such as arms control and environmental policy enforcement has been studied in [2], including analysis of whether inspectors can benefit from acting first. [16] also considered inspection games with sequential inspections, including compact recursive descriptions of these games. However, most of these works do not focus on concrete applications and thus, unlike our work, do not provide executable inspection schedules to inspectors.

Other areas of research have considered various models of patrolling strategies and scheduling constraints. These include patrolling games [1,3,5] and security games with varying forms of scheduling constraints on resources [6,12,19]. There has also been recent work on utilizing MDPs to represent strategies in security games [4,15]. However, none of these efforts have focused on environmental inspections and have not investigated topics important in this domain, such as the impact of fine structures on adversary behavior (i.e., compliance).

3   Motivating Domain

The pollution of India's rivers is a major concern. The waters of India's largest river, the Ganga (or Ganges) River, are used by over 400 million people – roughly one-third of India's population and more than the entire population of the United States. Unfortunately, the Ganga is ranked the fifth dirtiest river in the world. Generated from various sources such as sewage and industrial effluents, the pollution inflicts serious health conditions on all life that depends on the river. In Kanpur, villagers suffer from health conditions (e.g., cholera, miscarriages), and livestock yield less milk and die suddenly [9].

Situated around the city of Kanpur, the various leather tanneries are a major source of pollution in the Ganga River [9]. While there are a few sewage treatment plants (STPs) in Kanpur, they can neither treat the full volume nor the full range of produced pollutants [10]. In particular, treating heavy metals like chromium, mercury, arsenic, and nickel is costly and needs specialized personnel (in addition to the personnel required to operate the STPs). The government has put in regulations requiring the tanneries to own and operate effluent plants to remove the pollutants before they discharge their sewage. However, the tanneries have not been willing to undertake the additional cost of installing and operating the treatment units. Even when tanneries have installed the units, they avoid operating them whenever possible.

To address non-compliance issues, the government sends inspection teams to visit the tanneries. Inspecting the tanneries is a time-consuming, quasi-legal activity where the "as-is" situation is carefully recorded and samples are collected that can later be subjected to judicial scrutiny. It is also costly because, apart from the inspectors themselves, help from local police is requisitioned for safety, lab work is done for sample testing, and movement logistics are carefully planned; a full inspection is costly to conduct. Due to these costs, the number of inspectors that can be sent out on a patrol is very limited. Our application seeks to help by (1) generating randomized inspection patrols that maximize the effectiveness of available inspectors, and (2) introducing limited inspection teams which conduct simple inspections - a low-cost alternative to full inspection teams which conduct thorough inspections. While limited inspection teams cannot replace the needed capabilities of a full inspection team, they can still inspect tanneries and issue a fine for obvious violations (e.g., the site not owning an STP). We will refer to full inspection teams and limited inspection teams as thorough inspection resources and simple inspection resources, respectively.

4   Model

In this section, we model this pollution prevention problem as a defender-attacker Stackelberg Security Game (SSG). The task of the defender is to send resources to different tannery sites (i.e., the multiple adversaries) on a road network. The defender must devise a patrol strategy to maximize compliance among a number of sites (each site denoted by l), where each site has a number of factories f_l and each site's compliance cost increases with the number of factories. In addition, the defender must take into account the time it takes to travel to and inspect each site. We model the road network as a graph where the nodes represent sites and the edges represent the roads connecting each site. Each edge also has a cost, e_{ab}, associated with it that represents the travel time from a site a to another site b. Using publicly available data regarding tannery locations in Kanpur, we constructed a graph consisting of 50 sites.

The defender has two types of resources: r_1 number of thorough inspection resources and r_2 simple inspection resources. For thorough inspection resources, the inspector conducts a detailed inspection that takes i time units. We model imperfect inspections such that even if a violation exists, the inspectors will fail to detect it with a low probability γ_1. For simple inspection resources, the inspector will conduct a superficial inspection that takes d time units. Since the inspection is not detailed, simple inspection resources will not detect anything but obvious violations. Thus, such resources have a higher probability of failure γ_2. Each of the defender's resources (thorough and simple) have a maximum time budget, t_1 and t_2 respectively, to conduct inspections and travel to sites.

In the SSG framework, the defender will commit to a randomized patrol strategy (a mixed strategy) which is a probability distribution over the executable daily inspection patrols (the pure strategies for all resources). The adversaries (the sites) can fully observe the defender's mixed strategy and know the probability of being inspected by a thorough inspection team or a simple inspection team on a given day. Formulating the mixed strategy requires enumerating all feasible pure strategies for the defender. However, this approach is impractical for two main reasons: (1) for any realistically-sized patrolling problem, the defender pure strategy space is so large that it cannot fit into memory. For example, with our Kanpur graph of 50 tanneries, only one defender resource, and a time horizon of 10 h, the pure strategy space size would be too large to enumerate (approximately 50 choose 10). Therefore, we adopt a compact representation (a transition graph) that will allow our approach to scale to large problem sizes. (2) Inspectors must travel to sites via a road network (with potential delays), and the corresponding uncertainty cannot be handled by a standard SSG formulation. Rather than reasoning about mixed strategies, we instead use the compact representation to reason about spatio-temporal flow through a transition graph. To account for stochasticity and uncertainty in the outcome of actions, we use a Markov Decision Process (MDP) to represent the defender's inspection patrolling problem. We can solve the corresponding linear program (LP) to compute the optimal inspection strategy, i.e., the optimal MDP policy.

4.1   Compact Game Representation: Transition Graph

Brown et al. also faced the challenge of large state spaces for a traffic enforcement domain [6]. Since their game also takes place on a road network, there are sufficient similarities between our approach and theirs to apply their techniques, based on transition graphs, to improve the scalability of our model.

Instead of enumerating an exponential number of pure strategies, we need only enumerate a polynomial number of states and edges in the transition graph. We then compute the optimal probability flow (as seen in the next section), also called a marginal coverage vector, and sample from the vector to create inspection schedules. As the defender resource types (thorough and simple) have different time constraints, each has its own transition graph.

We discretize time into a granularity of h hours. In the thorough inspection resource transition graph, a vertex is added for each site l every h hours until the resource time budget t_1 has been expended. Similarly for the simple resource's transition graph, vertices are added until the time budget t_2 has been expended.

4.2   MDP Formulation

We present an MDP $\langle S, A, T, R \rangle$ to incorporate uncertainty into the transition graph. An example MDP is shown in Fig. 1 to illustrate these definitions.

- S: Finite set of states. Each state $s \in S$ is a tuple (l, τ), where l is the site that the resource is located, and τ is the current time step. For example, an inspector at site A at hour 1 is represented as $s_{A,1}$. Each vertex in the transition graph corresponds to a state s.
- A: Finite set of actions. $A(s)$ corresponds to the set of actions available from state s (i.e., the set of sites reachable from l) that the resource can travel to and inspect. For example, at site A at hour 1, the only available action is to move to site B (i.e., the solid arrow from A to B in Fig. 1).

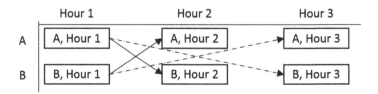

Fig. 1. Illustrative MDP example

- $T_1(s, a, s')$: Probability of an inspector ending up in state s' after performing action a while in state s. Travel time and inspection time are both represented here. As a simple example, there could be probability 0.7 for transition $T_1(s_{A,1}, a_B, s_{B,2})$: a transition from site A at hour 1 to move to and inspect site B will, with a probability of 0.7, finish at hour 2 (a travel + inspection time of 1 h). The dashed lines in Fig. 1 represent the remaining probability (0.3) that the same action will instead finish at hour 3 (due to a delay). Note that the two resource types have separate transition functions due to the difference in action times (i for thorough inspection resources and d for simple inspection resources).
- $R(s, a, s')$: The reward function for ending in state s' after performing action a while in state s. As we are interested in the game-theoretic reward, we define the reward in the LP and define R $= 0 \ \forall s, a, s'$.

5   Inspection Patrol Generation

We provide a linear program (LP) to compute the optimal flow through the MDP (i.e., the transition graph with uncertainty). By normalizing the outgoing flow from each state in the MDP, we obtain the optimal MDP policy from which we can sample to generate dynamic patrol schedules. In the following LP formulation, we make use of the following notation. A site l has a number of factories f_l, and if a site is caught violating during an inspection, they receive a fine, α_l. On the other hand, if a site wants to remain in compliance, they will need to pay a compliance cost β for each factory (total cost $= \beta f_l$). We represent the expected cost for each site l as v_l. As defined in the following LP, the expected cost corresponds to the lowest of either the site's expected fine or the site's full cost of compliance; we assume that these adversaries are rational and that they will choose to pay the lowest of those two values (expected fine or cost of compliance). Finally, we denote as S_l the set of all states that correspond to site l (i.e., all time steps associated with site l).

As discussed in the transition graph definition, the optimal flow through the graph corresponds to the optimal defender strategy, and that flow is represented by a marginal coverage vector. We denote the marginal probability of a resource type i (either thorough or simple inspection team) reaching state s and executing action a as $w_i(s, a)$. We also denote, as $x_i(s, a, s')$, the marginal probability of a resource type i reaching state s, executing action a, and ending in state s'.

$$\max_{w,x} \sum_{l} v_l \tag{1}$$

$$s.t. x_i(s,a,s') = w_i(s,a)T_i(s,a,s'), \forall s,a,s',i \tag{2}$$

$$\sum_{s',a',i} x_i(s',a',s) = \sum_{a,i} w_i(s,a), \forall s,i \tag{3}$$

$$\sum_{a,i} w_i(s_i^+,a) = r_i \tag{4}$$

$$\sum_{s,a,i} x_i(s,a,s_i^-) = r_i \tag{5}$$

$$w_i(s,a) \geq 0 \tag{6}$$

$$v_l \leq \alpha_l(p_{l1} + p_{l2}) \tag{7}$$

$$p_{l1} = (1 - \gamma_1) \sum_{s \in S_l,a} w_1(s,a) \tag{8}$$

$$p_{l2} = (1 - \gamma_2) \sum_{s \in S_l,a} w_2(s,a) \tag{9}$$

$$p_{l1} + p_{l2} \leq 1 \tag{10}$$

$$0 \leq v_l \leq \beta f_l \tag{11}$$

The objective function in Eq. 1 maximizes the total expected cost over all sites. Constraints 2–5 detail the transition graph flow constraints (for thorough inspections and simple inspections). Constraint 2 defines that x is equal to the probability of reaching a state s and performing action a multiplied by the probability of successfully transitioning to state s'. Constraint 3 ensures that the flow into a state s is equal to the flow out of the state. Constraints 4–5 enforce that the total flow in the transition graph, corresponding to the number of defender resources r_i, is held constant for both the flow out of the dummy source nodes s_i^+ and into the dummy sink nodes s_i^-.

Constraint 7 constrains the expected cost for site l. Constraints 8–9 define the probability of successfully inspecting a given site l and is the summation of probabilities of reaching any of l's corresponding states (thus triggering an inspection) and taking any action a. Note that the failure probability γ means that even if a violating site is inspected, there may not be a fine issued. Constraint 10 limits the overall probability of a site being inspected. If a site is visited by both thorough and simple inspection resources, the site will only have to pay a fine, at most, once. Constraint 11 defines the bounds for the adversary's expected cost; if the adversary's expected cost is at the upper bound ($v_l = \beta f_l$), we assume that the adversary would prefer to have a positive public perception and choose to comply rather than pay an equivalent amount in expected fines.

6   Evaluation

In order to explore the strategic tradeoffs that exist in our model of the tannery domain, we ran a series of experiments on our Kanpur tannery graph. For each experiment, we generated 3 distinct patrolling strategy types. 1. NECTAR's strategy, 2. the Uniform Random (UR) strategy: at each time step, every site has an equal probability of being chosen, and 3. an Ad-Hoc (AH) strategy: a deterministic strategy where sites are visited in numerical order (by ID number).

In order to analyze how different resource types affect performance, for each experiment we generated six defender strategies: the first three (NECTAR, UR, AH) correspond to when the defender had twice as many simple inspection resources as thorough inspection resources, and the last three (again NECTAR, UR, AH) correspond to when the defender had no simple inspection resources.

In addition to running experiments where each site l has the same fine (α), we ran a set of experiments where each site's fine α_l was: $\alpha_l = \alpha f_l$ or, in other words, the fine amount is a constant α multiplied by the number of factories f_l at that site – sites with more factories will be penalized for violations more harshly than sites with fewer factories. As this type of analysis requires heterogeneous sites, we randomize the number of factories at each site.

Ultimately, we are interested in inducing compliance in sites, and for our performance metric, we compute the number of sites that would be in full compliance given the defender strategy (i.e., how many sites' cost $v_l = \beta f_l$). The maximum number of sites in compliance for each experiment is 50 (i.e., the number of sites on our graph). The default parameter values for each experiment (unless otherwise specified) are listed in Table 1.

Table 1. Default experiment values

Variable	Value
Compliance cost β	10
Fixed fine amount α	100
Number of factories at each site f_l	2-5
Number of simple inspections r_2	2
Number of sites	50
Number of thorough inspections r_1	1
Patrol duration (hours) t_1, t_2	6
Simple inspection failure rate γ_2	0.6
Thorough inspection failure rate γ_1	0.1
Time granularity (hours) h	1
Time steps to complete simple inspection	1
Time steps to complete thorough inspection	2
Variable fine amount α_l	30

Fixed Fine Amount. In Fig. 2, we analyze the effects of the fixed fine amount α on the number of complying sites. The x-axis shows the fixed fine amount, and the y-axis shows the number of sites that are complying (i.e., $v_l = \beta f_l$).

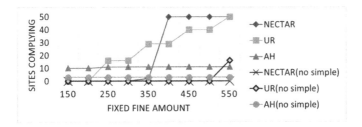

Fig. 2. Fixed fine: number of sites in compliance

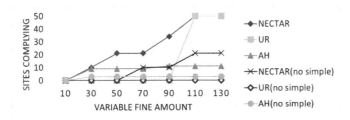

Fig. 3. Variable fine: number of sites in compliance

From the figure, we observe the following trends: (1) the NECTAR strategy does not achieve any compliance until the fine amount is 350, with all sites in compliance at 400. This is due to the objective function attempting to maximize expected cost over all sites simultaneously with a homogeneous fine. (2) While the UR and AH strategies achieve compliance from some of the sites for smaller fine amounts, they do not achieve compliance for all of the sites as quickly as the NECTAR strategy. (3) The inclusion of simple inspection resources improve performance for every strategy as expected.

Variable Fine Amount. In Fig. 3, we analyze the effects of the variable fine amount α_l on the number of complying sites. The x-axis shows the variable fine amount, and the y-axis shows the number of sites in compliance (i.e., $v_l = \beta f_l$).

From the figure, we observe the following trends: (1) both the NECTAR and UR strategies achieve compliance from all sites for the same variable fine amount; (2) as the fines are not homogeneous for all sites, it is beneficial for NECTAR to try to maximize expected cost in sites with many factories first (unlike with the fixed fine, there is no "water filling" effect); the NECTAR approach achieves faster compliance from larger sites, and (3) the NECTAR achieves compliance from the most sites at every point.

Number of Resources: Variable Fine. In Fig. 4, we analyze the effect of the number of resources when there is a variable fine amount α_l on the number of complying sites. The x-axis shows the number of thorough inspection resources, r_1 (for the strategies with simple inspection resources, the number of simple inspection resources is $r_2 = 2 \times r_1$), and the y-axis shows the number of sites that are complying (i.e., $v_l = \beta f_l$).

Fig. 4. Number of resources: variable fine: number of sites in compliance

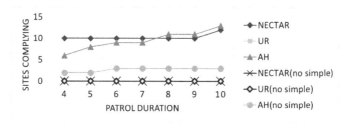

Fig. 5. Patrol duration: variable fine: number of sites in compliance

From the figure, we observe the following trends: (1) the NECTAR and AH strategies achieve compliance from some sites even with few thorough inspection resources, but NECTAR achieves compliance from the most sites at every point, (2) both the NECTAR and UR strategies achieve compliance from all sites for the same number of thorough inspection resources, and (3) even when there are many resources, the AH strategy does not achieve compliance from all sites.

Patrol Duration: Variable Fine. In Fig. 5, we analyze the effects of the patrol duration when there is a variable fine amount α_l on the number of complying sites. The x-axis shows the patrol duration, and the y-axis shows the number of sites that are complying (i.e., $v_l = \beta f_l$).

From the figure, we observe the following trends: (1) while the NECTAR strategy performs the best for lower values of patrol duration, it is eventually outpaced by the AH strategy, (2) regardless of the strategy, there is not much change in the number of sites in compliance as a function of patrol duration. For this experiment, the default values for the other parameters result in a low compliance rate regardless of the value of the variable of interest, and (3) having simple inspection resources is helpful for the NECTAR and AH strategies, but it is not very helpful for the UR strategy.

7   Discussion and Results Visualization

Based on these simulations, we make the following conclusions: (1) when the number of resources or variable fine amount is the experiment variable, NECTAR makes the most efficient use of its resources, regardless of whether it is using only thorough inspections or a combination of simple and thorough inspections; (2) having more resources (more manpower) is more useful than increasing the duration of patrols (longer work hours). This is intuitive when considering that each resource must spend time traveling to each site; two resources can each cover a separate sub-section of the graph whereas one resource will be forced to spend more time traveling. Finally, (3) using a variable fine (in which sites are fined according to their number of factories) leads to better compliance rates. This observation makes sense when put in the context of our LP's objective function: maximize the sum of the expected costs v_l over all sites.

Since our goal is to assist inspection agencies with patrol planning, it is useful to visualize the proposed inspection patrols. In Fig. 6, we show a simple graph and strategy visualization in Google Earth (a visualization for the Kanpur area is shown in Fig. 7). The lines represent edges on the graph (i.e., straight line connections between sites). Each line also has a time step and a coverage probability associated with it, where the probability represents the value of the MDP's transition function, $T(s, a, s')$. In other words, this information answers the question: "If the defender resource starts at site l at the beginning of this edge at time step t (i.e., state s), what is the probability that the defender resource will take action a and arrive at site l', at the end of this edge, in a following time step t' (i.e., state s')?" By clicking on an edge, the user can call up the aforementioned defender strategy information (shown in Fig. 6).

Fig. 6. Visualization example

Fig. 7. A Kanpur inspection patrol plan

NECTAR has been proposed to decision makers in governments, pollution control boards, and funding agencies that cover cleaning of large river basins. While field inspectors have not used randomized inspection schemes in the past, they have given positive feedback on this approach. These proposals are still in a preliminary state, and experience from literature suggests that the success of such initiatives, potentially lasting years, will greatly depend on the collaboration of multiple stakeholders so that the tannery industry and economy can continue to grow while the urgent need to protect the environment is also satisfied.

Acknowledgments. This research was supported by MURI Grant W911NF-11-1-0332.

References

1. Alpern, S., Morton, A., Papadaki, K.: Patrolling games. Operations Research **59**(5), 1246–1257 (2011)
2. Avenhaus, R., von Stengel, B., Zamir, S.: Inspection games. In: Handbook of Game Theory with Economic Applications, vol. 3, chap. 51, pp. 1947–1987 (2002)
3. Basilico, N., Gatti, N., Amigoni, F.: Patrolling security games: definition and algorithms for solving large instances with single patroller and single intruder. Artif. Intell. J. **184**, 78–123 (2012)
4. Bosansky, B., Jiang, A., Tambe, M., Kiekintveld, C.: Combining compact representation and incremental generation in large games with sequential strategies. In: AAAI (2015)
5. Bošanský, B., Lisý, V., Jakob, M., Pěchouček, M.: Computing time-dependent policies for patrolling games with mobile targets. In: AAMAS. pp. 989–996 (2011)
6. Brown, M., Saisubramanian, S., Varakantham, P.R., Tambe, M.: Streets: game-theoretic traffic patrolling with exploration and exploitation. In: IAAI (2014)
7. Dong, X., Li, C., Li, J., Wang, J., Huang, W.: A game-theoretic analysis of implementation of cleaner production policies in the chinese electroplating industry. Resour. Conserv. Recycl. **54**(12), 1442–1448 (2010)
8. Filar, J., et al.: Player aggregation in the traveling inspector model. IEEE Trans. Autom. Control **30**(8), 723–729 (1985)
9. Gupta, S., Gupta, R., Tamra, R.: Challenges faced by leather industry in kanpur (2007). http://home.iitk.ac.in/sgupta/tannery_report.pdf
10. India, P.C.o.: Evaluation study on the function of state pollution control boards (2013)
11. Institute, B.: Top ten toxic pollution problems: Tannery operations. Report (2011). http://www.worstpolluted.org/projects_reports/display/88
12. Jain, M., Conitzer, V., Tambe, M.: Security scheduling for real-world networks. In: AAMAS (2013)
13. Jainani, D.: Kanpur leather industry in danger as ngt cracks whip on pollution. In: Financial Express (2015)
14. Mwinyihija, M.: Emerging world leather trends and continental shifts on leather and leathergoods production. In: World Leather Congress Proceedings (2011)
15. Shieh, E., Jiang, A.X., Yadav, A., Varakantham, P., Tambe, M.: Unleashing Dec-MDPs in security games: enabling effective defender teamwork. In: ECAI (2014)
16. von Stengel, B.: Recursive inspection games. arXiv preprint (2014). arXiv:1412.0129
17. Tambe, M.: Security and Game Theory: Algorithms, Deployed Systems. Lessons Learned. Cambridge University Press, New York (2011)
18. Tapiero, C.S.: Environmental quality control and environmental games. Environ. Model. Assess. **9**(4), 201–206 (2005)
19. Yin, Z., Jiang, A., Johnson, M., Tambe, M., Kiekintveld, C., Leyton-Brown, K., Sandholm, T., Sullivan, J.: Trusts: scheduling randomized patrols for fare inspection in transit systems. In: IAAI (2012)

Combining Agent-Based and Social Network Analysis Approaches to Recognition of Role Influence in Social Media

Bogdan Gliwa[1], Jarosław Koźlak[1(✉)], Anna Zygmunt[1], and Yves Demazeau[2]

[1] AGH University of Science and Technology, Kraków, Poland
{bgliwa,kozlak,azygmunt}@agh.edu.pl
[2] CNRS, Laboratoire d'Informatique de Grenoble, Grenoble, France
Yves.Demazeau@imag.fr

Abstract. These days, different forms of social media play a significant role in the functioning of individuals and society, and social network analysis methodology ensures a better understanding of the structure and behaviour of societies forming in such environments. Including an agent–based approach to such analyses allows a more complete understanding of the specificity of given users as well as the local interactions between them. In this paper we introduce a multi–agent model of user organisations in social media, and analyse roles in social organisations based on distinguishing features of user behaviour such as activity, cooperativeness and group formation. We also analyse the range of influence of users playing given roles in the society, taking into consideration the consequences of removal of users with specific roles and carry out several experiments with data from the political blogosphere.

Keywords: Social multi–agent system organisation · Social network analysis (SNA) · Social group detection · Group dynamics

1 Introduction

In the modern world, different forms of social media play significant roles in the behaviour of individuals and society. The relations between users of social media are often represented as a network, which can be further analysed. A good understanding of the organisation structure and how society might evolve in the future using given media may bring significant benefits regarding choices of promising partners or acquiring useful knowledge.

However, various kinds of problems become apparent while trying to achieve this goal. One is that we often have to deal with an incomplete network: there are nodes and edges that are not represented, and some of these might have a significant impact on the behaviour of the whole network. Therefore, it is useful to identify these missing elements and take their influence on the network into consideration.

© Springer International Publishing Switzerland 2016
Y. Demazeau et al. (Eds.): PAAMS 2016, LNAI 9662, pp. 109–120, 2016.
DOI: 10.1007/978-3-319-39324-7_10

To achieve this goal, it is important to develop an approach that makes it possible to identify the influences of users playing different roles in society. Our approach, presented in the paper, combines multi-agent and social network approaches to identify the influence of users with given roles. We assume that the absence of important roles has a significant influence on the neighbouring users in the network, and multi-agent methods provide the possibility of analysing such local interactions. We define several types of roles, describing the importance and features of given social users, taking into consideration their activity, impact and cooperativeness. Each user in the social media system is represented by an agent. We analyse changes in the roles played by all agents in the network and changes in group memberships after the removal of agents with given roles. The system that we analyse uses data from the political blogosphere to build the network. In our approach we use a multi-agent model (where we represent users of a blog portal as agents) with social network elements (methods of group identification and social network analysis metrics for identification of significant users) for the analysis of data about social network evolution.

The aim of the paper is to find rules describing the changes/transitions of user roles after the removal from the network of these users with given roles.

The organisation of the rest of the paper is as follows. Section 2 contains a research domain description. In Sect. 3, we present a model of the social system under consideration. The obtained results are shown in Sect. 4, and Sect. 5 contains conclusions and proposals for future works.

2   Research Domain Description

The present work concerns methods that stem from two research domains: social network analysis (SNA) and multi-agent systems.

Social network analysis describes social relationships between users in the form of a network and provides effective methods for analysis, e.g., finding important users. Such a network, however, is not homogeneous and we can distinguish some parts (called groups) that are denser than others [7,15,22]. Many methods of finding groups exist in the literature – one of the most popular is the CPM (Clique Percolation Method) [15], which allows the extraction of overlapping groups, i.e. groups that share nodes with other groups. As a significant research activity, we can observe the lifecycle of groups and make predictions about their future states [14,16]. Additionally, users can play different roles [9,21].

Nowadays, most often, networks are built by crawling different types of social media (e.g., Facebook [www.facebook.com], Myspace [http://myspace.com]), blogging (e.g., HuffingtonPost [www.huffingtonpost.com]), forums, media sharing systems (e.g., YouTube [http://www.youtube.com], Flickr [www.flickr.com]), microblogging (e.g., Twitter [https://twitter.com]), wikis, social news (e.g., Digg [http://digg.com], Slashdot [http://slashdot.org], social bookmarking (e.g., Delicious [http://delicious.com]), Opinion, Review, and Ratings Websites (e.g., Epinions [www.epinions.com]). Because of the method of crawling (e.g., starting from the most active users) and the dynamic nature of social media, it is impossible to obtain a complete data set with all users and all relationships between them. The important problem is how to identify the important nodes that are lacking at a given time. Identifying missing members in the social network structure is a relatively new problem and is called the *Missing Node Identification Problem* [4]. The main research directions are based on clustering algorithms and metrics built for the missing information in social networks [17]. In [17], new algorithms are presented that combine the network structure with specific information about nodes.

Another approach to the problem of social analysis is provided by the domain of agent-based simulations [2], where the following features of multi-agent systems are especially taken into consideration: modelling of a simulated reality, maintaining an organisation structure and simulation of the proactive behaviour. There are several examples of applying the multi-agent approach to building, analysing or using a social network (e.g., [12,20]). The problem of modelling a society to better understand it is one of the significant problems in the in the multi-agent systems domain [1,3,5,10,18].

Possibilities of combined use of multi-agent and social network analysis approaches are presented in [6]. The authors notice that the analysis of different social structures is a significant topic in the domain of multi-agent research and distinguish two other versions of combined use of these methods: multi-agent simulations of social network evolution or implementations of multi-agent services for these networks.

One of the goals of our research is to provide a suitable aggregation of the representation of the state of the multi–agent system, to obtain the best form of it from the point of view of the information that we are able to acquire [13].

3 Social Agent-Based System Model

The system that we developed consists of agents (nodes) representing given users and social relations, produced by interactions, between them. Agents belong to given groups considering the strengths of their relations with neighbouring agents, and have assigned global (at the level of the whole society) and local (in each group they belong to) roles. For agents and groups, sets of measures are calculated, which describe their features. The application of the developed model is to analyse influences of agents with assigned given kinds of roles on their neighbouring agents and the whole network.

Model of Interaction. The identification of some of the aforementioned interaction types is burdened by a varying level of uncertainty, whether the assignment is correct or not. In our work we focus on the interactions caused by commenting on posts by other users, or by commenting on previously written comments to posts [7]. These interactions have varying characteristics that make them useful when analysing the dynamics of groups, and for a significant portion of them, it is possible to correctly identify who is being addressed.

The representation of the individual interaction, assumed by us, is as follows:

$$i_l = (N_i, N_j, N_p, t_z, k) \tag{1}$$

where: N_i – agent–interaction initiator (writer of post or comment), N_j – agent–the addressee of the comment (sometimes not specified), N_p – agent–author of post to which the comment/interaction is written, t_z – given time slot, k – type, which may be post, a comment to a post, or a comment to a comment.

Agent-Nodes and Relations. The main elements, agents and social relations, of the model are represented by the following sets:

- set of agent nodes N, where we can distinguish a set of known nodes N^K and a set of unknown nodes N^U, and each node from the set of unknown nodes needs to be linked to at least one node from the set of known nodes;
- set of relations R, in which it is possible to distinguish a set of known relations R^K and a set of unknown relations R^U (elements of unknown relations may connect two known nodes, one known and one unknown node or two unknown nodes);

Groups. Given agent–nodes may belong to one or several groups. Additionally, it is possible to build groups by taking into consideration either only known nodes and relations or all nodes and relations. In the case of groups containing only known nodes and relations, the representation of groups will be proceeded by letter 'K'. We introduce following symbols associated with groups:

- a group j exists in a time slot t that may contain both known and unknown nodes and relations – G_j^t or that contain only known nodes and relations KG_j^t;
- set of (temporary) groups containing all nodes and relations SG, or containing only known ones SKG;
- set of all (temporary) groups in time slot t – taking into considerations all or only known nodes and relations: SG^t and SKG^t;
- set of nodes belonging to a given group j in time slot t, for groups taking into consideration all or only known nodes and relations NG_j^t and NKG_t^k;
- set of all relations belonging to a given group j in a time slot t, for groups including all or only known nodes and relations: RG_j^t and RKG_t^k

Roles. Given agent–nodes have assigned roles, depending on their importance in the social network. The roles may be global (calculated on the level of the social network) or local (associated with groups to which the node belongs). We introduce the following symbols related to roles:

- a set of values of roles assigned to nodes in a given slot, locally or globally $\mathcal{R}$, where r_k is a role and k represents a kind of role;
- a function assigning a global role to a given node in a time slot t, $\rho_g(t, N_i)$;
- a function assigning a role to a node in a given group G_j, in a time slot t $\rho_l(t, N_i, G_j)$

– a set of pairs describing roles played by a given node i in a time slot t in the whole network and all groups to which it belongs: $\mathcal{RS}(N_i) = (r_a^t, G_a^t)$, r_a^t – subsequent roles of the node, G_a^t – subsequent groups to which it belongs, a – groups to which a node i belongs or the whole network.

Detailed definitions of used roles (elements of the $\mathcal{R}$ set) are given in [9]. The roles are differentiated according to their activity (expressed by numbers of written posts and comments), influence (calculated as the strength of response of other agents to their posts or comments) and cooperativeness (which distinguishes whether the agent writes comments mostly in the context of their own posts or in the contexts of posts written by other agents as well).

Two kinds of influential agents are distinguished: Users – which are influential both thanks to writing influential posts and comments and Bloggers who write mostly influential posts and whose commenting activity is not very high. In this group of Users and Bloggers we can distinguish the roles of *Influential User Social* (*InfUserSoc*), *Influential Blogger Social* (*InfBlogSoc*), *Influential Blogger Selfish* (*InfBlogSel*) and *Influential User Selfish* (*InfUserSel*), taking into consideration their high (Social roles) or low (Selfish roles) cooperativeness [9].

Among the remaining agents, it is possible to distinguish those who are not authors of significant posts, but actively comment on the posts of others: *Influential Commentator* (*ComInf*), who write influential comments, and *Standard Commentator* (*ComNotInf*), who write sufficiently numerous but not necessarily influential comments, and, rarely, posts. Users who write very few posts and comments are classified as *Not Active users*. The rest of the users, who are neither distinguished by a particular activity nor have entirely halted their activity on the portal, are assigned the role of *Standard Blogger*. Assignment to different roles was performed based on the *PostInfluence* and *CommentInfluence* metrics defined in [9].

Measures. We consider the following sets of measures in the model:

– a vector of measures assigned to a given node $M^N(t, N_i)$, where $m_k^N(t, N_i)$; is the k-th element in the vector of measures,
– a vector of measures assigned to a given group $M^G(t, G_j)$, where $m_k^G(t, N_i)$ is the k-th element in the vector of measures;
– measures of similarity calculated for a node in a network with only known nodes and relations and in the network with both known and unknown nodes and relations $M^{NS}(t, N_i)$, where $m_k^{NS}(t, N_i)$ is the k-th element in the vector of measures;
– measures of similarity between groups in the network with only known nodes and relations, and in the network with both known and unknown nodes and relations, where G_j represents a group identified in the network with only known nodes and relations, and G_k represents a group identified in the network also containing unknown nodes and relations $M_{GS}(t, G_j, G_k)$.

We calculate the following kinds of measures:

- measures for nodes: Page rank, betweenness centrality, input degree, output degree [19];
- measures for groups: density, cohesion;
- measures of similarity for nodes: differences and/or quotients of selected measures of nodes;
- measures of similarity for groups: Jaccard measure [11], modified Jaccard measure [8], differences and/or quotients of selected measures of groups.

Model of Social Organisation. We are describing the state of the social organisation in a given time slot t. Two social organisations are considered: a complete one (Org^C), and one with incomplete information regarding nodes and relations among them Org^{IC}.

The complete social organisation in a time slot t is represented as follows:

$$Org^C(t) = (N(t), R(t), SG^t, \mathcal{R}, \rho_g, \rho_l)$$

while the incomplete organisation is represented as follows:

$$Org^{IC}(t) = (N^K(t), R^K(t), SKG^t, \mathcal{R}, \rho_g, \rho_l)$$

Having the complete and incomplete organisations defined, we can identify differences between them. The incomplete organisation is an organisation with some nodes and relations between them lacking, because of limitations of data acquisition process or use of different, not considered by us, communication channels.

4   Results

4.1   Description of Experimental Environment

The analysed data set contains data from the portal *Salon24*[1], which is focused mainly on politics and news. Dates of written blogs and comments included in this dataset are from 4.04.2010 to 31.03.2012. The dataset consists of 190,323 posts, 2,854,253 comments and 20,143 users. The whole dataset was divided into time slots, each lasting 7 days and neighboring slots overlap each other by 4 days which resulted in 182 time slots. In each slot we used the comments model [7]: – the users are nodes and the relations between them are constructed in the following way: from the user who wrote the comment to the user who was commented on, or if the user whose comment was commented on was not explicitly referenced in the comment (by using @ and the name of the author of the comment), the target of the relation is the author of the post.

The aim of the experiments was to explore the influence of generated disturbances in the network on roles assigned to users. The disturbances are caused by

---

[1] www.salon24.pl.

the removal of one or more representatives of selected roles, decreasing according to the value of measure that decides their importance. We considered transitions between values of roles played by users before and after the removal of users with given roles. We intended to find which kinds of roles had the most significant impact on the change of state of the network when removed, expressed by the change of roles of the remaining users and the cutting of the connection of some users with the rest of the social network.

Thanks to this procedure it is possible to estimate the average influence of a user with a given role on the rest of the network.

4.2   Change of Distribution of Roles Caused by Disturbances

Removing Different Numbers of Users with Influential Roles. The set of Fig. 1a–h shows the results of removing some top users with defined roles (users with removed roles are shown as chart series) on the distribution of roles in the dataset. In other words, we wanted to know whether, if we removed some top nodes with an important role (i.e., with the word *Influential* in its name) from each time slot, there would be any difference in the distribution of the remaining roles. The selection of top users was chosen based on the values of the *PostInfluence* metrics for all roles except for *Commentator Influential* (in that case the selection was performed using the *CommentInfluence* metrics). These results are presented for slots that contain at least 3 users from each important role (16 slots).

One observation is that in all figures regarding influential roles (Fig. 1a, e, f, g and h), the biggest difference is in the number of roles that are removed which is intuitive. We can see in Fig. 1a that for the number of users with the role *Commentator Influential* the biggest impact (except for the same role) comes from the roles *Influential User Social* and *Influential Blogger Social*. The roles of *Influential User Selfish* and *Influential Blogger Selfish* have almost no effect. A different situation takes place for the number of roles of *Commentator Not-Influential* after removing users with different roles (see Fig. 1b). In this case, the biggest impact comes from the role *Influential User*, with a little less impact from *Influential Blogger* role. In the case of the number of users with role *Standard Blogger* (see Fig. 1c) we also notice that *Influential User* and *Influential Blogger* exhibit the biggest influence. Another interesting observation for both mentioned cases is that for removed roles, (i.e., *Standard Bloggers* and *Commentator NotInfluential*) *selfish* variants have a bigger impact than *selfish* ones, which is different than in the case of *Commentator Influential*, described earlier. This result means that for influential roles with the *selfish* variant, most users are not influential, i.e., *Standard Bloggers* and *Commentators NotInfluential*, but they are for ones with the *social* variant – *Commentators Influential*. For users with the role *NotActive* (see Fig. 1d), the biggest difference is observed when we remove nodes with the role *Influential User Selfish*. Surprisingly, there is almost no effect for the *social* variant of this role or for both variants of *Influential Bloggers*. For *Influential Blogger Selfish*, *Influential Blogger Social* and *Influential User Selfish* (see Fig. 1e, f, g) other important roles show very little effect.

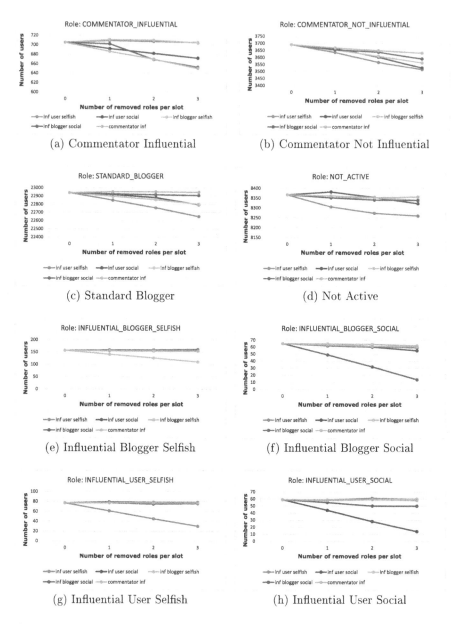

Fig. 1. Number of users with a role mentioned in chart's title after removing 0–3 top users per slot with roles marked in the chart's legend

In the case of *Influential User Social* (Fig. 1h) some effect is visible after removing *Influential Blogger Social*. For other roles, no differences appear.

Table 1. Matrices of changing user roles after removing one user with given role

source	ComInf	ComNotInf	StdBlog	NotActive	InfBlogSel	InfBlogSoc	InfUserSel	InfUserSoc	NotPresent
ComInf	0 /0	17/26	15/30	0/1	0/0	0/0	0/0	0/0	1/0
ComNotInf	16/7	0/0	140/123	3/0	0/0	0/0	0/0	0/0	4/0
StdBlog	8/4	0/0	0/0	208/166	0/0	0/0	0/0	0/0	124/64
NotActive	0/0	0/0	0/0	0/0	0/0	0/0	0/0	0/0	287/224
InfBlogSel	0/0	0/1	0/5	0/0	0/0	0/1	0/1	0/0	0/0
InfBlogSoc	0/0	0/3	0/1	0/0	1/1	0/0	1/0	1/2	0/0
InfUserSel	0/0	0/0	0/0	0/0	0/1	0/0	0/0	0/0	54/0
InfUserSoc	0/0	0/0	0/0	0/0	0/0	0/2	1/1	0/0	0/54

(b) Influential Blogger Selfish / Influential Blogger Social

source	ComInf	ComNotInf	StdBlog	NotActive	InfBlogSel	InfBlogSoc	InfUserSel	InfUserSoc	NotPresent
ComInf	0/0	5/24	10/26	1/0	0/0	0/0	0/0	0/0	1/1
ComNotInf	8/7	0/0	94/122	0/0	0/0	0/0	0/0	0/0	0/0
StdBlog	8/8	0/0	0/0	168/159	0/0	0/0	0/0	0/0	70/61
NotActive	0/0	0/0	0/0	0/0	0/0	0/0	0/0	0/0	201/189
InfBlogSel	0/0	0/2	0/3	0/0	0/0	0/0	0/0	0/0	54/0
InfBlogSoc	0/0	0/0	0/1	0/0	0/1	0/0	0/0	1/0	0/54
InfUserSel	0/0	0/0	0/0	0/0	0/0	0/0	0/0	0/0	0/0
InfUserSoc	0/1	0/0	0/0	0/0	0/1	1/0	2/3	0/0	0/0

(c) Commentator Influential

source	ComInf	ComNotInf	StdBlog	NotActive	InfBlogSel	InfBlogSoc	InfUserSel	InfUserSoc	NotPresent
ComInf	0	18	14	1	0	0	0	0	54
ComNotInf	6	0	50	0	0	0	0	0	0
StdBlog	2	0	0	38	0	0	0	0	18
NotActive	0	0	0	0	0	0	0	0	47
InfBlogSel	0	1	2	0	0	0	0	0	0
InfBlogSoc	0	0	6	0	1	0	0	0	0
InfUserSel	0	0	0	0	0	0	0	0	0
InfUserSoc	1	0	0	0	0	0	0	0	0

Table 2. User memberships to groups in all slots

Group membership	Number of users in all slots
1	22211
2	3038
3	497
4	69
5	10
6	2

Transition of Users' Roles After Removing Influential Roles. To more carefully assess the changes of roles after removing influential roles, we calculated appropriate matrices of roles transitions (Table 1a, b and c). The following results are presented for those slots that each contain at least two of each influential role (54 slots). In these experiments, we remove one influential role from each time slot. We can see (Table 1a and b) that for *selfish* variants of *Influential User* and *Influential Blogger* a smaller number of *Commentator Influential* changes their roles (they change their roles into *Commentator NotInfluential* and *Standard Blogger*, respectively) than their *social* variants. Furthermore, for *selfish* variants of influential roles we can also notice that more *Standard Bloggers* move from their original role into *NotActive* (they wrote only a single comment and still exist in the network) and *Not Present* (they are removed completely from the network) than for their *social* variants. For *Commentator NotInfluential*, more users change their role for *Influential User Selfish* than *Influential User Social*, and more for *Influential Blogger Social* than *Influential Blogger Selfish* (*Commentators NotInfluential* mostly move into *Standard Bloggers*). Moreover, more *NotActive* users are removed from the network when we remove *Influential Users* than *Influential Bloggers*.

Table 1c describes transitions in the case when we remove *Commentator Influential*. We can notice that the transitions are similar to those described above for *Influential Bloggers* and *Influential Users*, only their scale is smaller.

4.3 Change of Groups and User Memberships Caused by Disturbances

We also wanted also to investigate the impact of removing users with influential roles on groups and user memberships. The initial (before roles' removal) memberships of users (we take into account only users belonging to groups) are shown in Table 2 (sum of memberships from all time slots). It can be seen that there are only a few users with high membership values. The results described in this section are presented for the same time slots as in the previous experiment, i.e., on 54 time slots.

Figure 2 demonstrates the change in the total number of user memberships after removing a single node with an influential role. The total number of user memberships is calculated by multiplying a user membership with a number of users with this membership. The largest difference is observed for *Influential Users* (both *social* and *selfish* exhibit similar behaviour) and for *Influential*

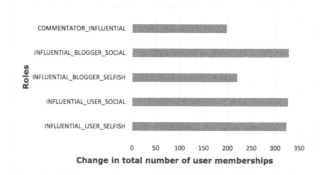

Fig. 2. Change between initial total number of user memberships and after removing a single user with a given role

Blogger Social. A significantly smaller change takes place for *Influential Bloggers Selfish* and *Commentators Influential.*

5   Conclusion

In this paper the agent–based model of a social media system was introduced. The model defines significant elements useful for conducting a wide scope of analyses, and helps to address the problem analysed in this work.

The performed experiments provide valuable information regarding the significance of users playing given roles, and the strengths of their influence on their neighbourhood. We assessed the impact of the removal of users with influential roles on the changes in the network. We focused in this study on the changes in the distribution of roles, the transitions between roles and the changes of users' memberships to groups. The results show that we can observe a significantly higher impact of agents with the most influential roles (*Influential User* and *Influential Blogger*) on other roles. Differences in behaviour between *social* and *selfish* variants of roles are also noticeable, especially for a higher number of removed roles. *Selfish* variants tend to have more influence on weaker roles such as *Commentators NotInfluential* and *Standard Bloggers*, but *social* ones tend to influence the more important roles of *Commentator Influential.* Furthermore, different characteristics of influential roles on groups can be observed: – *Influential Users* and *Influential Blogger Social* have more impact on the changes of users' memberships to groups after their removal.

In the future we are planning to more carefully assess the characteristics of groups after removing important roles from the network. Future work will also cover a detailed study of the impact of agents with local roles (roles defined on the level of a single group) and their removal on the structure of groups. The final goal we would like to achieve is the prediction of missing information in the network so we want to investigate the impact of removing roles on the network and, whether we can then infer from the network that some roles are missing.

References

1. Costa, A., Demazeau, Y.: Towards a formal model of multi-agent systems with dynamic organizations. In: Proceedings of the International Conference on Multi-Agent Systems, Kyoto, Japan. MIT Press publisher, Cambridge (1996)
2. Davidsson, P.: Multi agent based simulation: beyond social simulation. In: Moss, S., Davidsson, P. (eds.) MABS 2000. LNCS (LNAI), vol. 1979, pp. 97–107. Springer, Heidelberg (2001)
3. Demazeau, Y., Costa, A.R.: Populations and organizations in open multi-agent systems. In: 1st National Symposium on Parallel and Distributed AI (PDAI 1996) (1996)
4. Eyal, R., Rosenfeld, A., Sina, S., Kraus, S.: Predicting and identifying missing node information in social networks. ACM Trans. Knowl. Discov. Data **8**(3), 14:1–14:35 (2013)

5. Fox, M.: An organizational view of distributed systems. IEEE Trans. Syst. Man Cybern. **11**(1), 70–80 (1981)
6. Franchi, E., Poggi, A.: Multi-agent systems and social networks. In: Business Social Networking: Organizational, Managerial, and Technological Dimensions. IGI Global (2011)
7. Gliwa, B., Koźlak, J., Zygmunt, A., Cetnarowicz, K.: Models of social groups in blogosphere based on information about comment addressees and sentiments. In: Aberer, K., Flache, A., Jager, W., Liu, L., Tang, J., Guéret, C. (eds.) SocInfo 2012. LNCS, vol. 7710, pp. 475–488. Springer, Heidelberg (2012)
8. Gliwa, B., Saganowski, S., Zygmunt, A., Bródka, P., Kazienko, P., Koźlak, J.: Identification of group changes in blogosphere. In: IEEE/ACM International Conference on Advances in Social Networks Analysis and Mining, ASONAM 2012, Istanbul, Turkey, 26–29 August 2012. IEEE Computer Society (2012)
9. Gliwa, B., Zygmunt, A., Koźlak, J.: Analysis of roles and groups in blogosphere. In: Burduk, R., Jackowski, K., Kurzynski, M., Wozniak, M., Zolnierek, A. (eds.) CORES 2013. AISC, vol. 226, pp. 303–312. Springer, Heidelberg (2013)
10. Horling, B., Lesser, V.: A survey of multi-agent organizational paradigms. Knowl. Eng. Rev. **19**(4), 281–316 (2004)
11. Jaccard, P.: The distribution of the flora in the alpine zone.1. New Phytol. **11**(2), 37–50 (1912)
12. Lacomme, L., Camps, V., Demazeau, Y., Hautefeuille, F., Jouve, B.: Middle age social networks: a dynamic organizational study. In: Demazeau, Y., Pěchouček, M., Corchado, J., Pěrez, J. (eds.) Advances on Practical Applications of Agents and Multiagent Systems. Advances in Intelligent and Soft Computing, pp. 211–216. Springer, Heidelberg (2011)
13. Lamarche-Perrin, R., Demazeau, Y., Vincent, J.-M.: How to build the best macroscopic description of your multi-agent system? In: Demazeau, Y., Ishida, T., Corchado, J.M., Bajo, J. (eds.) PAAMS 2013. LNCS, vol. 7879, pp. 157–169. Springer, Heidelberg (2013)
14. Leskovec, J., Huttenlocher, D., Kleinberg, J.: Predicting positive and negative links in online social networks. In: Proceedings of the 19th International Conference on World Wide Web, WWW 2010, pp. 641–650. ACM, New York (2010)
15. Palla, G., Derényi, I., Farkas, I., Vicsek, T.: Uncovering the overlapping community structure of complex networks in nature and society. Nature **435**(7043), 814–818 (2005)
16. Saganowski, S., Gliwa, B., Bródka, P., Zygmunt, A., Kazienko, P., Koźlak, J.: Predicting community evolution in social networks. Entropy **17**(5), 3053–3096 (2015)
17. Sina, S., Rosenfeld, A., Kraus, S.: Sami: an algorithm for solving the missing node problem using structure and attribute information. Soc. Netw. Analys. Min. **5**(1), 54:1–54:20 (2015)
18. Tambe, M.: Towards flexible teamwork. J. Artif. Int. Res. **7**(1), 83–124 (1997)
19. Wasserman, S., Faust, K.: Social Network Analysis: Methods and Applications, vol. 8. Cambridge University Press, Cambridge (1994)
20. Weerdt, M.M., Zhang, Y., Klos, T.: Multiagent task allocation in social networks. Auton. Agent. Multi-Agent Syst. **25**(1), 46–86 (2011)
21. Zygmunt, A.: Role identification of social networkers. In: Alhajj, R., Rokne, J. (eds.) Encyclopedia of Social Network Analysis and Mining, pp. 1598–1606. Springer, New York (2014)
22. Zygmunt, A., Bródka, P., Kazienko, P., Koźlak, J.: Key person analysis in social communities within the blogosphere. J. UCS **18**(4), 577–597 (2012)

A Multiagent-Based Technique for Dialog Management in Conversational Interfaces

David Griol[(✉)] and José Manuel Molina

Computer Science Department, Carlos III University of Madrid,
Avda. de la Universidad, 30, 28911 Leganés, Spain
{david.griol,josemanuel.molina}@uc3m.es

Abstract. With the advances in Language Technologies and Natural Language Processing, conversational interfaces have begun to play an increasingly important role in the design of human-machine interaction systems in a number of devices and intelligent environments. One of the most demanding tasks when developing a dialog system consists of selecting the next system response considering the user's actions and the dialog history, which is the fundamental task related to dialog management. In this paper we present an multiagent-based technique for the development of dialog managers. In our proposal, a multiagent system with specialized dialog agents is designed to deal with each specific subtask of dialog objective for which the dialog system has been designed. The practical application of the proposed technique to develop a dialog system acting as a customer support service shows that the use of these specialized dialog agents increases the quality and number of successful interactions with the system in comparison with developing a single agent to manage the dialog for the complete domain.

Keywords: Human-agent interaction · Dialog systems · Agent-based dialog management · Spoken interaction · Statistical methodologies

1 Introduction

Natural human-computer interaction is a complex problem that requires work on multiple levels, such as speech and feedback recognition, natural language processing, dialog management or speech generation. Dialog systems are computer programs that address these processes to engage the user in a dialog that aims to be similar to that between humans [9,13,14].

Recent advances in conversational interfaces has been propelled by the convergence of three enabling technologies. First, the Web emerged as a universal communications channel. Web-based dialog systems are scalable enterprise systems that leverage the Internet to simultaneously deliver dialog services to large populations of users. Second, the development of mobile technologies and intelligent devices, such as smartphones and tablets, have made it possible to deploy a large number of sensors and to integrate them into dialog systems that provide multimodal interaction capabilities (i.e., use of different modalities for the input

© Springer International Publishing Switzerland 2016
Y. Demazeau et al. (Eds.): PAAMS 2016, LNAI 9662, pp. 121–132, 2016.
DOI: 10.1007/978-3-319-39324-7_11

and/or output of the system) and allow their access in almost every place and at any time. Third, computational linguistics, the field of artificial intelligence that focuses on natural language software, has significantly increased speech recognition, natural language understanding and speech synthesis capabilities [14].

These advances have extended the initial application domains of dialog systems to complex information retrieval and question answering applications [10], surveys applications [17], e-commerce systems [19], recommendations systems [15], e-learning and tutoring systems [8], in-car systems [5], spoken dialog within vehicles [12], remote control of devices and robots in smart environments [11], Ambient Assisted Living systems [2], or virtual companions [6].

The dialog management process of a dialog system relies on the fundamental task of deciding the next action of the system, interpreting the incoming semantic representation of the user input in the context of the dialog. In addition, it resolves ellipsis and anaphora, evaluates the relevance and completeness of user requests, identifies and recovers from recognition and understanding errors, retrieves information from data repositories, and decides about the next system's response.

The design of the dialog manager has been traditionally carried out by handcrafting dialog strategies tightly coupled to the application domain in order to optimize the behavior of the dialog system in that context. This has motivated the research community to find ways to develop dialog management strategies that have a more robust behavior, better portability, generalizable and are easier to adapt to different user profiles or tasks [4].

In the agent-based paradigm for dialog management, dialog is viewed as interaction between two agents, each of which is capable of reasoning about its own actions and beliefs. Agent-based dialog management is suitable for the design of more natural dialog systems in which the system and the user can share the initiative of the dialog [7]. Thus, the dialog manager takes the preceding context into account and the dialog evolves dynamically as a sequence of related steps that build on top of each other. Automating the learning of agent-based dialog managers by using statistical models trained with real conversations also allows us to model the variability in user behaviors and explore a wider range of strategies and dialog movements, also reducing the time and effort required to develop the dialog manager [3,4].

In this paper we present a novel agent-based methodology for dialog management, in which a multiagent system with specialized agents is employed to deal with each one of the dialog domains and/or dialog subtasks that form the complete set of functionalities provided by the dialog system. The statistical dialog model learned for each specialized agent is based on a classification process that provides the probabilities of selecting each one of the system actions (i.e., system responses) for the current state of the dialog. To do this, the training data is divided into different subsets, each covering a specific dialog objective or subtask. Each specific dialog agent is trained using the corresponding training subset and it is selected during the dialog once the specific dialog subtask has been detected.

We have applied the proposed methodology to develop two versions of a practical dialog system acting as a customer support service to help solve simple and routine software/hardware repairing problems, both at the domestic and professional levels. The first dialog system uses a single agent to complete the dialog management task and the second one integrates a multiagent system with specialized agents for each dialog objective. An in-depth comparative assessment of the developed dialog systems has been completed with recruited users. The results of the evaluation show that the use of the multiagent system allows a better selection of the next system responses, thus increasing the number and quality of successful interactions with the dialog system.

The rest of the paper is organized as follows. Section 2 describes our proposal to develop a multiagent system for dialog management in dialog systems. Section 3 shows the practical implementation of our proposal to develop the two systems for the customer support service. In Sect. 4 we discuss the evaluation results obtained by comparing the two developed systems. Finally, in Sect. 5 we present the conclusions and outline guidelines for future work.

2 Our Proposal for Multiagent Dialog Management

Figure 1 shows the complete architecture of a dialog system integrating our proposal for the use of a multiagent system with specialized agents to manage the dialog. As can be observed, the architecture consists of a set components, linked together by communication channels, that can be classified into System Components, Input and Output Components, and Natural Language Processing and Dialog Components.

The system components of the architecture are based on the proposal described in [16] for the use of AgentSlang components. The *Debug/Log* component allows the logging mechanism to be entirely distributed and independent. The logger manages the reception of debug messages in a centralized way. The *System Monitor* receives status messages from all subscribing components. These status messages are re-broadcasted to its subscribers, providing the source feedback.

User inputs are processed in the proposed architecture by the *Text Inputs* and the *Automatic Speech Recognition* Components. The *Text Inputs* Component allows to collect text inputs provided by means of the keyboard and tactile screen of portable devices. Moreover, it can subscribe to any channel and displays the received message as plain text.

The goal of speech recognition is to obtain the sequence of words uttered by a speaker. It is a very complex task, as there can be a great deal of variation in the input the recognizer must analyze, for example, in terms of the linguistics of the utterance, inter and intra speaker variation, the interaction context and the transmission channel [20]. Once the dialog system has recognized what the user uttered, it is necessary to understand what they said. Natural language processing generally involves morphological, lexical, syntactical, semantic, and pragmatical knowledge [21].

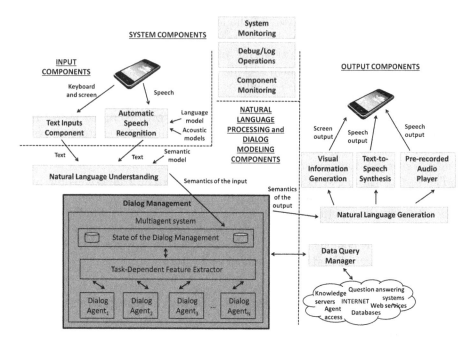

Fig. 1. Scheme of the complete architecture of a dialog system with the integration of the proposed multiagent dialog management technique

2.1   Multiagent System for Dialog Management

As described in the introduction section, to develop the *Dialog Manager*, we propose the use of a multiagent system with specialized agents dealing with each one of the subdomains or subtasks for which the dialog system has been designed. Each one of these specialized agents integrates a statistical dialog model to deal with the corresponding subtask or dialog objective.

Our proposed technique for statistical dialog modeling represents dialogs as a sequence of pairs (A_i, U_i), where A_i is the output of the system (the system response or turn) at time i, and U_i is the semantic representation of the user turn (the result of the understanding process of the user input) at time i; both expressed in terms of dialog acts [4]. This way, each dialog is represented by:

$$(A_1, U_1), \cdots, (A_i, U_i), \cdots, (A_n, U_n)$$

where A_1 is the greeting turn of the system (e.g. Welcome to the system. How can I help you?), and U_n is the last user turn (i.e., semantic representation of the last user utterance provided by the natural language understanding component in terms of dialog acts).

The lexical, syntactic and semantic information associated with the speaker u's ith turn (U_i) is denoted as c_i^u. This information is usually represented by:

- the words uttered;
- part of speech tags, also called word classes or lexical categories. Common linguistic categories include noun, adjective, and verb, among others;
- predicate-argument structures, used by SLU modules in various contexts to represent relations within a sentence structure.
- named entities: sequences of words that refer to a unique identifier. This identifier may be a proper name (e.g., organization, person or location names), a time identifier (e.g., dates, time expressions or durations), or quantities and numerical expressions (e.g., monetary values, phone numbers).

Our model is based on the one proposed in [1]. In this model, each system response is defined in terms of the subtask to which it contributes and the system dialog act to be performed.

The term A_i^a denotes the system dialog act (i.e., system action) in the ith turn, and ST_i^a denotes the subtask label to which the ith turn contributes. The interpretation process is modeled in two stages. In the first stage, the system dialog act is determined from the information about the user's turn and the previous dialog context, which is modeled by means of the k previous utterances. This process is shown in Eq. (1).

$$A_i^a = \operatorname*{argmax}_{A^a \in \mathcal{A}} P(A^a | ST_i^a, ST_{i-1}^{i-k}, A_{i-1}^{i-k}, c_{i-1}^{i-k}) \qquad (1)$$

where c_i^u represents the lexical, syntactic, and semantic information (e.g., words, part of speech tags, predicate-argument structures, and named entities) associated with speaker u's ith turn; ST_{i-1}^{i-k} represents the dialog subtask tags for utterances $i - 1$ to $i - k$; and A_{i-1}^{i-k} represents the system dialog act tags for utterances $i - 1$ to $i - k$.

In a second stage, the dialog subtask is determined from the lexical information, the dialog act computed according to Eq. (1), and the dialog context, as shown in Eq. (2).

$$ST_i^a = \operatorname*{argmax}_{s^a \in \mathcal{S}} P(s^a | ST_{i-1}^{i-k}, A_{i-1}^{i-k}, c_{i-1}^{i-k}) \qquad (2)$$

The prediction of the dialog subtask (ST_i^a) by means of Eq. (2) is carried out by a specific component in the architecture, which we have called the *Task-Dependent Feature Extractor*. This module is connected with the State of the Dialog Management component, which updates the current state of the dialog according to the semantic information provided by the *Natural Language Understanding* module after each user utterance. This information is provided to the Task-Dependent Feature Extractor for the prediction of the dialog subtask. According to this prediction, the *Task-Dependent Feature Extractor* selects the specialized dialog agent that will be used by the dialog manager in the following turn of the dialog. Then, the selected specialized agent employs the corresponding statistical dialog model to select the next action of the dialog system.

In our proposal, we consider static and dynamic features to estimate the conditional distributions shown in Eqs. (1) and (2). Dynamic features include the dialog act and the task/subtask. Static features include the words in each utterance, the dialog acts in each utterance, and predicate-arguments in each utterance. All pieces of information are computed from corpora using n-grams, that is, computing the frequency of the combination of the n previous words, dialog acts, or predicate-arguments in the user turn.

The conditional distributions shown in Eqs. (1) and (2) can be estimated by means of the general technique of choosing the maximum entropy (MaxEnt) distribution that properly estimates the average of each feature in the training data [1]. This can be written as a Gibbs distribution parameterized with weights λ as Eq. (3) shows, where V is the size of the label set, X denotes the distribution of dialog acts or subtasks (DA_i^u or ST_i^u) and ϕ denotes the vector of the described static and dynamic features used for the user turns from $i - 1 \cdots i - k$.

$$P(X = st_i|\phi) = \frac{e^{\lambda_{st_i} \cdot \phi}}{\sum_{st=1}^{V} e^{\lambda_{st_i} \cdot \phi}} \tag{3}$$

Such calculation outperforms other state of the art approaches [1], as it increases the speed of training and makes possible to deal with large data sets. Each of the classes can be encoded as a bit vector such that, in the vector corresponding to each class, the ith bit is one and all other bits are zero. Then, V-one-versus-other binary classifiers are used as Eq. (4) shows.

$$P(y|\phi) = 1 - P(\overline{y}|\phi) = \frac{e^{\lambda_y \cdot \phi}}{e^{\lambda_y \cdot \phi} + e^{\lambda_{\overline{y}} \cdot \phi}} = \frac{1}{1 + e^{-\lambda_{\overline{y}}' \cdot \phi}} \tag{4}$$

where $\lambda_{\overline{y}}$ is the parameter vector for the anti-label $\overline{y}$ and $\lambda_{\overline{y}}' = \lambda_y - \lambda_{\overline{y}}$.

3   Practical Application

We have applied our proposal to the problem solving domain of the *Facilisimo* dialog system, which acts as a customer support service to help solving simple and routine software/hardware repairing problems, both at the domestic and professional levels.

The definition of the system's functionalities and dialog strategy was carried out by means of the analysis of 250 human-human conversations (7215 user turns) provided by real assistants attending the calls of users with a software/hardware problem at the City Council of Leganés (Madrid, Spain). The labeling defined for this corpus contains different types of information, that have been annotated using a multilevel approach similar to the one proposed in the Luna Project [18]. The first levels include segmentation of the corpus in dialog turns, transcription of the speech signal, and syntactic preprocessing with POS-tagging (i.e., word-category disambiguation) and shallow parsing (i.e., identification of the different constituents in a sentence). The next level consists of the annotation of main information using attribute-value pairs. The other levels of the annotation show contextual aspects of the semantic interpretation.

The attribute-value annotation uses a predefined domain ontology to specify concepts and their relations. The attributes defined for the task include *Concept*,

Computer-Hardware, Action, Person-Name, Location, Code, TelephoneNumber, Problem, etc.

Dialog act (DA) annotation was performed manually by one annotator on speech transcriptions previously segmented into turns. The DAs defined to label the corpus are the following: (i) Core DAs: *Action-request, Yes-answer, No-answer, Answer, Offer, ReportOnAction, Inform*; (ii) Conventional DAs: *Greet, Quit, Apology, Thank*; (iii) Feedback-Turn management DAs: *ClarificationRequest, Ack, Filler*; (iv) Non interpretable DAs: *Other*.

The original FrameNet[1] description of frames and frame elements was adopted for the predicate-argument structure annotation, introducing new frames and roles related to hardware/software only in case of gaps in the FrameNet ontology. Some of the frames included in this representation are *Telling, Greeting, Contacting, Statement, Recording, Communication, Being operational, Change operational state*, etc.

The basic structure of the dialogs is usually composed by the sequence of the following tasks: *Opening, Problem-statement, User-identification, Problem-clarification, Problem-resolution*, and *Closing*. This set of tasks contains a list of subtasks, such as *Problem-description, Problem-Request, Problem-Confirmation, Brand-Identification, Model-Identification, Help-Request, Message-Confirmation, Name-Identification, Resolution-Confirmation*, etc. The shared plan is represented as a data register that encapsulates the task structure, dialog act structure, attribute-values and predicate-argument structure of utterances. Figure 2 shows the transcription of a dialog included in the training corpus.

During the *Problem-statement* task, the caller explains the problem the reasons why he/she calls the help-desk. In the *User-identification* task, the operator asks for additional information regarding the identity of the caller. Once the caller has described the problem, the operator can ask for additional information to clarify it during the *Problem-clarification* task.

During the *Problem-resolution* task, the operator asks the user to perform specific tests. We have defined nine different subtasks inside this generic segment, given that our goal is to detect not only that the dialog is in this segment, but also what are the specific problem that has to be resolved: *Printer* (P4), *Network connection* (P5), *PC going slow* (P6), *Monitor* (P7), *Keyboard* (P8), *Mouse* (P9), *CD-DVD player* (P10), *Power supply* (P11), and *Virus* (P12). The operator assigns a ticket number for the current call if the problem has not been solved after this task. The user must take note of this number and inform about this to the operator. The dialog ends at the *Closing* phase, in which the operator also tries to give a useful advice related to the described problem.

The complete set of human-human dialogs were manually labeled including this task/subtask information. This information was incorporated for each user and system turn in the dialogs. Two versions of the dialog system have been developed. The first one (*Generic Agent*) uses a generic dialog agent for the task, which employs a dialog model learned with the complete training corpus to select the next system response. The second one (*Multiagent System*) employs

---

[1] https://framenet.icsi.berkeley.edu/fndrupal/.

A_1: Welcome to the Facilisimo system. How may I help you?
U_1: Hello, my printer does not print correctly.
A_2: Tell me your name and surname.
U_2: My name is Ricardo Santamaria.
A_3: Can you tell me your phone extension?
U_3: Nine four sixty-three.
A_4: Can you tell me the brand and model?
U_4: HP Officejet Pro 8610.
A_5: Is the printer on now?
U_5: It is on.
A_6: Can you tell me the message on the printer display?
U_6: Paper jam is written.
A_7: Can you see the active printer from the control panel of your PC?
U_7: It is active.
A_8: Please try the following steps. Say next after each step. Turn the printer off, and then on.
U_8: Next.
A_9: Print a Printer Status Report.
U_9: Next.
A_{10}: Has this process solved your problem?
U_{10}: No.
A_{11}: Remove any loose paper from the main and optional trays.
U_{11}: Next.
A_{12}: Clear any jammed paper from the rear of the printer.
U_{12}: Next.
A_{13}: Has this process solved your problem?
U_{13}: Yes.
A_{14}: Anything else?
U_{14}: No, thank you.
A_{15}: Most of these steps will also work for troubleshooting an office copier. Have a nice day!

Fig. 2. Example of a dialog acquired with recruited users and the *Facilisimo* dialog system (translation from Spanish to English)

a multiagent system with 27 specialized dialog agents developed according our proposal for dialog management. Each one of the specialized dialog agents deals with a specific subtask of the dialog (from the opening task, the problem statement, user identification, practical resolution of each specific problem, out of the task conversations, and closing of the dialog).

4   Experiments and Results

We have completed a comparative evaluation of the two practical dialog systems developed for the task using a set of 25 scenarios covering the different problems that users can formulate to the system. A total of 150 dialogs were recorded from interactions of six recruited users for our department employing the two dialog systems. These users selected the specific scenarios in a random order and using a random assignment of both systems. An objective and subjective evaluation were carried out.

The following measures were defined in the objective evaluation to compare the dialogs acquired with the dialog systems: (i) Dialog success rate; (ii) Dialog length: average number of turns per dialog, number of turns of the shortest dialog, number of turns of the longest dialog, and number of turns of the most observed dialog; (iii) Different dialogs: percentage of different dialogs with respect to the total number of dialogs, and number of repetitions of the most observed dialog; (iv) Turn length: average number of actions per turn; (v) Participant activity: number of turns in the most observed, shortest and longest dialogs; (vi) Confirmation rate, computed as the ratio between the number of explicit confirmation turns and the total number of turns in the dialog; and (vii) Error correction rate, computed as the number of errors detected and corrected by the dialog manager divided by the total number of errors.

Table 1 presents the results of the objective evaluation. As can be observed, both dialog systems could interact correctly with the users in most cases for the two systems. However, the *Multiagent System* obtained a higher success rate, improving the initial results by a 6 % absolute. Using the *Multiagent System*, the average number of required turns is also reduced from 29.1 to 24.3.

Table 1. Results of the high-level dialog measures for the *Generic Agent* and the *Multiagent* system

	Generic agent	Multiagent system
Dialog success rate	89.0 %	95.0 %
Average number of turns per dialog	29.1	24.3
Percentage of different dialogs	84.6 %	88.7 %
Repetitions of the most observed dialog	4	3
Average number of actions per turn	1.2	1.5
Number of user turns of the most observed dialog	12	10
Number of user turns of the shortest dialog	9	6
Number of user turns of the longest dialog	15	11
Confirmation rate	38 %	36 %
Error correction rate	0.89 %	0.94 %

It can also be observed that when *Multiagent System* was used, there was a reduction in the average number of turns and in the number of turns in the longest, shortest and most observed dialogs. These results show that the use of specialized dialog agents made it possible to reduce the number of necessary system actions to attain the dialog goals for the different tasks. In addition, the results show a higher variability in the dialogs generated with *Multiagent System* as there was a higher percentage of different dialogs and the most observed dialog was less repeated. There was also a slight increment in the mean values of the turn length for the dialogs collected with *Multiagent System* due to the better selection of the system actions in the improved strategy.

The confirmation and error correction rates were also improved by using *Multiagent System* as it required less data from the user, thus reducing the number of errors in the automatic speech recognition process. A problem occurred when the user input was misrecognized but it had high confidence score, in which case it was forwarded to the dialog manager. However, as the success rate shows, this problem did not have a remarkable impact on the performance of the dialog systems.

Table 2. Proportions of dialog spent on-goal directed actions, ground actions and other possible actions

	Generic agent	Multiagent system
Goal-directed actions	68.21 %	74.35 %
Grounding actions	30.76 %	24.76 %
Rest of actions	1.03 %	0.89 %

Table 3. Results of the subjective evaluation with recruited users (1 = lowest, 5 = highest)

	Generic agent	Multiagent system
Q1	4.7	4.8
Q2	4.3	4.4
Q3	4.2	4.7
Q4	4.2	4.6
Q5	4.1	4.3
Q6	4.4	4.7

Additionally, we grouped all user and system actions into three categories: "goal directed" (actions to provide or request information), "grounding" (confirmations and negations), and "other". Table 2 shows a comparison between these categories. As can be observed, the dialogs provided by the *Multiagent System* have a better quality, as the proportion of goal-directed actions is higher than the values obtained for the *Generic Agent*.

We also asked the users to complete a questionnaire to assess their subjective opinion about the system performance. The questionnaire had six questions: (i) Q1: *How well did the system understand you?*; (ii) Q2: *How well did you understand the system messages?*; (iii) Q3: *Was it easy for you to get the requested information?*; (iv) Q4: *Was the interaction with the system quick enough?*; (v) Q5: *If there were system errors, was it easy for you to correct them?*; (vi) Q6: *In general, are you satisfied with the performance of the system?* The possible answers for each one of the questions were the same: *Never/Not at all, Seldom/In some measure, Sometimes/Acceptably, Usually/Well*, and *Always/Very Well*. All the answers were assigned a numeric value between one and five (in the same order as they appear in the questionnaire).

Table 3 shows the average results of the subjective evaluation using the described questionnaire. It can be observed that using either *Generic Agent* or *Multiagent System* the users perceived that the system understood them correctly. Moreover, they expressed a similar opinion regarding the easiness for correcting system errors. However, users said that it was easier to obtain the information specified for the different objectives using *Multiagent System*, and that the interaction with the system was more adequate with this dialog manager. Finally, the users were more satisfied with the system employing *Multiagent System*.

5 Conclusions and Future Work

In this paper, we have described a multiagent-based technique for dialog management in dialog systems. Our proposal is based on dealing with each one of the dialog subtasks or dialog objectives by means of specific dialog agents specialized in each one of them. A statistical dialog model has been defined for the practical implementation of these agents. This model, which considers the previous history of the dialog, is used for the selection of each specialized dialog agent according to the predicted dialog subtask, and the decision of the next system action. Although the construction and parameterization of the dialog model depends on expert knowledge of the task, by means of our proposal, we facilitate to develop dialog systems that have a more robust behavior, better portability, and are easier to be extended or adapted to different user profiles or tasks.

The results of the evaluation of our proposal for a dialog system acting as a help-desk system show that the number of successful dialogs is increased in comparison with using a generic dialog agent learned for the complete task. Also, the dialogs acquired using the specific dialog agents are statistically shorter and present a better quality in the selection of the system responses. For future work, we want to consider the incorporation of additional information regarding the user, such as specific user profiles adapted to the each application domain.

Acknowledgements. This work was supported in part by Projects MINECO TEC2012-37832-C02-01, CICYT TEC2011-28626-C02-02, CAM CONTEXTS (S2009/TIC-1485).

References

1. Bangalore, S., DiFabbrizio, G., Stent, A.: Learning the structure of task-driven human-human dialogs. IEEE Trans. Audio Speech Lang. Process. **16**(7), 1249–1259 (2008)
2. Bickmore, T., Puskar, K., Schlenk, E., Pfeifer, L., Sereika, S.: Maintaining reality: relational agents for antipsychotic medication adherence. Interact. Comput. **22**, 276–88 (2010)
3. Ferreira, E., Lefevre, F.: Reinforcement-learning based dialogue system for human-robot interactions with socially-inspired rewards. Comput. Speech Lang. **34**(1), 256–74 (2015)
4. Griol, D., Callejas, Z., López-Cózar, R., Riccardi, G.: A domain-independent statistical methodology for dialog management in spoken dialog systems. Comput. Speech Lang. **28**(3), 743–68 (2014)
5. Hofmann, H., Silberstein, A., Ehrlich, U., Berton, A., Muller, C., Mahr, A.: Development of speech-based in-car HMI concepts for information exchange internet apps. In: Mariani, J., Rosset, S., Garnier-Rizet, M., Devillers, L. (eds.) Natural Interaction with Robots, Knowbots and Smartphones: Putting Spoken Dialog Systems into Practice, pp. 15–28. Springer, New York (2014)
6. Horchak, O., Giger, J.C., Cabral, M., Pochwatko, G.: From demonstration to theory in embodied language comprehension: a review. Cogn. Syst. Res. **29–30**, 66–85 (2014)

7. Knott, A., Vlugter, P.: Multi-agent human-machine dialogue: issues in dialogue management and referring expression semantics. Artif. Intell. **172**(2–3), 69–102 (2008)
8. Kopp, K., Britt, M., Millis, K., Graesser, A.: Improving the efficiency of dialogue in tutoring. Learn. Instr. **22**(5), 320–0 (2012)
9. Lee, G., Kim, H.K., Jeong, M., Kim, J.: Natural Language Dialog Systems and Intelligent Assistants. Springer, Switzerland (2015)
10. Metze, F., Anguera, X., Barnard, E., Davel, M., Gravier, G.: Language independent search in mediaeval's spoken web search task. Comput. Speech Lang. **28**(5), 1066–1082 (2014)
11. Minker, W., Heinroth, T., Strauss, P., Zaykovskiy, D.: Spoken dialogue systems for intelligent environments. In: Aghajan, H., Delgado, R.L.-C., Augusto, J.C. (eds.) Human-Centric Interfaces for Ambient Intelligence, pp. 453–478. Elsevier, Amsterdam (2010)
12. Misu, T., Raux, A., Gupta, R., Lane, I.: Situated language understanding for a spoken dialog system within vehicles. Comput. Speech Lang. **34**, 186–200 (2015)
13. Ota, R., Kimura, M.: Proposal of open-ended dialog system based on topic maps. Procedia Technol. **17**, 122–9 (2014)
14. Pieraccini, R.: The Voice in the Machine: Building Computers that Understand Speech. MIT Press, Cambridge MA (2012)
15. Reschke, K., Vogel, A., Jurafsky, D.: Generating recommendation dialogs by extracting information from user reviews. In: Proceedings of the ACL 2013, pp. 499–504 (2013)
16. Serban, O., Pauchet, A.: Agentslang: a fast and reliable platform for distributed interactive systems. In: Proceedings of the ICCP 2013, pp. 35–42 (2013)
17. Stent, A., Stenchikova, S., Marge, M.: Reinforcement learning of dialogue strategies with hierarchical abstract machines. In: Proceedings of the SLT 2006, pp. 210–213 (2006)
18. Stepanov, E., Riccardi, G., Bayer, A.: The development of the multilingual LUNA corpus for spoken language system porting. In: Proceedings of the LREC 2014, pp. 2675–2678 (2014)
19. Tsai, M.: The VoiceXML dialog system for the e-commerce ordering service. In: Proceedings of the CSCWD 2005, pp. 95–100 (2005)
20. Tsilfidis, A., Mporas, I., Mourjopoulos, J., Fakotakis, N.: Automatic speech recognition performance in different room acoustic environments with and without dereverberation preprocessing. Comput. Speech Lang. **27**(1), 380–95 (2013)
21. Wu, W.L., Lu, R.Z., Duan, J.Y., Liu, H., Gao, F., Chen, Y.Q.: Spoken language understanding using weakly supervised learning. Comput. Speech Lang. **24**(2), 358–82 (2010)

Activity Qualifiers in an Argumentation Framework as Instruments for Agents When Evaluating Human Activity

Esteban Guerrero[1(✉)], Juan Carlos Nieves[1], Marlene Sandlund[2], and Helena Lindgren[1]

[1] Computing Science Department, Umeå University, 901 87 Umeå, Sweden
{esteban,jcnieves,helena}@cs.umu.se
[2] Physiotherapy Unit, Department of Community Medicine and Rehabilitation, Umeå University, 901 87 Umeå, Sweden
marlene.sandlund@umu.se

Abstract. Theoretical frameworks have been developed for enabling software agents to evaluate simple activities such as walking and sitting. However, such frameworks typically do not include methods for how practically dealing with uncertain sensor information. We developed an argument-based method for evaluating complex goal-based activities by adapting two qualifiers: *Performance* and *Capacity* defined in the health domain. The first one evaluates what a person does, and the second one how "well" or "bad" an activity is executed. Our aim is to deal with uncertainty and inconsistent information; generate consistent hypotheses about the activity execution; and resemble an expert therapist judgment, where an initial hypothesis assessment can be retracted under new evidence. We conducted a pilot test in order to evaluate our approach using a Physiotherapy assessment test as a goal-based activity. Results show that skeptic argumentation semantics are may be useful for discriminating individuals without physical issues by considering Performance and Capacity; conversely, credulous semantics may be suitable for obtaining information in the evaluation of activity, which an intelligent agent may use for providing personalized assistance in an ambient assisted living environment.

Keywords: Ambient assisted living · Intelligent agents · Argumentation theory · Argumentation semantics · Complex activities · Evaluation

1 Introduction

Recognition and evaluation of low-level physical activities such as walking, sitting or sleeping is typically being done by agents or multi-agents considering statistical methods ([1,5] among others). Such methods are dependent on a substantial amount of data. This work aims at developing methods for evaluating more complex goal-based activities, which requires a semantic logic-based approach.

© Springer International Publishing Switzerland 2016
Y. Demazeau et al. (Eds.): PAAMS 2016, LNAI 9662, pp. 133–144, 2016.
DOI: 10.1007/978-3-319-39324-7_12

These methods are aimed to be used by intelligent agents in ambient assisted living (AAL) environments for reasoning about an individuals actions and goals. Theoretical frameworks have been developed in this area *e.g.*, [14] however, they typically do not include methods for how practically dealing with uncertain sensor data when inferring qualities of performed goal-based activities. Therefore, this work aims at develop generic methods for detecting and evaluating goal-based complex activities, based on a particular goal-based activity performed in health care, in particular, we aim to investigate which argumentation semantics are suitable for measuring performance and capacity.

The rest of the paper is structured as follows: in Sect. 2 we present the theories and methods used. In Sect. 3, we present key definitions of argumentation theory as well as we present some contributions for reasoning about complex activities using an argumentation approach. The notions of Performance and Capacity qualifiers are defined in Sect. 4. In Sect. 5, we present results from a pilot study. Our contributions are discussed in Sect. 6.

2   Methods

In this section, we present the pilot study design, the underlying language used for capturing the activity knowledge, and the type of complex activities that we deal with in this paper.

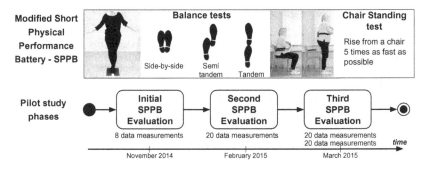

Fig. 1. Pilot study workflow

2.1   Study Design and Data Set

The pilot study included three data collection phases using a modified version of the Short Physical Performance Battery (SPPB) test, as is represented in Fig. 1. Sensor data was collected in the three phases by using a sensor-based mobile application called *Balansera* (https://github.com/esguerrero/Balansera-mob) which collects acceleration data. The mobile phone with the Balansera application was placed in the lower back using a belt for maintaining its position. The population sample inclusion criteria was: people over 65 years, ability to rise from a chair with a seat height of 45 cm., with his arms crossed over her/his chest and the ability to understand instructions on Swedish language, all the participants were assessed in laboratory conditions. The first group, 8 participants (7 female, 1 male) was assessed in balance and chair-standing using the SPPB. Similarly, the second group of 20 participants (11 female 9 male) was assessed in balance and chair-standing tasks; and, a third group of 20 participants (11 female 9 male) was assessed in chair-standing twice. In each occasion data measurements was obtained, in total, the data set contains 68 measurements from 28 different older adults. For our calculations, in this study, subsets of that corpus were used, which is further described in Sect. 4. Balansera's categorization and evaluation of sub-actions was validated by comparing the results with the assessments done independently by three physiotherapists [19].

2.2 Complex Activities

We adapt, for representing complex goal-based activities, a general and systemic model developed as a part of Activity Theory in the Social Science and Psychology fields [12]. In our approach, complex activities refers to hierarchical systems of human praxis, Activity theory defines a three-layer hierarchy for such systems: *activity*, consisting of a set of goal-based *actions*, which in turn may consist of actions and *operations* at the lowest level in a nested structure. In our model, observations level corresponds to operations (see Fig. 2). Our study is framed on the evaluation of such hierarchical activities where the following holds: (1) activities consists of sets of actions directed to a goal[1]; (2) goals and actions cannot exist outside of an activity; (3) goals have subgoals with more granularity which are associated to sub-actions; and (4) at the lowest level observable operations are identified which do not have goals.

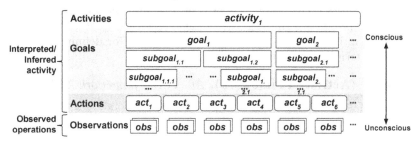

Fig. 2. Activity theory hierarchical structure.

2.3 Underlying Logical Language

In our approach, we use extended logic programs (ELP) [9] for capturing incomplete information as well as exceptions, using strong negation and negation-as-failure (NAF) represented by *not*. We use a propositional logic with a

---

[1] Actions have goals and are executed by a human agent at a conscious level, in contrast with operations which do not have a goal of their own and which are executed at the lowest level as automated, unconscious processes.

syntax language constituted by propositional symbols: $p_0, p_1, \ldots$; connectives: $\wedge, \leftarrow, \neg, not, \top$; and auxiliary symbols: (,), in which $\wedge, \leftarrow$ are 2-place connectives, $\neg, not$ are 1-place connectives and $\top$ is a 0-place connective. Propositional symbol $\top$ and symbols of the form $\neg p_i (i \geq 0)$ stand for indecomposable propositions which we call *atoms*, or *atomic propositions*. Atoms of the form $\neg a$ are called *extended atoms* in the literature. An *extended normal clause*, C, is denoted:$a \leftarrow b_1, \ldots, b_j, not\ b_{j+1}, \ldots, not\ b_{j+n}$ where $j + n \geq 0$, a is an atom and each $b_i (1 \leq i \leq j + n)$ is an atom. When $j + n = 0$ the clause is an abbreviation of $a \leftarrow \top$ such that $\top$ always evaluates true. An *extended normal program* P is a finite set of extended normal clauses. By $\mathcal{L}_P$, we denote the set of atoms which appear in a program P. ELP use both strong negation $\neg$ and *not*, representing common-sense knowledge through logic programs. On programs with NAF, the consequence operator: $\leftarrow$ is not monotonic, which means that the evaluation result, may change as more information is added to the program. Two major semantics for ELP have been defined: (1) answer set semantics [9], an extension of *Stable model semantics*, and (2) a version of the Well-Founded Semantics (WFS) [20]. WFS performs a *skeptical* reasoning approach being both polynomial time computable and always defined. In contrast to Stable, WFS satisfies the *relevance* property which allows us infer consistent conclusion and avoiding problems associated with the so-called *conflict propagation* [8].

3   Extension of an Argumentation Framework for Reasoning About Activity

In this section, we present some key properties of argumentation theory and we propose an extension to the work presented in [14], novel Definitions 1, 2, 3 and 5 are used for representing the cognitive dynamics of an agent when imperfect information and inconsistent goals are considered, and for defining an activity framework in terms of logic programs.

Definition 1 (Activity Framework). *An activity framework ActF is a tuple of the form* $\langle P, \mathcal{H}_A, \mathcal{G}, \mathcal{O}, Acts \rangle$ *in which:*

- *P is a logic program. $\mathcal{L}_P$ denotes the set of atoms which appear in P.*
- *$\mathcal{H}_A = \{d_1, \ldots, d_i\}$ is a set of atoms such that $\mathcal{H}_A \subseteq \mathcal{L}_P$. $\mathcal{H}_A$ denotes the set of hypothetical actions which an agent can perform in a world.*
- *$\mathcal{G} = \{g_1, \ldots, g_j\}$ is a set of atoms such that $\mathcal{G} \subseteq \mathcal{L}_P$. $\mathcal{G}$ denotes a set of goals of an agent.*
- *$\mathcal{O} = \{o_1, \ldots, o_k\}$ is a set of atoms such that $\mathcal{O} \subseteq \mathcal{L}_P$. $\mathcal{O}$ denotes a set of world observations of an agent.*
- *$Acts \subset 2^{\mathcal{G}}$. Acts denotes a set of goal-based activities.*

An activity framework (Definition 1) is a knowledge structure for an intelligent agent to be able of reasoning about hierarchical activities. Fragmentary explanations of an activity can be obtained by considering an argument structure, we present a definition of the so called hypothetical fragments [14] in terms of ELP. The novelty of our approach lies on the method to generate such fragments, dealing with inconsistent goals and incomplete observations by using an answer-set programming approach for building arguments first introduced in [10].

Definition 2 (Hypothetical Fragment of an Activity). *Let $ActF = \langle P, \mathcal{H}_A, \mathcal{G}, \mathcal{O}, Acts \rangle$ be an activity framework. A hypothetical fragment of an activity is of the form $HF = \langle S, O', a, g \rangle$ such that:*

1. *$S \subseteq P$, $O' \subseteq \mathcal{O}$, $a \in \mathcal{H}_A$, $g \in \mathcal{G}$,*
2. *$S \cup O' \cup \{a\}$ is consistent[2],*
3. *$g \in T$ such that $WFS(S \cup O' \cup \{a\}) = \langle T, F \rangle$,*
4. *S and O' are minimal w.r.t. set inclusion.*

$WFS(S)$ is a function inferring the Well-Founded Semantics (WFS) [20].

Intuitively, a fragment (Definition 2) is an argument-based explanation of an activity, fulfilling different principles of quality for rule-based argumentation systems [4,8]. We can denote $\mathcal{HF}$ the set of all the hypothetical fragments obtained by applying Definition 2 to a program P. $\mathcal{HF}$ can be seen as a set of activity explanations in a given situation. The support of a fragment can be an assembled substructure of other fragments, the so called *sub-fragments*. In order to define this concept we introduce some auxiliary functions Supp and Concl which return the support and conclusion of a given fragment respectively, *e.g.*, given the fragment $HF = \langle S, O', a, g \rangle$ we have $\mathsf{Supp}(HF) = S \cup O' \cup \{a\}$ and $\mathsf{Concl}(HF) = \{g\}$.

Definition 3 (Sub-fragment). *Let $HF_1 = \langle S_1, O'_1, a_1, g_1 \rangle$, $HF_2 = \langle S_2, O'_2, a_2, g_2 \rangle$ be two fragments of an activity. HF_1 is a sub-fragment of HF_2 iff $\mathsf{Supp}(HF_1) \subseteq \mathsf{Supp}(HF_2)$.*

Different types of attack relationship among fragments and sub-fragments can be defined.

Definition 4 (Attack Relationships). *Let $ActF = \langle P, \mathcal{H}_A, \mathcal{G}, \mathcal{O}, Acts \rangle$ be an activity framework. Let $HF_1 = \langle S_1, O'_1, a_1, g_1 \rangle$, $HF_2 = \langle S_2, O'_2, a_2, g_2 \rangle$ be two fragments such that $HF_1, HF_2 \in \mathcal{HF}$. $WFS(\mathsf{Supp}(HF_1)) = \langle T_1, F_1 \rangle$ and $WFS(\mathsf{Supp}(HF_2)) = \langle T_2, F_2 \rangle$ denote the semantic evaluation of the support, then HF_1 attacks HF_2 if one of the following conditions hold: (1) $\alpha \in T_1$ and $\neg\alpha \in T_2$.; (2) $\alpha \in T_1$ and $\alpha \in F_2$.*

In Definition 4, the two conditions of attack between fragments resembles the well-known notions of *undercut* and *rebut* [3,18].

An argumentation-based activity framework establishes a method for reasoning about activities by considering argumentation as inference method as follows:

---

[2] In argumentation literature, a set $S \subseteq P$ is *consistent* iff $\nexists \psi$, $\phi \in P$ such that $\psi = \neg\phi$, Definition 6. *Consistent set* in [4].

Definition 5 (Activity Argumentation Framework). *Let $ActF$ be an activity framework of the form $\langle P, \mathcal{H}_A, \mathcal{G}, \mathcal{O}, Acts \rangle$; let $\mathcal{HF}$ be the set of fragments w.r.t. $ActF$ and $Att_{\mathcal{HF}}$ or simply Att the set of all the attacks among $\mathcal{HF}$. An activity argumentation framework AAF with respect to $ActF$ is of the form: $AAF = \langle ActF, \mathcal{HF}, Att \rangle$.*

Dung in [7] introduced a set of *patterns of selection* of arguments, the so called *argumentation semantics* are a formal methods to identify conflict outcomes for any argumentation framework (AF). The sets of arguments suggested by an argumentation semantics are called *extensions* which can be regarded as "the best" explanation for the current situation. We can denote $SEM(AF) = \{Ext_1, \ldots, Ext_k\}$ as the set of k extensions generated by an argumentation semantics (SEM) w.r.t. an argumentation framework AF. This final step is defined as the *justified conclusions* generation of an argument-based system (ABS) in [4].

Definition 6 (ABS Output and Conclusions Set). *Let $AAF = \langle ActF, \mathcal{HF}, Att \rangle$ be an activity argumentation framework and SEM be an argumentation semantics, then if $SEM(AAF) = \{E_1, \ldots, E_n\}(n \geq 1)$ and HF be a fragment, then:* $\mathsf{Concs}(E_i) = \{Concl(HF) \mid HF \in E_i\}(1 \leq i \leq n);$ *and* $\mathsf{Output}_{SEM} = \bigcap_{i=1\ldots n} \mathsf{Concs}(E_i).$

In Definition 6, we can differentiate the scope of Concs and Output, being the later a skeptical approach. Skepticism is related with making more or less committed evaluations about the justification state of fragments in a given situation: a more skeptical attitude corresponds to less committed evaluations of an activity [2]. Intuitively, a skeptical view is opposed to a credulous position.

Definition 7. *Let $AF := \langle AR, attacks \rangle$ be an argumentation framework. An admissible set of arguments $S \subseteq AR$ is: (1) stable if and only if S attacks each argument which does not belong to S; (2) preferred if and only if S is a maximal (w.r.t. inclusion) admissible set of AF; (3) complete if and only if each argument, which is acceptable with respect to S, belongs to S; and (4) the grounded extension of AF if and only if S is the minimal (w.r.t. inclusion) complete extension of AF.*

The stable, preferred, complete and grounded semantics are instances of SEM, hence, without lost of generality, the stable, preferred, complete and grounded semantics can be applied to an activity argumentation framework.

4   Introduction of Qualifiers for Evaluating Activity

In this section, we propose two quantifiers to evaluate complex activities: Performance and Capacity based on quantifiers defined in the International Classification of Functioning, Disability and Health (ICF) [16]. Our interpretation of an activity qualifier considering an argumentation approach is based on the set of extensions of ABS.

4.1 Performance Qualifier

According to the ICF, Performance describes what an individual "really does". In this sense, our interpretation of this qualifier is based on the set of goals that an ABS prescribes, as follows:

Definition 8 (Performance Qualifier). *Let $AAF = \langle ActF, \mathcal{HF}, Att \rangle$ be an activity argumentation framework; let $SEM(AAF) = \{E_1, \ldots, E_n\}(n \geq 1)$ be the set of extensions inferred by the argumentation semantics SEM and let $Act \in Acts$ be an activity. The performance qualifier w.r.t. Act is given by:*

$$Perf_{Act} = \frac{\mid Perf_{max} \mid}{\mid Act \mid}$$

Where $Perf_{max} = \mathcal{M}_{act}(\mathsf{Concs}(SEM(AAF)), Act)$ infers a mapping of goals between $SEM(AAF)$ and Act.

$Perf_{Act}$ in Definition 8 calculates the Performance qualifier by considering goals in $SEM(AAF)$ (*e.g.*, the number of achieved goals for each assessment test) *w.r.t.* a reference number of goals in a given activity Act. Intuitively, $\mathcal{M}_{act}$ in Definition 8 is a mapping which depends on the activity evaluation focus, *e.g.*, in the SPPB case the Performance goal is counting the "positive" goals achieved, being $\mathcal{M}_{act}$ a maximization function selecting "positive" goals.

4.2 Capacity Qualifier

A criterion-referenced test is a test that examines the ability of an individual executing a task, against pre-defined criteria [6]. The Capacity qualifier measures how "well" or "bad" an individual executes an activity by following a criterion-referenced approach. In order to define Capacity qualifier we introduce an auxiliary function Obser which returns the set of observations O' of a given fragment *i.e.*, given the fragment $HF = \langle S, O', a, g \rangle$ we have $\mathsf{Obser}(HF) = O'$.

Definition 9 (Capacity Qualifier). *Let $AAF = \langle ActF, \mathcal{HF}, Att \rangle$ be an activity argumentation framework; let $SEM(AAF) = \{E_1, \ldots, E_n\}(n \geq 1)$ be the set of extensions inferred by SEM, and let $Act \in Acts$ be an activity. The Capacity qualifier w.r.t. Act is given by:*

$$Capacity = \frac{\mid Capac_{ref} \mid}{\mid \mathcal{R}ef \mid}$$

where $Capac_{ref} = \mathcal{M}_{ref}(\mathsf{Obser}(SEM(AAF)), \mathcal{R}ef)$ infers a mapping of observations between SEM and $\mathcal{R}ef$; $\mathcal{R}ef = \{O_1, \ldots, O_j\}$ is a set of reference observations given by a criterion-referenced test.

In Definition 9, $\mathcal{M}_{ref}$ defines a mapping among inferred observations *w.r.t.* a reference set. This function depends on the evaluation focus of the activity and it can be seen as a maximization or minimization functions, *e.g.*, in our SPPB test, Balansera tries to maximize the capturing of "correct" observations considering an initial assessment which is the reference set.

5   Results of the Physical Assessment Study

In this section, we present results obtained in our pilot test. We explore: (1) the method for capturing uncertain sensor data using ELP; and (2) variation of the qualifiers calculation using different argumentation semantics. The modified SPPB test was analyzed as a hierarchical activity with four goals and a set of observations, as Table 1 illustrates.

Table 1. Activity structure of the SPPB test.

5.1   Capturing Uncertain Sensor Data Using ELP

In six measurements from the second and third session of the study, the data obtained from the chair test shows that there is no detectable pattern in the rising or sitting data peaks (see Fig. 3 as example of one of the cases). This lack of evidence was confirmed by the manual annotations of the therapist (see extra data in Balansera Web site https://github.com/esguerrero/Balansera-mob). We capture this lack of observable evidence using the NAF symbol: *not*, *e.g.*, the observation: *Little_Sway$_o$ ← not Much_Sway$_o$*, describing: *given that **there is no evidence** that much sway is present in the test, **then** is assumed that a light sway is present.* In this manner, the SPPB test was captured as a logic program as is presented in Fig. 3. We also obtain a set of fragments by using Definition 2 to the program P, as a result we generate hypothetical fragments with the form:

$$F_2 = \langle \{correctRise_g \leftarrow Fast\_Rise_o, Slow\_Sit_o, Little\_Sway_o, Congrats\_mess_a;$$
$$Fast\_Rise_o \leftarrow not\ Slow\_Rise_o;\ Slow\_Sit_o \leftarrow not\ Fast\_Sit_o\},$$
$$\{Fast\_Rise_o, Slow\_Sit_o, Little\_Sway_o\},$$
$$Congrats\_mess_a,$$
$$correctRise_g \rangle$$

where $Congrats\_mess_a$ is the action taken by the system (an intelligent agent implementing our argumentation framework) directed to achieve the $correctRise_g$ goal. An intuitive reading about the hypothetical fragment F_2 would be: *"An individual has achieved a correct rise **given that**, there is no evidence that she sat down quickly, **therefore** she sat down slowly, **and** there is no evidence that she got up slowly, **therefore** she got up quickly, **and** she had little sway, **and** an alert message was displayed warning."* As a result, a fragment describes a complex explanation of a current situation given different observations of the world and an action performed by an agent.

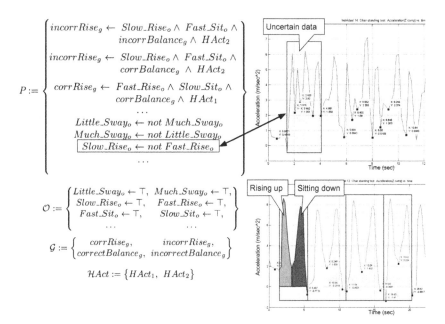

Fig. 3. Partial structure of a logic program capturing the sit-to-stand test of the SPPB for an individual (left); uncertain data for capturing starting ending data peaks (right).

5.2 Qualifiers Using Different Argumentation Semantics

In the calculus of Performance and Capacity argumentation semantics have a major impact. Grounded semantics among the Dung's semantics has a skeptical behavior [7], it belongs to the unique-status approach *i.e.*, $|SEM(AAF)| = 1$ and it prescribes a maximal number of undefined fragments among Dung's semantics. By considering a most *credulous* approach such as stable, we can obtain a contrary behavior than grounded, minimizing the number of fragments without a justified state. Stable belongs to the multiple-status approach, *i.e.*, $|SEM(AAF)| > 1$ being not universally defined, may in particular be the case that $|SEM(AAF)| = \emptyset$.

Results presented in Fig. 4 represent the calculation of the two qualifiers using Stable and Grounded semantics [7]. The results show that credulous semantics such as Stable and Preferred coincide and provide valuable information about the Performance and Capacity, *i.e.*, under a credulous semantics evaluation, our qualifiers provide different options for assessing an activity generating a qualification even for unlikely but reasonable hypotheses (fragments). On the other hand, by considering Grounded our qualifiers have a more skeptical attitude, generating frequently the lowest qualification: 0, possibly due to the character of the activity. Qualifiers provide a measurement between 0 to 1, which intuitively can be seen as, 0: a "severe problem" and 1: "no problem" or "negligible" in the execution of an activity (see [17] for a review of how to apply generic qualifiers in rehabilitation). In Fig. 4 most of the Grounded qualifiers calculations have a value 0.

6 Discussion

In this paper, we explore a novel approach based on argumentation theory for evaluating physical activities from the perspective of rational agents by resembling the kind of assessment reasoning performed by clinicians: (1) gathering data through observations; (2) handling ambiguous and uncertain observation information; (3) generating current function status hypothesis; (4) deduce an explanatory outcome of explanation; and (5) retracting the explanation under new evidence. Hypothetical fragments, as were defined in Definition 2, represent a novel approach for obtaining goal-based hypotheses about an activity considering uncertain information. We propose a method using ELP to capture uncertain data obtained from sensors, by analyzing signal peaks of the acceleration data and building rules with NAF. Some other approaches [11, 15] capture incomplete information and exceptions as well. On programs with NAF the evaluation result may change as more information is added to the program, this non-monotonic process in some sense, follows the natural treatment of lack of evidence performed by a therapist in an assessment process. As a result of our pilot test, ELP allowed us describe scenarios with incomplete information such as sensor-based contexts.

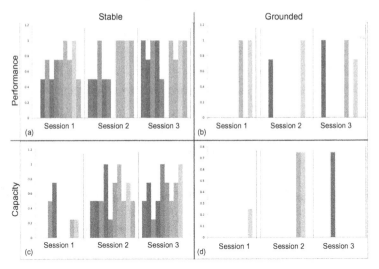

Fig. 4. (a) Performance using Stable; (b) Performance using Grounded; (c) Capacity using Stable; and (d) Capacity using Grounded semantics.

We introduce a quantifier called Performance to evaluate the achievement of goals obtained as output of an argument-based system (ABS). Goals are part of hypothetical fragments of activities, which are the output of ABS, and comes in the form of a set of fragment-based explanations. Intuitively, Performance can be understood as a quantifier of goal fulfillment and from the experimental practical view, it can show the change in the achievement of goals during a period of time. Capacity qualifier shows observation-based details of activity execution compared to an expected or referenced set of observations. These qualifiers depend on the output of an ABS, particularly described on the set of goal-based conclusions suggested by the extensions. In this setting, as Fig. 4 suggests and the theory predicts, a more skeptical attitude corresponds to *weaker* (*less committed* in [2]) evaluations of an activity. As future work, we will explore relationships between our qualifiers and different skepticism criteria of argumentations semantics, [2] among others.

The SPPB test is a comparable simple goal-oriented activity. In future work we will apply the results of this paper on more complex activities, with more levels of sub-actions and sub-actions overlapping by time. An interesting observation was made, that when the Grounded semantics give a high value on Capacity and Performance for an individual in the first action (initial assessment), this seems to indicate that the person is well equipped both with capacity and performance skills. If Grounded does not give the output, this could be interpreted as an increased risk for falling down. This could contribute to an automatic risk assessment in older adults. The Balansera application will be extended with agent-based reasoning utilizing the results of the work presented in this paper applied to an AAL environment, which will be subjected to feasibility studies with groups of older adults in the near future. The main purpose of the study and the AAL environment is to prevent falls and promote active living [13].

7   Conclusions

In this paper, we present theoretical and practical methods for an agent to use when detecting and evaluating human activities in an ambient assisted living environment. The methods were applied in a case study for evaluating the methods. We use accelerometer data collected by a mobile application called Balansera to evaluate physical condition in older adults. The contributions of this paper can be summarized as follows: (1) an extended version of an argumentation-based activity framework [14] in terms of logic programs, to reason with complex activities dealing with uncertainty from sensor data as well as inconsistent knowledge, *e.g.,* two contradictory goals to be achieved in the same activity; (2) a method for capturing uncertain sensor data in a knowledge base using logic programs, particularly ELP; (3) we introduce two qualifiers: Performance and Capacity to evaluate activity execution by resembling the assessment of physical activities that is performed by a therapist; and (4) credulous argumentation semantics provide valuable information when analyzing performance and quality, and stable semantics may be useful for identifying individuals who are at risk of falling. This and other characteristics of different semantics and of complex human activities will be studied in future work.

Acknowledgment. The authors are grateful to the participants in the user studies and to Marianne Silfverskiöld who conducted the case study. Silfverskiöld's study was approved by the ethical committee (2014/113-31Ö).

References

1. Aggarwal, J.K., Ryoo, M.S.: Human activity analysis: a review. ACM Comput. Surv. (CSUR) **43**(3), 16 (2011)
2. Baroni, P., Giacomin, M.: Skepticism relations for comparing argumentation semantics. Int. J. Approx. Reasoning **50**(6), 854–866 (2009)
3. Besnard, P., Hunter, A.: A logic-based theory of deductive arguments. Artif. Intell. **128**(1–2), 203–235 (2001)
4. Caminada, M., Amgoud, L.: On the evaluation of argumentation formalisms. Artif. Intell. **171**(5), 286–310 (2007)
5. Chen, L., Hoey, J., Nugent, C.D., Cook, D.J., Yu, Z.: Sensor-based activity recognition. IEEE Trans. Syst. Man Cybern. Part C Appl. Rev. **42**(6), 790–808 (2012)
6. Crocker, L., Algina, J.: Introduction to Classical and Modern Test Theory. ERIC, Princeton (1986)
7. Dung, P.M.: On the acceptability of arguments and its fundamental role in nonmonotonic reasoning, logic programming and n-person games. Artif. Intell. **77**(2), 321–357 (1995)
8. Dung, P.M., Thang, P.M.: Closure and consistency in logic-associated argumentation. J. Artif. Intell. Res. **49**, 79–109 (2014)
9. Gelfond, M., Lifschitz, V.: Classical negation in logic programs and disjunctive databases. New Gener. Comput. **9**(3–4), 365–385 (1991)
10. Guerrero, E., Nieves, J.C., Lindgren, H.: Semantic-based construction of arguments: an answer set programming approach. Int. J. Approximate Reasoning **64**, 54–74 (2015)
11. Kakas, A.C., Kowalski, R.A., Toni, F.: Abductive logic programming. J. Logic Comput. **2**(6), 719–770 (1992)
12. Leont'ev, A.N.: Activity, Consciousness, and Personality. Prentice-Hall, Englewood Cliffs (1978)
13. Lindgren, H., Surie, D., Nilsson, I.: Agent-supported assessment for adaptive and personalized ambient assisted living. In: Corchado, J.M., Pérez, J.B., Hallenborg, K., Golinska, P., Corchuelo, R. (eds.) Trends in Practical Applications of Agents and Multiagent Systems. AISC, vol. 90, pp. 25–32. Springer, Heidelberg (2011)
14. Nieves, J.C., Guerrero, E., Lindgren, H.: Reasoning about human activities: an argumentative approach. In: Twelfth Scandinavian Conference on Artificial Intelligence, SCAI 2013, Aalborg, Denmark, 20–22 November, 2013, pp. 195–204 (2013)
15. Nute, D.: Defeasible logic. In: Bartenstein, O., Geske, U., Hannebauer, M., Yoshie, O. (eds.) INAP 2001. LNCS (LNAI), vol. 2543, pp. 151–169. Springer, Heidelberg (2003)
16. World Health Organization. How to use the ICF: A practical manual for using the International Classification of Functioning, Disability and Health (ICF). WHO (2013)
17. Peterson, B.D.: International classification of functioning, disability and health: an introduction for rehabilitation psychologists. Rehabil. Psychol. **50**(2), 105 (2005)
18. Pollock, J.L.: Defeasible reasoning. Cogn. Sci. **11**(4), 481–518 (1987)
19. Silfverskiöld, M.: Development and validation of an application for mobile phone with a self-test of standing up from a chair. Master's thesis, Umeå University, Physiotherapy Department (2015, to appear)
20. Van Gelder, A., Ross, K.A., Schlipf, J.S.: The well-founded semantics for general logic programs. J. ACM **38**(3), 619–649 (1991)

Agent-Based Semantic Business Process Management Methodology

Hüseyin Kir[(✉)] and Nadia Erdoğan

Istanbul Technical University, Istanbul, Turkey
{hkir,nerdogan}@itu.edu.tr

Abstract. Business complexity is growing exponentially and current business process management (BPM) systems that depend on static process definitions are becoming inadequate to adept complex and dynamic nature of this new business environment. Multi agent and semantic technologies based solutions are natural candidates for a solution towards more flexible ways of working, shortening organizational reaction times and fully embracing business unpredictability. This paper presents an agent based semantic business process management methodology that aims at the integration of business process management lifecycle and agent oriented software engineering methodologies. Specifically, the proposed methodology enables the intelligent agent based self-adaptation of business processes via goal and semantic technologies based enhancement of processes specifications.

Keywords: Semantic business process management · Agent based BPM · BPM methodology

1 Introduction

Through the seventies and eighties data-driven approaches have dominated the information systems landscape. The focus of information technology has been on storing and retrieving information and as a result data modeling has become the starting point for building an information system. However, with the managerial tendencies toward process optimization and improvement, it has become clear that processes are equally important and need to be supported in a systematic manner. As a consequence, process oriented approaches to software design and development have started to come into prominence [20,22].

Today we are witnessing a new wave in information technology named cloud computing and this is barely the beginning. The rise of utility computing services delivered over the internet will continue to disrupt markets, spawn new business models, blur industry boundaries and enable multi-company virtual business networks and ecosystems. Complexity is growing exponentially and current business process management (BPM) systems, that depend on static process definitions, are becoming insufficient to meet the complexity and dynamism that

© Springer International Publishing Switzerland 2016
Y. Demazeau et al. (Eds.): PAAMS 2016, LNAI 9662, pp. 145–156, 2016.
DOI: 10.1007/978-3-319-39324-7_13

are required by this new business environment. New tools and methods are desperately needed to build businesses that are complex adaptive systems capable of bringing order out of the chaos [19].

Industrial process management research towards more flexible ways of working, shorter organizational reaction times and fully embracing market and business unpredictability has resulted in new concepts such as Agile BPM, Dynamic BPM, Intelligent BPM and even Event-driven SOA that aim to deal with current business challenges [4]. The common vision of these concepts is the construction of a knowledge-based (not just information-based) and adaptive business system that meets the needs of the moment and copes with the incompleteness and ambiguity of real business processes and workflows. While this vision of versatility is appealing, the underlying enterprise framework is getting extremely complex and simply needs intelligent infrastructure to manage and hide the complexity.

This business case is bringing intelligent agent technology out of the research lab and repurposing it as new-generation information technologies infrastructure. While it is naturally merging adaptive and knowledge-based technologies, its autonomous, problem-solving, collaborative and context-aware essence making it necessary to scale and manage the chaos [19].

In this paper, we propose a novel business process management methodology that is rigorously interoperable with the multi-agent theory. With this methodology we characterize the essential aspects and modelling phases of agent-based BPM and formalize the design procedure of such systems. The rest of the paper is organized as follows. The next section focuses on the current state of agent-based business process management research. In Sect. 3 we propose a unified methodology for agent based process management. Finally in Sect. 4 we conclude by highlighting the important aspects of our work.

2   Agent-Based Business Process Management

Both BPM technology and agent paradigms focus on addressing change and complexity. Intelligent agent technology is the next logical step in moving the BPM technology paradigm forward and overcoming some of its shortcomings [1]. Promising advantages of integrating these technologies have already been seen by researchers [12, 19] and studies have taken place in this direction.

In the literature agent-based business process agility is attempted through various approaches. In [13], authors utilize agents to perform dynamic web service composition in order to form adaptive business processes in runtime. Some studies [2, 5, 17] establish an abstraction on process definitions with goals, to decouple that which should be addressed from the method of its achievement. In this manner the responsibility of deciding which task to execute to fulfill the goal is postponed until run-time. Finally, Wang and Wang [21] define a business process as a set of business rules to reactively perform appropriate actions according to runtime perceptions via using normative reactive agents.

However, multi-agent technology is beyond being just a distributed software development infrastructure, it is also a next-generation software engineering paradigm. In this regard, agent-based business process management needs purpose built methods to interoperate with multi-agent theory. The three main design principles of the agent-based business process management methodology that we proposed are as follows. Firstly, accepted methods of industrial software development depend on standard representations for business processes that act as a contract between business and implementation viewpoints. Therefore any proposed methodology should support de facto business process management notations. Secondly, the new paradigm of business process management needs new methods of considering collaborative processes so as to build on the concepts of collaboration, evolution and the business context; not just messages, service calls and tasks. So goal based abstractions should be provided by the process models. Finally, new business dynamics require on-demand establishment of economic structures such as virtual organizations. Hence, process models should be semantically enriched in order to embrace this business heterogeneity.

3   Agent-Based Semantic BPM Methodology

Agent-based BPM system development methodology provides a sequence of activities for system designers and developers to follow. It consists of a set of phases wherein each phase uses the results of the previous one (see Fig. 1). In this section, the system development life cycle is illustrated step-by-step on a real world software system in order to clarify the applied models. A conference management system, which is frequently used in literature, will be considered for the case study. The outline of the case study scenario is as follows:

I. *Submission Phase:* Program committee calls for paper submissions. Researchers register their papers to the system. Researchers receive a notification which states that their papers are registered.

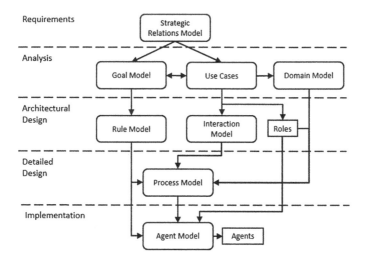

Fig. 1. Methodology phases

II. *Review Phase:* At the end of the submission deadline, the program committee asks pre-determined reviewers to review a number of the papers. Reviewers accept or reject the offer to review the paper according to their interests. Each reviewer reviews the accepted papers and reports back to program committee. The program committee accepts or rejects the paper in accordance with the reviews and notifies the authors.

III. *Publishing Phase:* Authors, who receive an acceptance notification, edit their papers in accordance with the reviews and submit the final version of the paper to system. Finally, all final copies are collected and printed in the conference proceedings.

3.1 Requirements Specification

The main objective of the proposed methodology is to enable development of process management systems that can adapt to changing conditions autonomously. In order to achieve this adaptability, the system should be able to perceive the deviance between the expectations (requirements) and runtime performance and change its actions to compensate for this divergence. Therefore, unlike object-oriented analysis, the software requirements need to be represented as knowledge which is used by agents not only during the analysis phase but also at runtime [14,17].

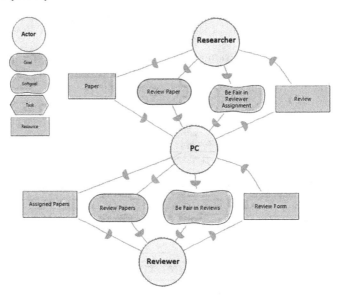

Fig. 2. Conference management strategic relations model

Goal Oriented Requirements Engineering (GORE) [23] approach provides a natural machine-processable specification of requirements in social organizations. The first phase of the proposed methodology utilizes GORE to define system requirements via modeling the organizational context, stakeholders, plus their objectives and relationships via a **Strategic Relations Model.**

The Strategic Relations Model is represented by a directed graph where business participants are modeled as nodes and their dependencies represent the agreements between participants. These agreements may stand for a task to be performed, a resource to be shared, a mutual goal to be achieved or a non-functional requirement (softgoal) to be satisfied. These relations represent system requirements from each actor's viewpoint.

As presented in Fig. 2, conference management organization comprises of three primary actors and their relations are defined as follows. The researcher sends a paper to the program committee (PC) requiring them to review the paper via a fair reviewer assignment. Likewise, the program committee expects reviewers to review assigned papers adequately and deliver the review forms. As a result this model provides an abstract definition of actor's expectations both from the system and from each other.

3.2   Analysis

While the strategic relations model focuses on relations between the actors, the motivations behind these dependencies are detailed with **Goal Models**. A goal model reveals the operational goals for each actor via detailing strategic goals that are based on the strategic relations model.

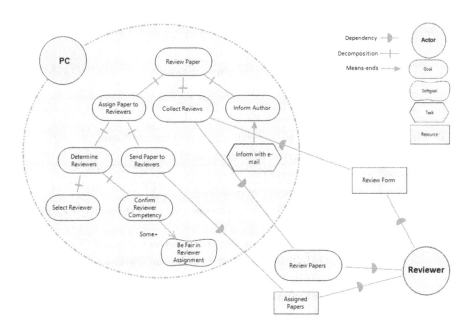

Fig. 3. Program Committee (PC) goal model

Based upon conventional social modeling frameworks [24] and popular Agent-Oriented Software Engineering (AOSE) methodologies [3,8,15] a goal model is designed which, allows a deeper understanding of each process participant's needs and how these needs are met. Operational goals are modeled through each actor's perspective via means-ends analysis, contribution analysis and task/goal decomposition methods. *Means-ends relations* are mostly used with goals and specify alternative ways of achieving them. Positive or negative contribution of goals and tasks on accomplishment of soft-goals are defined via *contribution relations*. Goals are further resolved into subgoals that need to be satisfied in order to achieve the main goal through *decomposition links*.

Figure 3 presents the Program Committee (PC) role's goal model in regard of the case study. Within this direction, the Review Paper goal is decomposed into three sub-goals: *assign paper to reviewers, collect reviews*, and *inform author* by using "and decomposition". Similarly, the *assign paper to reviewers* goal is further decomposed into fine-grained sub-goals. Also confirmation of reviewer competencies is identified as positively contributing to the *be fair on reviewer assignment* soft-goal. Lastly, a "means-ends" relation is used to identify whether the author informing goal has been achieved via an e-mail notification task.

Use Cases are formed in tandem with goal models, in order to define detailed scenarios to achieve system goals and, possibly, to identify any unrevealed goals. In accordance with methodology design principles, use case scenarios that are defined in a goal-driven fashion based on existing AOSE methodologies [15].

The use case scenario consists of a sequence of steps where each step is either a goal, a percept (incoming information from the environment), an action, another use case scenario, or an "other" step (e.g. waiting for an event). Every scenario

Table 1. Review paper use case

Use case	Review Paper
Main actor	Program Committee
Goal of main actor	Determine papers that set conference conditions
Focus actor's goal	Securing review of written paper
Success scenario	Authors receive the reviews
Triggering behavior	SENSE: Submission deadline
Main flow	1- GOAL: Select the reviewers related to the paper (Program Committee)
	2- GOAL: Confirm reviewer competency (Program Committee)
	3- GOAL: Send the paper to reviewers (Program Committee)
	4- OTHER: Wait for the review results (Program Committee)
	5- GOAL: Review the paper (Reviewer)
	6- GOAL: Send Review result (Reviewer)
	7- GOAL: Collect reviews (Program Committee)
	8- GOAL: Inform author about reviews (Program Committee)

step also lists the actor which will take the step. Table 1 shows an example use case scenario for the "review paper" system goal.

The analysis phase ends with construction of a **Domain Model** which defines the environment that the agent can sense and process upon. Ontologically defined domain model entities are utilized for instituting a common vocabulary amongst the system participants and for defining the resources that are consumed during the goal achievement process.

3.3 Architectural Design

There are inevitable dependencies and relationships between process participants and these interactions obviously need to be captured and represented in the architectural design phase. Instead of using conventional message-oriented interaction modeling approaches, a goal-oriented approach will enable a focus on the essential nature and purpose of the interaction, rather than on the precise ordering of particular message exchanges [6,15]. Also goal-oriented interaction modeling empowers autonomous behaviors, instead of following predefined steps mechanically.

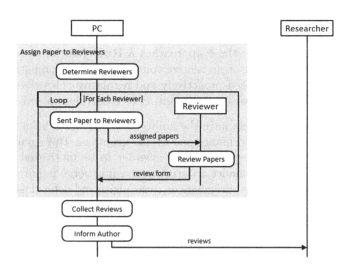

Fig. 4. Paper review scenario interaction model

In accordance with the **Interaction Model** (see Fig. 4), the agent determines its actual actions and messages at runtime to achieve the collaborative goals. Even messaging protocols can change dramatically in accordance with these goal achievement decisions. For example, the goal of *Determine Reviewers* consists of *Select Reviewer* and *Confirm Reviewer Competency* sub-goals, and it can be accomplished with different action sequences;

I. Program Committee scans all the papers and makes assignments based on its own preferences. The accuracy of assignments is confirmed by reviewers' feedback.

II. The system makes a keyword-based automatic assignment. The accuracy of assignment is confirmed by reviewers' feedback.

III. All papers' titles and abstracts are published. Reviewers make their selections by bidding according to their research interests. The program committee makes paper assignments after evaluating reviewers' preferences and expertise.

As seen, enacted behavior and messaging protocols can change significantly depending on the selected goal achievement approach. Interaction models designed independently of action and messaging details provide great flexibility on decision making and exception handling to agents.

As mentioned on previous methodology steps, multi-agent systems consist of autonomous agents that interact with each other. While every agent tries to achieve its individual goal, making a multi-agent system act on common interest is only possible via organizing agent behaviors and interactions in a normative way.

Also, in addition to studies on applying rules in the context of multi-agent systems [7,9,11], there are studies on applying law, regulation, and organizational rules to corporate processes in the field of business processes management [18]. With the unification of these approaches a **Rule Model** is constructed. The rule model is composed of preventive rules that ensure compatibility with the legislation by being tracked proactively and regulative rules which are used for optimizing business processes and adapting to constraints reactively.

– **Regulative Rules:** Agents have the ability to adjust their behavior at runtime to increase their performance and avoid exceptions. But agents are need to be aware of their underperformance in order to be motivated to change. In fact these target performance criteria are non-functional requirements that are identified during the requirements analysis phase and defined as soft-goals. In the context of the regulative rules modeling, the aimed is to include soft-goals in the agent's knowledge base through representing them as rules. During this conversion, rules are planned to be represented along with the compensation steps as in similar studies in the literature [10]. For example, in case of the failure of the *"Be Fair on Reviewer Assignment"* soft-goal, the re-planning of related behavior is defined as:

$$reviewerAssignments(p) \Rightarrow O_{PK} acceptableSuccessRatio(p) \otimes$$
$$O_{PK} replanGoal (DetermineReviewers)$$

In this statement, the O_{PK} deontic operator defines the obligations of program committee and the connective $\otimes$ operator associates the soft-goal and compensation behaviors.

Respectively, following the assignment of all papers to reviewers, the agent proportionally checks the performance. If the accept/deny ratio of paper assignments are below the desired accuracy, one of the methods mentioned during the Interactions Modeling phase (e.g. reviewers' bidding) is executed via re-planning the *'Determine Reviewers'* goal.

- **Preventive Rules:** Another set of rules aimed to be added to the rule model consists of organizational norms and regulations such as *"Reviewers shall not review their own papers"* and *"Papers should be reviewed by at least three different reviewers"*. These rules are proactively controlled by the agents to keep the plans' conformity with the regulations. However, in order to protect its autonomy, it is the agent's decision to apply or ignore the rule [10, 16].

  Preventive rules can also be defined using design control units (decision nodes, cycles etc.). For example, the *"Reviewers shall not review their own papers"* rule can be adopted by adding a decision node following the reviewer assignment task. But, handling rules at a cognitive level, as suggested in this methodology, provides greater flexibility through designing rules and process flows independently of each other.

3.4 Detailed Design

While interaction models define communication between roles at a bird's-eye-view, **Process Models** elaborate the process through the interacting roles' perspective in order to model the behavior of the roles. As a result, for each interacting role in the interaction model a process model is designed. For instance, the review papers interaction model (Fig. 4) encompasses communications between the Program Committee, Reviewer and Researcher roles. While the Researcher role is played by human actors, the Program Committee and Reviewer roles are supported by the agent-based process management system.

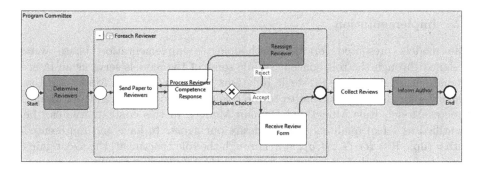

Fig. 5. Program committee role process model (Color figure online)

The process model for the Program Committee role is presented on Fig. 5. In addition to standard BPMN building blocks, goal tasks (emphasized in yellow) are used for process modeling. Identification of actions that fulfill these goals are postponed until to the runtime. In this way, behaviors that will be used for reviewer selection and researchers notification are dynamically determined in runtime via evaluating agent's beliefs (rules, facts, etc.) and environmental conditions.

While some of the tasks are processed entirely by the agent (*"background tasks"*), some are processed by the user (*"user task"*) through the process interface that the agent provides as a part of a decision support service. For example, in the *Send Paper to Reviewer* background task, without troubling the program committee member with operational details, the agent accomplishes delivery in background by attaching paper to an ACL message. Similarly, in the *Reassign Reviewer* task, the assignment is accomplished by the program committee member, the and agent offers suggestions to the member through a process GUI via providing assignable reviewers through different strategies (e.g. finding reviewers who have similar profiles to reviewers who have accepted the paper).

While it is not represented on the process's visual representation, in accordance with the WSMO[1] meta-model, a set of metadata are also defined in the process model. Firstly, the process is associated with a goal; in the presented example process is associated with Review Paper goal (see Fig. 5). Also, preconditions (e.g. completion of paper delivery phase) and effects (all authors receive reviewers' reviews of their papers) of the process are defined semantically. Afterwards, in order to designate the knowledge flow between process steps, inputs and outputs of each process step are identified using Domain Model concepts. For example, the input of the "Determine Reviewers" goal task is defined as paper and the output is defined as a set of reviewer assignments. Finally, goal tasks are associated with a goal in the Goal Model.

Compliance with WSMO enables the integration of semantic web services into the process. Goal tasks can be accomplished either by an agent behavior or a semantic web service transparently and this decision can be made on the fly.

3.5   Implementation

The models presented for the methodology's implementation phase were designed through the role concept. While some of the models serve as an intermediate product (such as Strategic Relations Model, Interaction Model and Use Cases), some directly contributes to the role's knowledge (such as Goal Model, Process Model, Rule Model and Domain Model). In this context, role can be identified as set of qualities that we desire our agents to have and represented with a tuple $R = \langle G, G_s, B, \sigma_r, \pi_r \rangle$. Through the role enactment, the agent gains a series of new goals (G), a set of soft-goals (G_s), behaviors required to accomplish these goals (B), rules applied to the role (σ_r), and basic beliefs required to play the role (π_r).

As the final phase of the methodology, agents are identified and roles are assigned to them through the **Agent Model**. This model is utilized at the instantiation of the agent based business process management systems and roles are deployed to the agents accordingly.

---

[1] http://www.wsmo.org/.

4   Conclusion

The new realities of the business have created new imperatives for business information systems. Today's business systems must be knowledge based to cope with the incompleteness and must be adaptive to bring productivity to business. In this paper, we have presented the agent based semantic business process management methodology that restates business process management lifecycle in compliance with the agent oriented software engineering methodologies. In this direction, process design products are reformulated and semantically enriched in accordance with agent based systems requirements. Also, self-adaptation is provided by the possibility to inject goals into the system at design-time and the ability of agents to create a bridge between their capabilities and the expected results. The Conference Management System is used as a representative example to demonstrate the overall business process design procedure.

References

1. Bergenti, F., Caire, G., Gotta, D., Long, D., Sacchi, G.: Enacting bpm-oriented workflows with wade. In: Fortino, G., Garro, A., Palopoli, L., Russo, W., Spezzano, G. (eds.) WOA. CEUR Workshop Proceedings, vol. 741, pp. 112–116. CEUR-WS.org (2011)
2. Braubach, L., Pokahr, A., Jander, K., Lamersdorf, W., Burmeister, B.: Go4Flex: goal-oriented process modelling. In: Essaaidi, M., Malgeri, M., Badica, C. (eds.) Intelligent Distributed Computing IV. SCI, vol. 315, pp. 77–87. Springer, Heidelberg (2010)
3. Bresciani, P., Perini, A., Giorgini, P., Giunchiglia, F., Mylopoulos, J.: Tropos: an agent-oriented software development methodology. Auton. Agent. Multi-Agent Syst. **8**(3), 203–236 (2004)
4. Bruno, G., Dengler, F., Jennings, B., Khalaf, R., Nurcan, S., Prilla, M., Sarini, M., Schmidt, R., Silva, R.: Key challenges for enabling agile bpm with social software. J. Softw. Maint. Evol. **23**(4), 297–326 (2011)
5. Burmeister, B., Arnold, M., Copaciu, F., Rimassa, G.: Bdi-agents for agile goal-oriented business processes. In: Proceedings of the 7th International Joint Conference onAutonomous Agents and Multiagent Systems: Industrial Track, AAMAS 2008, pp. 37–44. International Foundation for Autonomous Agents and Multiagent Systems, Richland (2008)
6. Cheong, C., Winikoff, M.: Hermes: designing goal-oriented agent interactions. In: Müller, J.P., Zambonelli, F. (eds.) AOSE 2005. LNCS, vol. 3950, pp. 16–27. Springer, Heidelberg (2006)
7. Dastani, M., Grossi, D., Meyer, J.-J.C., Tinnemeier, N.: Normative multi-agent programs and their logics. In: Meyer, J.-J.C., Broersen, J. (eds.) KRAMAS 2008. LNCS, vol. 5605, pp. 16–31. Springer, Heidelberg (2009)
8. DeLoach, S.A., Garcia-Ojeda, J.C.: O-mase: a customisable approach to designing and building complex, adaptive multi-agent systems. IJAOSE **4**(3), 244–280 (2010)
9. Esteva, M., Rosell, B., Rodriguez-Aguilar, J.A., Arcos, J.L.: Ameli: an agent-based middleware for electronic institutions. In: AAMAS, pp. 236–243. IEEE Computer Society (2004)

10. Governatori, G., Rotolo, A.: How do agents comply with norms? In: Boella, G., Noriega, P., Pigozzi, G., Verhagen, H. (eds.) Normative Multi-Agent Systems. Dagstuhl Seminar Proceedings, vol. 09121. Schloss Dagstuhl - Leibniz-Zentrum für Informatik, Germany (2009)

11. Hübner, J.F., Boissier, O., Kitio, R., Ricci, A.: Instrumenting multi-agent organisations with organisational artifacts and agents. Auton. Agent. Multi-Agent Syst. **20**(3), 369–400 (2010)

12. Jennings, N.R., Faratin, P., Johnson, M.J., Norman, T.J., O'Brien, P., Wiegand, M.E.: Agent-based business process management. Int. J. Cooperative Inf. Syst. **5**(2&3), 105–130 (1996)

13. Castellanos-Garzón, J.A., Garcia Coria, J.A., Corchado, J.M.: Intelligent business processes composition based on multi-agent systems. Expert Syst. Appl. **41**(4), 1189–1205 (2014)

14. Jureta, I.J., Borgida, A., Ernst, N.A., Mylopoulos, J.: The requirements problem for adaptive systems. ACM Trans. Manage. Inf. Syst. **5**(3), 17:1–17:33 (2014)

15. Khallouf, J., Winikoff, M.: The goal-oriented design of agent systems: a refinement of prometheus and its evaluation. IJAOSE **3**(1), 88–112 (2009)

16. Kır, H., Ekinci, E.E., Dikenelli, O.: Knowledge management in role based agents. In: Aldewereld, H., Dignum, V., Picard, G. (eds.) ESAW 2009. LNCS, vol. 5881, pp. 181–196. Springer, Heidelberg (2009)

17. Sabatucci, L., Lodato, C., Lopes, S., Cossentino, M.: Towards self-adaptation and evolution in business process. In: Giordano, L., Montani, S., Dupré, D.T. (eds.) AIBP@AI*IA. CEUR Workshop Proceedings, vol. 1101, pp. 1–10. CEUR-WS.org (2013)

18. Sadiq, S., Governatori, G.: Managing regulatory compliance in business processes. In: vom Brocke, J., Rosemann, M. (eds.) Handbook on Business Process Management 2. International Handbooks on Information Systems, pp. 265–288. Springer, Heidelberg (2015)

19. Sinur, J., Odell, J., Fingar, P.: Business Process Management: The Next Wave. Meghan-Kiffer Press, Tampa (2013)

20. van der Aalst, W.M.P., ter Hofstede, A.H.M., Weske, M.: Business process management: a survey. In: van der Aalst, W.M.P., Weske, M. (eds.) BPM 2003. LNCS, vol. 2678, pp. 1–12. Springer, Heidelberg (2003)

21. Wang, M., Wang, H.: Intelligent agent supported business process management. In: HICSS. IEEE Computer Society (2005)

22. Weske, M.: Business Process Management: Concepts, Languages, Architectures. Springer-Verlag New York Inc., Secaucus (2007)

23. Yamamoto, S., Kaiya, H., Cox, K., Bleistein, S.J.: Goal oriented requirements engineering: trends and issues. IEICE Trans. **89–D**(11), 2701–2711 (2006)

24. Yu, E.S.K.: Social Modeling and i^*. In: Borgida, A.T., Chaudhri, V.K., Giorgini, P., Yu, E.S.K. (eds.) Conceptual Modeling: Foundations and Applications. LNCS, vol. 5600, pp. 99–121. Springer, Heidelberg (2009)

An Agent-Based Model of Labor Market Participation with Health Shocks

Alessandro Moro[✉] and Paolo Pellizzari[✉]

Department of Economics, Ca' Foscari University,
Cannaregio 873, 30121 Venice, Italy
{alessandro.moro,paolop}@unive.it

Abstract. This paper presents an agent-based model of labor market participation, in which a population of agents is affected by adverse health shocks that impact the costs associated with work efforts, and decides whether to leave the labor market. This decision is simply taken by looking at the working behaviors of the other agents, comparing the respective levels of well-being and imitating the more advantageous decision of others. The analysis reveals that such mechanism of social learning suffices to replicate the existing empirical evidence regarding the decline in labor market participation of older people. As a consequence, the paper demonstrates that it is not necessary to assume perfect and unrealistic rationality at the individual level to reproduce a rational behavior in the aggregate.

Keywords: Labor market participation · Health shocks · Bounded rationality · Agent-based modeling

1 Introduction

This paper presents an agent-based model of labor market participation, in which a population of agents is naturally affected over time by adverse shocks that reduce their health and magnify the costs associated with work efforts. Agents decide whether or not to leave the labor market and retire (or access an otherwise available source of support, like a social security benefit). This decision is made by looking at the working behaviors of other randomly met agents and comparing the respective levels of well-being, rather than maximizing the utility function in a standard and fully rational way.

The analysis reveals that such mechanism of learning-by-meeting and imitation, even in the presence of otherwise entirely naive agents, can replicate some of the existing empirical evidence regarding the decline in labor market participation of older people. As a consequence, the paper shows that it is not necessary to assume full rationality at the individual level to reproduce a rational behavior in the aggregate.

The relevance of this claim can be understood by considering that the mainstream literature on labor supply and retirement choices is dominated by structural models, in which fully rational agents take decisions by maximizing their

© Springer International Publishing Switzerland 2016
Y. Demazeau et al. (Eds.): PAAMS 2016, LNAI 9662, pp. 157–168, 2016.
DOI: 10.1007/978-3-319-39324-7_14

life-time utility. Examples of this kind of modeling approach, that also incorporates health shocks, are Bound et al. (2010), Burkhauser et al. (2004), French (2005), Gilleskie (1998), Gustman and Steinmeier (2002), Heyma (2004), Rust and Phelan (1997). To give some flavor, the agents in the paper by Rust and Phelan optimize their behavior working backward the optimal employment decision (i.e. how much to work) at any time t between the age of 57 and 102 and choose whether to apply for Social Security. The situation faced by workers is described by 7 state variables, and optimality is determined in principle in each of 14,400 possible future occurrences maximizing the value of expected discounted utility.[1]

There is overwhelming evidence in experimental economics and psychology that shows how framing effects and contextual factors limit human rationality (Rabin 1998) and how poorly humans behave in problems that involve backward induction (Camerer 1997). Whether the previously described rational optimization can be performed by realistic agents is a no-brainer: consumer decision making is affected by information overload as soon as more than 10 options and 15 information items are provided (Lurie 2004), (Malhotra 1982), and it is well known that humans do not have good performances when dealing with (non trivial) probabilistic setups.

An alternative view, that incorporates the main findings of the empirical literature and much better accommodates with the psychological limitations of real agents, makes use of agent-based models where most often boundedly rational agents act using heuristics and cognitively sound adaptive rules of thumb. For instance, Lettau (1997) presents a model of portfolio decisions with agents that learn through a genetic algorithm how to behave based on random innovations and imitation. In particular, it is shown that investors in mutual funds exhibit the same patter of investments of the adaptive agents described in the paper and that the model closely matches the mutual fund data. Recently, Goudet et al. (2015) have developed an agent-based model with boundedly rational workers simulating the effects of suppression of fixed duration contracts in the French labor market.

More germane to our topic, Axtell and Epstein (1999) describe a model where a relatively small number of workers are rational, whereas a small proportion of them retire at random, and the vast majority just imitates the behaviors of the other agents in their social network. Again, high levels of optimal behavior can result in the aggregate despite low levels of individual rationality. Our paper supports a similar conclusion in a framework that also incorporates health shocks and proposes a different mechanism of social learning.

---

[1] This is an Herculean task requiring, among other things, to estimate transition probabilities from one state to all possible future states based on beliefs which, in turn, depends on 26 parameters to be determined. Other questionable assumptions include "rational expectations", a notion according to which all individual subjective probabilities equate the "objectively estimable population probability" and the capability to anticipate regulatory changes. The paper acknowledges several times that only some justification for such assumptions can be provided.

It is worth stressing that the present paper proposes a mechanism of imitation of behaviors. This is the main difference with respect to the dispositional contagion framework proposed by Epstein (2014), in which each agent is not influenced by the actions of his peers, but by their dispositions. In our study the former approach is preferred because behaviors are more easily observed than dispositions.

The rest of the paper is organized as follows: the next section illustrates the main stylized facts that the model is able to reproduce, it describes the model, its calibration as well as the results of the simulations; finally, the last section concludes stressing the reasons why the present model can be considered a valid alternative to the mainstream approaches.

2 Analysis

This section of the paper is divided in three parts: the first one describes a few traits of the empirical evidence regarding the decline in the labor market participation of elderly workers affected by adverse health shocks; the second subsection describes in detail the proposed agent-based computational model; the last part shows the results of the model simulation and, in particular, how the model is able to capture some relevant stylized facts.

2.1 Stylized Facts

Data from the first wave of the English Longitudinal Study of Ageing (ELSA) are chosen in order to illustrate the empirical evidence regarding the labor market participation of elderly people and the main stylized facts that the model is able to replicate. This dataset contains information on both economic and labor supply variables, as well as on self-assessed health status.

The ELSA sample is representative of people aged 50 and over, living in private households in England. The interviews of the first wave began in March 2002 and spanned 12 months, completing in March 2003.

Figure 1 shows how labor market participation, measured as the proportion of people employed or self-employed, declines with the age of individuals. In particular, each curve is associated with a different level of health.[2]

Although labor market participation decreases with age in each health group, it is evident that people affected by poor health conditions have much lower participation rates than the individuals with a good health status, and this is true in every age group. In fact, people affected by adverse health shocks who are eligible to disability benefits or retirement have a strong incentive to leave the labor market. Issues related to the effects of various benefits are still debated by policymakers as they may artificially alter the participation to the labor market or offer awkward incentives to workers.

---

[2] These statistics include people both in and outside the labor force. The data used to draw the curves in Fig. 1 are taken from the Table 4 A.3 in the Annex 4.1 - Tables on Work and Retirement of the first wave of the ELSA survey. http://www.elsa-project. ac.uk/reportWave1.

Labor Market Participation

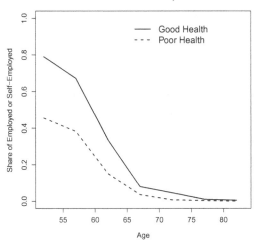

Fig. 1. Labor market participation by age and health. The solid line represents the participation of people with a good health, while the dashed line shows the participation of people affected by poor health conditions. Source: first wave of the English Longitudinal Study of Ageing.

2.2   The Model

In the model two types of agent, workers and pensioners, interact in a bidimensional torus space. At the beginning of the simulations ($t = 0$), the proportion of pensioners is equal to p. Workers receive a labor income y^l, which is greater than the pension y^p, but their work effort e^l is bigger than the one of pensioners e^p.[3]

Each agent i starts with an age $a_{i,0}$, randomly drawn from a uniform distribution on the (50, 89) interval, and receives a health $h_{i,0}$, drawn from uniform distribution on the $\left(0, \frac{50}{a_{i,0}}\right)$ interval.

Agents derive well-being $U_{i,t}^s$ from their working decisions that assumes the following expression:

$$U_{i,t}^s = y_{i,t}^s - \frac{e_{i,t}^s}{h_{i,t}} \tag{1}$$

where $s \in \{l, p\}$ denotes the state, labor or pension, of the individual. Thus, the well-being is an increasing function of income, whereas it decreases when the working effort increases. Moreover, the negative effect of exerting effort is greater when an agent suffers from a bad health, i.e. when $h_{i,t}$ is low.

---

[3] As mentioned previously, pensioners and pension income can also be interpreted as people who decide to leave the labor market and receive a subsidy or a disability benefit.

This definition of well-being is consistent with the framework proposed by the OECD (2013). In particular, this institution measures well-being in terms of outcomes achieved in two broad domains: material living conditions (income and wealth, jobs and earnings, ...) and quality of life (physical and mental health, work-life balance, ...).

In each time step, an agent is randomly selected (asynchronous activation) and he moves to a random site of the bidimensional space, where he can meet another agent. The movement rule is very simple: the agent turns right at an angle that is randomly picked in $\{0, 1, 2, \ldots, 359\}$ degrees and moves forward f patches (steps). If the moving agent "lands" on a patch hosting another person and the two are similar in terms of age and health status, they exchange information about their working choices, represented by the vector (y, e), and their levels of well-being U. The similarity between the agents i and j is established if the following inequality holds:

$$w \frac{\mid a_{i,t} - a_{j,t} \mid}{100} + (1 - w) \mid h_{i,t} - h_{j,t} \mid < d, \tag{2}$$

where $0 \leq w \leq 1$ measures the relative importance of age with respect to health, and d represents a similarity threshold. A low (high) value of w means that agents are more likely to imitate the behaviors of those with similar health conditions (age). Additionally, a higher value of the threshold d implies that agents are more willing to copy the working choices of dissimilar players. The difference of ages is divided by 100 to obtain a measure, whose magnitude can be compared to that of the difference of health levels.

Once inequality (2) is satisfied (and only in this case), the two agents compare their respective well-being. Then, if $U_{i,t}^s < U_{j,t}^s$, agent i will imitate the working choices $(y_{j,t}^s, e_{j,t}^s)$ of agent j, and vice versa. Social learning is therefore implemented with this kind of imitation mechanism involving no optimization or information processing on the part of the agents, who resemble walkers that randomly encounter other hikers and have a chance to discuss different experiences related to working satisfaction and opportunity to retire.

It is worth emphasizing that the movement in the bidimensional space can also be interpreted in metaphoric terms as the intensity of the social relationships of each agent: according to this view, a low value of the movement parameter f means that agents are shy and more likely to often meet the same close peers and, accordingly, their social network is very limited; conversely, more mobile and lively agents have higher chances of stumbling upon different peers, their acquaintances' network is more widespread and can, on average, obtain more information about retirement decisions.

Quite naturally, age evolves deterministically over time ($a_{i,t+1} = a_{i,t} + 1$), while health is affected by random shocks over the life cycle:

$$h_{i,t+1} = g h_{i,t} + (1 - g) x_{i,t+1} \tag{3}$$

where $0 \leq g \leq 1$ is a parameter capturing the persistence of health status, and $x_{i,t+1}$ is a random variable distributed with a uniform distribution on the

$\left(0, \frac{50}{a_{i,t+1}}\right)$ interval: thus, the future level of health is a weighted average of the current health status and the random shock. This expression implies that an older agent is more likely to experience bad health shocks and, consequently, a decreasing level of health.

Finally, it is assumed that agents die at age 90 and they are replaced by new agents with an age equal to 50 and a health drawn from uniform distribution on the $\left(0, \frac{50}{a_{i,0}}\right)$ interval. Moreover, these new agents are pensioners or workers with a probability equal to p and $1-p$, respectively.

The model is implemented in NetLogo (Wilensky 1999). The user can choose the values for the model parameters, agents are randomly located in the bidimensional torus space, and each agent receives a random age, health and working condition. The code is available at http://tinyurl.com/paams16health and a screenshot of the Netlogo's graphical user interface is provided in Fig. 2.

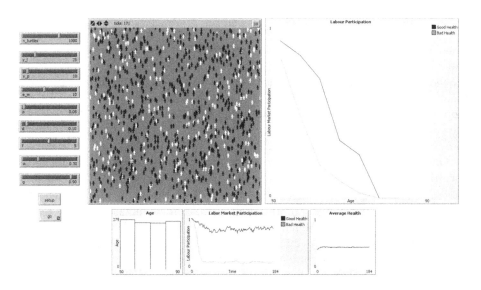

Fig. 2. Screenshot of Netlogo's graphical user interface.

In every time period the simulation evolves through the following steps:

1. an agent is randomly selected;
2. the chosen agent, following the movement rule, moves to a random site, where he/she may meet another agent;
3. if there is an encounter and the two agents are reasonably similar in terms of age and health conditions, the one with the lowest level of well-being will imitate the working choices of the agent with the highest well-being.

These simple rules are replicated for all agents. Then, once all agents have performed their tasks, the age and health status of each player is updated.

Agents with an age equal to 90 "die", they are replaced by new ones endowed with a random health, time advances by one unit and the procedure starts again until the user quits the simulation or some specified time is reached. It is possible to monitor the evolution of the system by looking at some time series graphs that show the dynamics of the main model variables, as well as in the bidimensional space, in which workers and pensioners are depicted with different colors.

2.3   Calibration and Results

The model is simulated many times and under different conditions. On the one hand, it is assumed that the work effort of pensioners e^p is equal to 0 and the benefits pensioners receive y^p are kept constant and equal to 10: seen from the perspective of the workers, this means that the option of retirement is independent from health conditions and assumes a value of 10. The parameter g is also constant and equal to 0.9: this implies that the health status of agents resembles a persistent and slowly decaying AR(1) process, which appears a rather sensible assumption. On the other hand, the other parameters vary in the following sets: $y^l \in \{25, 30, 35\}$, $e^l \in \{5, 10, 15\}$, $w \in \{0.3, 0.5, 0.7\}$, $d \in \{0.1, 0.2, 0.3\}$, $f \in \{1, 5, 20\}$, and $p \in \{0.05, 0.15, 0.25\}$.[4]

For every combination of these values the model is simulated 100 times, for a total of 72,900 runs, and in each simulation the proportion of workers in the age range [50, 54], [55, 59], [60, 64], [65, 69], [70, 74], [75, 79], [80, 89] is recorded,[5] distinguishing between agents with a good health, defined as those agents with $h_{i,t} \geq 0.5$, and the ones with a bad health, i.e. those with $h_{i,t} < 0.5$. All simulations are halted after 200 time steps and the proportion of workers in the different age and health groups is evaluated at the end of the simulation. Then, for each combination of parameter values, the average proportion is calculated employing the respective 100 simulations, for each age range and health status.

The values of the parameters are selected in order to minimize the absolute distance between the (ELSA) observed labor market participation rates $lmp_{a,h}^{obs}$, in the different age and health groups (a, h), and those predicted by the model $lmp_{a,h}^{pred}$, divided by the product between the total number of age A and health H classes. Formally:

$$D = \frac{1}{AH} \sum_{a,h} | \, lmp_{a,h}^{obs} - lmp_{a,h}^{pred} \, | \tag{4}$$

The smallest value for D is 0.036, attained at the values listed in Table 1. This means that, on average, the absolute deviation between observed and simulated labor market participation rates is about 3.6 %.

---

[4] Simulations are performed using the BehaviorSpace tool in NetLogo, which allows to specify the grid of parameter values and the number of simulations for each point of the grid.

[5] These seven classes of age correspond to the ones presented in the Table 4 A.3 in the Annex 4.1 - Tables on Work and Retirement of the first wave of the ELSA survey.

Table 1. Calibrated values of the model parameters.

Parameter	Description	Value
p	Initial share of pensioners	0.15
y^l	Workers' income	30
y^p	Pensioners' income	10
e^l	Workers' effort	15
e^p	Pensioners' effort	0
f	Movement	5
w	Age weight	0.7
d	Similarity threshold	0.1
g	Health persistence	0.9

Figure 3 plots the labor market participation rates predicted by the model for the different age and health groups when the values contained in Table 1 are assigned to the parameters. Clearly, the model nicely fits the decreasing trend of the labor market participation curves with respect to age.

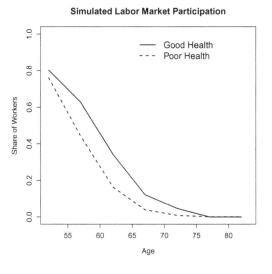

Fig. 3. Simulated labor market participation by age and health. The solid line represents the participation of agents with a good health ($h_{i,t} \geq 0.5$), while the dashed line shows the participation of agents affected by poor health conditions ($h_{i,t} < 0.5$).

Real and simulated data are listed in Table 2, together with the absolute differences that build the error measure D. Values in the third row of the table and visual comparison of Figs. 1 and 3 show that most of modeling error is due to

Table 2. Real and estimated labor market participation rates. The columns of the table in both health conditions correspond to the following age bins: [50, 54], [55, 59], [60, 64], [65, 69], [70, 74], [75, 79], [80, 89].

Data	Good health							Bad health						
Real	0.79	0.67	0.34	0.08	0.05	0.01	0.01	0.46	0.38	0.15	0.04	0.01	0.00	0.00
Simulated	0.80	0.63	0.34	0.12	0.05	0.00	0.00	0.76	0.44	0.16	0.04	0.01	0.00	0.00
Abs. diff	0.01	0.04	0.01	0.04	0.00	0.01	0.01	**0.31**	0.06	0.01	0.00	0.00	0.00	0.00

a unique entry (0.31, boldfaced), the participation rate of workers aged [50, 54] with bad health. We lack additional information for that age/health group, but a more carefully chosen initial condition for the simulations may greatly reduce the mismatch.

Moreover, the participation of agents affected by adverse health shocks decreases more rapidly than that of agents with a good health. Both these aspects are consistent with the empirical evidence contained in the ELSA survey. In fact, given the functional form chosen for the well-being function, a worker with a bad health who meets a similar and already retired agent is more likely to change his status than a worker with a good health. Conversely, a retired agent with a good health may decide to enter again in the labor market when meeting a worker more easily than a pensioner with a bad health. This explains the differences in participation between agents with good and bad health conditions and the reason why labor market participation declines in both groups as health deteriorates due to the ageing of the population.

One of the main contributions of this paper is indeed the demonstration that no hyper-rational agent is needed in the model to replicate the existing evidence as it is sufficient to assume that simple agents randomly and repeatedly meet and mimic each other's behavior.

In order to illustrate the effects of changes in the values of the model parameters and prove the robustness of the obtained results, Fig. 4 compares the baseline calibration, reported in the first panel of the figure, with other scenarios characterized by some deviations from the values contained in Table 1.

Panel 4b shows the effect of a higher income, i.e. y^l equals 35: it is evident that the labor market participation curves decline more slowly, especially for workers with a good health, because higher salaries make the outside option of retirement less attractive in relative terms. In fact, in an even more transparent way, the same pattern is observed in Panel 4c, in which work effort e^l is reduced to 10 (keeping income fixed at 30).

A lower value of the age weight w means that agents are more likely to imitate the behaviors of those who are similar in terms of health conditions than the ones with the same age. This leads to an increase in the divergence of the labor market participation curves with respect to the baseline scenario, as shown in Panel 4d. A higher value of the similarity threshold is associated with steeper participation curves, as can be seen in Panel 4e, because workers tend to imitate the behaviors of more dissimilar agents that may have already decided to retire.

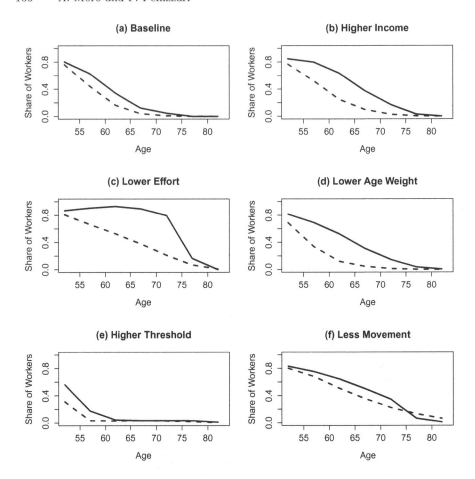

Fig. 4. Simulated labor market participation by age and health in different scenarios: (a) baseline calibration: values of Table 1 assigned to the model parameters; (b) higher labor income: $y^l = 35$; (c) lower work efforts: $e^l = 10$; (d) lower age weight: $w = 0.3$; (e) higher threshold: $d = 0.3$; (f) less movement: $f = 1$. In each panel, the solid line represents the participation of agents with a good health ($h_{i,t} \geq 0.5$), while the dashed line shows the participation of agents affected by poor health conditions ($h_{i,t} < 0.5$).

The last panel of the figure illustrates the effect of the mobility parameter f, showing that less mobile (or less socially connected) agents enjoy more infrequent meetings and, consequently, flatter labor market participation curves. Remarkably, nearly all of the graphs contained in Fig. 4 always preserve the same pattern, i.e. participation rates that decline when age increases, and in which workers affected by adverse health shocks are more likely to leave the labor market. The results of the model are therefore robust to different values of the parameters.

3   Conclusion

The simple model described in this paper is able to replicate some relevant stylized facts contained in the ELSA survey, concerning the labor market participation of elderly people.

The core of the model is represented by naive agents moving in a bidimensional torus space, exchanging information on their work and health conditions, and making labor market choices according to this information: although extremely simple, the proposed mechanism of imitation and social learning is able to reproduce an aggregate behavior that can be considered rational and consistent with the empirical evidence, despite the bounded rationality of the individual agents.

It has already been stressed that the dynamics underlying the model can be interpreted in figurative terms: for instance, the movement in the bidimensional space is a measure of the intensity of the social relationships of each agent. Following this idea, agents that explore less the surrounding space are more likely to meet too often the same peers and fail to be faced with alternative and possibly better decisions regarding retirement. Conversely, more mobile agents have higher chances of seeing in their more widespread network diverse examples to imitate and improve their own well-being.

The model captures the most prominent stylized facts regarding the decline in labor market participation of aged workers, and well fits the participation curves with relatively few parameters. This parsimony is in sharp contrast with the mainstream structural models, which usually require numerous parameters to replicate the empirical evidence (John von Neumann famously stated that "With four parameters I can fit an elephant. And with five I can make him wiggle his trunk." Our model also would definitely be considered inadequate if you look at Table 1 . . .)

Moreover, it is reasonable to think that more sophisticated forms of interaction between agents, such as the dispositional contagion mechanism assumed in the Epstein's (2014) notion of Agent_Zero, may probably deliver an outcome similar to our results.

In conclusion, all these considerations should allow to consider the model presented in this paper as a behaviorally plausible alternative to the standard modeling approaches that unrealistically assume the full rationality of individuals, despite an overwhelming psychological and experimental literature showing the limits of human reasoning.

References

Axtell, R.L., Epstein, J.M.: Coordination in transient social networks: an agent-based computational model of the timing of retirement. In: Aaron, H.J. (ed.) Behavioral Dimensions of Retirement Economics, pp. 161–183. Brookings Institution Press, Washington, DC (1999)

Bound, J., Stinebrickner, T.R., Waidmann, T.A.: Health, economic resources and the work decisions of older men. J. Econometrics **156**, 106–129 (2010)

Burkhauser, R.V., Butler, J.S., Gumus, G.: Dynamic programming model estimates of social security disability insurance application timing. J. Appl. Econometrics **19**, 671–685 (2004)

Camerer, C.F.: Progress in behavioral game theory. J. Econ. Perspect. **11**, 167–188 (1997)

Epstein, J.M.: Agent_Zero: Toward Neurocognitive Foundations for Generative Social Science. Princeton University Press, Princeton (2014)

French, E.: The effects of health, wealth, and wages on labour supply and retirement behaviour. Rev. Econ. Stud. **72**, 395–427 (2005)

Gilleskie, D.B.: A dynamic stochastic model of medical care use and work absence. Econometrica **66**, 1–45 (1998)

Goudet, O., Kant, J.D., Ballot, G.: Forbidding fixed duration contracts: unfolding the opposing consequences with a multi-agent model of the french labor market. In: Amblard, F., Miguel, F.J., Blanchet, A., Gaudou, B. (eds.) Advances in Artificial Economics. Lecture Notes in Economics and Mathematical Systems, vol. 676, pp. 151–167. Springer, Switzerland (2015)

Gustman, A.L., Steinmeier, T.L.: Retirement and the stock market bubble. NBER Working Paper No. 9404, National Bureau of Economic Research, Cambridge (2002)

Heyma, A.: A structural dynamic analysis of retirement behaviour in the Netherlands. J. Appl. Econometrics **19**, 739–759 (2004)

Lettau, M.: Explaining the facts with adaptive agents: the case of mutual fund flows. J. Econ. Dyn. Control **21**, 1117–1147 (1997)

Lurie, N.H.: Decision making in information-rich environments: the role of information structure. J. Consum. Res. **30**, 473–486 (2004)

Malhotra, N.K.: Information load and consumer decision making. J. Consum. Res. **8**, 419–430 (1982)

OECD: How's Life? 2013: Measuring Well-being. OECD Publishing, Paris (2013)

Rabin, M.: Psychology and economics. J. Econ. Lit. **36**, 11–46 (1998)

Rust, J., Phelan, C.: How social security and medicare affect retirement behavior in a world of incomplete markets. Econometrica **65**, 781–831 (1997)

Wilensky, U.: NetLogo. Center for Connected Learning and Computer-Based Modeling, Northwestern University, Evanston (1999). http://ccl.northwestern.edu/netlogo/

A Dynamic Emotional Model for Agent Societies

J.A. Rincon[1](✉), A. Costa[2], P. Novais[2], V. Julian[1], and C. Carrascosa[1]

[1] D. Sistemas Informáticos y Computación, Universitat Politècnica de València,
Valencia, Spain
{jrincon,vinglada,carrasco}@dsic.upv.es
[2] Centro ALGORITMI, Escola de Engenharia,
Universidade do Minho, Guimaraes, Portugal
{acosta,pjon}@di.uminho.pt

Abstract. This paper presents a first approximation of a dynamic emotional model to be employed in agent societies. The proposed model is based on the *PAD* emotional model and allows the representation of the emotional contagion phenomena of a heterogeneous group of agents which are capable of express emotions. Moreover, the proposal allows the definition of the social emotion of this group of agents. The model is mainly based on three elements: personality, empathy and affinity. These elements allow the characterization of each individual, causing them susceptible to vary in some degree the emotions of other individuals.

1 Introduction

What is an emotion? Some psychologists as *William James* define the emotions as, a representation of physiological change produced by the different stimulus of the environment [1]. Changes in the environment make humans change their emotional states, helping them to make decisions. From a computational perspective, emotions have been employed as a way to improve social simulation processes which require human interactions, but very little work has been done on representing collective emotions and emotion's atomicity. These states can be affected by an extensive number of internal or external factors. Internal factors are the personality and the cognitive processes such as attention; and external factors are related with the environment, which includes relationships among persons and culture expectations [2]. Over the last few years, different approaches have been proposed trying to model the concept of emotion as well as all of the related elements that affect it. There are already some tested emotional and personality models that can be used to recognize and simulate emotions, such as: *OCEAN* model [3], *OCC* emotional models [4], *Plutchiks* theory [5] and the *PAD* model [6]. The employment of these models allows the creation of intelligent entities capable of detect and communicate emotions between agents or between humans and agents. In the communication among agents, they can perceive the environment and the emotional state of other agents. In the same sense, if agents interact with humans, agents can perceive the human emotions using different devices such as cameras [7], speech analysis [8], bio-sensors [9], etc.

© Springer International Publishing Switzerland 2016
Y. Demazeau et al. (Eds.): PAAMS 2016, LNAI 9662, pp. 169–182, 2016.
DOI: 10.1007/978-3-319-39324-7_15

In most of the existing proposals the emotions are typically modeled as static information which influences the decision of an individual entity without taking into account possible interactions with other agents which can give way to an emotion contagion. Emotion contagion may be possible when the model takes into account elements such as situation, affinity, empathy, etc. Until now, only a few works have tried to model the emotional contagion in computational entities: Saunier and Jones [10] model the emotional contagion suggesting in each agent the separation of the body and the mind; the spiral model by Bosse et al. [11] tries to give a solution to the emotional propagation, distinguishing different factors that influence the emotional contagion.

This paper tries to expand the modelization of emotional contagion, by proposing a dynamic emotional model. The proposed model is based on the *PAD* emotional model and represents the emotional contagion of a heterogeneous group of entities capable of express and/or communicate emotions. Moreover, it allows to define the social emotion of a group of agents. To define the model we employ concepts like empathy, affinity and personality of each entity.

The employed concepts open the door to the construction of scenarios highly related to real-life events. Projects like the iGenda [12,13] require virtual actors that have responses similar to human responses.

2   Related Work

The emotional states are defined as the way to express emotion by humans being in a period of time. These emotion are not static and can be propagated through the environment, begin widely used in crowd simulation. It is essential to these applications too have the ability of emulating emotion as they are used to the decision making process. In crowd simulation the most common emotional state is fear, which allows the creation of emergency evacuation simulations [14,15]. Nevertheless, these simulations try to predict the behavior of humans in distress. These simulations have helped to design buildings, evacuation routes and simulate how the police, firefighters and ambulance may optimally respond to a disaster situation [16]. However human being have a whole range of emotions that can be propagated to other agents, such as: happiness, sadness, anger among others. To propagate these emotions the *Newtonian Emotion System (NES)* [17] is designed for multi-agent system, establishing the three laws of motion presented by *Newton*. In the *Newton* dynamic the aim is study of movements of objects and the origin of these movements, where each object is represented by a particles system. Each one of these particles have internal properties which makes them different to the other particles properties as the mass, length, with and height, among others this provide to the object a different behavior when external forces are acting on it. The application of these forces on a particle can changes your direction and velocity or knows if this particle is attracted to another. The authors based on their model in the *Newton* laws and apply some of the concepts presented by *Newton*, concepts as *force, mass, acceleration* and *velocity*. Using this concepts the author defined two laws of emotion dynamics, this two law is based on the laws of dynamic of *Newton*.

Other works have tried to introduce the contagion effect that humans can feel in multiple situations. One of these works is the emotional contagion spiral model [18]. This model tries to give a solution to the emotional propagation, distinguishing among different factors that influence in the emotional contagion. This model is based on a emotional model that was proposed by *Barsade* [19], which includes six hypotheses about how is produced the propagation of emotions. This work is applied in an evacuation simulation scenario, taking into account how human behaviors are affected by the dynamicity and propagation of emotions. Nevertheless, the complexity of these analysis provoques that these approaches are limited to only one emotion, in this case fear. So, behaviors of simulated agents are also affected by only one emotion.

This work tries to pose a possible solution to this problem, pretending to give a first approximation of a dynamic emotional model which allows the representation of the emotional contagion of a heterogeneous group of entities capable of express and/or communicate emotions. In this sense, nexte section explains in detail the proposed model.

3   Dynamic Emotional Model

This section proposes a dynamic emotional model based on the PAD emotional model. This model will represent the emotional contagion of a heterogeneous group of entities capable of expressing and/or communicating emotions.

Before defining the dynamic emotional model, it is necessary to define the representation of an emotional state of an agent on the PAD model. The emotion of an agent ag_i in an instant t ($\overrightarrow{E}_t(ag_i)$) is defined as a vector in $\mathbb{R}^3$, represented by the components that make up the *PAD* emotional model. The variation of each component allows to modify the emotional state of the agent (Eq. 1).

$$\overrightarrow{E}_t(ag_i) = [P_t(ag_i), A_t(ag_i), D_t(ag_i)] \tag{1}$$

This representation in $\mathbb{R}^3$ allows us to see emotions as a system of particles. They attract or repel depending on the internal properties of each one of them. These particles have the ability to move around the space because these particles have internal properties as *Mass*. The mass in a particle is a measure of the amount of matter that has a body, and one of the properties related to it is that it is proportional to the resistance to be attracted by others.

The attraction carried out in the *PAD* space reflects the emotional contagion between entities. An entity will be more easily suffer from contagion of other emotions according to different factors. The main factor, depending on the own entity is called *Empathy*. The empathy is a psychological motivator for helping others in distress [20]. The empathy could be defined as the ability to feel what other people feel. The empathy denotes a deep emotional understanding of another's feelings or problems, while sympathy is more general and can apply to small annoyances or setbacks. Our dynamical model uses this psychological concept, allowing agents to have an empathy level. The *Empathy Level* of an agent ag_i, denoted $\varepsilon(ag_i)$, represents a value in the range $[0, 1]$ indicating the ability of agent ag_i to perceive what another agent may feel. In the PAD space, the mass of agent ag_i $(m(ag_i))$ is defined as the inverse of empathy (Eq. 2) as an indicator of the difficult to be attracted by others, that is to be contagied by other emotions as $m(ag_i)$ increases.

$$m(ag_i) = \frac{1}{|\varepsilon(ag_i)|} \qquad (2)$$

Another important factor in the emotional contagion is the relationship between the emotion source and the emotion receiver, that is, the *Affinity* existing between them. It is not the same to perceive the emotions of a close acquaintance than a stranger. The Affinity Level between two agents ag_i and ag_j at instant t $(Af_t(ag_i, ag_j))$ is a value between $[-1, 1]$ that describes the level of affinity between agents ag_i and ag_j, being -1 the value dedicated to sworn enemies, 0 to perfect strangers and 1 to best of friends. The last factor to take into account in the emotion dynamics is the physical distance between the emotion source and the emotion receiver $(D_t(ag_i, ag_j)$ to denote the physical distance between entities ag_i and ag_j at instant $t)$.

The emotional dynamics described is based on the *Newton* universal attraction law. Newton's law of universal gravitation states that any two bodies in the Universe attract each other with a force that is directly proportional to the product of their masses and inversely proportional to the square of the distance between them. Based on this theory, we define the force that an agent ag_j makes over an agent ag_i at instant t $(\overrightarrow{F}_t(ag_i, ag_j))$ to attract or repulse it in the PAD space, that is, this force will control the emotion contagion between all the agents. The emotional force is a vector in $\mathbb{R}^3$ space. This vector measures the emotional change in the PAD space (Eq. 3).

$$\overrightarrow{F}_t(ag_i, ag_j) = \frac{\varepsilon(ag_i) \cdot Af_t(ag_i, ag_j)}{2^{D_t(ag_i, ag_j)}} \cdot ||\overrightarrow{E}_t(ag_i) - \overrightarrow{E}_t(ag_j)|| \qquad (3)$$

$\overrightarrow{F}_t(ag_i, ag_j)$ represents the force vector, which help us to know if the emotion of the agent ag_i is attracted by the agent ag_j. $\varepsilon(ag_i)$ represents the emphatic level of entity ag_i, and $Af_t(ag_i, ag_j)$ represents the affinity level between ag_i and ag_j at instant t. $D_t(ag_i, ag_j)$ is the physical distance between ag_i and ag_j at instant t and $\overrightarrow{E}_t(ag_i)$ represents the emotion of the ag_i at instant t and $\overrightarrow{E}_t(ag_j)$ represents the emotion of the ag_j at instant t. According to this, we define the *Emotional Attraction Force* of agent ag_i at instant t $(\overrightarrow{EAF}_t(ag_i))$ as the combination of all the attraction forces over agent ag_i at instant t (Eq. 4).

$$\overrightarrow{EAF}_t(ag_i) = \sum_{\forall ag_j \neq ag_i} \overrightarrow{F}_t(ag_i, ag_j) \qquad (4)$$

To calculate the new emotion of agent ag_i at instant $t + 1$ and assuming that there is no external stimuli that may change agent ag_i emotion out of the rest of entities in the system, it will be calculated according to movement in the PAD space. To get this new emotion it is necessary to use the second law of *Newton's* or the fundamental principle of dynamics. Based on this law, the $\overrightarrow{EAF}_t(ag_i)$ is used to calculate the emotional acceleration of agent ag_i at instant t ($\overrightarrow{a}_t(ag_i)$). This acceleration is the emotional variation per time unit of agent ag_i emotion (Eq. 5).

$$\overrightarrow{EAF}_t(ag_i) = m(ag_i) \cdot \overrightarrow{a}_t(ag_i) \tag{5}$$

Once the emotional acceleration $\overrightarrow{a}_t(ag_i)$ is calculated, the emotional velocity of entity ag_i at instant t can be obtained ($\overrightarrow{v}_t(ag_i)$). This is a measure of the emotional propagation velocity within the PAD space (Eq. 6).

$$\overrightarrow{v}_t(ag_i) = \overrightarrow{a}_0(ag_i) + (\overrightarrow{a}_t(ag_i) \cdot t) \tag{6}$$

Finally, it is necessary to calculate the new PAD emotion for entity ag_i at instant $t + 1$ ($\overrightarrow{E}_{t+1}(ag_j)$) (Eq. 7).

$$\overrightarrow{E}_{t+1}(ag_j) = \overrightarrow{E}_t(ag_j) + (\overrightarrow{v}_t(ag_i) \cdot t) \tag{7}$$

It is important to consider that emotions within the PAD space do not present any opposition by the environment, e.g., there is no friction causing a reduction of speed. There is no inercia affecting the emotions within the PAD space thus, there are no oscillations. This swing up was eliminated by adding this restriction to the model **if $\overrightarrow{EAF}_t(ag_i) = 0$ then $\overrightarrow{v}_t(ag_i) = 0$.**

The proposed dynamic model allows us to model and represent the emotional contagion phenomena among different intelligent agents. Nevertheless, these entities typically are not alone in the environment but are part of a group of agents. Our proposal is to model not only how an agent is influenced by other agents but also how the group of agents as a whole can be emotionally affected by its components. To do this, we need to define a social emotional model, which allows to calculate and represent the social emotion of a group of intelligent entities. Next subsection presents the proposed model for representing social emotions.

3.1   Social Emotional Model

The aim of the social emotional model is to obtain the social emotion of a group of heterogeneous agents in an specific instant. This model is composed by a triplet that allows us to define the social emotion (SE) [21] for a group of n agents $Ag = \{ag_1, ag_2, ..., ag_n\}$ at instant t (Eq. 8).

$$SE_t(Ag) = (\overrightarrow{CE}_t(Ag), \overrightarrow{m}_t(Ag), \overrightarrow{\sigma}_t(Ag)) \tag{8}$$

where $\overrightarrow{CE}_t(Ag)$ is a vector in the PAD space, where each one of its components is calculated averaging the P, A, and D values, respectively of the n agents forming the set Ag (Eq. 9). These averages will enable us to determine where the central emotion (CE) of this group of agents is and to visualize it in the PAD space.

$$\bar{P}_t(Ag) = \frac{\sum_{i=1}^{n} P_t(ag_i)}{n}, \bar{A}_t(Ag) = \frac{\sum_{i=1}^{n} A_t(ag_i)}{n}, \bar{D}_t(Ag) = \frac{\sum_{i=1}^{n} D_t(ag_i)}{n},$$
$$\overrightarrow{CE}_t(Ag) = [\bar{P}_t(Ag), \bar{A}_t(Ag), \bar{D}_t(Ag)] \tag{9}$$

The $\overrightarrow{m}_t(Ag)$ can indicate if there exist agents having their emotional state far away from the central emotion. The Euclidean distance is used to calculate the maximum distances between the emotion of each agent respect to the $\overrightarrow{CE}$ (Eqs. 10, 11, 12 and 13) as follows.

$$mP_t(Ag) = max \left(\sqrt{(P_t(ag_i) - \bar{P}_t(Ag))^2} \right), \forall ag_i \in Ag \tag{10}$$

$$mA_t(Ag) = max \left(\sqrt{(A_t(ag_i) - \bar{A}_t(Ag))^2} \right), \forall ag_i \in Ag \tag{11}$$

$$mD_t(Ag) = max \left(\sqrt{(D_t(ag_i) - \bar{D}_t(Ag))^2} \right), \forall ag_i \in Ag \tag{12}$$

$$\overrightarrow{m}_t(Ag) = [mP_t(Ag), mA_t(Ag), mD_t(Ag)] \tag{13}$$

The $\overrightarrow{\sigma}(Ag)$ or standard deviation (SD) allows the calculation of the level of emotional dispersion of this group of agents around the central emotion $\overrightarrow{CE}(Ag)$ for each component of the PAD (Eq. 14).

$$\sigma P_t(Ag) = \sqrt{\frac{\sum_{i=1}^{n}(P_t(ag_i) - \bar{P}_t(Ag))^2}{n}}, \forall ag_i \in Ag$$
$$\sigma A_t(Ag) = \sqrt{\frac{\sum_{i=1}^{n}(A_t(ag_i) - \bar{A}_t(Ag))^2}{n}}, \forall ag_i \in Ag \tag{14}$$
$$\sigma D_t(Ag) = \sqrt{\frac{\sum_{i=1}^{n}(D_t(ag_i) - \bar{D}_t(Ag))^2}{n}}, \forall ag_i \in Ag$$

The result of each of the above equations can be represented as a vector (Eq. 15), which allow to determine the level of emotional dispersion.

$$\overrightarrow{\sigma}_t(Ag) = [\sigma P_t(Ag), \sigma A_t(Ag), \sigma D_t(Ag)] \tag{15}$$

From this definition, it can be deduced that:

1. if $\overrightarrow{\sigma}_t(Ag) >> [\mathbf{0,0,0}]$, the group has a high emotional dispersion, i.e. the members of the group have different emotional states.
2. if $\overrightarrow{\sigma}_t(Ag) \cong [\mathbf{0,0,0}]$, the group has a low emotional dispersion, this means that individuals have similar emotional states.

This model takes into account that at some stage you may have two or more agent groups and each group has its own social emotion or have a single group which wants to move to a target emotion. This will allow to measure the emotional distance between the current social emotional group and a possible emotional target. This approach can be used as a feedback in the decision making process in order to take actions to try to move the social emotion to a particular area of the *PAD* space or to allow that the emotional state of a group of agents can be approached or moved away from other groups of agents (Eq. 16).

$$\Delta_{SE} : SE_t(Ag^i), SE_{t'}(Ag^j) \rightarrow [0,1] \tag{16}$$

According to this profile, Eq. 17 shows how we calculate this emotional variation. The equation calculates three distances corresponding to the three components of the *SE*.

$$\Delta_{SE}(SE_t(Ag^i), SE_{t'}(Ag^j)) = \frac{1}{2}\Big(\omega_c\Delta(\overrightarrow{CE}_t(Ag^i), \overrightarrow{CE}_{t'}(Ag^j)) $$
$$+ \omega_d\Delta(\overrightarrow{m}_t(Ag^i), \overrightarrow{m}_{t'}(Ag^j)) \tag{17}$$
$$+ \omega_v\Delta(\overrightarrow{\sigma}_t(Ag^i), \overrightarrow{\sigma}_{t'}(Ag^j))\Big)$$

$$where \quad \omega_c + \omega_d + \omega_v = 1; \quad \omega_c, \omega_d, \omega_v \in [0,1] \tag{18}$$

and Δ calculates the distance between two vectors. As every dimension of the *PAD* space is bounded between $[-1,1]$, each Δ will give values between $[0,2]$. Therefore, Δ_{SE} will have a range between $[0,1]$. Calculating the distance among social emotions allows the study of the behaviour of emotional-based agents, either minimizing or maximizing the $\Delta_{SE}(SE_t(Ag^i), SE_{t'}(Ag^j))$ function. This way, it can be extrapolated the knowledge about if an agent group approaches or moves away from a specific emotional state. To achieve this, it is necessary to modify through stimuli the individual emotions of each agent and therefore changing the social emotion.

Using this model is possible to determine the emotional distance among different groups of agents or between the same group in different instants of time. This will allow us to measure the emotional distance between the current social emotional group and a possible emotional target. Moreover, the combination of the presented models allows us to model and represent the emotional contagion of a heterogeneous group of agents and observe how it influences the social emotion of that group of agents.

4   Case Study

Different tests have been done in order to validate the proposed model. Concretely, a simulation prototype was implemented in Python (using a *jupyter*[1] notebook with *numpy* and *matplotlib* libraries). The simulation experiments were conducted to evaluate different aspects and to try to show the correct behavior of the proposed model. Visualization of results has been done using three different kind of images:

- PAD space representation: a 3D representation of the emotional states in the PAD space. In each graphic current emotional states of each agent and the social emotion of the existing groups are represented.
- Physical space position representation: a 2D representation of the different agents, similar to a graph where each agent is a node situated in its physical coordinates (x,y). The size of the agent is inversely proportional to its empathy and if there is any affinity between agents, it will be represented by a link joining them. Finally, a sequence of colors (see Fig. 1) is defined as a way for representing the current emotion of each agent.
- Social emotional evolution: a 2D representation of the evolution of the different values composing the Social Emotion ($SE_t(Ag)$):
  - $\overrightarrow{CE}_t(Ag) = [\bar{P}_t(Ag), \bar{A}_t(Ag), \bar{D}_t(Ag)]$, represented in the figure as *CE P*, *CE A* and *CE D*, respectively.
  - $\overrightarrow{m}_t(Ag) = [mP_t(Ag), mA_t(Ag), mD_t(Ag)]$, represented in the figure as *maxDistP*, *maxDistA* and *maxDistD*, respectively.
  - $\overrightarrow{\sigma}_t(Ag) = [\sigma P_t(Ag), \sigma A_t(Ag), \sigma D_t(Ag)]$, represented in the figure as *stdP*, *stdA* and *stdD*, respectively.

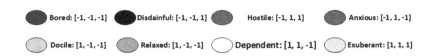

Fig. 1. Color representation for the different emotions. (Color figure online)

The experiments have been grouped into three situations changing the characteristics of the agents' groups. Moreover, each experiment includes different cases changing the affinity and empathy levels of the agents and also the physical distance among agents. The different proposed experiments are listed in Table 1.

4.1   First Experiment

The first experiment tried to evaluate how a group of heterogeneous agents evolve in the emotional space according to the dynamic model. To do this, we

---

[1] http://jupyter.org.

Table 1. Summary of proposed experiments

Experiment	# agents	Empathy		Affinity	Physical distance	
					Case 1	Case 2
1st	1 group of 10 agents	(a)	0	0	All agents have distance 0	All agents have random distances between 0 and 20
		(b)	0	1		
		(c)	1	0		
		(d)	1	1		
2nd	1 group of 10 agents (one agent with Empathy and Affinity = 0)	(a)	0	0	All agents have distance 0	All agents have random distances between 0 and 20
		(b)	0	1		
		(c)	1	0		
		(d)	1	1		
3rd	1 group of 5 agents and 1 group of 10 agents	(a)	0	0	All agents have distance 0	All agents have random distances between 0 and 20
		(b)	0	1		
		(c)	1	0		
		(d)	1	1		

implemented a set of 10 agents with a randomized initial emotional state. In order to evaluate the emotional behavior in the agent group, different situations have been defined changing the empathy and affinity values of each agent. Moreover the physical distance has also changed from a minimum distance of 0 m up to a maximum distance of 20 m. For reasons of brevity only two of the combinations are described.

First one is the corresponding to all the empathies and affinities between agents to 0, that is, a set of agents that has not any relationship between them and that are not moved by the emotions they feel around them. In this situation, the model works as expected, as the agents do not change their emotions.

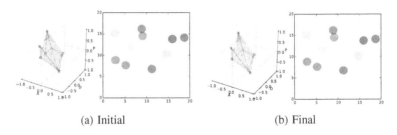

(a) Initial   (b) Final

Fig. 2. One group of 10 agents (with Empathy = 0, Affinity = 0 and distance between agents > 0)

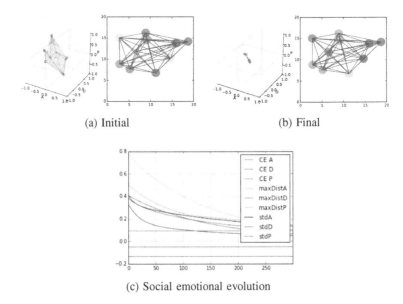

(a) Initial   (b) Final

(c) Social emotional evolution

Fig. 3. One group of 10 agents (with Empathy = 1, Affinity = 1 and all the agents with distance > 0)

Figure 2 shows one execution of this first situation of this example by a PAD space representation and a Physical space position representation for the initial and final stages of the execution.

Alternatively, Fig. 3 represents a situation where agents have a maximum value of the empathy and affinity levels. As we can see, the initial stage for the PAD values of the agents is the same of the previous situation (as can be observed in the corresponding PAD space representation). As this situation has different affinities and empathies, there exist links connecting agents in the Physical space position representation. This situation represents a group of agents that can be considered good friends and very sensitive to their friends emotions. As they are close enough (in a range of [0, 20] meters), their emotions are contaged tending to collapse in the PAD space (as is observed in the Fig. 4b - left). This evolution can be observed, at individual level, in the evolution of the PAD space representation, and in the evolution of the colors of the agents in the PAD space representation and in the Physical space position representation. On the other hand, Fig. 4c shows how fast is the convergence of the social emotional values during the experiment. The relevance of these experiments is the validation that all the situations have the expected behavior according to the proposed model.

4.2   Second Experiment

The second experiment is trying to observe how the emotional state of the group is disturbed by an odd agent without empathy and affinity with any agent. Scenarios proposed in this experiment are affected in the emotional states of the group due to the emotional response generated by the odd agent. As an example we can see the scenario proposed in Fig. 5a where all the agents of the group have the maximum value of the empathy and affinity levels except the odd agent (an initial situation similar to the one used in the Fig. 4a). As we can see, the final situation shows a non perfect grouping of all the agents due to the distorsion caused by the odd agent. This can be observed too in the temporal evolution of the social emotional values, if compared with Fig. 3.

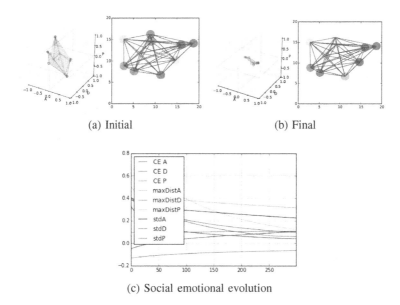

(a) Initial   (b) Final

(c) Social emotional evolution

Fig. 4. One group of 10 agents with an odd agent (with Empathy = 1, Affinity = 1 and all the agents with distance > 0). (Color figure online)

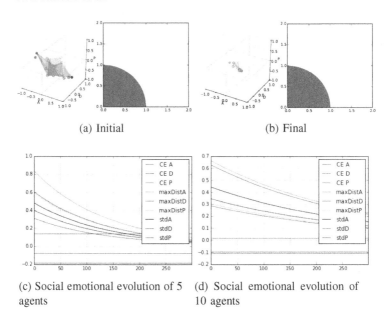

(a) Initial   (b) Final

(c) Social emotional evolution of 5   (d) Social emotional evolution of
agents   10 agents

Fig. 5. One group of 10 agents and another group of 5 agents (with Empathy = 1, Affinity = 1 and all the agents with distance = 0)

4.3   Third Experiment

Finally, the third experiment was centered in analyzing how two dissimilar groups of agents change their emotional states following the proposed model.

Figure 5 represents a scenario where there exists one group of ten agents and another group of five agents with the maximum level of empathy and affinity inside the group and the minimum distance between them. In this case, agents of each group are close to each other as can be expected. Regarding the temporal evolution, it is more evident in the case of the smallest group, where the social emotional parameters are more homogeneous than in the largest group.

5   Conclusions and Future Work

A new model for representing the emotional contagion has been presented in this paper. The goal of this model is to give a first approach for traction and emotional contagion in a group of intelligent entities. In this model the emotions of each agent are represented using PAD emotional model, which allows the representation of individual emotions in intelligent entities. The proposed model of dynamic emotion uses the individual emotions of each entity of a group, to obtain the level of emotional attraction between them. This model use the dynamic *Newton Law* and universal gravitation law, to calculate the attraction level $(\overrightarrow{EAF}_t(ag_i))$ and the new emotion of each agent $(\overrightarrow{E}_{t+1}(ag_j) = \overrightarrow{E}_t(ag_j) + (\overrightarrow{v}_t(ag_i) \cdot t))$. These definitions allow to calculate the emotional attraction between entities or groups.

Moreover, it is possible to obtain the resulting emotion of the attraction in a $(t + 1)$, as well as the emotional propagation velocity $(\overrightarrow{v}_t(ag_i))$. Considering these elements is possibly to know how is the emotional distribution among the agent group and to use this information to take on a decision and change your behaviour.

As future work, we want to introduce emotion recognition using face and physiological signals, using this information to allow us to obtain the human emotion and to simulate emotional contagion between humans and agents.

References

1. James, W.: What Is an Emotion? Wilder Publications, Radford (2007)
2. Fox, N.A., Calkins, S.D.: The development of self-control of emotion: intrinsic and extrinsic influences. Motiv. Emot. **27**(1), 7–26 (2003)
3. McCrae, R.R., John, O.P.: An introduction to the five-factor model and its applications. J. Pers. **60**(2), 175–215 (1992)
4. Ortony, A.: The Cognitive Structure of Emotions. Cambridge University Press, Cambridge (1990)
5. Plutchik, R.: A general psychoevolutionary theory of emotion. In: Kellerman, H., Plutchik, R. (eds.) Emotion: Theory, Research, and Experience. Theories of Emotion, vol. 1, pp. 3–33. Academic Press, New York (1980)
6. Mehrabian, A.: Analysis of affiliation-related traits in terms of the PAD temperament model. J. Psychol. **131**(1), 101–117 (1997)
7. Busso, C., Deng, Z., et al.: Analysis of emotion recognition using facial expressions, speech and multimodal information. In: Proceedings of the 6th International Conference on Multimodal Interfaces, ICMI 2004, pp. 205–211. ACM, New York (2004)
8. Palo, H.K., Mohanty, M.N., Chandra, M.: Use of different features for emotion recognition using MLP network. In: Sethi, I.K. (ed.) Computational Vision and Robotics. Advances in Intelligent Systems and Computing, vol. 332, pp. 7–15. Springer, India (2015)
9. Bos, D.O.: EEG-based emotion recognition. In: The Influence of Visual and Auditory Stimuli, pp. 1–17 (2006)
10. Saunier, J., Jones, H.: In: Proceedings of the 2014 International Conference on Autonomous Agents and Multi-agent Systems, pp. 645–652 (2014)
11. Bosse, T., Duell, R., Memon, Z.A., Treur, J., Van Der Wal, C.N.: A multi-agent model for emotion contagion spirals integrated within a supporting ambient agent model. In: Yang, J.-J., Yokoo, M., Ito, T., Jin, Z., Scerri, P. (eds.) PRIMA 2009. LNCS, vol. 5925, pp. 48–67. Springer, Heidelberg (2009)
12. Costa, Â., Castillo, J.C., Novais, P., Fernández-Caballero, A., Simoes, R.: Sensor-driven agenda for intelligent home care of the elderly. Expert Syst. Appl. **39**(15), 12192–12204 (2012)
13. Costa, A., Novais, P., Simoes, R.: A caregiver support platform within the scope of an ambient assisted living ecosystem. Sensors **14**(3), 5654–5676 (2014)
14. Van Minh, L., Adam, C., Canal, R., Gaudou, B., Tuong Vinh, H., Taillandier, P.: Simulation of the emotion dynamics in a group of agents in an evacuation situation. In: Desai, N., Liu, A., Winikoff, M. (eds.) PRIMA 2010. LNCS, vol. 7057, pp. 604–619. Springer, Heidelberg (2012)

15. Banarjee, S., Grosan, C., Abraham, A.: Emotional ant based modeling of crowd dynamics. In: Symbolic and Numeric Algorithms for Scientific Computing, 2005, SYNASC, p. 8. IEEE (2005)

16. Hawe, G.I., Coates, G., Wilson, D.T., Crouch, R.S.: Agent-based simulation for large-scale emergency response: a survey of usage and implementation. ACM Comput. Surv. (CSUR) **45**(1), 8 (2012)

17. Lungu, V.: Newtonian emotion system. In: Fortino, G., Badica, C., Malgeri, M., Unland, R. (eds.) Intelligent Distributed Computing VI. Studies in Computational Intelligence, vol. 446, pp. 307–315. Springer, Heidelberg (2013)

18. Bosse, T., Hoogendoorn, M., et al.: Modelling collective decision making in groups and crowds: integrating social contagion and interacting emotions, beliefs and intentions. JAAMAS **27**(1), 52–84 (2013)

19. Barsade, S.G.: The ripple effect: emotional contagion and its influence on group behavior. Adm. Sci. Q. **47**(4), 644–675 (2002)

20. McDonald, N.M., Messinger, D.S., Acerbi, A., Lombo, J.A., Sanguineti, J.J.: The development of empathy: how, when, and why. In: Moral Behavior and Free Will: A Neurobiological and Philosophical Aprroach, pp. 341–368 (2011)

21. Rincon, J.A., Julian, V., Carrascosa, C.: Social emotional model. In: Demazeau, Y., Decker, K.S., Pérez, J.B., De la Prieta, F. (eds.) PAAMS 2015. LNCS, vol. 9086, pp. 199–210. Springer, Heidelberg (2015)

Decentralized Group Analytical Hierarchical Process on Multilayer Networks by Consensus

Miguel Rebollo[(✉)], Alberto Palomares, and Carlos Carrascosa

Universitat Politècnica de València, Camino de Vera s/n, 46022 Valencia, Spain
{mrebollo,apalomares,carrasco}@dsic.upv.es

Abstract. The analytical hierarchical process (AHP) is a multi-criteria, decision-making process that has demonstrated to be of a high utility to achieve complex decisions. This work presents a method to apply it in grupal decisions, where the weights that each user assigns to the criteria are different and private. A combination of consensus process and gradient ascent is used to reach a common agreement that optimizes the utility of the decision using the information exchanged in the local neighborhood exclusively.

The AHP problem is modeled through a multilayer network. Each one of the criteria are negotiated by consensus with the direct neighbors on each layer of the network. Furthermore, each node performs a transversal gradient ascent and corrects locally the deviations from the personal decision to keep the best option.

The process locates the global optimal decision, taking into account that this global function is never calculated nor known by any of the participants. If there is not a global optimal decision where all the participants have a not null utility, but a set of suboptimal decisions, they are automatically divided into different groups that converges into these suboptimal decisions.

Keywords: Complex networks · Consensus · Gradient descent · Analytical hierarchical process

1 Introduction

The Analytic Hierarchical Process (AHP) is a muli-objective optimization method. The decision makers provide subjective evaluations regarding to the relative importance of the different criteria and the preference of each alternative for each criteria [12]. The result is a ranking of the considered alternatives that includes the relative score assigned to each one of these alternatives. The main advantage of this process is that it allows (i) to organize the information in a efficient and clear way, even for complex problems; and (ii) synthesize and visualize the effects of changes in the levels or preferences. Furthermore, it is possible to measure the consistence of the model, since a perfect consistency is very difficult to be achieved due to the subjectivity introduced to judge the relative importance of each criteria.

© Springer International Publishing Switzerland 2016
Y. Demazeau et al. (Eds.): PAAMS 2016, LNAI 9662, pp. 183–194, 2016.
DOI: 10.1007/978-3-319-39324-7_16

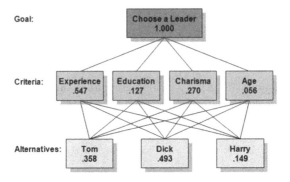

Fig. 1. Example of criteria hierarchy for a AHP

The AHP can be used for a single used to take a decision, but also for a group of people, such as a committee or a group of experts, to achieve a common agreement. There are works that extends the original AHP problem. But these approaches assume that all the actors are able to exchange information. This work proposes a method for group decision making based on AHP, where the participants are connected though a network and they interact exclusively with their direct neighborbors. A combination of consensus [18] and gradient ascent is used as optimization method [14].

The proposed solution considers each criterion as a layer in a multiplex network. A consensus process is performed in each layer, trying to achieve a common decision for the corresponding criteria for all the participants. Simultaneously, a gradient ascent is executed across the layers, trying to keep the preferred value for each one of the participants in the decision. This joint process converges to the desired, agreed decision. This decision is the optimal decision of the group if some conditions are fulfilled.

The rest of the paper is organized as follows. Section 2 explains the related techniques that have been combined and used to define the final proposed method to solve AHP in a decentralized and distributed way. The method is detailed and analyzed in Sect. 3 and, finally, Sect. 4 shows the results. Section 5 closes this work with the conclusions.

2 Related Works

2.1 The AHP Process

The AHP begins with the definition of the criteria used to evaluate the alternatives, organized as a hierarchy. The importance of each criteria is defined through its weight $w^\alpha \in [0, 1]$. For example, let's assume that a new leader has to be chosen among three candidates: Tom, Dick and Harry. To evaluate them, their age, experience, education and charisma are going to be considered. The criteria hierarchy and the weights associated to each criterion α are show in Fig. 1.

Table 1. (left) Local priority matrix with the relative importance of each candidate regarding to their experience. (right) Final priorities for the selected candidates. Dick is selected candidate, with the higher global value

	Tom	Dick	Harry	Priority (l_i^α)
Tom	1	1/4	4	**0.217**
Dick	4	1	9	**0.717**
Harry	1/4	1/9	1	**0.066**

Candidate	Exp	Edu	Char	Age	Goal
Tom	0.119	0.024	0.201	0.015	*0.358*
Dick	0.392	0.010	0.052	0.038	**0.492**
Harry	0.036	0.093	0.017	0.004	*0.149*

Once the criteria are defined, a pairwise matrix is created, assigning a relative judgement or preference value to each pair of alternatives. The value a_{ij} represents the preference of the alternative i over the alternative j for the considered criteria, and $a_{ij} = 1/a_{ji}$.

From this pairwise matrix, the local priority l_i^α is calculated, which defines the preference of the alternative i for the criterium α. The local priority is calculated as the values of the principal right eigenvector of the matrix (Table 1).

Finally, all the local priorities are synthesize across all the criteria in order to calculate the final, global priority p_i for each alternative. There exist many methods to calculate the priorities. The most usual ones are the mean of the rows of he pairwise matrix to calculate l_i^α, and the weighted average $p_i = \sum w^\alpha l_i^\alpha$ for the global priority.

There are approaches to extend AHP into grupal decision problems, but they are centralized solutions and use complete information. In this work, the participants are connected through a network that bounds the possible information exchanges. An agreement in the final decision is reached through a combination of a consensus process and a gradient ascent (see Fig. 2).

2.2   Consensus on Networks

Consensus means reaching an agreement on the value of a variable which might represent, for example, a physical quantity, a control parameter, or a price. Agents are connected through an acquaintances network whose topology constraints the possible interaction between them. This is one of the most promising research subjects in the MAS area that is currently emerging [8,9,11,13,21].

The theoretical framework for solving consensus problems in agent networks was formally introduced by Olfati–Saber and Murray [17,18]. Let G be a graph of order n with the set of entities E as nodes. Let (G, X) be the state of a network, where $X = (x_1, \ldots, x_n)^T \in \mathbb{R}^n$ and x_i is a real value that is associated with the node $e_i \in E$. A consensus algorithm is an interaction rule that specifies the information exchange between the agents and all of their neighbors in the network in order to reach the agreement. Consensus is reached in the network when $x_1 = \ldots = x_n$. It has been demonstrated that a convergent and distributed consensus algorithm in discrete-time exists and it converges to the average of their initial values.

$$x_i(t+1) = x_i(t) + \varepsilon \sum_{j \in N_i} (x_j(t) - x_i(t)) \tag{1}$$

where N_i denotes the set formed by all nodes connected to the node i (neighbors of i) and ε is the step size, $0 < \varepsilon < \min_i 1/d_i$, being d_i the degree of node i. This expression, when is executed by the agents, converges to the average of their initial values.

An interesting modification of the consensus introduces weights in the agents, which represent their importance in the system. Let $w = (w_1, w_2, \ldots, w_n)^T$ be a vector with the weight associated to each node. The following algorithm (see [17], p. 225) can be used to obtain the value of the weighted average consensus

$$x_i(t+1) = x_i(t) + \frac{\varepsilon}{w_i} \sum_{j \in N_i} (x_j(t) - x_i(t)) \tag{2}$$

where N_i denotes the set formed by all nodes connected to the node i (neighbors of i) and ε is the step size. The algorithm converges to the weighted average of the initial values of the state of each agent $x_i(0)$ if $\varepsilon < \min_i d_i/w_i$, being d_i the degree of node i [19].

Other works have extended the consensus algorithm for its application in large-scale systems [5], for its usage as a clustering technique [15], for treating problems derived from a failure in communications [10], or for applications in arbitrary directed graphs [7]. However, the application of the consensus algorithm to dynamic networks, where participants may enter and leave during the consensus process, is still an open issue.

2.3   Distributed Gradient Descent

Consensus leads to the average value of the network. But agreement processes frequently involve the optimization of some global utility function. Centralized methods usually require data fusion and distribution along the network, which supposes a high computational and communication cost when the systems scale. Decentralized approaches take advantage of scalability, adaptation to dynamic network topologies and can handle data privacy. Coupled optimization problems can be solved using a variety of distributed algorithms. A classical way is to iteratively refine an estimate of the optimizer using incremental subgradient methods [1]. It is used in static networks, where the topology does not change during the process. Matei [16] studies how the degree distribution in random networks affects the optimal value deviation, defining some metrics to evaluate the quality of the approximated solution. One way of accelerating the consensus process has been proposed by Pereira [20]. This new method is applied to random sensor networks. It is based on the study of the network spectral radius, requiring a complete view of the network to obtain that radius. The relation among the connection probabilities in a random network and the convergence speed has also been studied [20]. This relation also determines the optimal ε value that minimizes the convergence time. The work of Zanella [2] applies the Newton–Raphson method to distributed convex optimization problems. To minimize the optimization function, it uses a consensus process that converges to the exact solution in contrast to the subgradient–based methods. This last work has been

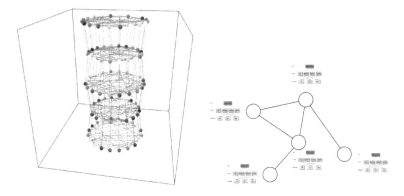

Fig. 2. (Left) Multilayer network example with 20 agents and 5 layers. (Right) Example of network, where each agent has its own values for the criteria an a preferred option.

extended to consider asynchronous transmission [3] and the multi-dimensional case in order to optimize an n-dimensional function [4].

The combination of consensus and gradient models can be expressed as a two step process [14]

$$x_i(t+1) = \sum_j w_{ij} x_j(t) - \alpha \nabla f_i(x_i(t)) \qquad (3)$$

where $W = [w_{ij}]$ is a symmetric, double stochastic matrix (note that it has the same properties demanded to the consensus process to converge) and $\nabla f_i(x_i(t))$ performs a gradient descent to minimize a cost function.

2.4   Multilayer Networks

Multilayer networks are a recent formalism created to model the phenomena that appears in complex networks in a more realistic way. Usually, relations do not occur isolated in one network and notions such as network of networks, multilayer networks, multiplex networks or interdependent networks are defined. In multilayer networks, links of different type exist among the nodes. For example, in a group of people, links representing friendship, working relations or family ties can be defined. Or in a communication model, different media, such as phone and mail, can be considered. Each one of this different links form a network in one layer. The interdependence among layers is defined through cross links between the nodes that represent the same entity in each network. These cross links models the transference of information that passes from one layer to the others.

A multilayer network (see Fig. 2, left) is formally defined [6] as a pair $M = (G, C)$ where $G = \{G^1, \ldots, G^p\}$ is a family of graphs $G^\alpha = (E^\alpha, L^\alpha), \forall \alpha \in [1, p]$ called layers, and $C = \{L^{\alpha\beta} \subseteq E^\alpha \times E^\beta, \forall \alpha, \beta \in [1, p], \alpha \neq \beta\}$ is the set of connections between two different layers G^α and G^β. The elements of each L^α

are called *intralayer* connections and the elements of C are the *interlayer* ones or *crossed layers*. The characteristic of the multilayer network is that all the layers have the same set of nodes $E^1 = \ldots = E^p = E$ and the cross layers are defined between equivalent nodes $L^{\alpha\beta} = \{(e^\alpha, e^\beta), \forall e \in E; \alpha, \beta \in [1, p]\}$.

In the present work, multilayer networks are used to represent the different criteria that form the decision. Each criterion will be negotiated in one layer.

3   Decentralized AHP Using Consensus in Multiplex Networks

Lets consider the participants connected in an undirected network. The topology is not relevant, but all the nodes must be connected in one component. Lets consider only the criteria that are the leafs of the hierarchy defined for the AHP problem, with $\sum w^\alpha = 1$, different and private for each one of the participants. Lets create a multilayer network, where each layer represents one of the final criteria. Each layer is weighted using the weight defined for the criteria. For example, the problem exposed in Fig. 1 has 4 criteria: experience, education, charisma and age. Therefore, a network with 4 layers is created. Furthermore, the weights associated to each one of them are 0.547, 0.127, 0.270 and 0.056 respectively. An utility function can be defined for each preference of the participants using a gaussian function with mean l_i^α and standard deviation $1 - w_i^\alpha$ (see Sect. 3.1). This function is used by the participant to perform the gradient ascent, trying to keep as near as possible to its preferred distribution.

Each participant has its own criteria and the goal of the system is to agree the best candidate according to all the agents involves in the decision. Therefore, a consensus process is executed in each layer in order to find the weighted average. But this process considers the criteria as independent and it does not converge in the value that optimize the decision. The combination of the consensus process with a gradient ascent, as it is defined in Eq. 4, corrects the deviation produced by the consensus and each participant tries to maintain the decision that maximizes its own local utility. This decentralized process leads to a consensus value near to the global optimum, considered as the sum of the local utility functions. Observe that this global utility function is never calculated and the participants reach this value exchanging information with their direct neighbors.

$$x_i^\alpha(t+1) = x_i^\alpha + \overbrace{\frac{\varepsilon}{w_i^\alpha} \sum_{j \in N_i^\alpha} (x_j^\alpha(t) - x_i^\alpha(t))} + \underbrace{\varphi \nabla u_i(x_i^1(t), \ldots, x_i^p(t))} \quad (4)$$

The result of the process is a common and agreed priority for the alternative evaluated in each layer. All the alternatives can be evaluated at the same time using independent consensus process if a vector of preferences is exchanged instead one alternative at a time.

If the global utility function is a smooth one and all the participants have an utility $u_i > 0$ for any final decision, the proposed method converges to the optimal decision for the group. But if there is no point in which all the participants have a positive utility, the resulting global utility function will have one (or more that one) local maximum that may alter the convergence process. In those cases, we allow the nodes to break the links with those neighbors that are pulling them to an undesired area. To do that, it is enough with breaking the communications and stopping exchange information with them. In this case, the network can be split in several groups and each one of them will reach a different decision.

The advantage of this distributed approach is that avoids the bottlenecks problems that arise in mediated solutions. Individual agents are not conscious of a final, global solution, but of the convergence to an agreed compromise among its near neighbors. Furthermore, the system is scalable since new nodes can be added without additional notifications to the rest of the network.

3.1   Utility Function

Utility functions have some common properties in any optimization problem: independence, completeness, transitivity and continuity. As we propose a model with cooperative agents, we'll assume that the utility functions have a maximum and this maximum will be the starting point for all the agents. Furthermore, the function must be a decreasing one. The normal distribution fulfills all this properties. Therefore, it has been the selected one for the utility function u_i of the agents. We can assume that agents are initially situated in its maximum value, which corresponds with the mean value of the utility function. The weight assigned to the term can be used in the dispersion measure. An agent does not desire changes in its more relevant term. Therefore, any change in its value must decrease drastically its utility. On the other hand, the agents would allow changes in terms with low importance, which might slightly decrease their utilities. In the case of a normal distribution, the standard deviation is the parameter that rules this behavior. If we use $\sigma_i^\alpha = 1 - w_i^\alpha$ we obtain the desired behavior. The utility function is defined as follows:

$$u_i^\alpha(x_i^\alpha) = e^{-\frac{1}{2}\left(\frac{x_i^\alpha - l_i^\alpha}{1 - w_i^\alpha}\right)^2} \tag{5}$$

All this individual functions are combined in one unique utility function for the agent.

$$u_i(x_i) = \prod_\alpha u_i^\alpha(x_i^\alpha) \tag{6}$$

This definition corresponds to a renormalized multi-dimensional gaussian distribution such that the maximum utility for the agent i is $u_i(x_i(0)) = 1$.

The global utility of the system is the sum of the individual utilities of the agents. This value is never calculated in the system directly and the function is known by none of the participants in the agreement.

$$U = \sum_i u_i(x_i) \tag{7}$$

4   Application Example

Lets consider a group of 9 agents that are going to take a decision using AHP. A bi-dimensional example has been chosen to be able to represent it graphically, so just 2 criteria will be considered. Figure 3 shows the utility function calculated from the initial preferences of each participant.

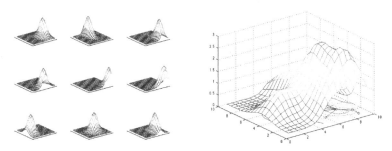

Fig. 3. (Left) Local utilities $u_i(x_i)$ as defined in Eq. 6 from the AHP criteria for each of one the 9 participants. (Right) Final global utility function U (Eq. 7) to locate the optimal decision, defined as the sum of the individual, local utility functions. These functions is not calculated, nor known by the participants, but the process converges to the maximum of this function.

Figure 4 shows the initial and final status of the process. When the combined process stops, all the participants have reached the same point, which corresponds to the common decision agreed by the agents. For this solution to exist, the only condition is that all the participants have a positive utility $u_i > 0$ along the complete solution space.

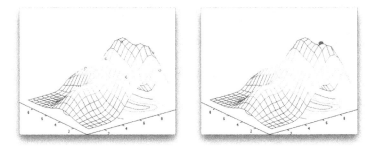

Fig. 4. Initial and final states for a decision in a group of 9 participants using two criteria. An agreed solution exists and it is located correctly by the group using local information only.

Figure 5 shows the evolution of the value for each criterion (left and right) for each one of the participants (in a different colour) along the process. It converges to the final decision. If these values are considered as the x and y coordinates, it matches with the point that corresponds to the solution in Fig. 4.

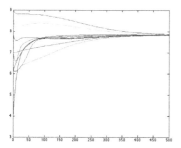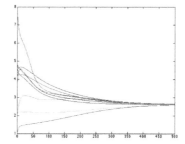

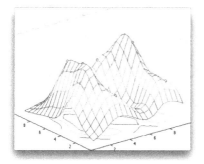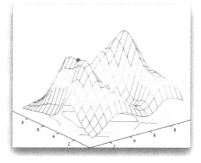

Fig. 5. Evolution of the values for each criteria for a each one of the participants. The convergence is guaranteed if $\forall i \; u_i > 0$ in all the solution space

Fig. 6. Example of convergence to a suboptimal solution because participants refuses to move towards the best solution for the group since its has zero-utility for some individual agent.

Nevertheless, when this condition is not fulfilled when some of the participants has an utility equal to zero in some areas of the solution space. In that case, the shape of the global utility function will show peaks and valleys, with local optimal values. Then, the convergence to the optimal solution is not guaranteed and, as it is shown in Fig. 6, the process halts on any value, depending on the initial preferences and the distribution of the utility functions over the solution space.

Our proposal to solve this additional problem is to allow break links among the participants. When a participant detects that the solution guides towards a point with zero-utility, the agent can decide to break the link to those neighbors who are pulling from the preferences. As Fig. 7 shows, in this case the network is broken into groups, each one of them converges to a different agreement. The optimal decision is located by the group formed by those participants whose utility function is positive in the best solution. Actually, this solution is reached if the agents with zero-utility are just removed from the system. Despite doing so, we allow this participants to reach another decision forming a separate group.

Figure 8 shows the evolution of the criteria in such a case. It can be clearly observed how more that one decision is taken. In this case, the network is divided

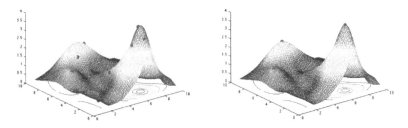

Fig. 7. Initial and final states for an AHP process allowing to break links and reconnect to near neighbors. This solutions guarantees the convergence of a subgroup to the best possible decision, along with another agreements around suboptimal solutions.

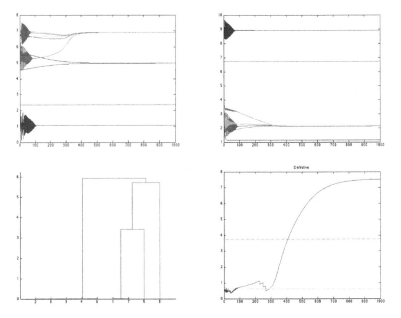

Fig. 8. (Top) evolution of the criteria and convergence into separated groups. (Bottom) Group division and global utility obtained by this process

into 4 groups: the bigger one arrives to the best decision, and another group formed by two agents arrives to another private agreement. Finally, another two participants remain isolated. The dendrogram of this figure shows the group formation, and the last graphic shows the global utility value, taking into account the sum of the solutions reached by the different groups.

Finally, the performance of the algorithm has been analyzed using networks of different sizes. The obtained results are shown in Fig. 9. Experiments were run in a 3.2 GHz Intel Core i5, with 8 Gb of RAM. Random networks from 100 to 1000 nodes have been generated, with 10 repetitions of each size. The AHP process has been executed over these networks and the obtained execution time has been averaged. The execution time takes into account the AHP process exclusively. The time needed to create the network and define the individual weights for the different criteria and alternatives are not included. The experiments show a quadratic cost for the algorithm in the studied network sizes. Bigger networks need to be analyzed. The main drawback of the current implementation is that the calculation of the φ parameter (see Eq. 4) to guarantee the convergence of the method is a centralized one (the φ parameter is related with the value of the Lipschitz constant for each utility function) and the cost is too high to be calculated in bigger networks (beyond 4 magnitude orders with respect to the execution time).

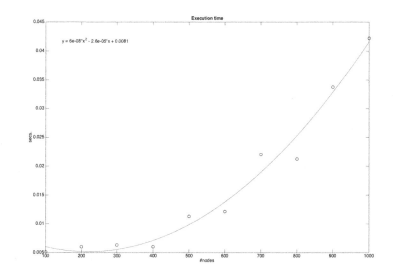

Fig. 9. Execution time of the algorithm with different network sizes

5   Conclusions

This work has presented a method based on a combination of consensus and gradient ascent to solve group AHP in a decentralized environment, where the participants in the decision making process exchanges their preferences with their direct neighbors to reach an agreement that allows the team to select the alternative with the highest utility for the group. This work can be easily extended to the case of having networks of preferences (ANP) or the case of changes in the local priorities or the weights of the criteria during the process.

Acknowledgements. This work is supported by the PROMETEOII/2013/019 and TIN2015-65515-C4-1-R projects of the spanish government.

References

1. Johansson, B., et al.: Subgradient methods and consensus algorithms for solving convex optimization problems. In: Proceedings of IEEE CDC 2008, pp. 4185–4190 (2008)
2. Zanella, F., et al.: Newton-raphson consensus for distributed convex optimization. In: Proceedings of IEEE CDC-ECC 2011, pp. 5917–5922 (2011)
3. Zanella, F., et al.: Asynchronous newton-raphson consensus for distributed convex optimization. In: Proceedings of IFAC NecSys 2012 (2012)
4. Zanella, F., et al.: Multidimensional newton-raphson consensus for distributed convex optimization. In: Proceedings of ACC 2012, pp. 1079–1084 (2012)
5. Askari-Sichani, O., Jalili, M.: Large-scale global optimization through consensus of opinions over complex networks. Complex Adapt. Syst. Model. **1**(1), 11 (2013)
6. Boccaletti, S., Bianconi, G., Criado, R., del Genio, C., Gómez-Gardeñesi, J., Romance, M., Sendiña-Nadalj, I., Wang, Z., Zanin, M.: The structure and dynamics of multilayer networks. Phys. Rep. **544**, 1–122 (2014)
7. Cai, K., Ishii, H.: Average consensus on arbitrary strongly connected digraphs with dynamic topologies. In: Proceedings of ACC 2012, pp. 14–19 (2012)
8. Cavalcante, R., Rogers, A., Jennings, N.: Consensus acceleration in multiagent systems with the chebyshev semi-iterative method. In: Proceedings of AAMAS 2011, pp. 165–172 (2011)
9. Elhage, N., Beal, J.: Laplacian-based consensus on spatial computers. In: AAMAS, pp. 907–914 (2010)
10. Frasca, P., Carli, R., Fagnani, F., Zampieri, S.: Average consensus on networks with quantized communication. Int. J. Robust Nonlin. **19**(16), 1787–1816 (2009)
11. Hu, H.X., et al.: Group consensus in multi-agent systems with hybrid protocol. J. Franklin Inst. **350**(3), 575–597 (2013)
12. Ishizaka, A., Labib, A.: Review of the main developments in the analytic hierarchy process. Expert Syst. Appl. **38**(11), 14336–14345 (2011)
13. Ji, Z., Lin, H., Yu, H.: Leaders in multi-agent controllability under consensus algorithm and tree topology. Syst. Cont. Lett. **61**(9), 918–925 (2012)
14. Yuan, K., Ling, Q., Yin, W.: On the convergence of decentralized gradient descent. Technical report. Report 13–61, UCLA CAM (2014)
15. Lancichinetti, A., Fortunato, S.: Consensus clustering in complex networks. CoRR abs/1203.6093 (2012)
16. Matei, I., Baras, J.: Performance evaluation of the consensus-based distributed subgradient method under random communication topologies. IEEE Sig. Proc. **5**(4), 754–771 (2011)
17. Olfati-Saber, R., Fax, J.A., Murray, R.M.: Consensus and cooperation in networked multi-agent systems. Proc. IEEE **95**(1), 215–233 (2007)
18. Olfati-Saber, R., Murray, R.M.: Consensus problems in networks of agents with switching topology and time-delays. IEEE TAC **49**(9), 1520–1533 (2004)
19. Pedroche, F., Rebollo, M., Carrascosa, C., Palomares, A.: On the convergence of weighted-average consensus. CoRR arxiv:1203.6093 [math.OC] (2013)
20. Pereira, S., Pages-Zamora, A.: Consensus in correlated random wireless sensor networks. IEEE Sig. Proc. **59**(12), 6279–6284 (2011)
21. Salazar-Ramirez, N., Rodríguez-Aguilar, J.A., Arcos, J.L.: Robust coordination in large convention spaces. AI Commun. **23**, 357–372 (2010)

Simulating Reputation with Regulatory Policies: The Case of San Jerónimo Vegetable Garden, Seville, Spain

Henrique Donâncio N. Rodrigues[1]([⊠]), Diana F. Adamatti[1],
Graçaliz P. Dimuro[1], Glenda Dimuro[2], and Esteban de Manuel Jerez[2]

[1] Centro de Ciências Computacionais, Universidade Federal do Rio Grande,
Rio Grande City, Brazil
henriquedonancio@gmail.com
[2] Depto de Expresión Gráfica Arquitectónica, Universidad de Sevilla, Seville, Spain

Abstract. This paper presents a reputation model applied to a multi-agent system for simulating regulatory policies and reputation of the social organization of San Jerónimo Vegetable Garden, located in Seville, Spain. We have used BDI agents with fuzzy beliefs for the investment and satisfaction analysis of services, as well as a reputation model as a performance measure of their activities within the project.

1 Introduction

This work is part of a project that aims at the development of MAS (Multi-Agent System) tools for simulating production processes and social management of urban ecosystems, in particular, the project of the Urban Vegetable Garden San Jerónimo (SJVG), located in Seville, Spain, coordinated by the ONG Ecologistas en Acción.

The project has the purpose to develop simulation tools to analyze, evaluate and/or experiment some processes to assist in fostering social participation in collective practices in urban organic agriculture. Currently, the beneficiaries of this project are retired gardeners, local school students and associations for scientific experiments [4–6].

In previous works of the research group, several aspects of the modeling of the social organization of the garden, modeling of the routines of the roles of this organization, special models of agents, modeling of normative policy, among other aspects, were introduced (see, e.g., [13,17–19]). These works were developed using JaCaMo platform (Jason, CArtAgO and Moise+) [1,2] and some extensions developed for the this specific modeling purpose (see, e.g., [14]).

This paper presents a reputation model applied to a MAS to simulate service exchanges that do not involve material goods, and also the internal normative policy of the organization of the SJVG, taking the metric of social performance, the reputation of the agent the project context. Exchanges that do not involve material goods are those related to hiring and/or performing services, generating only virtual debits and credits.

© Springer International Publishing Switzerland 2016
Y. Demazeau et al. (Eds.): PAAMS 2016, LNAI 9662, pp. 195–206, 2016.
DOI: 10.1007/978-3-319-39324-7_17

The reputation model adopted is an extension based on fuzzy logic of models such as REGRET [9,16]. The reputation analysis is divided into three dimensions: Social dimension, Individual Dimension and Ontological Dimension, as proposed in REGRET model. In the Social Dimension, the effectiveness of the agent is analyzed to its social group; in the Individual Dimension is analyzed the direct exchange between the agents. Finally, in the Ontological Dimension, the Social and Individual Dimension are combined for a final analysis.

We have implemented the model with Jason platform [3], an interpreter language of the AgentSpeak(L), based on BDI Architecture [10,11] together with the CArtAgO framework [12] and the MSPP (Modeling and Simulation of Public Policies) framework [20]. We used a hybrid agent model, namely, BDI-Fuzzy agents, introduced in [7,8].

The paper is organized as follows. Section 2 presents the technology support to this research, involving the JaCaMo platform and the MSPP framework. Section 3 presents the reputation model proposed and the Sect. 4 presents the preliminary simulations of MAS based on SJVG, as well as preliminary results. Section 5 concludes the paper.

2 Technological Tools

2.1 The JaCaMo Platform

The JaCaMo [2] platform is a framework for Multi-Agent Systems programming consists of three tools: Jason, CArtAgO and MOISE+. Jason [3] is an AgentSpeak(L) language interpreter based on the BDI architecture. An important aspect of this platform is its implementation in Java and therefore cross-platform. The communication between agents in Jason is based on the theory of speech acts. The agents to communicate, generate beliefs and these in turn can trigger plans.

CArtAgO framework (Common ARTifact infrastructure for AGents Open environments) [12] is based on Agents and Artifacts (A & A) to model and design Multiagent Systems. With this tool one can create structured artifacts in open spaces where agents can come together in order to work in conjunction. Artifacts are resources and tools, built dynamically, manipulated and used by agents to support/perform their individual and collective activities.

The MOISE+ organizational model [1] is a tool in order to model the organization of a MAS. Consists in the specification of three dimensions: structural, where roles are defined and linked inheritance and groups; functional, where a set for global plans and missions are established so that the goals are achieved; and deontic dimension, which is responsible for defining what role has obligation or permission to perform each task.

2.2 The Framework MSPP and Its Application in the SJVG

The MSPP framework [20] inserts public policies using the artifacts format in CArtAgO model. There are included in this framework two types of normative artifacts: NormObrig and NormPrb, modeling obligation and prohibition norms, respectively.

The framework also has pre-inserted agents to run/check those norms. They are the government agent, responsible for issuing the norms, social agents who are subject to the regulation and seek to achieve own goals, and also the detectors/effectors government agents responsible for detecting compliance of the norms as well as verify the use of the environmental resources, applying possible sanctions to actions that characterize the noncompliance of norms and regulating the resources available in the environment.

In a preliminary study, we have used the MSPP framework in the regulatory policies for the SJVG organization, with some modifications to the framework, which were discussed in [13]. Among those modifications, there was the inclusion of two new types of norms, namely, the permission norms and the right norms, and the composition of norms.

3   The Proposed Reputation Model

The participants of this project are gardeners and aspiring gardeners, who are the social agents. Technical and secretariat assume the role of government agents, responsible for verifying the norms applicable to social agents. The gardeners, once included in the project, have the right to use the plot (designated areas to cultivation and management of the garden) for a period of two years (renewable), subject to compliance of the norms and rules in the regulation set by the ONG. The regulation of the vegetable garden is a set which has a total of forty norms to establish better interaction between users and the administration, besides protect their rights and guide their actions.

The reputation model follows the structure adopted in REGRET [16], where the reputation is a composition of three dimensions: Social Dimension, Individual Dimension and Ontological Dimension.

Fuzzy reputation models already exist in the literature as [15] and others targeted to e-commerce and P2P networks. This approach however extends existing ones in the sense that Regret is able to provide metrics for public policies and collective environment scenarios.

3.1   Social Dimension

The social dimension evaluates collective aspects related to the agent. In [9], this evaluation is done by analyzing the effectiveness of the agent in relation to norms (obligations), the agent's participation and results.

When the agent to fulfill an obligation, participate in meetings, or its collective results are favorable, this indicates a positive and cumulative value $+1$, otherwise 0. The obligations are those related norms of the organization. Participation is on the convened meetings and assemblies that the agent participates. The results are the collective results that the agent gets.

In the SJVG project, agents must perform certain obligations, such as the monthly payment and renewal of their registration, besides the compliance of the norms. The participation is also a factor to be taken into account, because the project requires that the agents participate in meetings that are used to discuss and guide their practices. The results are all actions that the agent will perform collectively.

Each agent has a belief related to an individual value for the importance degree of these aspects to it, which are shared among the group. An individual evaluation is evaluated by [9]:

$$evaluation(\alpha) = \frac{\gamma p(\alpha) + \delta o(\alpha) + \epsilon r(\alpha)}{\gamma + \delta + \epsilon} \qquad (1)$$

where: the factors γ, δ and ϵ define the importance of participation, obedience and results, respectively.

These factors are independent between the social agents, and they may take values in the interval $[1, 10]$, thus defining the degree of relevance that the agent determines for the attribute multiplied by the factor. Therefore, the minimum value given for a particular reputation for the agent is 0 and the maximum value is 1.

3.2   Individual Dimension

The individual dimension is the result of direct interactions between the agents. In [16], this dimension is treated as the most reliable, because it expresses results of direct interactions with the target agent, i.e., an assessment given by the result of the interaction between the involved agents.

In our work, the agents exchange non-economic services which do not involve money or goods exchanges. The gardeners agents in SJVG project have, as valuation basis, the investment in performing a service and the satisfaction in receiving a service. When evaluating an investment, the agent takes into account three factors [8]:

- The *difficulty*, which represents how difficult it is for the agent to perform the requested service. It assumes values between 0 and 10, where values close to 10 illustrate a greater degree of difficulty.
- The *cost*, which represents the expenses to perform the service. It assumes values between 1 and 100, where values close to 100 indicate higher expenses in performing the service.
- The *time*, which represents the time spent performing the service. It assumes values between 1 and 90, where values close to 90 indicate a greater time spent in performing the service.

For example, Table 1 shows the fuzzy rule base for the evaluation of the investment when considering the difficulty.

For the analysis of satisfaction as a result of service received is taken into account [8]:

Table 1. Fuzzy rules base for investment analysis based on difficulty

Fuzzy rules base investment (Difficulty)
$R^{(1)}$: IF difficulty IS low THEN investment IS low
$R^{(2)}$: IF difficulty IS medium THEN investment IS medium
$R^{(3)}$: IF difficulty IS high THEN investment IS high

Table 2. Fuzzy rule base for debt analysis

Fuzzy rule base (Expect satisfaction X Real satisfaction)
$R^{(1)}$: IF expect sat. IS low AND real satisfaction IS low THEN debit IS medium
$R^{(2)}$: IF expect sat. IS low AND real satisfaction IS medium THEN debit IS high
$R^{(3)}$: IF expect sat. IS low AND real satisfaction IS high THEN debit IS high
$R^{(4)}$: IF expect sat. IS medium AND real satisfaction IS low THEN debit IS low
$R^{(5)}$: IF expect sat. IS medium AND real satisfaction IS medium THEN debit IS medium
$R^{(6)}$: IF expect sat. IS medium AND real satisfaction IS high THEN debit IS high
$R^{(7)}$: IF expect sat. IS high AND real satisfaction IS low THEN debit IS low
$R^{(8)}$: IF expect sat. IS high AND real satisfaction IS medium THEN debit IS low
$R^{(9)}$: IF expect sat. IS high AND real satisfaction IS high THEN debit IS medium

- The *quality*, which represents the degree of excellence of service. It assumes values between 0 and 10 where the higher the value the greater the degree of excellence of service.
- The *price*, which represents the value of expenditure on hiring the service. It assumes values between 0 and 100, with values near 0 indicate less expenses.
- The *time*, which is the time spent waiting for the execution of the service. It assumes values between 1 and 90, where the lower the number, the lower the expected time in performing the service.

When an agent requests to other agent a service, it calculates the expected satisfaction through a fuzzy membership function and a rule base and based on its "Service Evaluation Attitude" [8].

The Service Evaluation Attitude is the composition of one or more attributes that belong to this service. This means that, for example, the agent can analyze the investment in the realization of service "plant", based exclusively on the difficulty to perform this action, and on the other hand, it can analyze the satisfaction to receive this service, analyzing for example, the time and difficulty. Each agent has its Service Evaluation Attitude independently.

When receiving the service, the agent calculates the real satisfaction as well as the agent that made the investment calculates real investment. The relationship between expected satisfaction and real satisfaction, generates credit to who provided the service and debit for those who received the service.

For example, Table 2 shows the fuzzy rule base for the evaluation of the debts.

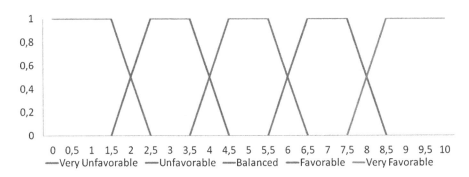

Fig. 1. Linguistic variables scale

3.3   Material and Virtual Balance

The material balance of an agent α, in the model BDI-Fuzzy is obtained through a fuzzy (qualitative) evaluation obtained by material values of investment Ra and satisfaction Sa, generated in the exchange of services with another agent, following a personal evaluation agent's [8].

The scale with linguistic terms to represent the material and virtual balance is represented as:

T_{bm} = < *very unfavorable, unfavorable, balanced, favorable, very favorable* > where the agents' normalized value is represented by the membership function given in Fig. 1.

In every performed exchange, where the agent provides a service (makes an investment), and receives a service (generates a satisfaction) with a target agent, a material balance is generated. In each exchange, the agent records the material balance in a vector v. This accumulated exchange generates the reputation with the target agent by:

$$\sum_{i=1}^{\text{size}(v)} \frac{v_i * a_n}{\text{size}(v)}, \tag{2}$$

where $a_n = a_1 + (n - 1) * \beta$, and β is given by

$$\beta = \frac{a_1 + 1}{\text{size}(v) + 1}$$

and $a_1 = 0.1$

It is important to note that the factor a_n generates weights that grow as new interactions are occurring. That's because new interactions should have more relevance to past experiences.

Once the agent provides a service, it generates credit for those who receives the service, and the agent who receives the service constricts a debit to other that provides the service. Once the exchange is realized, i.e., the agent performs an investment to provide a service and generates a satisfaction to receive a service, credit and debit values generated are analyzed using the "Virtual Balance".

Table 3. Fuzzy evaluation of virtual balance when the agent performs a service (Virtual Balance x Credit)

	Low	Medium	High
Very unfavorable	very unfavorable	unfavorable	balanced
Unfavorable	unfavorable	balanced	favorable
Balanced	balanced	favorable	very favorable
Favorable	favorable	very favorable	very favorable
Very favorable	very favorable	very favorable	very favorable

Table 4. Fuzzy evaluation of virtual balance when the agent receive a service (Virtual Balance x Debit)

	Low	Medium	High
Very unfavorable	very unfavorable	very unfavorable	very unfavorable
Unfavorable	unfavorable	very unfavorable	very unfavorable
Balanced	balanced	unfavorable	very unfavorable
Favorable	favorable	balanced	unfavorable
Very favorable	very favorable	favorable	balanced

The Virtual Balance is updated with each new credit and debit generated in the delivery or receipt of a service through the basic rules [8] given in Tables 3 and 4.

The agent will ask to perform one of two tasks that makes up the scenario of this study: plant and harvest, always requests aid to another agent. The criterion of choice about who may be required is based on Virtual Balance, according to the following steps:

1. Virtual balance *very unfavorable*: This type of balance is preferable because the agent has more credits than debits to the target agent.
2. Virtual balance *unfavorable*: A relationship with the target agent with unfavorable virtual balance is the second choice when there is not a relationship with virtual balance very unfavorable, because the agent has relatively greater credits in relation of that debts.
3. Virtual balance *balanced*: The agent has an equilibrated balanced relationship of exchanges with the target agent. This virtual balance is still preferable in relation to ask a stranger, since the agent will have to ask for help and therefore lead to a debit, but earlier exchanges reached a balance with the known target agent.
4. Virtual balance *favorable/very favorable*: When the agent does not even have a balanced balance with another agent, it will request to whom it contracted more debits to indicate other agent. The agent does not request the agent that has more debits because its balance is already negative and it seeks to achieve a balance.

Table 5. Expect/Real investment of Cicero agent

	Difficulty	Cost	Time
Crop service	6.3	50	47
Harvest service	5	40	60

Table 6. Expect/Real investment of Genaro agent

	Exp. Dif.	Exp. Cost	Exp. Time	Real Dif.	Real cost	Real time
Crop	8	70	62	9	88	75
Harvest	8.5	65	70	9.2	80	85

Table 7. Expect/Real investment of Pedro agent

	Exp. Dif.	Exp. Cost	Exp. Time	Real Dif.	Real cost	Real time
Crop	3.2	35	50	2.8	30	36
Harvest	2.3	20	28	1.7	10	11

- *Indication*: Agents, when they are requested to indicate someone to do a job, indicate someone that: (i) has a high satisfaction to receive the service; (ii) has a medium satisfaction to receive the service; OR (iii) has a low satisfaction to receive the service.

3.4 Ontological Dimension

The Ontological Dimension is the combination of social and individual dimensions. The Individual Dimension is more reliable than Social Dimension, since the first express direct relationships between agents. The equation which produces this combination is expressed in:

$$D_o(\alpha) = \frac{\vartheta D_s(\alpha) + \varphi D_i(\alpha)}{\vartheta + \varphi} \tag{3}$$

where the factors ϑ and φ define the importance of the Social Dimension and Individual Dimension respectively, and $\vartheta < \varphi$ applied to all agents. The value of these factors should be chosen according to the need to enhance the Individual Dimension for Social Dimension. It is noteworthy that D_i and D_s must be normalized.

4   Simulations and Preliminary Results

Each agent has expected investment values that at first it informed the agent that will receive the service, generating an expected satisfaction. In a second step, to complete the service, the agent generates a real satisfaction, which corresponds

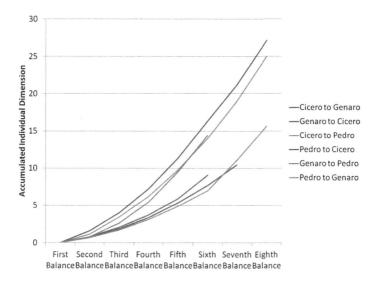

Fig. 2. Individual dimension evaluation based on cost and time for investment and time for satisfaction

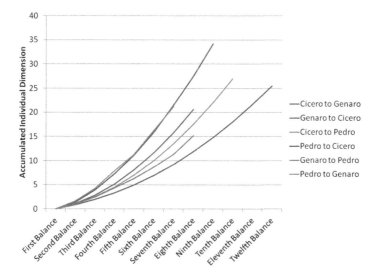

Fig. 3. Individual dimension evaluation based on cost and time for investment and quality and time for satisfaction

to the actual amounts invested in making the service assessed both at first and in the second step, according to the Service Evaluation Attitude of each involved part.

Consider a scenario where there are three agents (Cicero, Pedro and Genaro) that exchange services with each other. See Tables 5, 6 and 7. Exchanges, in

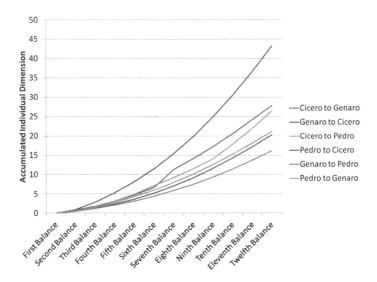

Fig. 4. Individual dimension evaluation based on difficulty for investment and quality and time for satisfaction

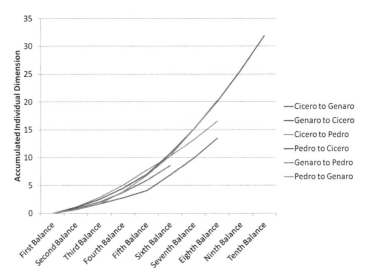

Fig. 5. Individual dimension evaluation based on difficulty for investment and time for satisfaction

this particular case, happen until the Virtual Balance reaches states by Partners Search Heuristic (favorable or very favorable conditions), whereupon the agent asks indication for the target agent about who can run the service. Note that depending on the Attitude of Service Evaluation, each agent may achieve a different performance, as shown in Figs. 2, 3, 4 and 5.

5   Conclusion

The initial simulations indicate that our hybrid reputation model includes both collective and individual performances about the agents involved in a satisfactory way, favoring those that best fulfill their roles, both in direct terms of exchanges as well as in the collective, in relation the normative policy (see [13]).

As future works, we will simulate our case study with more agents, exchanging information and indicating agents for services, as proposed in Partners Search Heuristic, as well as integrate collective social aspects, in order to obtain the Ontological Dimension.

Acknowledgments. This work was partially supported by CNPQ (Proc. 481283/2013-7, 306970/2013-9 and 232827/2014-1. G.P. Dimuro is in a sabatic year at Departamento de Automática y Computación, Universidad Pública de Navarra, under the Brazilian Program of Science without Borders, CNPq/Brazil.

References

1. Boissier, O., Bordini, R.H., Hubner, J.F., Ricci, A., Santi, A.: Multi-agent oriented programming with JaCaMo. Sci. Comput. Program. **78**(6), 747–761 (2013)
2. Bordini, R.H., Hübner, J.F.: Jacamo project (2014). http://jacamo.sourceforge.net/
3. Bordini, R.H., Hübner, J.F., Wooldridge, M.: Programming Multi-agent Systems in AgentSpeak using Jason. Wiley, New Jersey (2007)
4. Dimuro, G.: Sistemas urbanos: el estado de la cuestión y los ecosistemas como laboratorio. Arquitextos 124, 11 (2010). http://www.vitruvius.com.br/revistas/read/arquitextos/11.124/3594
5. Dimuro, G., Jerez, E.M.: Comunidades en transición: Hacia otras prácticas sostenibles en los ecosistemas urbanos. Cidades Comunidades e Territórios **20–21**, 87–95 (2010)
6. Dimuro, G., Jerez, E.M.: La comunidad como escala de trabajo en los ecosistemas urbanos. Revista Ciencia y Tecnología **10**, 101–116 (2011)
7. Farias, G.P., Dimuro, G.P., Costa, A.C.R.: BDI agents with fuzzy perception for simulating decision making in environments with imperfect information. In: Proceedings of the Multi-agent Logics, Languages, and Organisations Federated Workshops (MALLOW 2010), Lyon, France, 30 August–2 September 2010, vol. 627, pp. 41/23–41/30 (2010)
8. Farias, G.P., Dimuro, G., Dimuro, G., Jerez, E.D.M.: Exchanges of services based on Piaget's theory of social exchanges using a BDI-fuzzy agent model. In: 2013 BRICS Congress on Computational Intelligence and 11th Brazilian Congress on Computational Intelligence (BRICS-CCI and CBIC), pp. 653–658. IEEE, Los Alamitos (2013)
9. Hübner, J.F., Boissier, O., Kitio, R., Ricci, A.: Instrumenting multi-agent organisations with organisational artifacts and agents. Auton. Agents Multi-agent Syst. **20**(3), 369–400 (2010)
10. Rao, A.S.: AgentSpeak(L): BDI agents speak out in a logical computable language. In: Perram, J., Van de Velde, W. (eds.) MAAMAW 1996. LNCS, vol. 1038. Springer, Heidelberg (1996)

11. Rao, A.S., Georgeff, M.P.: An abstract architecture for rational agents. In: Proceedings of the 3rd International Conference on Principles of Knowledge Representation and Reasoning (KR 1992), Cambridge, MA, 25–29 October 1992, pp. 439–449 (1992)
12. Ricci, A., Piunti, M., Viroli, M.: Environment programming in multi-agent systems: an artifact-based perspective. Auton. Agents Multi-agent Syst. **23**(2), 158–192 (2011)
13. Rodrigues, H.D.N., Santos, F.C.P., Dimuro, G., Adamatti, D.F., Jerez, E.M., Dimuro, G.P.: A MAS for the Simulation of Normative Policies of the Urban Vegetable Garden of San Jerónimo, Seville, Spain. USP, São Paulo (2013)
14. Rodrigues, T.F., Costa, A.C.R., Dimuro, G.P.: A communication infrastructure based on artifacts for the JaCaMo platform. In: Proceedings of 1st International Workshop on Engineering Multi-agent Systems at AAMAS 2013, EMAS 2013. IFAMAS, Saint Paul (2013)
15. Rubiera, J.C., Lopez, J.M.M., Muro, J.D.: A fuzzy model of reputation in multi-agent systems
16. Sabater, J., Sierra, C.: Regret: a reputation model for gregarious societies. In: Proceedings of the Fourth Workshop on deception Fraud and Trust in Agent Societies, pp. 61–70 (2001)
17. Santos, F.C.P., Rodrigues, T.F., Dimuro, G., Adamatti, D.F., Dimuro, G.P., Costa, A.C.R., De Manuel Jerez, E.: Modeling role interactions in a social organization for the simulation of the social production and management of urban ecosystems: the case of San Jerónimo vegetable garden of Seville, Spain. In: 2012 Third Brazilian Workshop on Social Simulation (BWSS), pp. 136–139. IEEE, Los Alamitos (2012)
18. Santos, F.C.P., Rodrigues, T.F., Donancio, H., Dimuro, G., Adamatti, D.F., Dimuro, G.P., De Manuel Jerez, E.: Analyzing the problem of the modeling of periodic normalized behaviors in multiagent-based simulation of social systems: the case of the San Jerónimo vegetable garden of Seville, Spain. In: Kamiński, B., Koloch, G. (eds.) Advances in Social Simulation. AISC, vol. 229, pp. 61–72. Springer, Heidelberg (2014)
19. Santos, F., Rodrigues, T., Donancio, H., Santos, I., Adamatti, D.F., Dimuro, G.P., Dimuro, G., Jerez, E.D.M.: Towards a multi-agent-based tool for the analysis of the social production and management processes in a urban ecosystem: an approach based on the integration of organizational, regulatory, communication and physical artifacts in the JaCaMo framework. In: Adamatti, D., Dimuro, G.P., Coelho, H. (eds.) Interdisciplinary Applications of Agent-Based Social Simulation and Modeling, pp. 287–311. IGI Global (2014)
20. Santos, I., Costa, A.C.R.: Toward a framework for simulating agent-based models of public policy processes on the jason-cartago platform. In: Proceedings of the Second International Workshop on Agent-based Modeling for Policy Engineering in 20th European Conference on Artificial Intelligence (ECAI)- AMPLE 2012. Montpellier University, Montpellier (2012)

CloudAnchor: Agent-Based Brokerage of Federated Cloud Resources

Bruno Veloso[1,2], Benedita Malheiro[2,3(✉)], and Juan Carlos Burguillo[1]

[1] EET/UVigo – School of Telecommunication Engineering,
University of Vigo, Vigo, Spain
[2] INESC TEC, Porto, Portugal
[3] ISEP/IPP – School of Engineering,
Polytechnic Institute of Porto, Porto, Portugal
mbm@isep.ipp.pt

Abstract. This paper presents CloudAnchor, a brokerage platform conceived to help Small and Medium Sized Enterprises (SME) embrace Infrastructure as a Service (IaaS) cloud computing both as providers and consumers. The platform, which transacts automatically single and federated IaaS cloud resources, is a multi-layered Multi-Agent System (MAS) where providers, consumers and virtual providers, representing provider coalitions, are modelled by dedicated agents. Federated resources are detained and negotiated by virtual providers on behalf of the corresponding coalition of providers. CloudAnchor negotiates and establishes Service Level Agreements (SLA) on behalf of SME businesses regarding the provision of brokerage services as well as the provision of single and federated IaaS resources. The discovery, invitation, acceptance and negotiation processes rely on a distributed trust model designed to select the best business partners for consumers and providers and improve runtime.

Keywords: Federated resources · Multi-Agent System (MAS) · Infrastructure as a Service (IaaS) · Service Level Agreement (SLA) · Trust-based brokerage

1 Introduction

The IaaS cloud computing market, while still maturing, is already populated by major players, making it difficult for SME providers to thrive. In this scenario, brokers, which are entities that manage the use, performance and delivery of cloud services, and negotiate relationships between cloud providers and consumers [7], are emerging as the preferential middle-ware to match demand and offer. SME are still in the early stages of adopting the cloud paradigm or providing cloud services and, consequently, require support services and platforms to migrate to the cloud. For SME providers, brokers offer additional business opportunities and simplify the management and integration of disparate cloud services — potentially across different providers —fostering the creation of provider coalitions. In the case of SME consumers, brokers provide seamless provider lookup

© Springer International Publishing Switzerland 2016
Y. Demazeau et al. (Eds.): PAAMS 2016, LNAI 9662, pp. 207–218, 2016.
DOI: 10.1007/978-3-319-39324-7_18

and invitation as well as SLA negotiation services, increasing the chances of obtaining the desired resources at the best price and within the deadline. The ultimate goal of this research is to support the adoption and provision of IaaS by SME both as consumers and as providers.

This paper describes CloudAnchor, an SME business-to-business (B2B) brokerage platform regarding single and federated infrastructure resources. The federated resources must be decomposable in standard Virtual Machine (VM) packages. This problem is by nature distributed, decentralised, dynamic and involves multiple stakeholders (consumers and providers) continuously entering and leaving the system (open system). The stakeholders are loosely coupled, but, depending on the situation, can either compete (consumers and providers compete for getting and leasing resources) or cooperate (coalition of providers). Furthermore, businesses wish to retain autonomy, privacy and the control of their strategic knowledge, leading to the adoption of the agent-based paradigm.

In terms of contributions, the proposed brokerage platform provides: (*i*) decentralised trust models of partners (providers, consumers and platform) based on the outcome of partner invitation, partner acceptance, SLA negotiation and SLA enforcement; (*ii*) trust-based invitation/acceptance of potential partners; (*iii*) trust-based negotiation and establishment of brokerage, coalition and resource SLA instances; and (*iv*) federated resources through the creation of virtual providers, representing provider coalitions. In particular, the creation and application of such partner trust models is, as far as we know, a novel approach.

In terms of organisation, this document contains five sections. Section 2 is dedicated to cloud brokerage. It introduces the most relevant concepts of cloud brokerage as well as describes related agent-based cloud resource brokerage platforms. Section 3 describes our approach, including the platform architecture and services. Section 4 describes the tests and discusses the results obtained. Finally, Sect. 5 draws the conclusions and suggests future developments.

2   Cloud Brokerage

According to the NIST, a cloud broker may include service intermediation, aggregation and arbitrage [7]. Such tasks require the modelling of resources (single and federated), businesses and their relationships (SLA) as well as methodologies for partner discovery, resource negotiation and resource provision. Frequently, brokers build trust and/or reputation models to support SLA negotiation. In recent years, several agent-based cloud brokers were proposed by An *et al.* (2010) [3], Venticinque *et al.* (2011) [13], Ferrer *et al.* (2012) [6], Al Falasi *et al.* (2013) [1] and Pawar *et al.* (2014) [9]. While An *et al.* propose a platform for single resource SLA negotiation, the remaining platforms offer single and federated resource SLA negotiation services and adopt trust and/or reputation models of business partners. In terms of services, 80 % include partner discovery, 100 % include SLA negotiation and 40 % SLA enforcement.

Service Level Agreements. The establishment of Service Level Agreements (SLA) is the ultimate goal of a broker. The adoption of specifications and standards to represent SLA instances are essential to ensure interoperability. There are two major concurrent specifications: the Web Service Agreement (WS-Agreement)[1] created by the Open Grid Forum (OGF); and Web Service Level Agreement (WSLA)[2] created by International Business Machines (IBM). However, in the case of cloud federated resources, these specifications do not cover all the needs. Whereas Alhamad *et al.* (2010) rely on performance and business metrics to establish SLA contracts between consumers and providers [2], we adopt a trust-based performance metric. Moreover, we define brokerage, resource and coalition SLA to represent the different business relationships and their dependencies [11].

Peer Trust and Reputation. Trust is, by default, a subjective property of direct (one-to-one) relationships attributed by a trustor to a trustee and, according to Castelfranchi, implies a decision to rely on someone [5]. Built from the outcomes of past interactions, it is typically intended to be used in future interactions between trustor and trustee. Reputation is obtained from third parties and can be used to characterise new business partners or complement trust built from first hand information. Pinyol and Sabater (2013) classify reputation and trust models according to: (*i*) the paradigm, *i.e.* if the model is cognitive or numerical; (*ii*) the information sources; (*iii*) the visibility, *i.e.* if the trust can be observed by other agents; (*iv*) the granularity, *i.e.* the context of the trust information; (*v*) the source behaviour, *e.g.* credible or deceptive; and (*vi*) the type of information exchanged [10]. In the specific case of analysed agent-based cloud brokers, trust and/or reputation models have been used in the partner discovery stage by [6,13] or [9] and in the SLA negotiation stage by [1] (to specify rewards and penalties). In CloudAnchor, we apply the trust models in both stages: consumers use trust for partner lookup and invitation and for SLA negotiation, whereas providers for invitation assessment and SLA negotiation.

SLA Negotiation. For Bichler *et al.*, negotiation can be unstructured, semi-structured or structured and includes six main attributes: (*i*) the number of participants (bilateral, multilateral, multi-bilateral or arbitrary); (*ii*) the number of issues (single or multidimensional); (*iii*) the scope (restricted or open); (*iv*) the domain of the offers (private or public); (*v*) the scenario (competitive and/or cooperative); and (*vi*) the protocol [4]. In the case of SLA negotiation, An *et al.* (2010) adopt a cloud resources negotiation protocol composed of alternating offers, commonly used for bilateral bargaining, which includes the negotiation of SLA violation fines [3]. Venticinque *et al.* (2011) use the Iterated Contract Net Interaction Protocol (ICNIP) for SLA negotiation and take into account multiple constraints and parameters, including provider reputation [13]. CloudAnchor adopts two negotiation protocols – the one shot bilateral protocol for bSLA and the ICNIP for rSLA and cSLA – and implements a multidimensional negotiation, including partner trust as well as resource price and uptime.

---

[1] https://www.ogf.org/documents/GFD.107.pdf.
[2] http://www.research.ibm.com/people/a/akeller/Data/WSLASpecV1-20030128.pdf.

3   CloudAnchor Broker

CloudAnchor, when compared with the analysed cloud brokerage platforms, implements two distinctive features: (*i*) a business model contemplating the negotiation, establishment and enforcement of brokerage, coalition and resource agreements; and (*ii*) a decentralised trust model of the peers, taking into account all past interactions, including provider invitation/acceptance, SLA negotiation and SLA enforcement outcomes, and not just the usual SLA enforcement results. This novel approach allows consumers to invite providers based on the outcome of past provider/consumer invitation/acceptance ratios as well as provider and consumer SLA establishment/negotiation and enforcement. The SLA enforcement results are provided by the SLA monitoring and enforcement modules, which, in our case, are external to the platform.

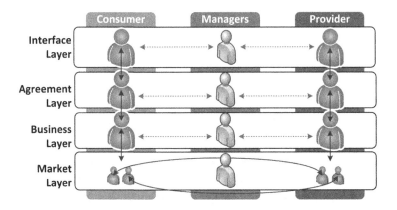

Fig. 1. CloudAnchor broker architecture

The broker architecture, which is detailed in [12], is organized in interface, agreement, business and market layers (Fig. 1) and comprises of five types of specialised dedicated agents: (*i*) interface agents to interact with consumer and provider SME businesses; (*ii*) agreement agents to manage SLA instances; (*iii*) business agents to model consumer and provider SME businesses; (*iv*) market delegate agents to negotiate specific resources on behalf of consumer and provider SME businesses; and (*v*) layer manager agents responsible for the management of platform layers (creation/removal of agents in the layer). Each business (consumer or provider SME) is represented in the platform by the corresponding: (*i*) interface agent located in interface layer; (*ii*) agreement agent located in agreement layer; (*iii*) business agent in the business layer; and (*iv*) an undetermined number of delegate agents involved in specific resource negotiations in the market layer. These agents are identified by a trading code, preventing third parties from intruding in undergoing negotiations [11]. To overcome the existing interoperability issues between different IaaS platforms, CloudAnchor interacts with the provider platforms through the Deltacloud abstraction framework [8].

The CloudAnchor brokerage platform implements an open event-driven multi-layered agent-based architecture. Businesses are represented by dedicated autonomous agents and are, thus, able to specify their self-models, by uploading their strategic knowledge (lookup, invitation, acceptance and negotiation strategies), resource offers (providers) or resource requests (consumers), as well as to build peer models of their business partners based on the outcomes of their previous interactions (local peer trust). The layered approach allows the distribution and delegation of the interface, agreement, business (knowledge and processes) and negotiation related tasks to corresponding dedicated agents, where each business is represented by a set of dedicated specialized agents rather than by a single agent to increase the overall responsiveness. In terms of external events, there are business registration/de-registration, resource request/offer and SLA fulfilled/violated events. These events drive the execution of the business registration service, business de-registration service, provider lookup and invitation service, provider resource publication service and SLA termination service. In particular, whenever a consumer requests a new resource via its interface agent (resource request event), it triggers the resource finding process. The consumer business agent automatically looks up and invites providers for negotiation. If the invited provider business agents accept the invitation, dedicated delegate market agents are created by both consumer and provider business agents to negotiate and establish the resource SLA (rSLA). If the providers are unable to provide the resource single-handedly, the platform attempts to create a virtual provider. Virtual providers are temporary coalitions of providers established on the fly to provide federated resources, *i.e.*, resources which were not offered by any single provider. When an rSLA terminates, the parties involved (consumer and provider) receive an agreement fulfilled or agreement violation event.

SLA Templates, Classes and Hierarchy. The platform contemplates the negotiation, establishment and termination of: (*i*) brokerage agreements – bSLA – which define the platform service provision terms for each business; (*ii*) resource agreements – rSLA — that specify the resource provisioning terms between businesses; and (*iii*) coalition agreements – cSLA — which details the platform coalition service provision terms between the businesses that form the coalition. A bSLA establishes a one-to-one relationship between a business and the brokerage platform; an rSLA establishes a one-to-one relationship between one consumer and one provider businesses; and a cSLA establishes a one-to-many binding relationship between a virtual provider and a collection of providers. The different agreements are described according to the WS-Agreement specification. There is a hierarchical dependency between the different types of SLA. A bSLA defines the general conditions which apply to any service performed on behalf of the business by the platform, including resource (rSLA) and coalition agreements (cSLA). As a result, when two businesses establish a resource provision contract (rSLA), they must fulfil the agreed brokerage, coalition (in the case of a federated resource) and service provision terms. Figure 2 describes the SLA life-cycle state: SLA template (Temp), SLA partially instanced (Inst), SLA under negotiation (Nego), SLA under enforcement SLA (Enfo) and SLA terminated (Term).

The state transitions are event-driven: (*i*) when a service becomes available, the provider partially instances an SLA (Temp to Inst); (*ii*) when a provider accepts a consumer invitation, they engage in the negotiation of the SLA terms (Inst to Nego); (*iii*) if they reach an agreement, the SLA is established and applied (Nego to Enfo), otherwise the SLA terminates (Nego to Term); (*iv*) when the enforcement succeeds or fails, the SLA terminates (Enfo to Term) and the service becomes available (Term to Temp).

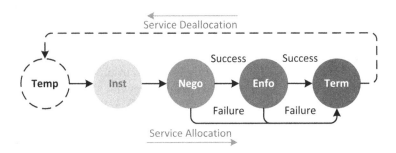

Fig. 2. SLA life-cycle

The provision of a resource results in several payments: (*i*) the consumer pays the established resource provisioning fee to the provider; (*ii*) the provider pays the accorded brokerage fee to the platform; and (*iii*) the consumer pays the negotiated brokerage fee to the platform. In the case of a federated resource, there is an additional brokerage fee that the federated providers pay to the platform. These fees are typically distinct. According to the default SLA terms, if a business fails to fulfil an established SLA, it reimburses the partner.

Distributed Trust Model. The platform creates and maintains a distributed decentralised self and acquaintances models of the business partners with the trust model. Each entity (platform, consumer, provider and virtual provider) builds these local models based on their past common interactions, *i.e.*, the ratio of successful invitations, negotiations and fulfilled SLA. While consumers, providers and virtual providers hold a partial incomplete trust model of their counterparts, the platform is in a unique position as it keeps a global and complete trust model of all businesses. The CloudAnchor distributed trust model implements, according to Pinyol and Sabater (2013) classification, a local (granularity), private (visibility) numerical approach (paradigm) based solely on direct interactions (sources). The trust model supports all brokerage stages: provider invitation (I), SLA negotiation (N) and SLA enforcement (E). Each business agent builds corresponding self and partner models. By default, at start up, businesses are fully trusted. For a given brokerage stage S, the local dynamic trustworthiness attributed by a trustor business a to a trustee partner b is given by Eq. 1:

$$T_S(a,b)_n = \frac{n-1}{n} \times T_S(a,b)_{n-1} + \frac{1}{n} \times Out_{S,n} \tag{1}$$

where n is the number of stage S interactions accomplished between a and b, and $Out_{S,n}$ is the boolean outcome of the last stage S interaction – success (1) or failure (0). As a result, each business agent builds local partner invitation (I), SLA negotiation (N) and SLA enforcement (E) models: (i) $T_I(a, b)_n$ corresponds to the ratio of acceptances versus invitations to negotiate; (ii) $T_N(a, b)_n$ is the ratio of established versus negotiated SLA; and (iii) $T_E(a, b)_n$ is the ratio of fulfilled versus established SLA. Additionally, businesses maintain their own I, N and E self models. Equation 2 represents, for a given brokerage stage S, the self trustworthiness of business a:

$$T_S(a)_n = \frac{\sum_{i=1}^{n} Out_{S,i}}{n} \qquad (2)$$

where n is the total number of stage S interactions accomplished with all business partners and $Out_{S,i}$ is the boolean outcome of the last stage S interaction. In the case of a virtual provider vp created on behalf of a consumer c, the initial self model values $T_S(vp)_0$ are obtained through Eq. 3, where $T_S(c, p_i)_n$ corresponds to the trustworthiness of provider p_i according to consumer c.

$$T_S(vp)_0 = \min_{i=1,\ldots m} T_S(c, p_i)_n \qquad (3)$$

Provider Lookup and Invitation. In this stage consumers discover and invite providers for negotiation and providers decide whether to accept or reject the invitations. Consumers select and invite the best provider candidates for negotiation by applying a cascade filter based on the enforcement, negotiation and invitation trustworthiness of the potential providers. Providers accept consumer invitations based on the consumer enforcement trustworthiness. The provider invitation algorithm (Algorithm 1) looks for providers (line 1) in the service registry, calculates the acceptance threshold for each filter (line 2, 6 and 12) and implements the T_E based filter (lines 3–5), the T_N based filter (lines 7–11) and the T_I based filter (lines 11–13). Algorithm 2 determines, on the provider side, when to accept a consumer invitation by calculating the mean enforcement trustworthiness – $\overline{T_E}$ (line 2) and $\overline{T_N}$ (line 3) – of all provider clients and verifying that $T_E(p, c) \geq \overline{T_E}$, where p represents the provider and c the consumer.

Algorithm 1. Lookup and invitation
```
1:  L[n] ← LookUp p
2:  T_E ← CalcT_E Mean(L[n])
3:  for p = 0; p < n; p++ do
4:      if L[p].T_E(c, p) ≥ T_E then
5:          L_E[p] ← L[p]
6:  T_N ← CalcT_N Mean(L_E[m])
7:  for p = 0; p < m; p++ do
8:      if L_E[p].T_N(c, p) ≥ T_N then
9:          L_N[p] ← L_E[p]
10: T_I ← CalcT_I Mean(L_N[l])
11: for p = 0; p < l; p + + do
12:     if L_N[p].T_I(c, p) ≥ T_I then
13:         L_I[p] ← L_E[p]
14: return L_I[p]
```

Algorithm 2. Acceptance
```
1:  L[c] ← ClientConsumerList
2:  T_E ← CalcT_E Mean(L[c])
3:  T_N ← CalcT_N Mean(L[c])
4:  if T_E(p, c) ≥ T_E then
5:      return accept
6:  return reject
```

SLA Negotiation. CloudAnchor implements a competitive, private, restricted (by invitation), multidimensional (uptime, price and trust) bilateral structured protocol – the ICNIP – for rSLA and cSLA negotiations and a private, restricted, multidimensional (time, price and trust) bilateral protocol - the one shot protocol – for bSLA negotiations. The negotiation of coalition and resource agreements takes place in the market layer between provider and consumer delegate agents. Provider delegates implement a dynamic price adaptation strategy according to Eq. 4c, where r represents the resource, p the provider, c the consumer and n the current negotiation round. First, they determine the maximum resource price to propose to the consumer $Pr(p, c, r)_{max,n}$ using Eq. 4a, which takes into account $T_E(c, p)_n$, i.e. the provider's enforcement trustworthiness as perceived by the consumer, the maximum resource price range $\Delta Pr(p, r)$ and the minimum resource price $Pr_{min}(p, r)$. Then, they determine the consumer's loyalty discount through Eq. 4b. The discount depends on the ratio between the uptime of the resources delivered to the consumer and the total number of provider's resource hours, the consumer's enforcement trustworthiness according to the provider $T_E(p, c)_n$ and the current resource price range $Pr(p, c, r)_{max,n} - Pr_{min}(p, r)$. Finally, Eq. 4c establishes the current price proposal $Pr(p, c, r)_n$ as the difference between the consumer's maximum price $Pr(p, c, r)_{max,n}$ and discount $Di(p, c, r)_n$.

$$Pr(p, c, r)_{max,n} = Pr_{min}(p, r) + T_E(c, p)_n \times \Delta Pr(p, r) \tag{4a}$$

$$Di(p, c, r)_n = \frac{\sum_{i=1}^{d} \Delta t_{up,i}}{n_r \times \Delta t} \times T_E(p, c)_n \times (Pr(p, c, r)_{max,n} - Pr_{min}(p, r)) \tag{4b}$$

$$Pr(p, c, r)_n = Pr(p, c, r)_{max,n} - Di(p, c, r)_n \tag{4c}$$

Consumer delegates determine the utility of provider proposals through Eq. 5, where $U(c, p, r)_n$ represents the utility of the provider's proposal according to the consumer, $T_E(c, p)_n$ is the current provider's enforcement trustworthiness as perceived by the consumer, $Pr(p, c, r)_n$ is the proposed resource price, $\Delta t_{up}(r)$ is the proposed resource uptime and, finally, the α_c parameter allows the consumer to define the relative importance between the price and uptime dimensions.

$$U(c, p, r)_n = T_E(c, p)_n \times (\alpha_c(1 - Pr(p, c, r)_n) + (1 - \alpha_c)(\Delta t_{up}(r)). \tag{5}$$

4   Tests and Results

We performed several tests to verify the correct operation of the platform and the impact of the trust-based invitation/acceptance and negotiation in terms of the negotiated resource price and negotiation time involving one consumer and multiple providers. The tests contemplated three provision – undersupply, equilibrium and oversupply – and three resource consumption scenarios: (i) single resources, i.e., when the demand can be met by any single provider; (ii) federated resources, i.e., when the demand can only be met by coalitions of providers; and (iii) mixed (single and federated) resource provision, i.e., when the demand includes both single and federated resources (Table 1). The resulting nine experiments were performed with the base algorithm and with the application of the

Trust-based Invitation/acceptance and Negotiation (TIN) model. In the base algorithm the peer trustworthiness remains 100 %. During these experiments, the consumer remains fully trusted and requests 1000 standard virtual machines (VM) in different combinations: (i) 1000 VM in the single resource provision scenario; (ii) 500 VM and 20 packages of 25 VM in the mixed resource provision scenario; and (iii) 40 packages of 25 VM in the federated resource provision scenario. In the case of the providers there are: (i) 25 providers holding 20 standard VM each in the under-supply market scenario; (ii) 50 providers holding 20 standard VM each in the supply and demand equilibrium market scenario; and (iii) 100 providers holding 20 standard VM each in the oversupply market scenario. During these tests, all providers violate 25 % of the established rSLA, ending up with 75 % trustworthiness. Providers implement identical price adaptation policies, i.e., they apply Eq. 4c with an initial maximum value of 47 € and a minimum value of 27 € per standard VM. In terms of hardware, the tests were executed on a platform with one quad-core i7-2600 3.40 GHz Central Processing Unit (CPU) with 2 threads per core, 16 GiB Random Access Memory (RAM) and a 1.8 TiB of storage capacity.

Table 1. Resource consumption and provision scenarios

Resource	Scenario	Businesses	VM/business	$\overline{T_E}$ (%)
Demand	Single	1 consumer	1000×1	100
	Mixed		$500 \times 1 + 20 \times 25$	
	Federated		40×25	
Offer	Undersupply	25 providers	20	75
	Equilibrium	50 providers		
	Oversupply	100 providers		

Figure 3 presents the base test results (without TIN). We can observe that the price depends solely on the resource type ($\overline{Pr_{fed}} > \overline{Pr_{sin}}$) and is independent of the number of providers. In terms of runtime, the negotiation time per VM decreases from single to federated resources ($\overline{\Delta t_{sin}} > \overline{\Delta t_{mix}} > \overline{\Delta t_{fed}}$) because federated resources are negotiated in packages.

Figure 4 groups the TIN results. We can observe that the average VM price increases with the number of providers ($\overline{Pr_{ove}} > \overline{Pr_{equ}} > \overline{Pr_{und}}$) and with the resource type ($\overline{Pr_{fed}} > \overline{Pr_{sin}}$). In terms of runtime, the negotiation time per VM decreases from single to federated resources ($\overline{\Delta t_{sin}} > \overline{\Delta t_{mix}} > \overline{\Delta t_{fed}}$) as expected. Table 2 presents the comparison between the base and TIN results. The TIN average VM price is lower in all cases and the TIN negotiation time decreases considerably when compared with the base values. These results show that the trust-based invitation/acceptance and trust-based negotiation grants faster negotiations, better proposals (lower prices) and selects the best providers in each negotiation.

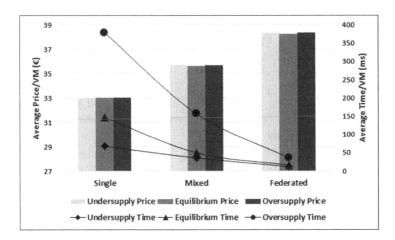

Fig. 3. Base results

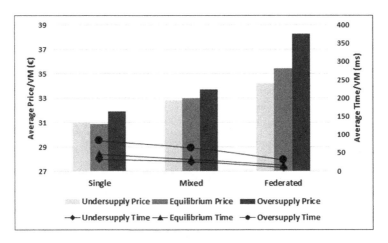

Fig. 4. TIN results

Table 2. TIN *versus* base results

	Single			Mixed			Federated		
	Under	Equi	Over	Under	Equi	Over	Under	Equi	Over
$\Delta Price$	−06.3%	−06.5%	−03.4%	−08.1%	−07.5%	−05.6%	−10.8%	−07.4%	−00.3%
$\Delta Time$	−52.9%	−68.7%	−78.1%	−27.7%	−36.0%	−59.2%	−16.6%	−06.3%	−13.9%

5 Conclusions

CloudAnchor offers cloud infrastructure brokerage services for SME vendors and consumers regarding single and federated resources, which must be decomposable in standard VM packages. The brokerage services include provider lookup and discovery, trust-based provider selection, invitation and acceptance as well as trust-based SLA negotiation.

The platform contemplates the negotiation and establishment of three different types of SLA – brokerage, resource and coalition – supported by the decentralised peer trust model. This novel model takes all past interactions into account, including provider invitation, resource negotiation and resource provision, and not just the SLA enforcement outcomes. Our approach allows: (i) consumers to invite providers based on the outcome of past invitations, SLA negotiations and SLA enforcements; and (ii) providers to decide whether or not to accept an invitation for negotiation based on the outcome of past SLA negotiation and SLA enforcement. The trust-based results demonstrate the usefulness of the model showing a considerable reduction of the average resource negotiation time and a slighter decrease of the average resource price paid by the consumers.

In terms of future developments, we plan to: (i) implement the renegotiation of bSLA and cSLA based on the trust model and on the success of the businesses within the platform; (ii) enrich SLA templates with new parameters to meet increasing business demands; and (iii) create virtual providers not only at the request of consumers, but also at the request of providers. Concerning the validation of the platform, we are performing experiments to assess the impact of the distributed trust model from the provider perspective, $i.e.$, when consumers violate agreements.

Acknowledgements. This work was partially financed by the ERDF – European Regional Development Fund through the Operational Programme for Competitiveness and Internationalisation - COMPETE Programme within project ≪FCOMP-01-0202-FEDER-023151≫ and project ≪POCI-01-0145-FEDER-006961≫, and by National Funds through the FCT – Fundação para a Ciência e a Tecnologia (Portuguese Foundation for Science and Technology) as part of project UID/EEA/50014/2013.

References

1. Al Falasi, A., Serhani, M.A., Elnaffar, S.: The sky: a social approach to clouds federation. Procedia Comput. Sci. **19**, 131–138 (2013)
2. Alhamad, M., Dillon, T., Chang, E.: Conceptual SLA framework for cloud computing. In: 2010 4th IEEE International Conference on Digital Ecosystems and Technologies (DEST), pp. 606–610. IEEE (2010)
3. An, B., Lesser, V., Irwin, D., Zink, M.: Automated negotiation with decommitment for dynamic resource allocation in cloud computing. In: Proceedings of the 9th International Conference on Autonomous Agents and Multiagent Systems, vol. 1, pp. 981–988. International Foundation for Autonomous Agents and Multiagent Systems (2010)
4. Bichler, M., Kersten, G., Strecker, S.: Towards a structured design of electronic negotiations. Group Decis. Negot. **12**(4), 311–335 (2003)
5. Castelfranchi, C., Falcone, R.: Principles of trust for MAS: cognitive anatomy, social importance, and quantification. In: Proceedings of the International Conference on Multi Agent Systems, pp. 72–79. IEEE (1998)

6. Ferrer, A.J., Hernández, F., Tordsson, J., Elmroth, E., Ali-Eldin, A., Zsigri, C., Sirvent, R., Guitart, J., Badia, R.M., Djemame, K., et al.: Optimis: a holistic approach to cloud service provisioning. Future Gener. Comput. Syst. **28**(1), 66–77 (2012)
7. Liu, F., Tong, J., Mao, J., Bohn, R., Messina, J., Badger, L., Leaf, D.: NIST Cloud Computing Reference Architecture: Recommendations of the National Institute of Standards and Technology (Special Publication 500–292). CreateSpace Independent Publishing Platform, USA (2012)
8. Meireles, F., Malheiro, B.: Integrated management of IaaS resources. In: Lopes, L., et al. (eds.) Euro-Par 2014, Part II. LNCS, vol. 8806, pp. 73–84. Springer, Heidelberg (2014)
9. Pawar, P.S., Rajarajan, M., Dimitrakos, T., Zisman, A.: Trust assessment using cloud broker. In: Zhou, J., Gal-Oz, N., Zhang, J., Gudes, E. (eds.) Trust Management VIII. IFIP AICT, vol. 430, pp. 237–244. Springer, Heidelberg (2014)
10. Pinyol, I., Sabater-Mir, J.: Computational trust and reputation models for open multi-agent systems: a review. Artif. Intell. Rev. **40**(1), 1–25 (2013)
11. Veloso, B., Malheiro, B., Burguillo, J.C.: Media brokerage: agent-based SLA negotiation. In: Rocha, A., Correia, A.M., Costanzo, S., Reis, L.P. (eds.) New Contributions in Information Systems and Technologies. AISC, vol. 353, pp. 575–584. Springer, Heidelberg (2015)
12. Veloso, B., Meireles, F., Malheiro, B., Burguillo, J.C.: Federated IaaS resource brokerage. In: Kecskemeti, G., Kertes, A., Nemeth, Z. (eds.) Developing Interoperable and Federated Cloud Architectures, Chap. 9. IGI Global, Pennsylvania (2016)
13. Venticinque, S., Aversa, R., Di Martino, B., Rak, M., Petcu, D.: A cloud agency for SLA negotiation and management. In: Guarracino, M.R., et al. (eds.) Euro-Par-Workshop 2010. LNCS, vol. 6586, pp. 587–594. Springer, Heidelberg (2011)

A MAS Approach for Group Recommendation Based on Negotiation Techniques

Christian Villavicencio[1], Silvia Schiaffino[1(✉)], J. Andres Diaz-Pace[1],
Ariel Monteserin[1], Yves Demazeau[2], and Carole Adam[2]

[1] ISISTAN (CONICET - UNCPBA), Campus Universitario, Tandil, Argentina
silvia.schiaffino@isistan.unicen.edu.ar
[2] IMAG, Grenoble, France

Abstract. Providing recommendation to groups of users has become a
promising research area, since many items tend to be consumed by groups
of people. Various techniques have been developed aiming at making recommendations to the group as a whole, but satisfying all group members
in an even way still remains as a challenge. We propose a multi-agent
approach based on negotiation techniques for group recommendation. In
this approach we use the multilateral monotonic concession protocol to
combine individual recommendations into a group recommendation. We
applied our proposal in the movies domain. The results obtained indicate that using this negotiation protocol, users in the groups were more
evenly satisfied than with traditional ranking aggregation approaches.

1 Introduction

Recommender systems provide assistance to users to deal with a variety of potentially interesting items in a given domain, by identifying those items that match
a user's needs, preferences, tastes, and goals. These systems can give item suggestions in domains, such as e-commerce, movies, and tourism, among others. Several recommendations techniques have been proposed, ranging from those based
on the analysis of the similarity of the content of the items being recommended,
collaborative filtering techniques that seek similar users in the community, to
hybrid techniques that combine different approaches [15].

In some cases, the kind of recommendations made requires techniques to
assist groups of users, instead of individual users. For example, in domains such
as movies, music or tourism, recommendations tend to serve groups of people
as well as individuals. The aim of a group recommender system is to make item
recommendations that are "good for" a group of users as a whole, i.e., satisfy, as
much as possible, the individual preferences of all group members [9]. Group recommendation brings challenges to the area, since generating recommendations
that satisfy a group of users with possible competing interests is not straightfor-
ward, and new issues (beyond individual recommendation) have to be considered.
Group recommendation approaches developed thus far are based on: (i) the generation of a group profile combining individual profiles [5], which is then used to

Y. Demazeau et al. (Eds.): PAAMS 2016, LNAI 9662, pp. 219–231, 2016.
DOI: 10.1007/978-3-319-39324-7_19

make recommendations considering this profile; (ii) the integration of recommendations obtained for each member separately, such as in ranking aggregation [1]; or (iii) the aggregation of individual ratings using, for example, approaches such as minimizing misery or maximizing average satisfaction [14]. However, these techniques often fail to satisfy the whole group in an even way and there is still no agreement on how to assess the utility of recommendations [1,11].

In this work, we propose a multi-agent approach called PUMAS-GR[1] for group recommendation. Our approach integrates recommendations previously obtained for each group member into a list of recommendations for the group. Each user (of a group) is represented by a personal agent that knows her preferences and acts on her behalf when looking for item agreements (with other agents). These agents rely on a cooperative negotiation process. In this context, we claim that the negotiation process can generate recommendations that satisfy more evenly the different group members than traditional approaches. In a real-life scenario, when a group of users has to choose some item (e.g., a movie, or a music track), the group members generally discuss and analyze their options for achieving a consensus. This consensus might not be easy to achieve, involving several rounds of (sometimes conflicting) negotiation. Thus, applying negotiation techniques to obtain group recommendations appears as an interesting approach, which has not been explored before in that research field. Particularly, we use the multilateral Monotonic Concession Protocol (MCP) [6], since it closely mirrors the way in which human negotiation seems to work [18]. Furthermore, the negotiation decentralizes the decision-making process of the recommender, allowing us to have heterogeneous agents that can personalize their negotiation strategies and recommendations according to each user profile.

We have applied PUMAS-GR in the movies domain (MovieLens), but the approach is applicable to other domains as well. We compared our proposal against traditional approaches for ranking aggregation. The effectiveness of the group recommendations was measured in terms of the average satisfaction of each group and the standard deviation of this group satisfaction. The results so far are promising, since the average group satisfaction was higher for the recommendations produced by PUMAS-GR and also the group members were satisfied in a "more uniform" way.

The rest of the article is organized as follows. In Sect. 2 we describe related works. In Sect. 3 we present the details of PUMAS-GR. Then, in Sect. 4 we report on the experiments we carried out to evaluate our approach. Finally, in Sect. 5 we give the conclusions and outline some future work.

2   Related Work

The problem of generating recommendations to groups began to be investigated in the last decade [4]. Group recommender systems can be classified into three main categories: (i) those that merge individual recommendations; (ii) those that perform an aggregation of individuals' preferences (ratings) to obtain a group

---

[1] Personalized User-centered Multi-Agent Systems, name of the supporting project.

evaluation for each candidate item; and (iii) those that perform an aggregation of individuals' models into a single group model, and then generate suggestions based on that model. Some techniques to aggregate individuals' ratings are multiplication, maximizing average satisfaction, and minimizing misery. Each of these techniques suits different goals such as total satisfaction or equity, so conflicts may arise when different goals are pursued. To create a group model reflecting the preferences of most members of a group, the systems often aggregate group members' revealed preferences. Suggestions are generated for the "virtual user" constructed upon the group model, by applying a classic recommendation technique for individual users. As regards merging of individual recommendations, Masthoff [10] analyzes different techniques such as average, average without misery, and least misery. In [1] the authors analyzed the effectiveness of ranked list recommendations tailored for a group of users. The analyzed methods are: Spearman footrule, Borda count, average and least misery.

Multi-agent systems (MAS) have been applied in various domains. When it comes specifically to recommendation systems, some approaches have proposed multi-agent techniques to generate recommendations, for example, on adaptive customization of websites [12], tourism [2], and games on mobile phones [17]. These works aim at making recommendations to individual users. Although negotiation has been used extensively in the area of personal assistants, most particularly in multi-agent meeting scheduling [13], only a few works have targeted group recommendation with MAS and negotiation. In [3] a group recommender system relying on the application of cooperative negotiation is presented. The authors propose a process in which agents, acting on behalf of group members, participate in a direct (alternating offers) or mediated (merging rankings) negotiation. This negotiation produces group recommendations, based on individual recommendations and user preference models. The approach has only been tested with simulations involving two agents while we will test our approach on bigger groups of users. In [8] an agent-based negotiation schema that uses alternating offers is developed, in which agents negotiate the preferences of the whole group. In [7] the authors propose a MAS where user agents negotiate with the aim of building a group profile that satisfies the users' requirements. A mediator governs the negotiation in order to facilitate the agreements. Our work differs from [7,8] in that they negotiate user preferences while we negotiate recommendations.

3   Proposed Multi-agent Approach

Our group recommendation approach, called PUMAS-GR, is based on a multi-agent system (MAS), in which each agent acts as a personal assistant for a member of the group. Each agent has a profile of the user's preferences and can generate a ranking of items of interest for its associated user. Furthermore, a novel aspect of PUMAS-GR is that these agents negotiate with each other in order to reach a consensus on the most satisficing items for the group. Our approach, as described in Fig. 1b, conceives the MAS as the group recommender system. This vision differs from traditional group recommendation systems that

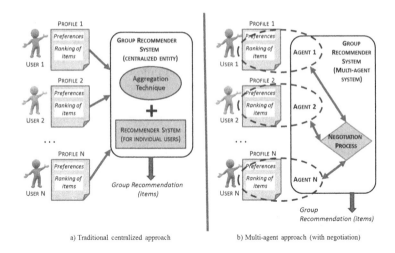

Fig. 1. From a centralized (a) to a MAS-based (b) recommender for groups.

work with a central entity that usually employs some aggregation technique (either for user profiles, or user rankings) in tandem with a single-user recommender system, as shown in Fig. 1a. Furthermore, in PUMAS-GR, we leverage on a Monotonic Concession Protocol (MCP) [6] with multiple parties (agents) in order to realize the multilateral negotiation process.

More formally, let $A = \{ag_1, ag_2, ..., ag_N\}$ be a set of N cooperative agents, and let $X = \{x_1, x_2, ...x_M\}$ be a finite set of items (potential agreements) that can be proposed by those agents. The set X can be interpreted as the union of the results of a recommender system R^i that returns an ordered list of items (i.e., a ranking) for every $ag_i \in A$. A ranking for a given ag_i will normally be a subset of X. The recommended items for ag_i are denoted as x_j^i, where j denotes the order of the recommended item in R^i. As a motivating example, let us assume the well-known domain of movie recommendation to (groups of) users. Along this line, let us have a group of 3 friends who want to watch a movie together. Let us also have a set of M possible movies to be chosen. Each user is equipped with her own personal agent that is able to access her user profile. For simplicity, a profile includes only ratings over (a subset of) the possible movies. A user rating $rt_i(item, satisfaction)$ assigns a valuation in $[0, 1]$ to a given movie, where 1 means high satisfaction of the user with the movie (item) and 0 means dissatisfaction. We have $A = \{ag_1, ag_2, ag_3\}$ as the MAS in which the negotiation for the "best" movie takes place. The (initial) situation is the following: ag_1 handles rating $< rt_1(M1, 0.8), rt_1(M5, 0.74), rt_1(M3, 0.56) >$ on behalf of user #1, ag_2 handles $< rt_2(M24, 0.85), rt_2(M10, 0.82), rt_2(M52, 0.65) >$ for user #2, and ag_3 handles $< rt_3(M3, 0.9), rt_3(M32, 0.88), rt_3(M46, 0.8) >$ for user #3.

The steps of the MCP protocol are summarized in Fig. 2. At the beginning, each agent makes an initial proposal with its "favorite" (top-ranked) movie. Then, the proposals are interchanged in order to determine if an agreement on

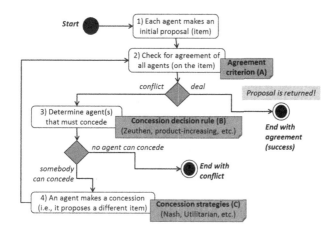

Fig. 2. Steps of the MCP for PUMAS-GR (adapted from [6])

the movie can be reached. The notion of *agreement* (also called deal) is defined in terms of the utility of a given proposal for the agents. To do so, a *utility function* $U_i : X \to \mathbb{R}_0^+$ is assumed in each agent $ag_i \in A$ that maps agreements to non-negative values. In the simplest case, the utility function corresponds to the ratings of the user for the different movies. Either actual or "predicted" ratings are allowed here. For instance, if a user did not rate a given movie, it is possible to compute an estimated ranking via a (single-user) recommendation technique. Thus, there is an agreement if one agent makes a proposal that is at least as good (regarding utility) for any other agent as their own current proposals [6,19]. If so, the proposal that satisfies all the agents is chosen (if several proposals meet this criterion, we simply pick one of them randomly). In our example, after the initial round of proposals, an agreement among the 3 agents is not possible, because each top movie in one ranking is ranked low in the others (Fig. 3a). Note that an agent will exclude from its proposals those movies that the user has already watched. Nonetheless, the movie proposed by a given agent might have been watched by some other user within the group. If so, the problem of avoiding such movies can be handled with the utility function.

rt(item, satisfaction)	M1	M24	M3
ag1	0,8	0,7	0,6
ag2	0,7	0,85	0,8
ag3	0,6	0,74	0,9

rt(item, satisfaction)	M1	M52	M3
ag1	0,8	0,53	0,6
ag2	0,7	0,65	0,8
ag3	0,6	0,82	0,9

rt(item, satisfaction)	M3	M52	M46
ag1	0,56	0,53	0,7
ag2	0,63	0,65	0,79
ag3	0,72	0,82	0,8

(a) Round 1: No agreement   (b) Round 2: No agreement   (c) Round k: Agreement

Fig. 3. Example of agent satisfaction with the item proposals during negotiation.

3.1   Multilateral Negotiation Protocol

As mentioned above, the agents basically engage in rounds of negotiation, each one making proposals (of items) that need to be assessed by the other agents, until an agreement is reached or the negotiation finishes with a *conflict*. Our agents abide by a set of predefined rules that specify the range of "legal" moves available at each agent at any stage of the negotiation process. In an MCP, these rules have to do with: (i) the agreement criterion, (ii) which agent makes the next concession (after a round with no agreement), and (iii) how much an agent should concede. The agreement criterion (step 2 of Fig. 2) is a generalization of the agreement for bilateral negotiations [6]: an agreement is reached iff there is an $ag_i \in A$ such that $U_k(x_j^i) \geq U_k(x_l^k)$ for all $ag_k \in A$.

In case a round of negotiation ends up in a conflict, one of the agents must make a *concession* (step 3). A concession means that an agent seeks an inferior proposal with the hope of reaching an agreement. If none of the agents can concede, the process finishes with no-agreement. Several concession strategies are possible (Sect. 3.2). In our example, let us imagine that ag_2 decides to make a concession and then proposes movie M52 (as $rt_2(M52, 0.65)$) to the group. At this point, the agreement criterion is re-assessed by the agents, but not consensus is reached yet (Fig. 3b). After a few rounds of negotiation, ag_1 makes a concession and proposes M3 (as $rt_1(M3, 0.56)$) to the group. Since the latter meets the criterion, the negotiation finishes with an agreement (Fig. 3c).

As it can be inferred from the example, the negotiation is not guaranteed to terminate successfully (with agreement) among all the agents. Furthermore, there are two properties of interest for MCP that must be analyzed: termination, and deadlock-freedom [6]. Ensuring these two properties depends on the concession strategies configured in the agents.

3.2   Concession Strategies

Selecting the agent(s) that must concede can be determined by applying the Zeuthen strategy [19] around the concept of *willingness to risk conflict* (WRC). In the bilateral MCP (i.e., two agents), both agents evaluate their WRC and the agent with the lower value makes the next concession. If we assume that the utility of the conflict deal is 0, the WRC of agent ag_i (in a negotiation with ag_j) is given by $WRC_i = (U_i(x^i) - U_i(x^j))/U_i(x^i)$. The justification of this strategy is that of utility optimization, as it leads to a final agreement that maximizes the product of the utilities of the two agents. The strategy can be directly generalized to a multilateral setting (i.e., more than two agents), in which Zeuthen evaluates the loss in utility in case of concession assuming the worst possible outcome for the agent[2]. The willingness to risk conflict (WRC) for ag_i is then given by Eq. 1:

$$WRC_i = \begin{cases} 1 & if\ U_i(x^i) = 0 \\ \frac{U_i(x^i) - min\{U_i(x^k)|k \in A\}}{U_i(x^i)} & otherwise \end{cases} \quad (1)$$

As for the concession itself (i.e., the new proposal made by the agent determined by the Zeuthen generalization), various strategies are discussed in the

---

[2] Although this generalization might lead to deadlock, some ways around to avoid the problem can be exploited.

literature [6]. For our work, we selected the so-called Nash concession, because it guarantees termination and deadlock-freedom. In the Nash strategy, an agent makes a proposal such that the product of utilities of the other agents increases (Nash product). When assessing the behavior of the Nash strategy in practical cases, we observed though that it sometimes leads to "early conflicts" during the negotiation, that is, situations in which all agents quickly exhaust their potential proposals and the MCP ends (with no deal). This is due to the way each agent computes the utility of its next concession with the Nash product. To mitigate this problem, we implemented a variation of the Utilitarian concession strategy called Desires Distance (DD). DD attemps to measure how far a candidate proposal is with respect to the desires of the other agents. Along this line, an agent makes a proposal that is "closer to the other agents' desires" (we denote the desires distance as dd_{value}) but also has a utility value lower or equal than the agent current proposal. DD guarantees termination and deadlock-freedom[3].

The DD strategy works as follows. Initially, we create a list with all the "elegible" candidate proposals (i.e., proposals with a lower utility value than the current proposal), we then select the first candidate from the list that has a dd_{value} lower or equal than the one of the current proposal. The dd_{value} is computed as explained in Eq. 2. This strategy requires $U_k(X_{ij}) - U_k(X_k)$ to be lower than 0, because otherwise agent ag_k is already satisfied and therefore it should not be considered in the distance computation.

$$dd_{value}(X_{ij}) = \sum_{k=0, k \neq i}^{N} |U_k(X_{ij}) - U_k(X_k)|$$

$$when\ U_k(X_{ij}) - U_k(X_k) < 0\ and\ X_k\ is\ the\ current\ proposal\ of\ ag_k. \quad (2)$$

4   Evaluation

The PUMAS-GR approach was implemented in Java. Internally, each agent relies on a basic (single-user) recommender system. For this recommender system, we chose the Duine framework[4] as it provides predefined prediction techniques for estimating the utility of items. To evaluate the effectiveness of PUMAS-GR, we compared the recommendations resulting from agent negotiation against those of a traditional group recommendation technique. Since the agents actually negotiate over rankings of items, we chose a technique based on aggregation of individual preferences – also known as *ranking aggregation* [1], as the baseline for our comparison. In addition, we implemented a variant of the MCP – known as the *one-step protocol* [16], in which all the negotiations happen in one single round: the agents simply interchange their proposals and seek for agreement but there is no concession. The effectiveness was measured in terms of the average satisfaction of a given group with the top-k items generated by the recommender.

---

[3] The demonstration follows from that for Utilitarian concession [6].
[4] http://www.duineframework.org/.

The group satisfaction was estimated as the average satisfaction of its members. In addition, we considered the standard deviation of the average group satisfaction, because we were interested in differences in satisfaction within a group.

We used the popular *MovieLens*[5] dataset with ratings of users for different movies to generate user groups of varying sizes. In particular, the experiments were performed with MovieLens100k that contains 100.000 ratings, 943 users and 1682 movies. We randomly sampled 120 users (without repetition) from this dataset and created 30 groups of 3, 4 and 5 people (10 groups per size).

4.1 Experimental Setting

The number of recommendations for a ranking was set to $k = 10$ items, since this is a common number for recommendations (top-ten). In the case of MCP (either one-step or multi-step variants), we ran the protocol k times, in order to produce the rankings. For a given run, we remove from the negotiation space the item that was agreed by the agents in the previous run. In all approaches, we conducted experiments with several configurations. For computing the ranking of items for each group with ranking aggregation, we used different aggregation methods [4]. Thus, we tested 6 variants in total, namely: three for PUMAS-GR (OneStep, Nash, and DD), and three for ranking aggregation (Average, Least Misery and Most Pleasure).

Given two group recommendation approaches (or variants) R_1 and R_2, we say that R_1 produces better recommendations than R_2 if the following criterion is met: $\sigma_{R_1} \leqslant \sigma_{R_2} \wedge \bar{U}_{R_1} > \bar{U}_{R_2}$. In this formula, σ_{R_1} and σ_{R_2} are the standard deviations of the group satisfaction for R_1 and R_2 respectively, and $\bar{U}_{R_1}$ and $\bar{U}_{R_2}$ are the average group satisfactions for both approaches. The interpretation of this criterion is that R_1 generates recommendations with higher satisfaction at the group level but smaller differences in the user satisfaction within the group.

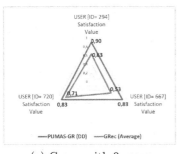

(a) Group with 3 users

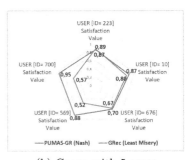

(b) Group with 5 users

Fig. 4. Example of user satisfaction for different group sizes

---

[5] http://grouplens.org/datasets/movielens/.

For instance, Fig. 4 shows typical outputs of PUMAS-GR (with Nash concession) and ranking aggregation (with Least Misery) for groups of different sizes using kiviat diagrams. We can see that PUMAS-GR produces more "balanced" recommendations, in terms of satisfaction of individual users, than the baseline approach (we refer to it as GRec).

4.2   Results and Lessons Learned

Figure 5 shows the average satisfaction of all groups in our sample with the 6 variants tested in our experiments. Average satisfaction here is measured as the satisfaction given by the group to the whole set of recommendations (i.e., the ranking of 10 movies). It can be noticed that the MAS-based variants produced better recommendations than those variants of the baseline approach. The average group satisfaction is about an 8–9% higher for the recommendations of PUMAS-GR with respect to the ones produced with the GRec variants. Furthermore, the standard deviations of the individual satisfaction of the members of a group are lower for the recommendations with PUMAS-GR, about a 25% better in terms of dispersion of the satisfaction with respect to GRec. This would indicate that the members of the groups were satisfied in a "more uniform" way than with the ranking aggregation approach. In these results, there is a chance that some recommended movies were watched already by at least one group member. The percentage of such movies in the outputs of PUMAS-GR ranged from 10–40%, depending on the group size.

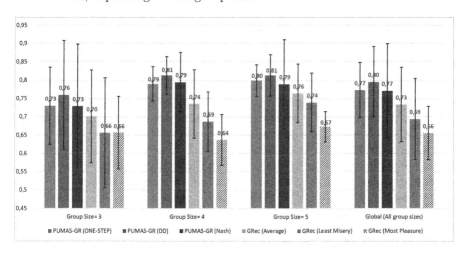

Fig. 5. Average group satisfaction with the different variants (the error bars denote the standard deviation of the average group satisfaction).

Figure 6 gives the distribution of the average group satisfaction of the 30 groups for the 6 different variants. We can see that the medians of the PUMAS-GR variants are higher than those of the traditional group recommendation variants, and we also notice a relative smaller variation in the distributions, with the exception of the Nash variant. Although the boxplots give descriptive insights, no conclusion can be made so far on whether there is a statistically significant difference among the approaches. Statistical tests are necessary for our claims. We derived hypotheses H_A (average group satisfaction) and H_B (satisfaction standard deviation) from the criterion in Sect. 4.1, which are analyzed next.

Analysis #1 (H_A). First, we tested the data series (average group satisfactions) for normality using the Shapiro–Wilks test and found that (some) data deviated from normality. Then, we used the Kruskal–Wallis one-way ANOVA test to determine if there were statistical differences among our 6 variants (alternative hypothesis). Since the null hypothesis was rejected, we concluded that (some of) the variants did have differences. We proceeded to check the 6 variants pairwise using Game-Howell as a post-hoc test. This testing revealed differences in PUMAS-GR (DD) and PUMAS-GR (Nash), and we defined the null hypothesis ($H_{A,0}$): the average satisfaction with variant R_1 is less or equal than the average satisfaction with variant R_2. The alternative hypothesis ($H_{A,1}$) is that the average satisfaction with R_1 is greater than the average satisfaction with R_2. After running a series of Mann-Whitney tests, we were able to reject the null hypothesis $H_{A,0}$ for the case of PUMAS-GR (DD) compared to the remaining variants, with the exception of PUMAS-GR (Nash), thus showing a statistically-significant evidence about the dominance of PUMAS-GR (DD) in terms of average satisfaction. We also found a statistically-significant evidence for PUMAS-GR (Nash) having a greater average satisfaction than the three ranking aggregation variants - GRec (Average), GRec (Most Pleasure) and GRec (Least Misery). Since the tests for statistically-significant differences between PUMAS-GR (DD) and PUMAS-GR (Nash) were inconclusive, we can assume that these two variants have equivalent (average) satisfaction values.

Analysis #2 (H_B). Once hypothesis $H_{A,1}$ (greater group satisfaction) was accepted, we analyzed the average standard deviations. Analogously, we initially tested the data series for normality using the Shapiro-Wilks test. Again, the data deviated from normality for some distributions, so we used the Kruskal-Wallis one-way ANOVA test to determine if there were statistical differences among our 6 variants (alternative hypothesis). The null hypothesis was rejected, and we concluded that (some of) the variants did have differences. The 6 variants were tested pairwise using the Game-Howell test. The results showed differences in PUMAS-GR (DD) and PUMAS-GR (Nash), and we defined the null hypothesis ($H_{B,0}$): the average satisfaction with variant R_1 is greater or equal than the average satisfaction with variant R_2. The alternative hypothesis ($H_{B,1}$) is that the average satisfaction with R_1 is less than the average satisfaction with R_2. After running several Mann-Whitney tests, we were able to reject the null hypothesis $H_{B,0}$ for the case of PUMAS-GR (DD) against the remaining variants, with the exception of PUMAS-GR (Nash). Therefore, we concluded (with statistical significance) that PUMAS-GR (DD) had less average standard deviation for group satisfaction. Like in the first analysis, PUMAS-GR (Nash) turned out to have less standard deviation than the three ranking aggregation variants based on statistically-significant evidence. However, we were not able to determine any statistically-significant differences between the standard deviations of PUMAS-GR (Nash) and PUMAS-GR (DD), so equivalence between the average values of these two variants was assumed.

Overall, we accepted $H_{1,A}$ (greater group satisfaction) and $H_{1,B}$ (less standard deviation) for the PUMAS-GR (DD) variant and partially for the PUMAS-GR (Nash) variant, when compared to the ranking aggregation variants. These results, although preliminary, confirm our presumption that both PUMAS-GR (DD) and PUMAS-GR (Nash) can produce more effective group recommendations with balanced user satisfaction within groups. Regarding performance, we found that the time needed for making a recommendation when using PUMAS-GR was slightly higher: the recommenders took 9–57 s. with the MAS-based approach and 8–10 s. with the baseline.

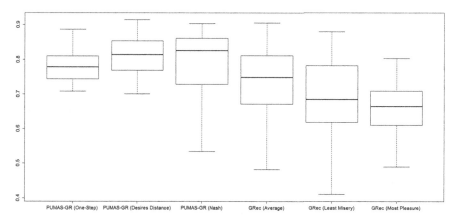

Fig. 6. Distribution of average group satisfaction (N = 30 groups)

5   Conclusions and Future Work

We have presented a MAS approach for group recommendation based on negotiation techniques. We have carried out experiments in the movies domain with promising results. We can conclude that due to the negotiation process, the items proposed by our (MAS-based) group recommender can satisfy the user preferences more evenly than traditional approaches. Furthermore, when specific concession strategies are selected, MCP can guarantee termination and deadlock-freedom properties. However, our experimental study involved some threats to validity, which are discussed next. A first threat to validity is that the user groups were selected randomly from the dataset, and we ignored any potential relationships of group members. However, it might be the case that "similarities" between particular users (e.g., friendship, common tastes, etc.) within the group might affect the recommendations, and thus, the resulting average satisfaction for some groups [11]. Also, user relationships of trust and influence might affect the movie selection. We plan to tackle these aspects in future work.

A second threat to validity is the high reliance of our current implementation on the movie scores generated by Duine. A third threat to validity is related to the way in which we compute each group utility by averaging the individual satisfaction of the group members. Different methods (others than the average) for integrating the individual satisfaction values into a group score might produce different results. The generation of a ranking of k items with MCP by simply running k times the negotiation algorithm might not consider item dependencies that might influence the negotiation. To deal with this limitation, we will explore adaptations of MCP to consider multi-issue negotiation.

Finally, we are planning to evaluate our approach in other domains and to compare it with other standard techniques for group recommendation.

Acknowledgments. This work has been funded by projects PICT2011-0366, PIP112-201101-00078, and by "PUMAS" CONICET-CNRS cooperation project.

References

1. Baltrunas, L., Makcinskas, T., Ricci, F.: Group recommendations with rank aggregation and collaborative filtering. In: Proceedings of the RecSys 2010, pp. 119–126. ACM (2010)
2. Bedi, P., Agarwal, S.K., Jindal, V., Richa: MARST: multi-agent recommender system for e-tourism using reputation based collaborative filtering. In: Madaan, A., Kikuchi, S., Bhalla, S. (eds.) DNIS 2014. LNCS, vol. 8381, pp. 189–201. Springer, Heidelberg (2014)
3. Bekkerman, P., Sarit, K., Ricci, F.: Applying cooperative negotiation methodology to group recommendation problem. In: ECAI Workshop on Recommender Systems (2006)
4. Cantador, I., Castells, P.: Group recommender systems: new perspectives in the social web. In: Cantador, I., Castells, P. (eds.) Recommender Systems for the Social Web. Intelligent Systems Reference Library, vol. 32, pp. 139–157. Springer, Heidelberg (2012)
5. Christensen, I., Schiaffino, S.: A hybrid approach for group profiling in recommender systems. J. Univ. Comput. Sci. **20**(4), 507–533 (2014)
6. Endriss, U.: Monotonic concession protocols for multilateral negotiation. In: Proceedings of the AAMAS 2006, pp. 392–399. ACM, New York (2006)
7. Garcia, I., Sebastia, L.: A negotiation framework for heterogeneous group recommendation. Expert Syst. Appl. **41**(4, 1), 1245–1261 (2014)
8. Garcia, I., Sebastia, L., Onaindia, E.: A negotiation approach for group recommendation. In: Proceedings of the International Conference on Artificial Intelligence, pp. 919–925 (2009)
9. Jameson, A., Smyth, B.: Recommendation to groups. In: Brusilovsky, P., Kobsa, A., Nejdl, W. (eds.) Adaptive Web 2007. LNCS, vol. 4321, pp. 596–627. Springer, Heidelberg (2007)
10. Masthoff, J.: Group modeling: selecting a sequence of television items to suit a group of viewers. User Model. User-Adap. Inter. **14**(1), 37–85 (2004)
11. Masthoff, J.R.: Group recommender systems: combining individual models. In: Ricci, F., Rokach, L., Shapira, B., Kantor, P.B. (eds.) Recommender Systems Handbook, pp. 677–702. Springer, New York (2011)

12. Morais, A.J., Oliveira, E., Jorge, A.M.: A multi-agent recommender system. In: Omatu, S., Paz Santana, J.F., González, S.R., Molina, J.M., Bernardos, A.M., Rodríguez, J.M.C. (eds.) Distributed Computing and Artificial Intelligence. AISC, vol. 151, pp. 281–288. Springer, Heidelberg (2012)
13. Mukherjee, R., Sajja, N., Sen, S.: A movie recommendation system - an application of voting theory in user modeling. User Model. User-Adap. Inter. **13**(1–2), 5–33 (2003)
14. O'Connor, M., Cosley, D., Konstan, J.A., Riedl, J.: PolyLens: a recommender system for groups of users. In: Prinz, W., Jarke, M., Rogers, Y., Schmidt, K., Wulf, V. (eds.) ECSCW 2001, pp. 199–218. Kluwer Academic Publishers, Netherlands (2001)
15. Ricci, F., Rokach, L., Shapira, B., Kantor, P.: Recommender Systems Handbook. Springer, New York (2010)
16. Rosenschein, J.S., Zlotkin, G.: Rules of Encounter Designing Conventions for Automated Negotiation Among Computers. MIT Press, Cambridge (1994)
17. Skocir, P., Marusic, L., Marusic, M., Petric, A.: The MARS – a multi-agent recommendation system for games on mobile phones. In: Jezic, G., Kusek, M., Nguyen, N.-T., Howlett, R.J., Jain, L.C. (eds.) KES-AMSTA 2012. LNCS, vol. 7327, pp. 104–113. Springer, Heidelberg (2012)
18. Wooldridge, M.: An Introduction to MultiAgent Systems, 2nd edn. Wiley, Hoboken (2009)
19. Zeuthen, F.L.B.: Problems of Monopoly and Economic Warfare. Routledge and Sons, London (1930)

Demo Papers

Automatic Detection System for Food Allergies and Intolerances in Recipes

José Alemany[(⊠)], Stella Heras, Javier Palanca, and Vicente Julián

Departamento de Sistemas Informaticos y Computacion,
Universitat Politècnica de València, Valencia, Spain
{jalemany1,sheras,jpalanca,vinglada}@dsic.upv.es

1 Introduction

Health is a very important aspect to keep in mind to lead a full and comfortable life. Physical exercise, rest, hygiene and food are some of the factors that help us achieve a healthy life. Food allergies are an issue that directly affect the health of people who suffer them, either by eating certain foods (which can damage your health) or by avoiding them (which can produce a nutritional imbalance due to the lack of some nutrients).

Recently there has been an increase in the population affected by food allergies and intolerances (up to 8 % of children and 2 % in adults)[1] [1]. Allergy-related organizations (WAO, AEPNAA and others) highlight the importance and impact of this problem in the society. Still, people with food allergies (especially those who have recently been diagnosed and need to retrain their eating habits) are forced to constantly review the composition of what they eat. This is an awkward situation. Furthermore, the lack of experience in nutrition prevents them from properly feed themselves with the appropriate nutrients that they are eliminating from their diet due to their food restrictions.

In order to facilitate the work of planning the daily diet of people with food allergies and intolerances we have designed a system based on our previous work [2], where we presented `receteame.com`, a persuasive social recommendation system whose goal is to recommend the most appropriated recipe to each specific user, taking into account their preferences, food restrictions and social context. This new system enhances the functionalities of `receteame.com` with the automatic detection of allergens in recipes, based on their ingredients composition (extracted from USDA Nutrient database). This prevents the system from recommending inappropriate recipes to people with specific food restrictions. Our solution implements a collaborative *multi-agent expert system* that is able to automatically detect food allergies in nutrients and label ingredients with their potential allergens.

---

[1] WAO World Allergy Organization, Food allergy statistics: http://www.worldallergy.org/public/allergic_diseases_center/foodallergy/.

© Springer International Publishing Switzerland 2016
Y. Demazeau et al. (Eds.): PAAMS 2016, LNAI 9662, pp. 235–238, 2016.
DOI: 10.1007/978-3-319-39324-7_20

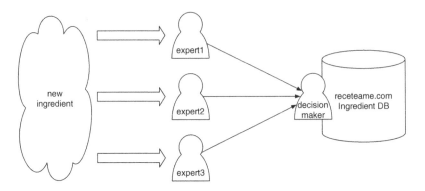

Fig. 1. Collaborative multi-expert-system.

2   Main Purpose

To improve our persuasive social recommendation system and take into account dietary restrictions due to food allergies or intolerances, we have designed the collaborative *multi-agent expert system* shown in Fig. 1. This system is able to identify and label potential allergens taking into account the detailed information (description and nutritional components) provided by nutrient databases like the USDA Nutrient and using machine learning techniques. In this way, it is able to provide additional nutritional information about the recipes.

With the incorporation of this improvement in our system it is able to avoid the recommendation of foods with nutrients likely to cause certain allergies and to offer other allergen free recipes able to supply the necessary nutrients for the user. Also, this new functionality helps the user to acquire new eating habits and trains him/her to maintain a healthy diet.

3   Demonstration

The implementation of the collaborative multi-expert system has been performed by creating several binary classifiers for each food allergy (a subset of the most common food allergies reported in the specialized literature). Each expert agent our collaborative system represents one of the machine learning techniques that we tested and that got a minimum threshold of 85 % in classification accuracy.

In order to train the classifiers, we created training and test sets using keyword dictionaries and the USDA Nutrient database. The keyword dictionaries have been developed taking into account the information provided by the World Allergy Organization (WAO) containing permitted and prohibited primary foods for each food allergy. With the sets defined, we tried a wide range of machine learning techniques including decision trees, linear regression, logistic regression, support vector machines and k-nearest neighbors. The machine learning techniques that achieved better classification results were decision trees, logistic regression and k-nearest neighbors. The experts agents that contain the classifiers

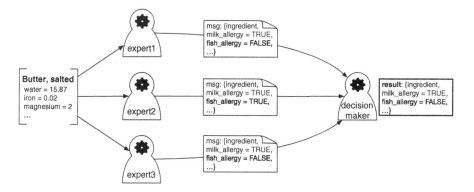

Fig. 2. Food allergy detection: Example of collaboration.

have been implemented using the `scikit-learn` and BigML software packages, which provide simple and efficient tools for data mining and analysis.

The operation of our collaborative multi-expert system is performed as follows: when a new ingredient is uploaded or updated in `receteame.com`, the three expert agents receive the ingredient and its composition. Then, to automatically detect potential allergens, they use the learned models to classify the ingredient (as causing or not such allergy) and send a message to the decision-maker agent with the results of the classifications. Finally, the decision-maker agent implements a voting system by which the classification agreed by the majority is selected as the final classification for each allergy in each ingredient (see Fig. 2 for an example). With the voting technique, our systems reaches good allergy-detection results and is robust against individual misclassification errors.

The collaborative multi-expert system described previously, has been built and integrated into `receteame.com` to provide the new functionality of allergy detection. In addition, the system implements other features such as the extraction of ingredients and the calculation of kilocalories in recipes. These functions are performed each time a new recipe is uploaded or updated in the system. The information extracted from the recipes that are included in `receteame.com` is stored in our database along with information about ingredients, recipes and users (personal information, tastes, preferences, allergies, etc.). The databases have been implemented using `mongodb` technologies, which provides a fast access and high load capacity for applications, and `neo4j` technologies, which provides flexibility and easy queries. The entire system can be seen in Fig. 3. It has been designed following the MVC (Model-View-Controller) model, where the databases represent the model, and the front-end (web interface) represents the view and the controller.

Thus, the front-end website allows the user to find recipes that best fit his/her tastes, preferences and dietary restrictions.

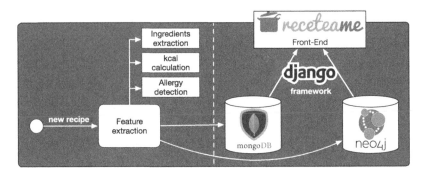

Fig. 3. Receteame.com platform: components and services.

4   Conclusions

This paper has presented a collaborative multi-agent system composed by experts that represent different machine learning techniques, able to automatically detect food allergies in nutrients. Moreover, the system includes a decision-maker agent that collects different opinions from the experts and, finally, labels ingredients with their potential allergens. With the integration of this new feature into `receteame.com` we improve our recipe recommender system offering a better and more personalized service. Furthermore, the daily task of feed is facilitated and re-educated helping the users (with some food allergy) to acquire new eating habits to follow a healthy diet.

Acknowledgements. This work was supported by the projects TIN2015-65515-C4-1-R and TIN2014-55206-R of the Spanish government and by the grant program for the recruitment of doctors for the Spanish system of science and technology (PAID-10-14) of the Universitat Politècnica de València.

References

1. Santos, A.F., Lack, G.: Food allergy and anaphylaxis in pediatrics: update 2010–2012. Pediatr. Allergy Immunol. **23**(8), 698–706 (2012)
2. Palanca, J., Heras, S., Botti, V., Julián, V.: receteame.com: a persuasive social recommendation system. In: Demazeau, Y., Zambonelli, F., Corchado, J.M., Bajo, J. (eds.) PAAMS 2014. LNCS, vol. 8473, pp. 367–370. Springer, Heidelberg (2014)

An ABM Java Applet to Explore the Free Market Equality/Efficiency Tradeoff

Hugues Bersini[⊠]

IRIDIA - Universite Libre de Bruxelles - CP 194/6,
50, av. Franklin Roosevelt, 1050 Bruxelles, Belgium
bersini@ulb.ac.be

1   Introduction

A classical disputed question regarding the effect of free market economy on the social welfare is the right balance between equality and efficiency called by Okun: the big tradeoff. *If both equality and efficiency are valued, and neither takes absolute priority over the other, then, in places where they conflict, compromises ought to be struck. In such cases, some equality will be sacrificed for the sake of efficiency and some efficiency for the sake of equality. But any sacrifice of either has to be justified as a necessary means of obtaining more of the other.*

Part of the problem lies in the difficulty to appropriately define these two notions. To help to understand this key trade-off, we propose an easy to use java applet allowing to compare two very different structures of market that potentially should drive the collective welfare to the two extremes: aggregative on one side and distributive on the other. These two structures are first a double auction competitive market (in which buyers and sellers compete to outbid each other) and a random market (in which the matching between buyers and sellers is done in a purely random way). The experimental outcomes are presented along three key dimensions: the Gini indices (regarding equality), the aggregate utility and the probability of market failures (both regarding efficiency).

2   Main Purpose

The model maps onto a Java object oriented applet (runnable at URL iridia.ulb.ac.be/bersini/research/Market) where the distinct responsibilities have been distributed through the many classes.

The competitive market is akin to a continuous double auction market in which agents bid to buy and sell products units. During a succession of steps, the market repeatedly invites two randomly selected agents to place asks and bids on one product they want to sell or purchase. At the first tick, the market is initialized with best-buying and best-selling offers for all the products on the market (bids at price null and asks at price max). Then a random seller is selected to place an ask for the most profitable product he has in stock (the proposed price should be below the best-selling offer and incurring the least

© Springer International Publishing Switzerland 2016
Y. Demazeau et al. (Eds.): PAAMS 2016, LNAI 9662, pp. 239–242, 2016.
DOI: 10.1007/978-3-319-39324-7_21

expense (i.e. selecting the product with the highest skill), this price is finally set between the producers skill and the current best-selling offer). The market then looks whether this ask crosses the current best-buying offer on that particular product. If so, the transaction occurs, if not, the ask becomes the best-selling offer and the market turns to the buying part. The randomly selected competitive buyer shows the very symmetrical behavior. He first selects the most desirable product (one with the highest taste above the best-buying offer) and places a bid limited by his reservation price (the proposed price is set between the best-buying offer and the reservation price). The market looks whether this bid crosses the current best-selling offer. Once two offers cross, the transaction price is fixed as the buying offer price. If following a determined number of trials, no transaction is to be found, a market failure is reported.

The random market is much simpler, since the sellers and the buyers behave without particular interest. In this version, a random seller places an ask on a random product, on which a random buyer is invited to react. If the buyer reservation price is higher than the price asked by the seller, a transaction takes place, the price being randomly set between the two offers. Here again, if following a determined number of trials, no transaction turns possible, a market failure is reported.

Whatever initial conditions being set: number of agents, number of products, vector of tastes and skills for every agent, initial endowment of money for all agents, they are obviously exactly equal for both market simulations, the objective being to compare the competitive version of the market (supposedly more efficient) with the random one (supposedly more equalitarian).

3   Demonstration

Four key metrics evolving in time can be measured and visualized out of the different simulations: utility (increasing by consumption), money (leaking out

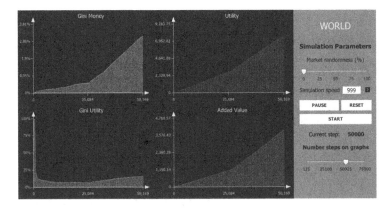

Fig. 1. Snapshot of the Free Market simulator. Four key metrics can be followed in time

by production and then fluctuating according to the transactions), added value (the difference between the price earned by the seller and the production cost) and market failures. For the first three, the aggregate value over all agents is used as an indicator of the market efficiency while the Gini coefficient (computed again for all three) testifies of how unequal this market turns out to be. The market failures (labeled MF in the following) is also used as an indicator of the market efficiency, but in the sense originally given by Hayek. Our simulations are always executed in the presence of a given number of agents, of products and during a sufficient number of simulation steps (500000). Once the simulation is launched, it is possible to follow how the metrics evolve in time, either for a market alone or for the two markets running in parallel.

As main result, the competitive market turns out to be much more efficient in aggregative terms but this superior efficiency comes at a very high price in terms of inequality, compared with a random market (the utility Gini index is much greater as a result of the competition). Distortions in utility and money tend to grow over time. The competitive market favors those with skill in demand and those with taste skillfully satisfied. If this difference in taste can be continuously expressed over the simulation, a self-amplifying pairing happens between the greedy consumers and their dedicate competent producers.

Fig. 2. Comparing the two markets in a same window, random in the right part (lower aggregate and better Gini), competitive in the left

Among many others, a further key aspect of the model to be explored is the influence of the budgetary constraint on the behavior of the market. The random version of the market simply stops executing at around an initial endowment of 25 (not the case for the competitive one) corrupted by a succession of market failures. Many agents go bankrupt and the simulation is being constantly interrupted by market failures. These outcomes testify of the inefficiency of the random market to map the producers onto the consumers. As Hayek nicely anticipates, competition allows the price to convey the right information. In its absence, the producers waste their money making products that the consumers are definitely not interested in.

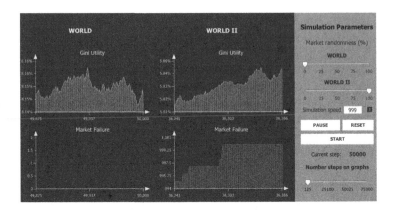

Fig. 3. The random market (right part) provokes a lot of market failures for a small initial budget

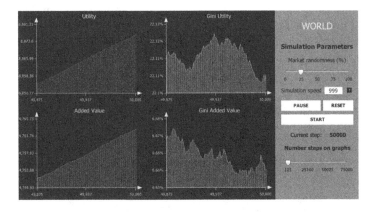

Fig. 4. Exploring mixtures of the two markets in search of the best compromise

4   Conclusions

The software proposes a stylized simulation exercise in which we compare a double auction, competitive market, with a pure theoretical abstraction that represents a market in which producer and consumer matching is purely made on a random basis. Our main results confirm the higher efficiency generally attributed to competitive markets first to simply map the consumers onto the producers then in maximizing the aggregative welfare. Our results equally show the inequality explosion, above all in the case of budgetary constraints, when only the best producers can survive, make money and consume. At last, the simulator makes possible to explore mixtures of the two markets to achieve the best compromise, the acceptable inequality level for the market to simply survive at the benefice of a bigger aggregate happiness.

U-Tool: A Urban-Toolkit for Enhancing City Maps Through Citizens' Activity

Elena del Val[✉], Javier Palanca, and Miguel Rebollo

Universitat Politècnica de València, Valencia, Spain
{edelval,jpalanca,mrebollo}@dsic.upv.es

1 Introduction

The study of the dynamics of cities has become a topic of particular relevance when planning the urban development or analyzing their influence on citizen activities and how citizens interact with the cities. The availability of updated data in real-time about what is happening in a city is of vital importance for the development of what is known as smart cities.

In this context, the main problem is the availability of real-time information for decision-making. However, the use of social networks through mobile devices turns citizens into mobile sensors and their movements and habits can be traced.

Nowadays, there are several tools to analyze user activity on different social networks. We will focus on Twitter. Twitter is an on-line social network that has been extensively studied due to the accessibility of the information that is posted by its users. It has millions of users around the world and all of them have a public profile where their messages can be seen by anyone or they can keep them in private. Most users usually have a public profile which allows other users to follow them and see their messages in their time line.

Twitter, through the application Twitter Analytics, provides users with statistics of their activity and the impact it has on their *friendship circles*. However, this tool only allows us to study the activity of the user itself, which can be useful to determine the impact of specific campaigns. Other tools provide the ability to follow the impact of hashtags (i.e., *SocialBro*, *Tweetbinder*, or *Sprout Social Topsy*). However, for urban analysis it is also necessary to analyze geo-located information. *Geofeedia*, *WeLink* and *HootSuite*, allow us to determine an area of study and analyze the activity of this area.

But there is still an open issue: the analysis is performed off-line, once all the information has been collected. In many cases, it is needed to incorporate the new information as it is received and to integrate it into the existing results, incrementally. This is particularly relevant if a live-event is going to be analysed, or if changes in the behaviour of the users have to be detected. In this sense, *Flocker* (of Outliers Collective), allows us to follow a label (word, user or hashtag) and perform online tracking, building the network that reflects the discussion taking place in real-time. However, this is a tool still under development and the final analyzed data provided is quite limited and does not include spatial information (geo-located) of the tweets.

© Springer International Publishing Switzerland 2016
Y. Demazeau et al. (Eds.): PAAMS 2016, LNAI 9662, pp. 243–246, 2016.
DOI: 10.1007/978-3-319-39324-7_22

2   Main Purpose

U-Tool performs a real-time analysis on the activity of a city through the messages that users exchange inside a social network. The objective of this application is to explore and analyse the spatial network of a city [1], in an intuitive and visual way, and the activity that takes place in the city to assist users in a decision-making process.

This tool will be useful both on a professional level, as is the analysis for urban planning, and users, citizens or tourists that move around a town and want to explore the activity of certain areas in real time. It can be applied to detect where an event is happening, mobility patterns (to detect where the population is moving to or to detect pedestrian flows), to detect which areas of the city receive greater attendance of visitors, to predict activity in a particular point of interest in the city, to find the optimum location for a new urban facility, to measure the spatial accessibility between different parts of the city and to detect alternative routes. In general, this type of urban analysis will help us to understand the social and economic impact of the cities planning.

3   Demonstration

The data used in this demonstrator is geotagged tweets and photos in a city. Access to information is done through the public API for developers of Twitter and Instagram (additional tools with public APIs can be easily added). Moreover, information about the infrastructure of the city can be integrated when local governments provide it through open data initiatives[1]. By knowing the infrastructure of the city, we can estimate the area of influence of each point of interest (PoI) through a set of proposed metrics.

Currently, the application considers the following metrics: (i) density of activity/users associated to each PoI of the city; (ii) metrics associated to the network structure generated using Delaunay's triangulation; (iii) "hot"/"cold" spots in the city that have an unusual activity compared to the expected values in a usual day; (iv) estimation of the attraction of each PoI in the city; (v) mobility patterns.

Density of Activity/Users of PoIs. Based on the set of PoIs (Points of Interest) identified in the city, a Voronoi map is generated. Geotagged messages are assigned to the corresponding polygon. The map is colored in response to the density and the number of messages generated in each area (i.e. buscafallas.com is a website that uses U-Tool to show the activity around the different monuments, called *fallas*, erected along the city; see Fig. 1). There are two ways of understanding the data. If we consider unique authors, (i.e., considering only a tweet/photo per user), it can be estimated how many people is near a PoI. Considering the general activity, (i.e., total number of messages generated by users located in the PoI) you can determine in which part of the city is an important activity going on.

---

[1] http://gobiernoabierto.valencia.es/en/.

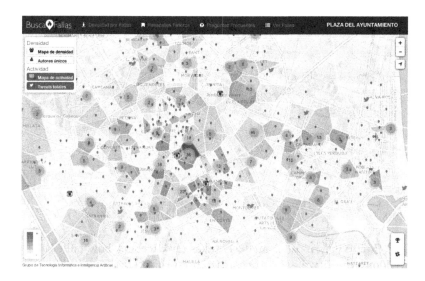

Fig. 1. www.buscafallas.com site, which uses U-Tool. (Color figure online)

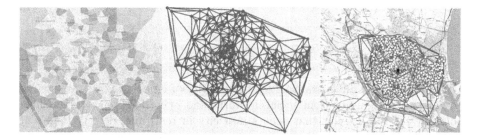

Fig. 2. Voronoi map and Delaunay triangulation

Structural Metrics. Based on the Voronoi diagram generated from the PoIs, a dual representation in a planar network is created using a Delaunay triangulation (see Fig. 2). Nodes of this network represent PoIs and links represent relations with other neighbour PoIs. Once the network is available, we consider structural measures such as diameter, degree of clustering, or index centrality measures (i.e., closeness, betweenness, and eigenvector).

Unusual Activity. We have applied the Local Moran Index. This index detects, given a set of weighted entities (PoIs), statistically significant spatial outliers. This index makes possible to determine "hot" or "cold" spots in the city that have an unusual activity compared to their expected values.

Attraction of PoIs. A complementary vision of the city is generated using a gravitational [2] potential model (see Fig. 3). In that case, each tweet is located over the map and the 'surface' of the city is deformed according to the distribution of tweets. Those dense areas will be more depressed and they will attract users (and activity) from its surroundings.

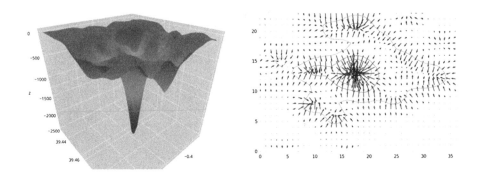

Fig. 3. Gravitational potential maps

Mobility Patterns. Another analysis takes into account how individual users move along the city, by creating trajectories that follow the position of each one of the tweets of each user. The combination of this information with the gravitational model help us to understand how people travel, the most used routes or to find potential bottlenecks among others.

4   Conclusions

U-Tool provides an analytical tool for the activity of cities using as data source the geo-located activity from social networks and open data repositories. This tool analyzes the activity that occurs in a city in real time, detects Points of Interest, flows of crowds, hotspots, events, or even prevents emerging situations geographically located in a city before they occur. This tool creates spatial network models of cities and applies techniques of complex networks analysis to study their properties and assist on decision-making to understand urban economic and social effects on city planning. This tool has been applied in a real case: the analysis of visitors activity in Valencia during a cultural event called Fallas.

Acknowledgements. This work is supported by the following projects: TIN2014-55206-R, TIN2012-36586-C03-01, PROMETEOII/2013/019, TIN2015-65515-C4-1-R.

References

1. Barthélemy, M.: Spatial networks. Physics Reports. **499**, 1–101 (2011)
2. Beir, M.G., et al.: Predicting human mobility through the assimilation of social media traces into mobility models (2016). arXiv:1601.04560

PriceCast Fuel: Agent Based Fuel Pricing

Alireza Derakhshan[1]([✉]), Frodi Hammer[1], and Yves Demazeau[1,2]

[1] A2I Systems A/S, Blangstedgårdsvej 8, 5220 Odense SØ, Denmark
{ad,fh}@a2isystems.com
[2] LIG — CNRS, 38000 Grenoble, France
yves.demazeau@imag.fr

Abstract. Setting the right price at a gas station is a complex task involving numerous parameters. By using a hybrid agent architecture based on BDI and ANN we can model a gas station agent that can learn to model its consumers. The gas station agent can then use the learning from it's consumer behavior to detect anomalies in the environment and autonomously set its own price to influence the consumer and thereby optimize e.g. gross margin without sacrificing volume.

1 Introduction

Pricing fuel at a gas station can be a complex task involving multiple dynamic parameters. Different brands use different pricing strategies depending on their market position. In general, these strategies can be divided into two major categories; namely, price setter and price follower. Price setters are used by the major oil companies which control the entire business chain – from upstream, midstream till downstream. Brands within this group are not sensitive to end product pricing; hence, their revenue stream is divided on the entire business chain. The price follower strategy is used by brands which are mainly positioned at the end of the downstream business chain by buying the fuel from the open markets, transporting it to it's gas stations and selling it to the consumer. This group is in particular sensitive to product pricing, due to the fact that the entire revenue stream comes from the consumer. The majority of brands in the price follower category emphasis competitor prices as the most important parameter; hence, the name "price follower". The reasoning behind this model lays in the nature of the product, since the same product is sold by different brands the competing parameter becomes the price [3] and therefore there is a high probability for the "price following" category to fall into an Edgeworth pricing cycle [7] which has the counter effect on maximizing revenue.

2 Main Purpose

Our proposal is that it is more profitable to emphasize on the consumer rather than the competitor; which, is directly linked to the revenue stream. This however is not trivial since the domain is a highly volatile and no consumer model

© Springer International Publishing Switzerland 2016
Y. Demazeau et al. (Eds.): PAAMS 2016, LNAI 9662, pp. 247–250, 2016.
DOI: 10.1007/978-3-319-39324-7_23

has been proven valid to mimic the dynamics of the environment. In addition, if the aforementioned could be accomplished could this modeled be used to utilize an autonomous agent for self maximization with respect to different properties i.e. maximizing profit while maintaining market share?

In [5] a novel agent model was proposed which consists of a BDI agent [4] with the use of ANN to model and learn from children's play on a playground within a controlled environmental setup. The knowledge gained from observing children's play was used to categorize the child's playing activity in 8 different categories and thereby adapt the playground to specific goals based hereby. In our domain two agent types can be defined with respect to [5]; namely the Gas Station Agent (GSA) and the Consumer Agent (CA). The GSA would by observing the behavior of CAs be able to learn and model CAs behavior. By applying the presented methodology in [5] to our GSA the three phases observation, learning and adaptation can be defined as the following:

Observation: Information is extracted from the available dataset e.g. gas station properties such as number of pumps, shop, carwash etc. and transactions (when was which product purchased by whom) and finally competitor prices. This phase corresponds to the perception of the BDI agent (the gas station).

Learning: The GSA agent is presented with the observation data and learns to correlate different inputs to a given output. E.g. learning how time of day vs. day of year vs. temperature vs. competitor prices vs. number of gas pumps vs. distance to nearest competitor vs. price etc. correlate to the amount of gasoline sold.

Adaptation: The outcome of the learning phase settles the foundation for the adaptation in order to achieve a given goal. The output of the adaptation phase is a price change of gasoline for a specific station. Thereby the price change (the adaptation effect) can be measured on the observations.

3   Demonstration

To demonstrate the application PriceCast Fuel (PCF) [1] has been developed as a commercial product. Due to legal issues the reference case of the company OK in Denmark is the only case among our consumers that can be disclosed. OK has a market share of approximately 25 % and has 700 gas stations which makes it the biggest company in Denmark measured by number of stations [2].

An agent has been designed by applying the methodology presented in [5] and has been able to observe and learn from data sets to find correlation and produce a consumer model in terms of amount of gasoline sold (volume). The chart depicted in Fig. 1(a) the consumer model for a given day for a given station as accumulated gasoline sold. The data related to this day has not been observed by the agent whereas the predicted volume is based on previous observations.

As illustrated by the chart on Fig. 1(a) the agent — based on it's consumer model — predicted the volume throughout the day (24 h) at the start of the day as illustrated by the model series. As time goes by the purchase of real consumers are depicted as a discrete chart illustrated by the actual series. There are several interesting parts of the consumer model. The agent has learned the consumer tendencies which are from 5 – 9 o'clock, 9 – 14 o'clock and 14 – 23 o'clock. If we examine the %-error at 9 o'clock, 14 o'clock and 23 o'clock we get 7.7 %, 2.6 % and 9.0 % respectively for this particular agent. However, it is also shown that the largest deviation gain is from 14 – 16 o'clock where the actual has a much greater slope than the model. Whereas from 16 – 23 the %-error is approximately constant.

Having a valid consumer model enables us to experiment with different adaptation strategies. A given scenario could be to use the consumer model as a reference and thereby detect anomaly in the behavior [6] to use as a trigger for adapting the price. This scenario is shown for a given gas station and product in the Fig. 1(b). Where the adaption of the price is directly inverse proportional by a given factor to the degree of the anomaly; hence the adaption results in a price which is directly linked to the price sign of the gas station.

The actual line in Fig. 1(b) indicates the actual price for this particular GSA running PCF. The symbol "◆" indicates competitor observations registered. In the depicted scenario four observations are made where the most interesting observation is the second (observed 4th Maj 2012 at 18:00 h) priced at 1,353 – which is quite aggressive compared to the first observation. In theory this price could have been set by the competitor in any point of time between the first observation and the second. The pricing pattern indicates that the GSA has detected unusual consumer behavior which results in negative fuel volume and uses lower pricing to correct this behavior; hence, it has learned the correlation between Δprice and Δfuel volume.

In order to validate PCF two groups, A and B, of similar gas stations was selected. Each group consisted of 15 stations representing the distribution of the entire brand. Group A was the test stations running PCF fully autonomously and group B was the control stations operated manually in a usual manner. All agents where given the goal to maintain market share and maximize margin. After 1 month when comparing the net margin of the two groups the fully autonomous

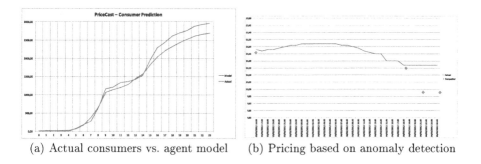

(a) Actual consumers vs. agent model   (b) Pricing based on anomaly detection

Fig. 1.

PCF gas stations performed on average 5 % better while keeping the market share [2]. OK in Denmark has been running PriceCast Fuel with approximately 700 autonomous GSAs pricing and optimizing 24/7/365 and handling a revenue stream of 1,5+ Billion USD per year for 4 years.

4 Conclusion

It has been demonstrated that the presented agent model [5] can be applied on a gas station and operate fully autonomously to achieve a given goal by learning and modeling Danish gasoline consumer behavior. Furthermore, it can be concluded that in Denmark the GSAs where able to achieve their given goal 5 % better than humans. PriceCast Fuel has been improving it's GSA model since 2011 where this demonstration is from; hence, the world expansion of PriceCast Fuel has shown that the environment of the GSA must be modeled to cope with elements such as legislation, government regulations etc. PriceCast Fuel is also now investigating the utilization of MAS concepts such as cooperation, completion, organization etc.

References

1. A2I Systems. Pricecast fuel. http://www.a2isystems.com/pricecast.html. Accessed 12 Feb 2016
2. A2I Systems. Pricecast fuel: Reference story. http://www.a2isystems.com/files/pdf/PriceCast%20Fuel%20Case%20Story%20('15).pdf. Accessed 12 Feb 2016
3. Angwin, J., Mattioli, D.: Coming soon: toilet paper priced like airline tickets. http://on.wsj.com/1QfNTMe. Accessed 12 Feb 2016
4. Bratman, M.E., Israel, D.J., Pollack, M.E.: Plans and resource-bounded practical reasoning. Comput. Intell. **4**, 349–355 (1988)
5. Derakhshan, A., Hammer, F., Lund, H., Demazeau, Y.: Mapping children and playgrounds into multi-agent systems (2006)
6. Lane, T., Brodley, C.E.: An application of machine learning to anomaly detection. In: Proceedings of the 20th National Information Systems Security Conference, pp. 366–380 (1997)
7. Noel, M.D.: Edgeworth price cycles. In: Durlauf, S.N., Blume, L.E. (eds.) The New Palgrave Dictionary of Economics. Palgrave Macmillan, Basingstoke (2011)

An Evolutionary Platform for Social Simulation in Case of Critical Hydrogeological Phenomena: The Authority's Role

Rino Falcone and Alessandro Sapienza[(⊠)]

ISTC-CNR of Rome, Rome, Italy
alessandro.sapienza@istc.cnr.it

Abstract. Starting from our previous work [1], we propose a study on cognitive agents that have to learn how to use their different information sources (their own evaluation, the authority communication, others' behavior) in different situations and with respect to different hydrogeological phenomena.

In particular we consider some specific situations in which the authority can be more or less trustworthy and more or less able to deliver its own forecasts to the agents. The simulations will show how, on the basis of a training phase in these different situations, the agents will be able to make a rational use of their different information sources.

Keywords: Trust · Social simulation · Cognitive analysis

1 Introduction

One of the main problems for understanding and foreseeing any domain and world, is not just to access to the different information sources about that domain, but also to be able to evaluate the trustworthiness of those sources: the same source not necessarily has the same degree of trustworthiness in any situation and context, but could change its own reliability on the basis of different external or internal factors. Are the agents able to learn the more trustworthy sources? Are the agents' performances coherent with the trustworthiness of the sources they are following? Are we able to extract useful information from these simulations for situations of real cases?

Exploiting NetLogo [3], we created a very flexible platform, taking into account a lot of parameters to model a variety of situations. For the sake of space, we are not going to report here the whole model. This work starts from a previous work of the authors in the same conference. Then for further details concerning information sources, events and agents' evaluation please look at [2].

2 Main Purpose

We used the simulative platform to investigate how different authority's behavior affects citizens' choice and the trust they have in their information sources. We believe that

© Springer International Publishing Switzerland 2016
Y. Demazeau et al. (Eds.): PAAMS 2016, LNAI 9662, pp. 251–255, 2016.
DOI: 10.1007/978-3-319-39324-7_24

authority's choices affect not only citizens individually, but also, by a social effect, citizens not directly reached by the authority. We study a series of scenarios, populated by equal populations but in presence of different authorities and we analyze how citizens respond to these changes, measuring their trust values and their choice in presence of possible risks.

2.1 Agents' Description

At the beginning, the agents have the same neutral **trust value** 0.5 for all their information sources. They are also characterized by a **decision deadline** determining when agents decide. Also not all the agents have the same abilities to read phenomena. We divided equally agents into three sets. **Good evaluators** are able to see 15 ticks of event. They will be quite always able to detect correctly the event. **Medium evaluators** see 14 ticks of event. They can detect the event, but not as good as the previous category. Finally **bad evaluators** see 13 ticks of event. Quite often, they will need another source to decide between two choices.

There is also the authority. Its aim is to inform promptly citizens about the phenomena. It is characterized by an **uncertainty**, expressed in terms of standard deviation σ, and by a **communicativeness value**, representing the probability that it will be able to inform each citizen.

2.2 Feedback on Trust

Agents need to adapt to the context in which they move. Starting from a neutral trust level they will try to understand how much to rely on each single information source. To do that, they need a way to perform feedback on trust. We propose to use weighted mean.

Given the two parameters α and β, the new trust value is computed as:

$$newTrustDegree = \alpha * oldTrustDegree + \beta * performanceEvaluation$$
$$\alpha + \beta = 1$$

Where *oldTrustDegree* is the previous trust degree and the *performanceEvaluation* is the objective evaluation of the source performance. This last value is obtained comparing what the source said with what actually happened. Considering the PDF (probability distribution function) reported by the source, we will have that: the estimated probability of the event that actually occurred is completely taken into account; the estimated probability of the event immediately near to the actual one is taken into account for just 1/3 (it is not completely wrong); the rest of the PDF is not considered.

3 Demonstration

In the world some weather phenomena happen, with a variable level of criticality, in a temporal window of 16 ticks. The cognitive agents (citizens) belonging to this world react to these situations, deciding how to behave, on the basis of the information sources they have and of the trustworthiness they attribute to these different sources: they can escape, take measures or evaluate absence of danger. Each simulation is divided into two steps. In the first one, called "**training phase**", agents make experience with their information sources, determining how much they are reliable. At the beginning of this phase the authority gives forecast for a future temporal window (composed by 16 ticks): critic = 3, medium = 2, light = 1. This information reaches each single agent with a probability given by the **authority communicativeness**. Being just a forecast, it is not sure that it is really going to happen. It depends on how much the authority is reliable (its standard deviation σ). However it allows agents to evaluate the situation in advance, before the possible event. Event in fact starts at t_1 and, as previously said, lasts for 16 ticks. During the decision making phase, agents check their information sources, aggregating the single contributes according to the corresponding trust values. They estimate the possibility that each event happens and decide accordingly. When this phase reaches the deadline, agents have to make a decision that cannot be changed anymore. This information is then available for the other agents (neighborhood), which can exploit it for their decisions. At the end of the event, agents evaluate the performance of the sources they used and adjust the corresponding trust values. If they haven't been reached by the authority, there will not be a feedback on trust but, as this source wasn't available when necessary, there will be a reduction of trust linked to the kind of event that happened: -0.15 for a critical event, -0.1 for a medium event, -0.05 for a light event.

This phase is repeated for 100 times so that agents can make enough experience to judge their sources. During this phase, in each quadrant each event has a fixed probability to happen: 10 % for critical event; 20 % for medium event; 70 % for light event.

After that, there is the "**testing phase**". Here we want to understand how agents perform, once they know how much reliable their sources are. To do that, we investigate how they perform in presence of a fixed map [3 1 3 2] and we compute the accuracy of their decision.

Simulation settings: **number of agents** = 200; **α and β** respectively 0.9 and 0.1; **authority reliability** high ($\sigma = 0.3$, its forecast are correct about the 90 % of time) or low ($\sigma = 0.9$, its forecast are correct about the 50 % of time); **authority communicativeness** 100 % (strongly communicative) or 30 % (weakly communicative); **training phase duration** 100 events; **probability of the events** 10 % critical event, 20 % medium

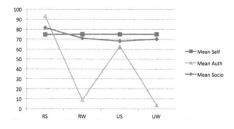

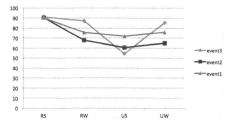

Fig. 1. The average trust value of all the agents on the three information sources in the four scenarios presented before.

Fig. 2. The average performances of all the agents for the three events in presence of four different authorities.

event, 70 % light event; **event map:** [3 1 3 2]. Simulations results are mediated through 500 cases (Figs. 1 and 2).

Where RS = reliable strongly communicative, RW = reliable weakly communicative, US = unreliable strongly communicative, UW = unreliable weakly communicative.

There will be a lot to say about these 4 cases, but for the sake of space we need to summarize results analysis. Let's then try to see the big picture, also comparing cases to each other.

In the first case (RS) we have the highest values of authority trust: it is a reliable available source, so that agents can rely on it. The authority trust has a good value also in the US case meaning that, in order to be trustworthy, it is important to be available to citizens, even if not always with correct information.

The RW and UW cases seem to be very similar: regardless of authority's reliability, trust on the authority is very low. Even the average social trust seems to be the same in the RW and UW cases. It reaches its maximal point in the RS case, being the other two sources quite always right, and its minimal point in the US, when the authority reaches all the agents, but it spreads incorrect information. Summarizing, **the US case seems to be good from the authority's point of view, but it seems to have a negative social impact.**

Taking into account performances the best case is the RS one; having just trustworthy sources, agents' performances are very high. Again the RW and UW cases, in which the authority is unavailable, are quite the same (actually the UW cases' values are a little bit lower) meaning that **if the authority is unavailable, it is no longer important how much competent it is.** The worst case is the US one. Here we have that all the agents' performances decreases to their lowest value.

Finally, one could ask if it is better to have a reliable authority but not always available (RW) or an unreliable authority that has a strong presence (US). These results clearly state that the RW case is better, considering citizens' performance. This is due to the fact that, even if each individual citizen will receive right information from the authority about the 27 % of the times in the RW case and about the 50 % of the times in the US case, in the RW case the positive effect of the authority is widespread by the social effect. Then even if the authority doesn't reach everyone directly, it can count on the social effect to do it.

4   Conclusion

We presented a platform for studying agents' choice in presence of critical weather phenomena, where agents evaluate and aggregate information from different information sources.

Through the training phase the agents learn to attribute to the different information sources the right values of trustworthiness and, as a consequence, they are able to perform quite effectively. In particular, two behaviors of the authorities are interesting: reliable and weakly communicative, not reliable and strongly communicative. They are a good simulation of the real cases in which the best prediction of a weather event is the more temporally close to the event itself (when becomes difficult to effectively spread the information: time for spreading is little). On the contrary, a prediction of a weather event can be effectively spread when there is big time for the spreading (far from the event), but this is in general a very inaccurate prediction.

Very interesting is the compensative and integrative role of the social phenomenon (observation of the others' behavior) that guides the performances of the agents upwards when just one of the two other sources results as reliable.

Acknowledgments. This work is partially supported by the project CLARA—CLoud plAtform and smart underground imaging for natural Risk Assessment, funded by the Italian Ministry of Education, University and Research (MIUR-PON).

References

1. Castelfranchi, C., Falcone, R.: Trust Theory: A Socio-Cognitive and Computational Model. Wiley, Chichester (2010)
2. Falcone, R., Sapienza, A., Castelfranchi, C.: Which information sources are more trustworthy in a scenario of hydrogeological risks: a computational platform. In: In Proceedings of PAAMS 2016
3. Wilensky, U.: Center for Connected Learning and Computer-Based Modeling. Northwestern University, Evanston (1999). NetLogo. http://ccl.northwestern.edu/netlogo/

Demo Paper: AGADE
Scalability of Ontology Based Agent Simulations

Thomas Farrenkopf[1]($\boxtimes$), Michael Guckert[1], Neil Urquhart[2], and Simon Wells[2]

[1] KITE - Kompetenzzentrum für Informationstechnologie,
Technische Hochschule Mittelhessen, Giessen, Germany
{thomas.farrenkopf,michael.guckert}@mnd.thm.de
[2] School of Computing, Edinburgh Napier University, Edinburgh, Scotland, UK
{n.urquhart,s.wells}@napier.ac.uk

Abstract. Simulations of real world scenarios often require considerably large numbers of agents. With increasing level of detail and resolution in the underlying models machine limitations both in the aspect of memory and computing power are reached. Even more when additional features like reasoning mechanisms of semantic technologies are used as in the AGADE framework where we have extended the principal BDI paradigm with an interface to OWL ontologies. We have observed that the extensive use of ontologies results in high memory consumption due to the large number of String objects used in the reasoning process and caching mechanisms of the OWL API. We address this issue by running simulations in a highly distributed environment. In this paper we demonstrate how we enabled AGADE to be run in such an environment and the necessary architectural modifications. Furthermore, we discuss the potential size of simulations that can be run in such a setting.

Keywords: Multi-agent system · BDI · OWL ontology · Market simulation · Distributed simulation

1 Introduction

Using OWL ontologies [7] in a usual single instance setting memory consumption is not a serious issue. But using ontologies in multi-agent simulations where each agent is equipped with its own ontology memory usage increases linearly due to the extensive use of String objects used in the reasoning process and caching mechanisms of the OWL API [4]. As AGADE keeps representations of social relations in the ontology the effect is enforced with increasing number of agents and consequently rising numbers of mutual connections. AGADE uses ontologies to flexibly model world knowledge in a BDI architecture. See [1] for detailed examples of how ontologies can be integrated into the BDI concept in general and the Jadex [6] framework in particular. Although, distributed agent platforms have long been available, but the support of crucial elements of multi-agent simulations e.g. schedulers for managing time, synchronising agents and

© Springer International Publishing Switzerland 2016
Y. Demazeau et al. (Eds.): PAAMS 2016, LNAI 9662, pp. 256–259, 2016.
DOI: 10.1007/978-3-319-39324-7_25

data collection is often not available [5]. Therefore AGADE been implemented in a non distributed environment at first and has then been extended. Multi-agent simulations can now be run in a network and offer full support of a model of time and elaborate communication mechanisms so that scenarios can be scaled up and run in the network or not.

2 Main Purpose

AGADE is a BDI based framework that supports the development of dynamic business scenarios with individual access to semantic reasoning for each agent [2]. AGADE agents are equipped with their own inference engine (reasoner) and private ontology using the OWL API [4]. The ontology allows a flexible architecture as aspects of the agent may be expressed in the rules rather than static code [1]. We distinguish between the abstract domain layer (ADL) containing general knowledge and the specific domain layer (SDL) shared by all agents and the individual domain layer (IDL) specific to each agent. AGADE allows scaling up the amount of agents participating in a simulation scenario using a directing agent that orchestrates the set of agents and controls the flow of time and communication. Each round (time step) of the simulation is structured into four phases (calculation, socialisation, action, control) with defined functionality and integration into the BDI paradigm.

3 Demonstration

AGADE implements a Java RMI (Remote Method Invocation) based communication mechanism with which the agents can send and receive messages. RMI is directly based on socket communication and is therefore more efficient than alternative technologies like Web Services or CORBA. We ran various benchmarks comparing the alternatives with results similar to what has been published before (e.g. [3]). Consequently, we decided to use RMI which is currently still the best technology for running distributed tasks in the context of multi-threaded applications in Java.

On an abstract level AGADE knows two different kinds of BDI agents: a single director type agent that acts as controlling instance of the simulation and performs central administrative tasks (e.g. controlling simulation rounds by triggering each agent), and a participant type agent that acts in the simulation (i.e. consumer or seller). The communication between participating agents and between participating agent and director agent uses RMI based services both in distributed and in non-distributed mode ensuring a unified architecture for the framework.

The typical RMI flow of execution starts with an initial registration of objects in the RMI registry of a server using a unique name which makes the objects available for client access. Clients can now query the lookup service of the *RMI registry* to get a reference to the objects. The client can then invoke appropriately published methods. In our AGADE implementation the role of server and client are interchangeable i.e. each node in the network can act as client and as server thus allowing two way communication with asynchronous method invocation (see Fig. 1). AGADE implements a `YellowPages` service in each node where agents and their node are published to be used in inter-agent communication. Note that two nodes in the network do not necessarily have to be connected through yellow page entries as they may not have to communicate at all during the simulation. But at least one distinguished central node must be aware of all other nodes and can then act as a broker and can enable communication if requested. Once communication between two nodes has been established mutual entries are made in the yellow pages. This lazy set up of communication information reduces initial messaging efforts and provides direct links only if requested. The director agent and the GUI communication with the user obviously have to be placed on the central node as well. The delivery process of inter-agent communication is therefore implemented as follows:

- query local yellow pages on client-side and deliver message directly if both address information is available
- request broker on central node to provide necessary information and initiate communication.

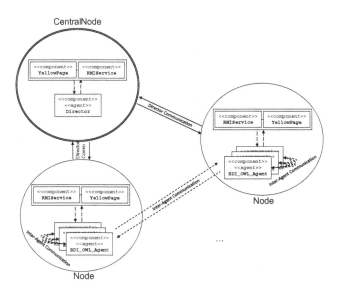

Fig. 1. AGADE nodes model.

In the inter-client communication scenario, the client is querying the server for the client-address and will then deliver the message to the specific client directly. RMI message mechanisms use Java serialisation to deliver objects. OWL components are represented as Strings and can therefore undergo the standard RMI serialisation process. Thus the content of each agent message is eventually a serialised instance of **String**. The typical message content size of an OWL concept is about 850 Byte = 0.0068 Mbit. Theoretically, a typical network bandwidth of 1000 MBit/s allows sending ~147,058 messages simultaneously with respect to the content size without limitations neglecting connection overhead usage. To reduce the amount of network traffic between clients, we further compress the message content by using *gzip* which reduces the size by roughly 50 percent.

This architecture allows to scale up simulations considerably. We successfully tested the robustness of this architecture by simulating a homogeneous crowd of buyers acting in a mobile phone market where we have run 100,000 agents over 100 rounds on 6 clients each connected with 100 MBits network speed and equipped with various hardware settings (RAM/CPU).

4   Conclusion

In this demonstration paper, we have presented an improved version of AGADE, where round-based multi-agent simulations with elaborate agent behaviour modelled in OWL can be scaled up considerably. We addressed the high memory consumption of the OWL reasoning process by running simulations in a distributed environment where full support of crucial characteristics of MAS (e.g. well defined phases, common model of time,...) are guaranteed. As a result, AGADE can now handle simulation scenarios with a much higher number of agents in a single architecture that can easily be configured to be run on a single machine or in a network with distributed nodes.

References

1. Farrenkopf, T., Guckert, M., Hoffmann, B., Urquhart, N.: AGADE how individual guidance leads to group behaviour and how this can be simulated. In: Müller, J.P., Weyrich, M., Bazzan, A.L.C. (eds.) MATES 2014. LNCS, vol. 8732, pp. 234–250. Springer, Heidelberg (2014). http://dx.doi.org/10.1007/978-3-319-11584-9_16
2. Farrenkopf, T., Guckert, M., Urquhart, N.: AGADE using personal preferences and world knowledge to model agent behaviour. In: Demazeau, Y., Decker, K.S., Bajo Pérez, J., De la Prieta, F. (eds.) PAAMS 2015. LNCS, vol. 9086, pp. 93–106. Springer, Heidelberg (2015). http://dx.doi.org/10.1007/978-3-319-18944-4_8
3. Gray, N.A.B.: Comparison of web services, java-rmi, and corba service implementation. In: Fifth Australasian Workshop on Software and System Architectures (2004)
4. Horridge, M., Bechhofer, S.: The owl api: a java api for owl ontologies. Seman. Web **2**(1), 11–21 (2011)
5. Mengistu, D., Troger, P., Lundberg, L., Davidsson, P.: Scalability in distributed multi-agent based simulations: the jade case. In: International Conference on Future Generation Communication and Networking Symposia, vol. 5, pp. 93–99 (2008)
6. Pokahr, A., Braubach, L., Jander, K.: The jadex project: programming model. In: Ganzha, M., Jain, L.C. (eds.) Multiagent Systems and Applications. Intelligent Systems Reference Library, vol. 45, pp. 21–53. Springer, Heidelberg (2013)
7. W3C OWL Working Group: OWL 2 Web Ontology Language: Document Overview. W3C Recommendation, 11 December 2012. http://www.w3.org/TR/2012/REC-owl2-overview-20121211/

A Framework to Evaluate Autonomic Behaviours for Intelligent Truck Parking

José F. García[1]([⊠]), Vicente R. Tomás[2], Luis A. García[2], and Juan J. Martínez[1]

[1] Institute of robotics and information and communication technologies (IRTIC),
University of Valencia, Valencia, Spain
{jfgarcia,juanjo}@irtic.uv.es
[2] Engineering and Computer Science Department, University Jaume I,
Castellón de la Plana, Spain
{vtomas,garcial}@uji.es

Abstract. This paper presents a multi-agent platform to evaluate different strategies to manage the negotiated management of parking spaces in road rest areas. The system dynamically adapts itself to the preferences and needs of the drivers of goods about parking requests. The system is shown to be robust to incidents regarding the closure of road rest areas and allows a conversational interaction of new parking requests through an Android based mobile application.

1 Introduction

Freight transport has a high relevance in the transportation domain and has a direct impact in long distance corridors which are used by any kind of drivers. Regulations regarding driving times and rest periods are very restrictive to ensure road safety [1]. Truck drivers need to know the parking availability in order to achieve their destination respecting laws, and, avoiding to be forced to park on ramps or shoulders decreasing road safety and being exposed to be fined.

In this context, the problem of finding a parking space is not merely a selection problem, or a "first-in problem". The system must ensure that the allocation of parking spaces is the best possible allocation according to the current truck location, Road driving Time (RT), and driver preferences. Drivers are confident with the system because it minimizes the number of drivers that are forced to park illegally or continue to the next parking area exceeding the Maximum driving Time (MT).

In this paper, we describe a multi-agent framework to evaluate different strategies to tackle the problem. The multi-agent system has been developed based on JADE [2], and, it uses a negotiation protocol to adapt dynamically the available parking spaces between trucks. The framework presented allows to simulate different scenarios along a road network populated with a set of areas and trucks. It also allows the dynamic reallocation of trucks when an area is temporally closed, or, reopened. An android application has been deployed to

© Springer International Publishing Switzerland 2016
Y. Demazeau et al. (Eds.): PAAMS 2016, LNAI 9662, pp. 260–264, 2016.
DOI: 10.1007/978-3-319-39324-7_26

simulate and incorporate new trucks. Using this tool is also possible to study the evolution of the system when new trucks enter in the system and request parking spaces.

2 Negotiation Protocol

The negotiation protocol is based on a voting system. Area agents confirm the requested reservations to truck agents while supplies free parking spaces. The negotiation process is fired when an agent area has all its parking spaces reserved and a new truck requests a parking space into the area. In most voting systems, voters have the same weight in their votes, but sometimes this rule is not applied. In Borda [3], voters provide a different score to each of the feasible solutions. First choices will have a higher score than later ones. The negotiation protocol used is conducted by a variation of Borda voting-based protocol. In this proposal, trucks will vote different solutions. These solutions are the set of possible distributions of parking spaces of the corresponding area between the trucks involved in the negotiation.

Since the main objective is minimizing the illegal parking, trucks with more RT must have a higher weight in their votes. These trucks need a high priority since they have less opportunities to reach other rest areas. At the same time, the weight of votes tries to avoid the reallocation of vehicles when they are close to the rest area. The weight of the vote of a truck j is defined by:

$$w_j = \frac{RT_j * 100}{MT} \tag{1}$$

Moreover, trucks will assign a greater value to solutions where the corresponding truck is allocated in its most preferred rest area and this value will be decreased when it is allocated in less preferred rest areas. So, in this approach weights are pondered regarding the position of the area where a truck is allocated in the solution according to the order in its list of preferences.

$$Preferences = [a_1, ..., a_n] : a_1 \succ a_2 \succ ... \succ a_n \tag{2}$$

$$Vote_j = w_j * [n, n - 1, ..., 1] \tag{3}$$

But, trucks with more candidate rest areas would get a higher score than other trucks on the same rest area with a less number of candidate rest areas. This problem is avoided by using a normalization process to the votes from each truck.

In this paper, two different methods are presented to normalize the vote of the values applied to each truck involved in a negotiation.

First method proposed the use of a Φ parameter to normalize the values of the votes regarding the set of solutions. This parameter is the maximum number of preferences from all trucks implied in the negotiation. Using this method we ensure that weights are pondered by the same value for the most preferred area of the trucks involved and decreasing homogeneously in the followings:

$$Vote_j = w_j * [\Phi - 0, \Phi - 1, .., \Phi - (n - 1)] : \Phi \geq n \tag{4}$$

Second method uses a percentage that depends on the number of preferred areas of the truck involved in a negotiation. The first preference will be pondered with a 100 %, and this percentage will be reduced gradually according to the number of preferences. Using this method trucks pondered again the most preferred area by the same value (100 %), but the next ones will be pondered according to the pending active preferences of the truck involved.

$$Vote_j = w_j * 100 * [\frac{n - 0}{n}, \frac{n - 1}{n}, ..., \frac{n - (n - 1)}{n}]. \tag{5}$$

3 Demonstration

A framework to evaluate the proposed negotiation protocol is presented in this section. The framework allows to define scenarios in a road network with different configuration of trucks and areas.

The scenario configuration parameters are the following:

- Initial position and final positions where trucks can be located along the road. The system will locate randomly each truck between these two positions.
- Maximum number of preferences. Number of preferences of truck drivers to park.
- Speed (km/h). Average speed of drivers along the road-network.
- Maximum driving time. Maximum driving time allowed by law.
- Initial and Final Driving Time. The system will assign randomly a driving time to each truck between the interval defined.
- The initial and final position where areas can be located along the road.
- The number of available parking spaces in the different areas.

The framework has been tested in a real road network: the E-15 motorway along the Valencian Community in Spain. The framework interface uses the Google Maps API to show the road network and the areas. 11 real rest areas has been included in the model including the position.

The framework allows to modify the configuration of the parameters of trucks and areas to test different scenarios. This configuration can be also saved in order to reproduce the same configuration with different methods.

Once the simulation is configured, the framework launches the interface agent, the area agents, and, the truck agents. The agent interface shows the evolution of assignations of parking spaces by the areas to the different truck agents. It also shows the evolution of the occupancy without the negotiation process, and the occupancy using the negotiation process selected in the configuration.

During the execution of the scenario, the framework allows to simulate the temporally closure of an area, and how the involved truck agents are reallocated in the neighbouring areas according to their preferences.

An Android based mobile application has been developed to improve the framework. The Android application represents a new truck agent in the system and recreates its functionalities: the current truck agent position, the request for the position of existing areas, the creation of its list of preferences, and the request for a reservation. Once the Android App has received the confirmation of the area assigned, the mobile application will drive the truck to the assigned area through a Google Maps route.

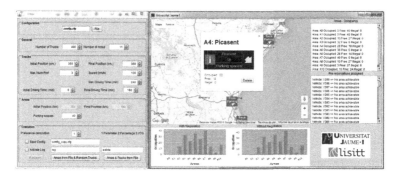

Fig. 1. On the left the configuration window is presented. On the right, a snapshot of the interface agent is shown. Areas are identified with icons showing the availability of free spaces or full occupancy. The exact occupancy of the area and the VMS panel to be shown on the road are presented when clicking on an area icon.

4   Conclusions

In this paper, a multi-agent framework to evaluate different strategies to allocate trucks along a set of rest areas is presented. The system tries to guarantee that all vehicles have a parking space when they reach the rest area. In this way, drivers comply laws about driving time and rest periods. The system takes into account not only the current parking places but also the preferences of drivers. So, drivers can know in advance if they have a parking place reserved in one of their preferred areas. The negotiation protocols are adapted to the dynamic behaviour of the traffic. When an area has more reservation than free parking spaces, the area start a negotiation protocol based on a voting system. Each truck votes his best option from a possible set of solutions. The voting system is a modification of the Borda protocol adapted to this specific problem. An android based mobile application has been developed to better observe the reaction of the framework when new trucks request for a parking space. The framework eases the evaluation and comparison of new approaches of the protocol to improve the solution of the problem. Simulation results based on a real scenario shows the benefits of allocating parking spaces using the negotiation protocol compared to the same scenario without negotiation following a first-come first-served bases.

References

1. Regulation (EC) No 561/2006 of the European Parliament and of the Council of 15 March 2006. Council Regulations (EEC) No 3821/85 and (EC) No 2135/98 (2006)
2. Java Agent Development framework (JADE), TILAB (2014). http://jade.cselt.it
3. Zahid, M.A., de Swart, H.: The borda majority count. In: SSEAC Workshop on Voting and Allocation Systems, Finland (2010)

Modeling Agents Working on ETL Processes

Nuno Gomes, Bruno Oliveira, and Orlando Belo[✉]

Department of Informatics, School of Engineering, ALGORITMI R&D Centre,
University of Minho, Campus de Gualtar, 4710-057 Braga, Portugal
obelo@di.uminho.pt

Abstract. All data warehousing systems architects know that is quite difficult to build a "perfect" ETL system without having primarily a model well founded on real operational requisites. Thus ETL modeling is crucial to the success of populating a data warehouse, independently from their natural complexity. Modeling will also reduce implementation costs once it allows for revealing eventual operational errors originated by misinterpreted requisites. In this demo we demonstrate the viability of modeling an ETL system, using a standard work-flow language and an ETL pattern approach implemented based on a cooperative community of opportunistic agents. The demo shows how we modeled, configured and executed an ETL system prototype in YAWL, and how we used agents to implement a self-organizing general purpose ETL system.

Keywords: Multi-agent systems · Data warehousing systems · ETL systems modeling · ETL patterns design · YAWL

1 Introduction

Usually, *Data Warehousing Systems* (DWS) [4] architects and engineers do not have a positive perspective about the utility of a well-supported conceptual schema. Based on some time restrictions, they use to adopt a more physical ETL (*Extract-Transform-Load*) [3] approach supported by realistic and strong specifications the logical level. In their point of view, conceptual models rarely are useful instruments in a practical ETL system implementation. However, we have a slightly different opinion – conceptual models are useful when used as a first schematic approach to ETL system implementation. We believe that a well-defined conceptual model can drive us quite balanced through the entire DWS life cycle, since it incorporated the most basic structures and tasks that will support the essential behavior of the future ETL system. So, this initial schema - an ETL sketch – when modeled appropriately is a useful instrument in the definition and validation of a preliminary version of an ETL system. Furthermore, if we have the possibility to see how the designed model will behave using simulation, it will be possible to observe ETL components working and evaluate their performance, either individually or jointly. ETL systems are very complex tasks in which planning and designing assume very important roles in their development. These tasks allow for sketching and validating different kinds of implementations accordingly all operational requirements presented, as well as contribute for reducing the occurrence of errors

© Springer International Publishing Switzerland 2016
Y. Demazeau et al. (Eds.): PAAMS 2016, LNAI 9662, pp. 265–268, 2016.
DOI: 10.1007/978-3-319-39324-7_27

avoiding jeopardizing the success of the system. Using workflow languages for speci-fying ETL systems is quite interesting, due to: (1) their understandable notations; (2) a well separation of concerns between operations orchestration; and (3) the data involved and the necessary meaning to instantiate more conceptual models to execution primi-tives. The YAWL language [1] is one of them. Using formalisms inherited by Petri Nets concepts and workflow patterns, it provides a formal but very intuitive way to represent workflows, being quite adequate to specify and validate ETL systems, at a very early stage of development, disposing powerful constructs that enable execution primitives in the definition of a workflow. With YAWL, we will demonstrate how to design a complete ETL system from scratch using an agent based approach to design and simu-lated an ETL system, using as basic building blocks a set of ETL patterns.

2   Main Purpose

In spite of existing a large diversity of tools in the market, it is a little bit difficult to find some having the ability to help us in the first stages of an ETL system project, especially at the conceptual modeling one. Many of the work done at this stage it can easily be disposed of. We have not yet the possibility to use it effectively in the next stages, where some tool gather and transform it in a way that could be analyzed, tested and validated. The majority of the tools starts immediately at physical level, having no kind of mech-anism for receiving conceptual specifications or even conceptual models. The main purpose of this work was to design and implement a way for evaluating the suitability of an ETL conceptual model, using the standard modeling and simulation means provided by YAWL. Basically, our goal was to use the conceptual specification of an ETL system just at the beginning of the process as a demonstration mean and a helping tool to reflect in functional terms the business requisites we are gathering. In order to reduce the complexity of the system specification we used ETL patterns [5] – e.g. *change data capture* (CDC), *data quality enhancement* (DQE), *slowly changing dimension* (SCD), or *intensive data loading* (IDL) –, implementing them in YAWL following an agent-based approach [2] - one agent for one ETL pattern. ETL patterns are reusable components that represent common ETL tasks, often used in DWS, which based on a set of configurable input parameters produce an output based on their internal configu-ration. They are autonomous components working in an isolation mode, not affecting other patterns' behavior and preserving the structure of the entire ETL system. Using agents, we got the possibility to model and simulate a self-regulate ETL system, which means that any ETL task definition, as well as their overall scheduling, can be done dynamically. As agents, ETL patterns can be used autonomously, being activated given a set of well-defined operational constraints, based on a specific working order, indi-cating as input a task of its competence, and when possible returning back the result of the task it just made to the entity that previously made the request – it may be another ETL agent. Thus, an ETL process would be achieved using a kind of opportunistic intervention of each of the agents available in the system that make together the work hosted for populating a data warehouse.

id	list_id	task_id	task_name	dim_name	task_stat	task_agent	task_timestamp
121	1	1	CDC	DIM_One	0	NULL	NULL
122	1	1	CDC	TF	0	NULL	NULL
123	1	2	SCD	DIM_One	0	NULL	NULL
124	1	3	SKP	TF	0	NULL	NULL
125	1	4	IDL DIM	DIM_One	0	NULL	NULL
126	1	5	IDL	TF	0	NULL	NULL

Fig. 1. An excerpt of an ETL job list.

3 Demonstration

To demonstrate an ETL system conceptual modeling and simulating process, we idealized a simple application scenario involving: (1) a community of agents, which are responsible to execute several ETL tasks of a given working package accordingly to a set of pre defined ETL patterns; and (2) a shared knowledge structure - a blackboard – that agents use to see what to do and to communicate results. The ETL process it is presented to the community of ETL agents as a job list (Fig. 1), with all the priorities associated with each defined ETL task. After posted into the blackboard, all active agents would observe the ETL job list in a continuous manner (Fig. 2a), performing the tasks of their competence and returning results timely and accordingly to the priorities established. When all the tasks presented in that list are finished, a monitoring agent will terminate the correspondent ETL process. In Fig. 2b it is depicted the YAWL model for an agent executing an SCD ETL pattern. Other agents were modeled and tested as well, namely the ones related to ETL tasks such as CDC, DQE, IDL, or SKP (*surrogate key pipelining*).

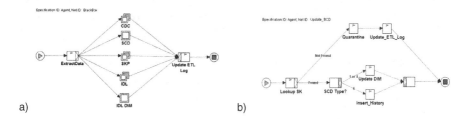

Fig. 2. Two YAWL Models – (a) The execution of agents; (b) The SCD Agent – update mode.

The SCD ETL pattern presented in Fig. 2b is one of the most used tasks in DWS populating processes. Receiving information about decision-makers analysis perspectives, slowly changing dimensions represent data structures whose attributes' values have the ability to change over time. They are used to track changes in dimension attributes, in order to maintain the history of the dimension, enabling the assignment of a proper dimension attribute's value for some date in the past. The YAWL model presented in Fig. 2b shows how a SCD ETL agent acts in case of detecting a SCD request in the ETL job list. Basically, it starts searching for a surrogate key that validates the record it has. If the surrogate key is a valid one, the agent identifies the variation type of the dimension, and (1) rewrite the record ("Update DIM"), or (2) move the old record to an auxiliary table and insert the new one in the correspondent dimension table

("Insert_History"). In case of the agent do not detect a valid surrogate key in the first task the record goes directly to a quarantine table ("Quarantine"). In Fig. 3 we can see also some screenshots of the process we modeled related to the definition of an ETL job (Fig. 3a), including three ETL tasks (two CDC and one SCD), the initial configuration of an agent (Fig. 3b), and the current status of an ETL job list (Fig. 3c).

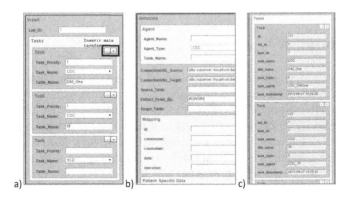

Fig. 3. Screenshots of the execution of the system modeled.

4   Conclusions

YAWL is a powerful tool to design and validate ETL systems during its conceptual design phase, allowing for creating *a priori* an ETL conceptual model that can be simulated and tested. The primitives and constructors that YAWL provides us today still are insufficient to provide a complete specification of an ETL system. However, the use of ETL patterns attenuated a little bit this disadvantage and allowed to demonstrate that YAWL conceptual models could be used to reduce the development time and as well as the computational resources necessary for the implementation of an ETL system. The use of agents allowed us for modeling a self-regulate ETL system.

References

1. Van der Aalst, W., Hofstede, A.: YAWL: yet another workflow language. Inf. Syst. **30**, 245–275 (2003)
2. van der Hoek, W., Wooldridge, M.: Multi-agent systems. In: van Harmelen, F., Lifschitz, V., Porter, B. (eds.) Handbook of Knowledge Representation, pp. 887–928. Elsevier, Amsterdam (2008)
3. Kimball, R., Caserta, J.: The Data Warehouse ETL Toolkit: Practical Techniques for Extracting, Cleaning, Conforming, and Delivering Data. Wiley, New York (2004)
4. Kimball, R., Ross, M.: The Data Warehouse Toolkit: The Complete Guide to Dimensional Modeling. Wiley, New York (2002)
5. Oliveira, B., Belo, O.: Pattern-based ETL conceptual modeling. In: Cuzzocrea, A., Maabout, S. (eds.) MEDI 2013. LNCS, pp. 237–248. Springer, Heidelberg (2013)

Providing Entertainment Services by Means of a User-Adapted Multimodal App

David Griol$^{(\boxtimes)}$ and José Manuel Molina

Computer Science Department, Carlos III University of Madrid,
Avda. de la Universidad, 30, 28911 Leganés, Spain
{david.griol,josemanuel.molina}@uc3m.es

Abstract. In this paper, we describe a context-aware multimodal conversational agent for Android-based mobile devices that dynamically incorporate user specific requirements and preferences as well as characteristics about the interaction environment, in order to improve and personalize the information and services that are provided. The developed App facilitates the interaction by means of speech or using the screen and virtual keyboard. The services that are provided by the App include accessing the latest local and international news, the weather forecast for the coming days for the current place, the results of different lottery contests and events, the movie listings and upcoming movies.

Keywords: Human-agent interaction · User interfaces · Conversational agents · Spoken and multimodal interaction · Mobile devices · Android

1   Introduction

Multimodal interactive systems offer the user combinations of input and output modalities for interacting with mobile devices, taking advantage of the naturalness of speech [5]. Different vendors offer APIs for the development of applications that use speech as a possible input and output modality, but developers have to design ad-hoc solutions to implement the interaction management.

Speech access is then a solution to the shrinking size of mobile devices (both keyboards to provide information and displays to see the results). Besides, speech interfaces facilitate the access to multiagent systems [1], especially in environments where this access is not possible using traditional input interfaces (e.g., keyboard and mouse). It also facilitates information access for people with visual or motor disabilities.

In this paper we describe a practical application showing how context-aware and user-adapted multimodal conversational interfaces can be easily integrated in hand-held Android mobile devices. The developed Android App provide entertainment services that are adapted to the users' preferences and location.

© Springer International Publishing Switzerland 2016
Y. Demazeau et al. (Eds.): PAAMS 2016, LNAI 9662, pp. 269–272, 2016.
DOI: 10.1007/978-3-319-39324-7_28

2   Main Purpose

Our proposal is focused on the development of multimodal conversational agents for mobile devices operating with the Android OS [4]. The Google Speech API is integrated to include the speech recognition functionality in a multimodal conversational agent. The development of multimodal systems involves user inputs through two or more combined modes, which usually complement spoken interaction by also adding the possibility of textual and tactile inputs provided using physical or virtual keyboards and the screen. In our contribution, we also model the context of the interaction as an additional valuable information source to be considered in the fusion process. We propose the acquisition of external context by means of the use of sensors currently supported by Android devices. The Android sensor framework (*android.hardware* package) allows to access these sensors and acquire raw sensor data.

The dialog manager of the system is based on a previously developed statistical methodology [2]. The visual structure of the user interface (UI) is defined by means of layouts, which are defined by declaring UI elements in XML or instantiating layouts elements at runtime. Finally, we propose the use of the Google TTS API to include the text-to-speech functionality. The *android.speech.tts* package includes the classes and interfaces required to integrate text-to-speech synthesis in an Android application.

3   Demonstration

We have developed a practical multimodal entertainment App for Android-based mobile devices. Users can interact with the developed application by means of their speech or using the screen and virtual keyboard. The App allows to access the latest local and international news, the weather forecast for the coming days and current place, the results of different lottery contests and events, and the movie listings and upcoming movies. The information is provided in Spanish. Users can also personalize the information that is provided by the App by means of specifying their preferences when accessing the different services.

In order to provide the functionalities described, the system engages in a dialog with the user to retrieve different pieces of information that are complemented with the context-awareness capabilities of the system. This way, the system response is adapted taking into account the specific preferences and suggestions selected by the users, as well as to the context in which the interaction takes place. The statistical models for the user's intention recognizer and dialog management modules were learned using a corpus acquired by means of an automatic dialog generation technique previously developed [3].

Figure 1 shows the main screen of the application, the screen that users can employ in order to personalize the services provided by the App, and an example of the information provided for a specific movie.

Figure 2 shows different examples corresponding to the access of the latest news, the results of a specific lottery contest for a given day, and the weather forecast corresponding to the date provided by the user.

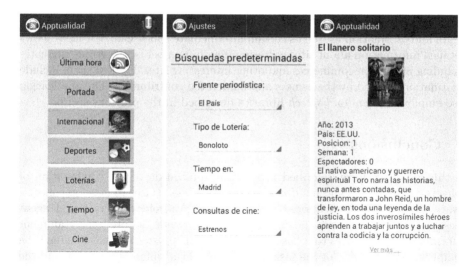

Fig. 1. Set of functionalities provided by the developed App (main screen, personalized user profiles, and movies listing)

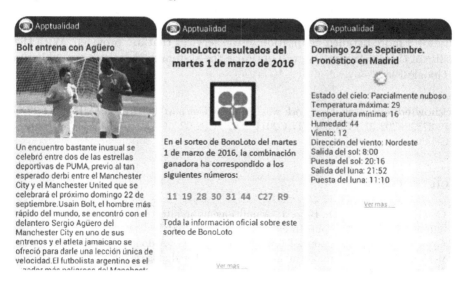

Fig. 2. Set of functionalities provided by the developed App (latest news, lottery contests, and weather forecast)

The developed multimodal App also uses Google Maps, Google Directions and Google Places. Google Maps Android API makes it possible to show an interactive map in response to a certain query. It is possible to add markers or zoom to a particular area, also to include images such as icons, highlighted areas and routes. Google Directions is a service that computes routes to reach a certain spot walking, on public transport or bicycle, and it is possible to specify the origin and destination as well as certain intermediate spots. Google Places shows detailed information about sites corresponding to number of categories currently including 80 million commerces and other interesting sites. Each of them include information verified by the owners and moderated contributors. The application also employs the *android.speech* libraries described in the previous section.

4   Conclusions

In this paper we have described a practical application of the combination of conversational agents and hand-held Android mobile devices to develop context-aware multimodal applications. The developed Android conversational agent uses geographical context and user profiles to provide adapted entertainment information and services to its users. To develop this system we have defined the complete requirements for the task and developed the different modules, and the necessary information sources to be incorporated in the user profiles.

We are currently undergoing the next phases in the deployment of the application. We want to include additional functionalities to facilitate the location of points of interest related to the provided user preferences, and to also consider additional information sources related to the users' emotional state and personality for a more detailed adaptation of the services that are provided. With the results of these activities, we will optimize the system, and make it available the in Google Play.

Acknowledgements. This work was supported in part by Projects MINECO TEC 2012-37832-C02-01, CICYT TEC2011-28626-C02-02, CAM CONTEXTS (S2009/ TIC-1485).

References

1. Corchado, J., Tapia, D., Bajo, J.: A multi-agent architecture for distributed services and applications. Comput. Intell. **24**(2), 77–107 (2008)
2. Griol, D., Callejas, Z., López-Cózar, R., Riccardi, G.: A domain-independent statistical methodology for dialog management in spoken dialog systems. Comput. Speech Lang. **28**(3), 743–768 (2014)
3. Griol, D., Sánchez-Pi, N., Carbó, J., Molina, J.: An agent-based dialog simulation technique to develop and evaluate conversational agents. In: Demazeau, Y., Pěchouček, M., Corchado, J.M., Pérez, J.B. (eds.) Advances on Practical Applications of Agents and Multiagent Systems (PAAMS 2011). Advances in Intelligent and Soft Computing, vol. 88, pp. 255–264. Springer, Heidelberg (2011)
4. McTear, M., Callejas, Z.: Voice Application Development for Android. Packt Publishing, Birmingham (2013)
5. Pieraccini, R.: The Voice in the Machine: Building Computers that Understand Speech. MIT Press, Cambridge (2012)

DRNS: Dynamical Relay Node Placement Solution

Roberto Magán-Carrión[1](✉), José Camacho[1], Pedro García-Teodoro[1],
Eduardo Feo Flushing[2], and Gianni A. Di Caro[2]

[1] Network Engineering & Security Group (NESG), Department of Signal Theory,
Telematics and Communications - CITIC, University of Granada,
18071 Granada, Spain
{rmagan,josecamacho,pgteodor}@ugr.es
[2] Istituto Dalle Molle di studi sull'intelligenza artificiale (IDSIA),
Galleria 2, Via Cantonale 2c, 6928 Manno, Switzerland
{eduardo,gianni}@idsia.ch

Abstract. Relay node (RN) placement is a challenging problem, specially in mobile ad hoc networks (MANETs) environments where the
locations of the nodes are continuously changing. In this context we propose here a novel, modular and adaptable RN placement solution based
on the joint maximization of the network connectivity and throughput.
For that, we use a combination of particle swarm optimization (PSO)
and model predictive control (MPC) inspired methodologies to drive the
RN movements. In order to corroborate the validity and applicability of
the approach we implement, deploy and test the proposed solution in a
real MANET environment where the nodes are mobile robots.

Keywords: Relay node placement · PSO · MPC · MANET

1 Introduction

In communication networks, the spatial distribution of the nodes is of primary
importance to achieve the desired performance. For instance, in wireless sensor networks (WSNs), the maximization of the coverage range of a monitored
area is a common objective highly depending on the node distribution. Unfortunately, in a WSN and in some other networks, it is often the case that not
all individual nodes can be controlled for their position. In such a cases, the
contribution of additional nodes under a explicit control can be helpful or even
needed to achieve the desired performance. For this purpose, the so-called *relay
nodes* (RNs) are used to relay the information among the network nodes [1].
The placement and/or movement of the RNs is controlled to fulfill some specific
given requirements [2]. This turns to be a challenging task, specially in dynamic
environment. In these scenarios, dynamic and adaptive RN placement solutions
are needed to maintain the services and performance provided by the network.
To address the previous concerns, the rest of the work introduces a novel RN
placement solution specially devised to be applied in real robotic mobile ad hoc
networks (MANETs).

© Springer International Publishing Switzerland 2016
Y. Demazeau et al. (Eds.): PAAMS 2016, LNAI 9662, pp. 273–276, 2016.
DOI: 10.1007/978-3-319-39324-7_29

2   Main Purpose

To tackle the aforementioned issues, it is necessary to consider two principal questions appearing in such a kind of environments and situations: *(i)* which are the RN optimum locations at a given time? and *(ii)*, how should they move towards those locations? That way, we propose a modular optimization solution to solve both issues that performs the joint maximization of the network connectivity and throughput. The proposed system builds on our previous research works [3,4] and solves some severe drawbacks introduced by the approach of Dengiz *et al.* [5]. In agreement with that approach, we use particle swarm optimization (PSO) and model predictive control (MPC) inspired methodologies to control the RN movements.

3   Demonstration: Dynamical Relay Node Placement Solution (DRNS)

As aforementioned we developed a novel RN placement solution, hereafter termed *Dynamical Relay Node placement Solution* (DRNS). DRNS is in charge of driving the available RNs throughout the network area to optimize connectivity and throughput among the *user nodes* (UNs) over time. The last ones are demanding the network services while the RNs try to guarantee that the UNs receive the best network service as possible. The functional and modular architecture of DRNS in shown in Fig. 1. In the figure, leftmost, the **DKS motion prediction** is in charge of inferring the UN positions in a receding horizon $(t + H)$. The UNs location prediction U^{t+H} is afterwards used to select the corresponding optimization action depending on the connectivity provided by the network through the evaluation of $O_1(G^U)$. Only for disconnected networks, we first need to compute an optimized set of *attraction points* (APs) $(A^{*(t+H)})$ by means of the execution of the **AP optimization** module. These points are the target points where the RNs should go. Afterwards, the **RN motion control** module comes into play by running a PSO algorithm that considers a cost function in accordance with the network status. For a partitioned network, DRNS leads the RNs towards the previous computed APs to restore or even increase the network connectivity. Otherwise, DRNS drives the RNs to maximize the overall network throughput. Once the entire procedure is completed, the new and optimized RN positions (R^{t+1}) are obtained, and the RNs can the move towards them. The process is iterated over time.

3.1   Real Environment Deployment: IDSIA Swarm Robotics Laboratory

In this work, we have used a robotic scenario to validate our proposal. Such a robotic scenario has been deployed at IDSIA Swarm Robotics Laboratory [6]. A number of issues had to be tackled when deploying the system. First, while moving, robots should avoid potential obstacles and others robots.

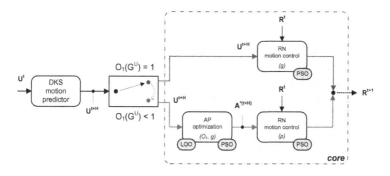

Fig. 1. Functional blocks of DRNS.

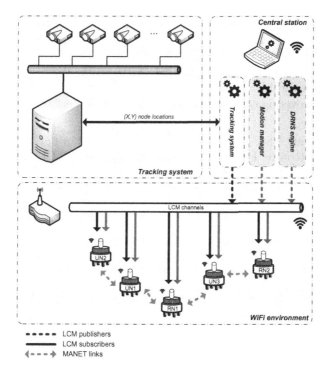

Fig. 2. Overall functional architecture of the real scenario (Color figure online)

Moreover, each one must know its own 2D location and has to be able to receive the new the coordinates of its new target position. For this, we devised and implemented an architecture based on the use of an existing tracking system including several software modules inside a central station allowing to control the robots movement. The developed architecture is shown in Fig. 2. Running inside the central station, the *motion manager* module is in charge of managing the UNs (blue robots) movement following known mobility patterns like random way point (RWP). In turn, the *tracker interface* module allows each robot to know its current 2D location, as computed by the tracking system. Finally, the *DRNS engine* implements our RN placement proposal to drive the RNs (red robots) in a optimized way according to the system performance goals and the current network topology.

In order to prove the successful deployment of our solution in a real robotic MANET environment, a video showing a specific real experiment carried out, can be seen in [7]. Such a video is intended to be a demonstration of the usability and applicability of DRNS in these kinds of scenarios.

4   Conclusions

In this work we have introduced a novel RN placement solution dealing with specially challenging scenarios. A positioning optimization procedure is carried out to determine the best positions of the relays over time to dynamically maximize the connectivity and throughput of the network. We tested our system by means of a real robotic scenario, that shows the success of the approach for maintaining, recovering or even improving the network performance over time.

Acknowledgment. This work has been partially supported by Spanish Government-MINECO (Ministerio de Economía y Competitividad) and FEDER funds, through project TIN2014-60346-R and by the FPU P6A grants program of the University of Granada.

References

1. Younis, M., Akkaya, K.: Strategies and techniques for node placement in wireless sensor networks: a survey. Ad Hoc Netw. **6**(4), 621–655 (2008)
2. Quesada, L., Sitanayah, L., Brown, K.N., OSullivan, B., Sreenan, C.J.: A constraint programming approach to the additional relay placement problem in wireless sensor networks. Constraints **20**(4), 433–451 (2015)
3. Magán-Carrión, R., Camacho-Páez, J., García-Teodoro, P.: A security response approach based on the deployment of mobile agents. In: Demazeau, Y., Ishida, T., Corchado, J.M., Bajo, J. (eds.) PAAMS 2013. LNCS, vol. 7879, pp. 182–191. Springer, Heidelberg (2013)
4. Magán-Carrión, R., Camacho-Páez, J., García-Teodoro, P.: A multiagent self-healing system against security incidents in MANETs. In: Corchado, J.M., et al. (eds.) PAAMS 2014. CCIS, vol. 430, pp. 321–332. Springer, Heidelberg (2014)
5. Dengiz, O., Konak, A., Smith, A.E.: Connectivity management in mobile ad hoc networks using particle swarm optimization. Ad Hoc Netw. **9**(7), 1312–1326 (2011)
6. IDSIA: IDSIA Swarm Robotics Lab. DRNS: Dynamical Relay Node placement Solution 5. Accessed 23 April 2016. http://robotics.idsia.ch/
7. Magán-Carrión, R., Camacho, J., García-Teodoro, P., Flushing, E.F., Di Caro, G.A.: Dynamical Node Placement Solution in MANETs. Accessed 23 April 2016. http://youtu.be/mW1Q_MUFYs4

Smart Grid Demonstration Platform for Renewable Energy Exchange

Mihail Mihaylov[1]([⊠]), Iván Razo-Zapata[2], Roxana Rădulescu[1], Sergio Jurado[3], Narcis Avellana[3], and Ann Nowé[1]

[1] Vrije Universiteit Brussel, Brussels, Belgium
mmihaylo@vub.ac.be
[2] Luxembourg Institute of Science and Technology, Esch-sur-Alzette, Luxembourg
[3] Sensing & Control Systems, Barcelona, Spain

1 Introduction

Offsetting cities' dependence on fossil fuels is one of the key factors for meeting the environmental targets set out by the European Commission (EC) by 2020 [3]. The penetration of small-scale renewable resources in domestic households (photovoltaic panels and micro wind mills) empowers dwellings to collectively reduce their carbon footprint. Incentivizing the injection and trade of locally-produced renewable energy is a step towards the decarbonisation of the power sector.

Nowadays many energy retailers apply feed-in tariffs to motivate prosumers to inject their produced energy, in order for the retailer to comply with environmental targets. With the growing decentralization of renewable energy production [4], it is a challenge to offer subsidies that ensure a profitable and balanced grid for all parties involved. There rises the need to design an incentive mechanism that aligns the objectives of individual prosumers, who are aiming for high profits from their investments, with the objectives of governments and policy makers seeking to reduce their spendings while still facilitating long-term positive environmental change.

2 Main Purpose

The solution offered so far in the smart grid domain for incentivizing production is to provide payments to prosumers in the form of subsidies. This mechanism comes at a financial burden for governments and policy makers, who seek ways to balance the economic incentives offered to agents with the need for a stable grid. In [5] we proposed the NRG-X-Change concept, which attempts to address this challenge using a novel decentralized digital currency called NRGcoin. When locally-produced renewable energy is fed into the grid, the NRG-X-Change protocol generates new NRGcoins that are awarded to prosumers based on their injected energy. These coins are then sold on a currency exchange market to consumers, who use them to pay their consumption. The billing is performed in real-time by the substation, where the energy cost takes into account total

Y. Demazeau et al. (Eds.): PAAMS 2016, LNAI 9662, pp. 277–280, 2016.
DOI: 10.1007/978-3-319-39324-7_30

supply and demand in the neighbourhood, rather than the individual's supply and demand, as currently done in practice.

During overproduction prosumers are paid proportionally to the injected energy that covers the total demand in the neighborhood, such that the over-produced energy is not remunerated. This payment protocol incentivizes the balance of local energy supply and demand in the neighborhood. The excess renewable energy is stored in batteries and injected when it is most profitable by relying on an intelligent battery control strategy, which incorporates a prediction algorithm.

The NRGcoin currency shares characteristics with Bitcoin and has numerous advantages in the smart grid [5]. Independently from injection and withdrawal of energy, NRGcoins are traded on an open currency exchange market for their monetary equivalent. Agents use Random Forest prediction algorithm to determine the quantity to trade and Adaptive Attitude (AA) bidding strategy [7] to determine the bid/ask price. AA allows agents to continuously update their eagerness to sell or buy NRGcoins depending on the market changes: a short-term attitude translates into profit desire (i.e., selling/buying at high/low prices), while a long-term attitude encourages more transactions (i.e., submitting low/high asks/bids).

The NRG-X-Change concept has been thoroughly tested on a smart grid multi-agent simulator using Repast Simphony [2]. To further validate the NRG-X-Change concept, we deploy it on hardware and use real data of energy consumption in a typical neighbourhood. The aim of our demonstration is fourfold: (i) to raise awareness about the challenges and impact of future smart grid scenarios; (ii) to highlight the potential of NRG-X-Change in decarbonizing the power sector; (iii) to demonstrate the weather influence on monetary incentives and market behavior; and (iv) to illustrate the impact of battery control strategies on the scenario dynamics, i.e., on market evolution and energy prices [6], as well as on prosumers' and substation's profits.

3   Demonstration

Our demo offers four types of interaction. *(1) Influence consumption:* Users can change the 'virtual' outdoor temperature, which influences the consumption of all houses. For example, decreasing the outdoor temperature will drive agents to increase their consumption proportionally, relative to their real-world consumption. *(2) Reduce production:* Users can cast shadows over the solar panels of prosumers using cardboard clouds. This simulation of weather conditions allows users to observe their effect on the overall energy balance and on the incentives of agents for exchanging renewable energy. *(3) Increase production:* Users can install extra panels to observe the influence of big producers on the real-time energy price and on the currency market. Similarly, equipping a consumer with solar panels increases the percentage of prosumers and therefore changes the energy balance in the neighborhood. *(4) Install battery storage:* Users will be able to observe the effect of equipping prosumers with battery storage and thereby understanding the influence of storage systems on prosumer's profits and market conditions.

Within the demo we use real-life data, provided by Eandis — a Belgian Distribution System Operator (DSO). For this demo we have selected a typical Belgian neighborhood consisting of 6 prosumers and 56 consumers (cf. Fig. 1). To find a typical substation in the data, we applied a two level clustering that considers global features such as total trimester consumption, and local features such as daily consumption [1]. The measurements that we use in this demonstration are collected between 1st of March 2014 and 31st of May 2014.

The substation and the six prosumers are represented by software agents running on individual Raspberry Pi boards. Prosumers produce energy in real-time using mini solar panels. A dimmable spotlight projector is automated to simulate the day/night cycle using a z-Wave controller. All 56 consumer agents are running in individual threads on two Raspberry Pi boards. Energy consumption of both prosumers and consumers is read from the real data. The boards allow agents to submit orders for buying and selling NRGcoins to an online market hosted and running in Azure Cloud. Orders are matched in real-time using continuous double auction, as employed by the New York Stock Exchange. Thus, our demo represents a multi-agent system that autonomously exchanges renewable energy using the NRG-X-Change incentive mechanism. Since the currency market is hosted

Fig. 1. Demo setup

in the Cloud, it allows agents to place bids from anywhere in the world. Thus, multiple neighbourhoods running in different parts of the world can seamlessly interact in the same scenario and demonstrate the scalability of our concept. All software agents are developed in Java, while the exchange market is developed in C# using Azure Service Bus for synchronizing actions. All components communicate using the RESTful Microservice architecture.

Each prosumer is equipped with a 3.7 V lithium-polymer (LiPo) rechargeable battery of 2.6 Wh. We scale the capacity of the physical batteries in software with factors between 1500 and 5000 to match that of real commercial batteries, which can range between 4 kWh and 13.2 kWh. The battery is charged by the mini solar panels and discharged using a heater resistor to simulate self-consumption or injection in the grid. The battery control strategy infers at every time slot whether it is most profitable to inject the excess green energy in the grid or to store it in the battery for later use, depending on the predicted energy balance in the neighborhood.

Prosumer houses have LCD screens showing in real-time: (i) individual energy production and consumption in kWh; (ii) NRGcoin balance of prosumer; (iii) NRGcoin transactions and payments; (iv) market orders for buying and selling the currency; and (v) the state of charge of the battery. Likewise, substation's screens show aggregated information about: (a) total energy production and consumption of all houses; (b) NRGcoin balance of the substation; (c) all unmatched buy and sell orders in the currency market; (d) the evolution of the NRGcoin price.

While in reality measurements are taken every 15 min, we speed up our demonstration by a factor of 300 to arrive at 3 s time slots. Thus, charts are updated every 3 s, allowing users to observe in less than 5 min the behavior of a real neighborhood in a whole day. Users are also able to pause the execution of the entire demonstration (including the day/night cycle) in order to analyze the plots. This functionality is available via the user interface in the substation's LCD display.

4   Conclusions

We present here a demonstration setup of a smart grid scenario showing how green energy exchange can take place in a typical neighborhood, under the NRG-X-Change incentive mechanism, using real life consumption data. We also highlight the effect of weather conditions and battery control strategies. Incentive mechanisms for local energy trade are a vital stimulus in the race to meet our environmental targets. We believe digital currencies for energy are a promising newcomer in the smart grid scene and may prove to be an important ingredient in the design of future-compatible incentive mechanisms.

References

1. Arco, L., Cases, G., Nowé, A.: Two-level clustering methodology for smart metering data using global and local patterns. In: Fifth International Workshop on Knowledge Discovery, Knowledge Management and Decision Making (2015)
2. Collier, N.: Repast: An extensible framework for agent simulation. The University of Chicagos Social Science Research, vol. 36 (2003)
3. European Commission: Europe 2020: A strategy for smart, sustainable and inclusive growth. COM (2010)
4. Lesser, J.A., Su, X.: Design of an economically efficient feed-in tariff structure for renewable energy development. Energy Policy 36(3), 981–990 (2008)
5. Mihaylov, M., Jurado, S., Van Moffaert, K., Avellana, N., Nowé, A.: NRG-X-Change: a novel mechanism for trading of renewable energy in smart grids. In: Proceedings of the 3rd International Conference on Smart Grids and Green IT Systems, pp. 101–106, April 2014
6. Prüggler, N., Prüggler, W., Wirl, F.: Storage and Demand Side Management as power generators strategic instruments to influence demand and prices. Energy 36(11), 6308–6317 (2011)
7. Vytelingum, P., Cliff, D., Jennings, N.: Strategic bidding in continuous double auctions. Artif. Intell. 172(14), 1700–1729 (2008)

Demonstration of ALBidS: Adaptive Learning Strategic Bidding System

Tiago Pinto[✉], Zita Vale, Isabel Praça, and Gabriel Santos

Institute of Engineering – Politechnic of Porto (ISEP/IPP), GECAD – Knowledge Engineering and Decision-Support Research Center, Porto, Portugal
{tmcfp,zav,icp,gajls}@isep.ipp.pt

1 Introduction

Current worldwide electricity markets are strongly affected by the increasing use of renewable energy sources [1]. This increase has been stimulated by new energy policies that result from the growing concerns regarding the scarcity of fossil fuels and their impact in the environment. This has also led to an unavoidable restructuring of the power and energy sector, which was forced to adapt to the new paradigm [2]. The restructuring process resulted in a deep change in the operation of competitive electricity markets. The restructuring made the market more competitive, but also more complex, placing new challenges to the participants, which increases the difficulty of decision making. This is exacerbated by the increasing number of new market types that are being implemented to deal with the new challenges. Therefore, the intervenient entities are relentlessly forced to rethink their behaviour and market strategies in order to cope with such a constantly changing environment [2].

So that these entities can deal with the new challenges, the use of decision support tools becomes crucial. The need for understanding the market mechanisms and how players' interaction affects the outcomes of markets has contributed to the emergence of several simulation tools [3]. Multi-agent based software is the most widely adopted solution as this paradigm is particularly suitable to analyse dynamic systems with complex interactions among its elements, such as electricity markets. Current software tools allow studying different electricity market mechanisms and analysing the relationships between market entities; however, they are not prepared to provide suitable decision support to the negotiation process of electricity market players [4].

This gap motivates the development of this work, which arises with the purpose of providing a solution to enable electricity market players to take the best possible outcomes out of each market context. This contribution is provided by ALBidS (Adaptive Learning strategic Bidding System), a decision support system that includes a large number of distinct market strategies, and learns which should be used in each context in order to provide the best expected response [5]. ALBidS is also integrated with

This project has received funding from the European Union's Horizon 2020 research and innovation programme under the Marie Sklodowska-Curie grant agreement No 641794.

Y. Demazeau et al. (Eds.): PAAMS 2016, LNAI 9662, pp. 281–285, 2016.
DOI: 10.1007/978-3-319-39324-7_31

MASCEM (Multi-Agent Simulator of Competitive Electricity Markets), which enables the simulation of realistic scenarios using real data [6].

2   Main Purpose

The literature offers a large variety of strategic approaches that aim at providing decision support in auction-based electricity market negotiations [7]. However, none of the proposed strategies has shown to be clearly better than the others. Case studies show that there is no strategy that presents the best performance in all environments and contexts, *i.e.* strategies that have performed well in one situation may have mediocre performances in different circumstances [5].

The main goal of ALBidS is to take the most advantage out of the alternative market strategies that have been introduced in the literature. With this purpose, the general concept behind ALBidS is the integration of as many distinct market strategies as possible, whose performance is evaluated under different contexts of negotiation. This evaluation is used by the system to learn which strategies are the most adequate and present the highest chance of success in each different context.

The learning process is undertaken by means of reinforcement learning algorithms, namely the Roth-Erev algorithm and an algorithm based on the Bayesian theorem of probability [5]. Additionally, a 2E balance management mechanism has been developed to enable controlling the efficiency and effectiveness of the large variety of algorithms that are executed simultaneously. This method allows ALBidS to adapt the execution time of the system to the purpose of each simulation, *e.g.* if the expected results from ALBidS are as best as it is able to achieve, or if the main requirement is for the system to be executed rapidly to analyse issues other than player's optimal performance in the electricity market.

ALBidS incorporates a large variety of market decision support strategies with different natures and perspectives, such as data mining techniques, forecasting methods, artificial intelligence methodologies, application of electricity market directed strategies, mathematic approaches, economic theory based models, the adaptation of physics theories, game theory, metalearners, among others. This way, the system is able to take advantage of the characteristics of each approach whenever they show to be advantageous. The system is, thus, prepared to deal with different contexts and scenario situations, guaranteeing a large scope of approaches, which offer a greater chance of having appropriate responses even in very distinct situations.

The context awareness capabilities of ALBidS are provided by the context analysis methodology proposed in [8]. Different characteristics of each negotiation period and day are analysed so that different negotiation contexts are identified and defined. This methodology enables the learning process of ALBidS to be dependent on the negotiation context by adapting the responses to each current context. Strategies can, this way, be evaluated and chosen depending on their performance in each context.

The interaction with the MASCEM electricity market simulator provides the means for experimenting the developed decision support methods under realistic simulation conditions [6]. MASCEM makes use of the RealScen scenarios generator [9], to create simulation scenarios that are the representation of real markets. RealScen uses real data that is available online, which is gathered in real time, as soon as it is made available by each different source, using an automatic data extraction tool [9].

3 Demonstration

ALBidS is connected with the MASCEM simulator, providing a response to the negotiating players when they require intelligent support to act in the market. The connection between the two systems is managed by the Main Agent. This agent acts as an intermediary between the two systems. It receives requests from the negotiating players when they require decision support, and provides them the corresponding answers. These answers are provided after managing the ALBidS internal mechanism, including the interactions with the strategy agents. Figure 1 presents the user interface of ALBidS, which allows defining the inputs of the system and where the outputs of the decision support process can be consulted and analysed.

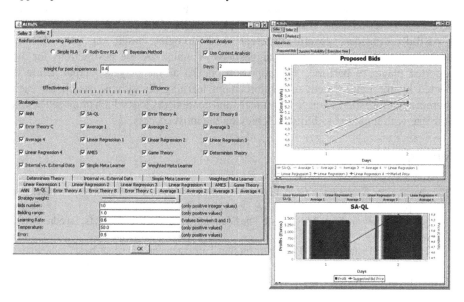

Fig. 1. ALBidS' user interface

From Fig. 1 it is visible that ALBidS enables choosing the desired reinforcement learning algorithm and defining its parameters. It is also possible to define the efficiency/ effectiveness balance preferences and to set up the context analysis. In the strategy panel, it is possible to select the strategies to use, and define their parameters.

After all parameterizations are defined, and the simulation is started, the ALBidS interface displays the graphs presenting the simulation data. The interface displays two types of graphs: the global stats graphs, providing a global view of the simulation; and the strategy individual graphs, presenting the information regarding each of the strategies. In the global stats panel, three graphs are displayed, presenting: all strategies' bids and the actual market price, comparing the different strategies' proposals; the performance of each strategy; and the comparison of the execution times of all strategies. The second panel presents the individual strategy graphs, displaying for each one the bid prices and the obtained profits.

4 Conclusion

The constant growth in electricity markets unpredictability resulted in an amplified need for market intervenient entities in foreseeing market behaviour. The need for understanding the market mechanisms and how the involved players' interaction affects the outcomes of the markets contributed to the growth of usage of simulation tools. Multiagent based software is particularly well fitted to analyze dynamic and adaptive systems with complex interactions, such as electricity markets.

This paper presents a demonstration of ALBidS, a multiagent system created to provide decision support to market negotiating players. This system is integrated with the MASCEM electricity market simulator, so that its advantage in supporting market players can be tested using cases based on real markets' data.

ALBidS considers several different methodologies based on very distinct approaches, to provide alternative suggestions of which are the best actions for the supported player to perform. The approach chosen as the players' actual action is selected by the employment of reinforcement learning algorithms, which for each different situation, simulation circumstances and context, decides which proposed action is the one with higher possibility of achieving the most success.

References

1. Sioshansi, F.P.: Evolution of Global Electricity Markets – New Paradigms, New Challenges, New Approaches. Academic Press, USA (2013)
2. Biggar, D.R., Hesamzadeh, M.R. (eds.): The Economics of Electricity Markets, 1st edn. Wiley, New York (2014)
3. Li, H., Sun, J., Tesfatsion, L.: Testing institutional arrangements via agent-based modeling: a U.S. electricity market application. In: Dawid, H., Semmler, W. (eds.) Computational Methods in Economic Dynamics. Dynamic Modeling and Econometrics in Economics and Finance, vol. 13, pp. 135–158. (2011)
4. Pinto, T., Barreto, J., Praça, I., Sousa, T.M., Vale, Z., Solteiro Pires, E.J.: Six thinking hats: a novel metalearner for intelligent decision support in electricity markets. Decis. Support Syst. **79**, 1–11. Elsevier (2015)
5. Pinto, T., Vale, Z., Sousa, T.M., Praça, I., Santos, G., Morais, H.: Adaptive learning in agents behaviour: a framework for electricity markets simulation. Integr. Comput.-Aided Eng. **21**(4), 399–415. IOS Press (2014)
6. Praça, I., Ramos, C., Vale, Z., Cordeiro, M.: MASCEM: a multi-agent system that simulates competitive electricity markets. IEEE Intell. Syst. Spec. Issue Agents Markets **18**(6), 54–60 (2003)
7. David, A.K., Wen, F.: Strategic bidding in competitive electricity markets: a literature survey. IEEE Proc. Power Eng. Soc. Summer Meet. **4**, 2168–2173 (2000)

8. Pinto, T., Vale, Z., Sousa, T.M., Praça, I.: Negotiation context analysis in electricity markets. Energy **85**, 78–93. Elsevier (2015)
9. Teixeira, B., Silva, F., Pinto, T., Praça, I., Santos, G., Vale, Z.: Data mining approach to support the generation of realistic scenarios for multi-agent simulation of electricity markets. In: 2014 IEEE Symposium on Intelligent Agents (IA) at the IEEE SSCI 2014 (IEEE Symposium Series on Computational Intelligence), Orlando, Florida, USA, 9–12 December 2014

Detecting Social Emotions with a NAO Robot

J.A. Rincon[1](✉), A. Costa[2], P. Novais[2], V. Julian[1], and C. Carrascosa[1]

[1] D. Sistemas Informáticos y Computación, Universitat Politècnica de València,
Valencia, Spain
{jrincon,vinglada,carrasco}@dsic.upv.es
[2] Centro ALGORITMI, Escola de Engenharia, Universidade do Minho,
Guimarães, Portugal
{acosta,pjon}@di.uminho.pt

Abstract. This article aims to give an approach of a dynamic and emotional propagation, which allows to calculate the propagation of the emotion of a group of humans and/or intelligent entities. The dynamic model is based on the *Newton laws* in order to calculate the emotional attraction among them. To obtain the emotions we use a *NAO* robot as a tool to move around of a real environment for interacting with the humans. The robot obtains the emotions through image processing. Moreover, the robot can start a dialogue game with humans in order to estimate the personality of a new individual.

1 Introduction

Human beings manage themselves in different environments, either in the working place, at home or in public places. In each of these places the human interacts with other human beings. In this interaction the humans can express and/or perceive the emotion of the other humans that have around them. In this perception is possible that a human could be influenced by the emotion expressed for other human. In such a scenario if you could distinguish two elements that could influence the emotional contagion, the first is the level of affinity that have both individuals and the second is how empathetic is the agent that perceives the emotion. This two situations have been taken into account in our dynamic emotional model. The empathy has a correlation with the personality [1], the empathy is related with *Agreeableness*. The empathy level can be extracted using the *OCEAN* test estimating the personality of the human beings. This test allows to know which is the personality of the human and to use these values to get a personality estimation. Intelligent agents technology have emerged as a way for the development of autonomous entities in order to act on behalf of people anticipating their decision-making processes. Therefore, these artificial intelligent entities may include the capabilities and required elements that will help them to recognize and simulate emotions [2].

2 Dynamic Emotional Model

This section proposes a dynamic emotional model based on the PAD emotional model. This model will represent the emotional contagion of an heterogeneous

© Springer International Publishing Switzerland 2016
Y. Demazeau et al. (Eds.): PAAMS 2016, LNAI 9662, pp. 286–289, 2016.
DOI: 10.1007/978-3-319-39324-7_32

group of entities capable of expressing and/or communicating emotions. The emotional representation of an emotional state of an agent on the PAD model, the emotion of an agent ag_i in an instant t $(\vec{E}_t(ag_i))$ is defined as a vector in $\mathbb{R}^3$. The variation of each component allows to modify the emotional state of the agent (Eq. 1).

$$\vec{E}_t(ag_i) = [P_t(ag_i), A_t(ag_i), D_t(ag_i)] \tag{1}$$

The emotional dynamics described is based on the *Newton* universal attraction law. Based on this theory, we define the force that an agent ag_j makes over an agent ag_i at instant t $(\vec{F}_t(ag_i, ag_j))$ to attract or repulse it in the PAD space, that is, this force will control the emotion contagion between all the agents (Eq. 2).

$$\vec{F}_t(ag_i, ag_j) = \frac{\varepsilon(ag_i) \cdot Af_t(ag_i, ag_j)}{2^{D_t(ag_i, ag_j)}} \cdot ||\vec{E}_t(ag_i) - \vec{E}_t(ag_j)|| \tag{2}$$

$\vec{F}_t(ag_i, ag_j)$ represents the force vector, which contains all the mathematical properties of vectors as, direction and magnitude. Using these elements help us to know if the emotion of the agent ag_i is attracted by the agent ag_j. $\varepsilon(ag_i)$ represents the emphatic level of entity ag_i, and $Af_t(ag_i, ag_j)$ represents the affinity level between ag_i and ag_j at instant t. $D_t(ag_i, ag_j)$ is the physical distance between ag_i and ag_j at instant t and $\vec{E}_t(ag_i)$ represents the emotion of the ag_i at instant t and $\vec{E}_t(ag_j)$ represents the emotion of the ag_j at instant t. According with this, we define the *Emotional Attraction Forces* of agent ag_i at instant t, as summation of all forces over agent ag_i at instant t. Using this forces and following the *Newton* laws we calculate the velocity ans finally using this velocity we calculate the new emotion. This new emotion is a PAD vector for entity ag_i at instant $t + 1$ $(\vec{E}_{t+1}(ag_j))$ (Eq. 3).

$$\vec{E}_{t+1}(ag_j) = \vec{E}_t(ag_j) + (\vec{v}_t(ag_i) \cdot t) \tag{3}$$

The proposed dynamic model allows us to model and represent the emotional contagion phenomena among different intelligent agents. Nevertheless, these entities typically are not alone in the environment but are part of a group of agents. Our proposal is to model not only how an agent is influenced by other agents but also how the group of agents as a whole can be emotionally affected by its components. To do this, we employ the social emotional model defined in [3]. Due to space limitations, please refer to that work for a detailed explanation of the model. Using this model, it is possible to determine the emotional distance among different groups of agents or between the same group in different instants of time. This will allow us to measure the emotional distance between the current social emotional group and a possible emotional target. Next subsection shows an application where a mobile robot implements the two models allowing the robot to estimate and represent the emotional contagion of a heterogeneous group of people and observe how the robot can influence over the social emotion of that group of people.

3   Demo

The application example has been developed in a real environment, where there is a *NAO* robot[1] in charge of interacting with humans in a room. The main goal of the proposed example is the automatic recognition of the emotional states of a group of individuals in order to enhance the wellbeing of these individuals. To do this, the robot is moving around the room and tries to interact with any detected person. The robot calculates the emotional states of the group of identified individuals and, according to the proposed model, it estimates possible emotional contagions among individuals. In order to make this process it uses different tools to communicate with its environment and to obtain the information that surrounds it:

- Speech recognition, the robot speaks with people to try to change their emotional states. Moreover, if the robot does not know the person, it estimates his personality using a dialogue game that follows the OCEAN test.
- Robot movement, the robot is continually moving around the room trying to interact and animate any individual presented in the room.
- Image processing, used to detect the emotional state of people around the room. To detect the emotional states, the robot employs the API presented in the *project oxford*[2]. This project can support the detection and evaluation of around 64 faces extracting the emotion of each one of them. We use these results in order to calculate the emotional dynamic according to the previously presented dynamic emotional model.

Figure 1 shows a simulated environment of the proposed application where we can see the NAO robot interacting with a group of three individuals.

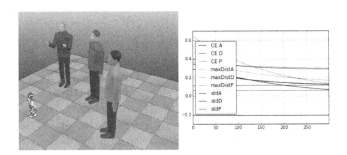

Fig. 1. Simulation of the proposed application

With this information, the robot tries to animate and stimulate people which is in the room. This stimulation actions are performed when the robot detects

---

[1] https://www.aldebaran.com/en.
[2] https://www.projectoxford.ai/.

emotional changes that lead to social emotion to move away from a target emotion (happiness, usually). This continuous sensorization of the robot environment, allows to estimate the emotional dynamics of the group and thus the robot is able to react performing different actions like telling a joke, asking what happens to them or make a funny action. One of the possible applications of this system is in nursing homes, where they have to perform tasks playful. The robot would be responsible for carrying out these tasks while analyzing emotions and modifying its actions according to the emotion of the group [4].

4   Conclusions and Future Work

A new model for the calculation of dynamic emotions has been presented in this paper, giving a first approach for the emotional contagion and simulation of dynamic social emotions into a group of intelligent entities. The proposed model uses the personality of each entity and the affinity level between entities in order to calculate and represent the emotional dynamic of a group. The dynamic emotional model of a group of agents not only allows a global view of the emotional dynamic of the group, also can improve the decision making based on the attraction level between entities. The paper introduces also a demo about how to calculate, represent and use the dynamic emotional model into a real environment. The proposed application consists of a NAO mobile robot which uses the proposed emotional model to enhance its decision-making process.

Acknowledgments. This work is partially supported by the MINECO project TIN2015-65515-C4-1-R and the FPI grant AP2013-01276 awarded to Jaime-Andres Rincon.

References

1. Graziano, W.G., Habashi, M.M., Sheese, B.E., Tobin, R.M.: Agreeableness, empathy, and helping: a person x situation perspective. J. Pers. Soc. Psychol. **93**(4), 583–599 (2007)
2. Rincon, J.A., Julian, V., Carrascosa, C.: Applying a social emotional model in human-agent societies. In: Bajo, J., Hallenborg, K., Pawlewski, P., Botti, V., Sánchez-Pi, N., Duque Méndez, N.D., Lopes, F., Vicente, J. (eds.) PAAMS 2015 Workshops. CCIS, vol. 524, pp. 377–388. Springer, Heidelberg (2015)
3. Rincon, J.A., Julian, V., Carrascosa, C.: Social emotional model. In: Demazeau, Yves, Decker, Keith S., Bajo Pérez, Javier, De la Prieta, Fernando (eds.) PAAMS 2015. LNCS, vol. 9086. Springer, Heidelberg (2015)
4. Niewiadomska-Szynkiewicz, E., Sikora, A.: Progress in automation, robotics and measuring techniques. Adv. Intell. Syst. Comput. **351**, 181–190 (2015)

Multi-agent Supply Scheduling System Prototype for Energy Production and Distribution

Alexander Tsarev[✉] and Petr Skobelev

Smart Solutions, Ltd., Samara, Russia
mail@identifier.at, petr.skobelev@gmail.com

Abstract. Smart grids actively develop around the world providing new possibilities for energy market and require new ways of management in the dynamic environment. This paper addresses the economically efficient management of production, accumulation and distribution of the energy in smart grids. Recent works consider many separate aspects of smart grids including constraints and effective use of energy storages. However, these works usually consider only simplified grid topologies and focus on time-consuming optimisation methods. This work proposes the energy supply scheduling system prototype for real-time management oriented on economic efficiency of energy supply.

Keywords: Distributed generation · Energy storage · Energy production · Smart grid · Real-time scheduling · Energy market · Multi-agent approach

1 Introduction

Smart grids actively develop in the recent years raising many issues related to distributed generation and reverse power flow from local microgrids [1, 2], use of renewable sources, such as photovoltaic and wind generators operated simultaneously with traditional generators, use of batteries and fuel-cells [3]. Smart grids provide new possibilities for interactive customer and supplier communication, and building new market structure with direct participation of smaller customers and suppliers.

In such open market environments, it is assumed that energy demand (expected load) is defined as a set of orders, each with its own price and amount of energy required in a specific time interval (load is assumed constant on this time interval). In simplified cases, the price can be fixed (at least for a certain time interval), but in general, several orders with different price can be placed for the same time interval. This feature is important to let end-customers in smart grids participate in the open market as it happens in many countries between big suppliers and consumers [4].

There are many unpredictable events that can disrupt smooth delivery of energy, the most important being the change of the production capacity (due to weather conditions, equipment breakdowns or lack of fuel), arrival of an unexpected order (sudden increase of demand in the nearest time) and cancellation or modification of a previously defined demand. With the intensive flow of events, which is normal in modern life, our planned and actual reality will always quickly diverge.

© Springer International Publishing Switzerland 2016
Y. Demazeau et al. (Eds.): PAAMS 2016, LNAI 9662, pp. 290–293, 2016.
DOI: 10.1007/978-3-319-39324-7_33

Modern grids tend to grow in scale and integrate with the outside world, so that the optimal management requires a coordinated scheduling of many interconnected electrical networks. Large-scale grids have so many diverse variables that no current optimiser based on the batch processing principle can possibly produce an optimal solution that will last. And all current systems work in batch mode. Real-time grid management is achievable in some cases, but only if it is limited to the control of the current situation, without scheduling of future operations. This becomes a serious drawback when we deal with energy accumulation facilities and production facilities that need time to change the mode (e.g. power output). In these cases, much better results can be achieved using real-time scheduling of all operations for a specific horizon. But the currently proposed schedule optimization methods do not work well for large grids [5].

2   Main Purpose

The purpose of this research and development is to obtain a technology that allows users of future smart grids to achieve higher economic efficiency in energy consumption, production, accumulation and distribution using real-time scheduling.

We propose to use the multi-agent approach to achieve real-time processing on large or interconnected smart grids. An individual software agent represents each unit (site) of the electrical network. Depending on the type of the unit, its agent can request energy supply (with demand and price defined for each time interval) from other agents, or provide energy (with limitations and costs defined for each time interval) to other requesting agents, or both.

Agents run in parallel and process input data and requests from other agents until they either find a way to satisfy the requests or decide that it is not possible within the current limitations. The quality of the result (the cost of requests satisfaction) can be different depending on the time available for processing. The proposed approach is that the agent takes the fastest solution first, and if no new requests come before the next agent processing time, it tries a next, potentially more profitable solution. This way, we keep the balance between the task solution time and the quality of the result, depending on the intensity of changes in the network.

The most basic act of multi-agent communication can be described as three steps:

1. In order to achieve a result (plan of energy production and distribution) the consumer agents start to request the power supply from the less expensive supplier sites (including generators, storages, energy routers, external networks). The expected cost of supply from each connected site is based on the agent experience of previous negotiations.
2. In response to the consumers' requests, the supplier builds its own internal plan of supply for the full time horizon considering the constraints and the possibility to store energy. When the plan is ready, the site agent sends sub-requests to other suppliers and costs with limitations to the consumers.
3. If the consumer receives limitations (the energy cannot be fully supplied) or additional costs (including the cost of supply from the next site in the network and cost of all energy losses) it may change the orders fully or partially and request energy from another directly connected site.

Using these three basic steps, all agents asynchronously communicate with each other. The energy supply requests propagate through the network accumulating the costs and limitations until a solution is found. If a specific agent has several options of demand satisfaction, it explores them by trying suppliers subsequently over the processing iterations.

The developed multi-agent supply scheduling system prototype allows analysis of different cases of energy production and distribution in smart grids from the economic efficiency point of view. It considers many aspects that affect the efficiency in open market smart grids, and are not yet completely considered in any existing software, including:

- order based energy distribution (each customer can place orders for a specific amount of energy, specific time interval, and define the price);
- energy production capacities and costs (each producer can define the limits and minimal costs on different time intervals);
- energy accumulation capacities, efficiency and costs;
- electrical lines capacities, efficiency and energy delivery costs;
- fuel supply limitations and costs.

3   Demonstration

The demonstration of the system prototype includes the demonstration of interactive network design features (user can add nodes, electrical lines, change costs and limitations of production and delivery). The key aspect is that the changes are processed automatically, and the user always have a valid schedule and achieved KPIs at hand to compare with other network designs (Fig. 1).

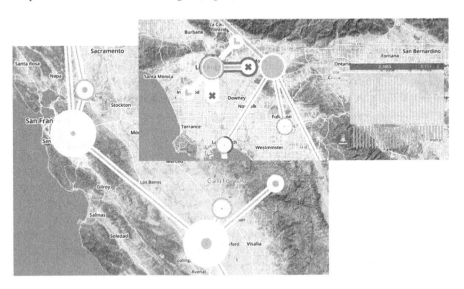

Fig. 1. Electrical network management user interface.

The demonstration shows how the supply orders are managed and scheduled in real-time, and how the change of the future demand affect the current activity in the network. The user interface allows producers and consumers to negotiate the prices, production and demand volumes. The demonstration cases clearly show how the scheduling in advance allows users to improve economic efficiency.

The demonstration shows how the system deals with different power production and accumulation equipment, how it proposes to switch the production on and off at different capacities depending on the situation.

The demonstration shows the system features for micro-economic analysis, results explanation, how the user can partially fix or manually rework the result to consider the external factors and limitations.

4   Conclusions

The developed prototype shows good potential for the multi-agent scheduling and grid management.

The industry-ready version of the system will let the users to interact in real time and negotiate their consumption and production based on realistic schedules considering current and expected grid limitations and demands. The system can be used to manage the grid hardware in real time to optimize the overall economy by deciding:

- when and which production capacity in the grid to use;
- when and where to start and stop accumulation;
- which consumption orders to satisfy;
- where from and where to deliver energy.

This work was carried out with the financial support of the Ministry of Education and Science of the Russian Federation (contract 14.579.21.0084, project unique id RFMEFI57914X0084).

References

1. Vasquez, J.C., Guerrero, J.M., Miret, J., Castilla, M., de Vicuña, L.G.: Hierarchical control of intelligent microgrids. IEEE Ind. Electron. Mag. **4**, 23–29 (2010)
2. Barklund, E., Pogaku, N., Prodanovic, M., Hernandez-Aramburo, C., Green, T.C.: Energy management in autonomous microgrid using stability-constrained droop control of inverters. IEEE Trans. Power Electron. **23**(9), 2346–2352 (2008)
3. Arai, J., Iba, K., Funabashi, T., Nakanishi, Y., Koyanagi, K., Yokoyama, R.: Power electronics and its applications to renewable energy in Japan. IEEE Circ. Syst. Mag. **8**, 52–66 (2008)
4. Ministry of Energy of the Russian Federation. 2010. Energy Strategy of Russia for the Period of up to 2030. Approved by Decree No. 1715r of the Government of the Russian Federation dated 13 November 2009
5. Levron, Y., Guerrero, J.M., Beck, Y.: Optimal power flow in microgrids with energy storage. IEEE Trans. Power Syst. **PP**(99), 1–9

PUMAS-GR: A Negotiation-Based Group Recommendation System for Movies

Christian Villavicencio, Silvia Schiaffino[✉], Jorge Andres Diaz-Pace, and Ariel Monteserin

ISISTAN (CONICET - UNCPBA), Campus Universitario, Tandil, Argentina
silvia.schiaffino@isistan.unicen.edu.ar

Abstract. Providing recommendations to groups of users has become popular in many applications today. Although several group recommendation techniques exist, the generation of items that satisfy all group members in an even way still remains a challenge. To this end, we have developed a multi-agent approach called PUMAS-GR that relies on negotiation techniques to improve group recommendations. We applied PUMAS-GR to the movies domain, and used the monotonic concession protocol to reach a consensus on the movies proposed to a group.

1 Introduction

Recommender systems provide assistance to users by identifying items that match a user's needs, preferences, and goals from a usually long list of potentially interesting items. Several recommendation techniques have been proposed in the literature [3]. The aim of a group recommender system is to make item recommendations that are "good" for a group of users as a whole, i.e., the items satisfy the individual preferences of each group member [2]. Group recommendation brings new challenges, since users might have competing interests within a group, and thus issues beyond individual recommendation have to be considered.

In this work, we present a multi-agent approach, called PUMAS-GR, for group recommendation. The novelty of our approach is that leverages on negotiation techniques in order to integrate recommendations (previously) obtained for each group member into a list of recommendations for the group. Each user is represented by a personal agent that works on her behalf. The agents carry out a cooperative negotiation process based on the multilateral Monotonic Concession Protocol (MCP) [1]. We argue that this negotiation process can generate recommendations that satisfy the different group members more evenly than traditional group recommendation approaches, since it mirrors the way in which human negotiation seems to work [4]. We have applied PUMAS-GR to the movies domain (MovieLens), but the approach is applicable to other domains as well.

2 Main Purpose

Our approach conceives the multi-agent system (MAS) as the group recommender system, according to the client-server architecture of Fig. 1. The user

© Springer International Publishing Switzerland 2016
Y. Demazeau et al. (Eds.): PAAMS 2016, LNAI 9662, pp. 294–298, 2016.
DOI: 10.1007/978-3-319-39324-7_34

interacts with a Web-based client, which can make different functional requests to a server, such as: log into a session, rate sequences of movies presented by the system, or ask for a group recommendation. The latter is what actually triggers the agent negotiation. On the server side, the *Group Recommender*, hosts a collection of *Agent* instances along with a *Moderator* component. This *Moderator* is responsible for coordinating the agents according to the MCP rules. Information about user credentials, membership to different groups, and movies watched by users are stored in the *User Profiles* repository. Information about available movies for recommendation are kept in a separate repository. The *Movies Dataset* contains data from MovieLens[1].

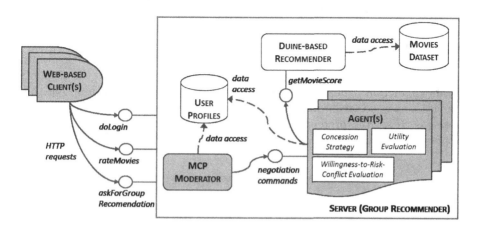

Fig. 1. Architecture of PUMAS-GR

Each *Agent* is a process that implements a number of negotiation commands, which are enacted by the *Moderator*. The negotiation commands refer to three aspects: (i) computation of the agent utility function, which is used for determining agreements; (ii) computation of the agent "willingness" to risk a conflict, and (iii) the concession strategy (e.g., Nash, egocentric), in case the *Moderator* decides that the agent must concede. Furthermore, each agent is able to generate a ranking of movies of interest for its associated user. Internally, each agent relies on a basic (single-user) recommender system that generates the rankings. To do so, we rely on the Duine framework[2], as it provides predefined prediction techniques for estimating movie scores. These techniques use item and user similarity models to feed predictors, which are then able to estimate the rating a user would have given to a movie.

---

[1] http://grouplens.org/datasets/movielens/.
[2] http://www.duineframework.org/.

3   Demonstration

The basic functionality of the PUMAS-GR prototype is illustrated in Fig. 2. A user logs into the system and can rate different movies presented randomly by the system (a). The user can configure a given group of users (b) and ask for a recommendation of k movies for the group (c). These k movies are the result of the MCP-based negotiation process.

At the beginning, each agent makes an initial proposal with its favorite (top-ranked) movie, which is the movie with the highest score. Then, proposals are interchanged among the agents in order to determine if an agreement can be reached. The notion of agreement is defined in terms of the utility of a given proposal for the agents. To do so, each agent computes a utility function that maps agreements to non-negative values. If the user already watched a given movie, then she probably assigned a score (utility) to it. If a user did not rate (or watched) a movie, an estimated utility is computed via Duine. Specifically, the utility is the product of the prediction score for the movie and the certainty of that prediction. There is an agreement if one agent makes a proposal that is at least as good (regarding utility) for any other agent as their own current proposals. If so, the proposal that satisfies all the agents is chosen (if several proposals meet this criterion, the *Moderator* simply picks one of them randomly).

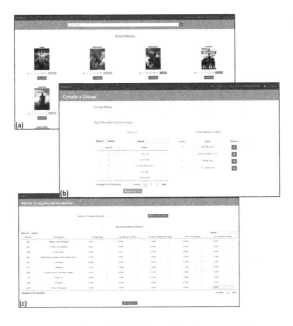

Fig. 2. PUMAS-GR application at work

If an initial agreement is not possible, the agents engage in rounds of negotiation, each one making movie proposals that need to be assessed by the other agents, until an agreement is reached or the negotiation finishes with a conflict. The agents abide by a set of predefined MCP rules, which correspond to the negotiation commands discussed for the Fig. 1. In case a round of negotiation ends up in a conflict, one of the agents must make a concession. A concession means that an agent seeks an inferior proposal with the hope of reaching an agreement. If none of the agents can concede, the process finishes with no-agreement.

Selecting the agent that must concede is determined by applying the Zeuthen strategy [5] around the concept of willingness to risk conflict (WRC). In the bilateral MCP (i.e., two agents), both agents evaluate their WRC value and the agent with the lowest value makes the next concession. The strategy can be generalized to a multilateral setting (i.e., more than two agents), in which Zeuthen evaluates the loss in utility in case of concession assuming the worst possible outcome for the agent. As for the concession itself, various strategies are discussed in the literature [1]. For our work, we selected the so-called Nash concession, because it guarantees termination and deadlock-freedom. Based on Nash concession, an agent makes a proposal such that the product of utilities of the other agents increases.

4 Conclusion

PUMAS-GR is a MAS approach for group recommendation based on negotiation techniques. Preliminary experiments with our prototype in the movies domain have shown promising results in terms of satisfaction of group members, when compared to traditional rank aggregation techniques. A limitation of our prototype is the high reliance on movie scores predicted by Duine as the main source of rankings for individual users. In addition, Duine often presents performance problems when recommender system is used constantly by several users. However, our architecture is flexible to admit other scoring strategies or (single-user) recommender systems. Currently, we are in the process of substituting Duine by Mahout[3], in order to improve the performance of the prototype. Finally, we plan to evaluate our approach in other domains involving groups (e.g., tourism, software architecture decision making), and to compare it with other standard techniques for group recommendation.

Acknowledgements. This work has been partially supported by projects ANPCyT-PICT2011-0366 and CONICET-PIP112-201101-00078 (Argentina), and also by "PUMAS" CONICET-CNRS cooperation project.

References

1. Endriss, U.: Monotonic concession protocols for multilateral negotiation. In: Proceedings of AAMAS 2006, pp. 392–399. ACM, New York (2006)

---

[3] http://mahout.apache.org/.

2. Jameson, A., Smyth, B.: Recommendation to groups. In: Brusilovsky, P., Kobsa, A., Nejdl, W. (eds.) Adaptive Web 2007. LNCS, vol. 4321, pp. 596–627. Springer, Heidelberg (2007)
3. Ricci, F., Rokach, L., Shapira, B., Kantor, P.: Recommender Systems Handbook. Springer, New York (2010)
4. Wooldridge, M.: An Introduction to MultiAgent Systems, 2nd edn. Wiley, Chichester (2009)
5. Zeuthen, F.L.B.: Problems of Monopoly and Economic Warfare. Routledge and Sons, London (1930)

Building Prototypes Through 3D Simulations

Jorge J. Gómez-Sanz, Marlon Cardenas, Rafael Pax,
and Pablo Campillo

Departamento de Ingeniería del Software e Inteligencia Artificial,
Facultad de Informática, Universidad Complutense de Madrid,
28040 Madrid Spain
{jjgomezm,marlonca,rpax,pabcampi}@ucm.es

Abstract. The demo introduces a fast prototyping method based on 3D simulations and the kit AIDE. The system is part of a development philosophy called Virtual Living Lab, where part of the experimentation is made against simulated 3D worlds which show a behavior close to the real one. The demo will illustrate the capabilities of this development philosophy applied to two basic functions working into two different environments: a house and a large installation, such as a faculty building or a mall center.

Keywords: Multi-agent based simulation · Crowd simulation · Inferring population composition · People tracking

1 Introduction

The development of Ambient Assisted Living (AAL) systems is a challenging one. Its is inherently expensive because of, among others, the necessary experimentation and availability of hardware, the uncertainty in the determining the necessary functionality which leads to longer development periods, the need of incorporating the end-user in the development so as to have early feedback, and, at the same time, the complexity of preserving the end-user dignity, privacy, and integrity.

By transferring the development work of the AAL solution to the computer, several benefits are achieved. The main one is the cost reduction since the development environment is not a demanding one and computers designed for gaming will be sufficient. A secondary one is the easiness of experimentation, with the capability of running batteries of tests in a deterministic way. This development philosophy is what we call *Virtual Living Lab*

This transfer has to exist in both directions. It is not only bringing the problem to the computer. It is also being capable of taking out a working solution from the computer. Both transfers are challenging because they imply reproducing the hardware inside the simulation in a convincing way. Past works focused on the Android platform, which was a limiting decision. This iteration of this solution will open the development environment to linux based platforms with enough sensor/actuator availability.

The demo uses software which now is part of the Ambient Intelligence Development Environment (AIDE), which is distributed as free software from

© Springer International Publishing Switzerland 2016
Y. Demazeau et al. (Eds.): PAAMS 2016, LNAI 9662, pp. 299–301, 2016.
DOI: 10.1007/978-3-319-39324-7

http://grasia.fdi.ucm.es/aide. This work bases on previous results, some of them defended in PAAMS [1, 3].

2   Main Purpose

The demo intends to prove the feasibility of a development using these methods using two platforms: Android, and Beagle Bone. The first platform corresponds to the initial work in this line [1, 2], which targeted Android as deployment platform. This decision was based in the widespread adoption of android technology in most homes and looking for reusing existing hardware in most homes. Nevertheless, this strongly limits the application on other hardware platforms more popular of the Internet of Things, such as Arduino, and reduces the number of sensors/actuators available only to those of Android. Hence, for realizing the *Virtual Living Lab* concept, more hardware platforms need to be considered.

Achieving this goal is not trivial. The variety of operating systems in embedded hardware is appealing. An extensive coverage is too ambitious, so, instead, the goal is to target linux based devices, which are cheap to create and to host, while keeping computing power. Enough power to run some of the open platforms for AAL, such as UniversAAL.

From existing linux based platforms, Beagle Bone (BB) has been chosen for this project. The reason is being BB open hardware and having an extensive collection of pluggable sensors and actuators. This makes this platform suitable for quick prototyping AAL devices with different configurations.

3   Demonstration

The demo consists in the elaboration of example systems oriented towards aiding the user using a variety of sensors. The demo bases on the extensive use of Beagle Bone (BB) for showing several use cases of interest for people with special needs. The demonstration will show cooperation among two or more devices in the simulation and also in the real world, as well as deployment capabilities that enable developers to move software in both directions: from the simulation to the BB devices and vice-versa. The developed functionalities for this demo will cover the following:

– Recognition of activities. The demo will show learning the activities in the simulated world, preparing a control based on this knowledge, and testing this control both in the simulated and the real world. In the demo, the character in the simulation will perform a number of actions with sufficient variations. This will serve to learn and test activity recognition for simple situations.
– Guidance to the user. Through displays, capacitive buttons, and speakers, the user will receive assistance about the activities being performed. In particular, the user is reminded the need of going on with a previously planned scheduled adapted to the user daily activities. This reminder is important for people with diseases

affecting their cognitive abilities, such as Alzheimer's disease. Also, if the user does not follow the advices, it will decide whether to take further action, for instance, contacting relatives or a caregiver, just in case the person is having a disorientation episode.

These two basic functions will be applied in two different scenarios. One will be a house where the user develops a particular daily living activity. The other will be a large installation, such as faculty building or a mall centre, where the user needs assistance to not loose the focus.

4   Conclusions and Reference

The development of AAL solutions is an expensive one, but approaches such as the *Virtual Living Lab* may help to reduce development costs as well as increasing the quality of the developed solution. So far, this was achieved for the Android platform, though this platform has limited possibilities in terms of available sensors and actuators. To overcome this limitation and facilitate the widespread adoption of this philosophy, this demo will prove the feasibility of this approach to more generic linux based platforms. In particular, this demo will focus on the Beagle Bone platform, which is an open hardware platform with an extensive availability of sensors and actuators.

Acknowledgements. We acknowledge support from the project "SOCIAL AMBIENT ASSISTING LIVING - METHODS (SociAAL)", project "Collaborative Ambient Assisted Living Design (ColoSAAL)", and mobility grant EEBB-I-15-10097, supported by Spanish Ministry for Economy and Competitiveness, with grant TIN2011-28335-C02-01 and TIN2014-57028-R respectively; and MOSI-AGIL-CM (S2013/ICE-3019) co-funded by Madrid Government, EU Structural Funds FSE, and FEDER.

References

1. Campillo-Sanchez, P., Gómez-Sanz, J.J.: Agent Based simulation for creating ambient assisted living solutions. In: Demazeau, Y., Zambonelli, F., Corchado, J.M., Bajo, J. (eds.) PAAMS 2014. LNCS, vol. 8473, pp. 319–322. Springer, Heidelberg (2014)
2. Campillo-Sanchez, P., Gómez-Sanz, J.J.: A framework for developing multi-agent systems in ambient intelligence scenarios. In: Proceedings of the 2015 International Conference on Autonomous Agents and Multiagent Systems. AAMAS 2015, Istanbul, Turkey, May 4–8, 2015. pp. 1949–1950 (2015)
3. Gómez-Sanz, J.J., Sanchez, P.C.: Achieving parkinson's disease patient autonomy through regulative norms. In: 13th International Conference on Trends in Practical Applications of Agents, Multi-agent Systems and Sustainability - The PAAMS Collection. PAAMS 2015, Salamanca, Spain, June 3–4, 2015, Special Sessions. pp. 97–104 (2015)

Author Index

Printed in the United States
By Bookmasters